ESSAYS IN THE
FUNDAMENTAL THEORY OF MONETARY ECONOMICS AND MACROECONOMICS

ESSAYS IN THE
FUNDAMENTAL THEORY OF MONETARY ECONOMICS AND MACROECONOMICS

John Smithin

York University, Canada

 **World Scientific**

NEW JERSEY · LONDON · SINGAPORE · BEIJING · SHANGHAI · HONG KONG · TAIPEI · CHENNAI

Published by

World Scientific Publishing Co. Pte. Ltd.

5 Toh Tuck Link, Singapore 596224

USA office: 27 Warren Street, Suite 401-402, Hackensack, NJ 07601

UK office: 57 Shelton Street, Covent Garden, London WC2H 9HE

Library of Congress Cataloging-in-Publication Data
Smithin, John N.
    Essays in the fundamental theory of monetary economics and macroeconomics / by John
Smithin (York University, Canada).
        p. cm.
    Includes bibliographical references and index.
    ISBN 978-9814289160
    1. Money. 2. Monetary policy. 3. Economic policy. 4. Macroeconomics. I. Title.
HG221.S6435 2013
339.5'3--dc23

                                                                    2012036393

British Library Cataloguing-in-Publication Data
A catalogue record for this book is available from the British Library.

In-house Editors: Sandhya Venkatesh/Dipasri Sardar

Typeset by Stallion Press
Email: enquiries@stallionpress.com

Printed in Singapore.

To my step-daughters, Jana Campbell and Sylva Zyba.

CONTENTS

About the Author   ix

Introductory Remarks   xi

1. Money, Debt and Credit in the Enterprise Economy   1

2. The Recurring Debates in Monetary Economics   33

3. Variations on the Theme of the Quantity Theory of Money   61

4. Wicksellian and Neo-Wicksellian Models
    of Monetary Economics   103

5. Keynes, Samuelson, Hicks and the Fate
    of Keynesian Economics   139

6. Long-Run Models of Monetary Growth, Forced Saving,
    Wealth, Time Preference, and the Neoclassical
    Theory of Capital   185

7. An Alternative Monetary Model of Economic Growth,
    the Business Cycle, Inflation and Income Distribution   219

8. Capitalism in One Country?: A Re-examination
    of Monetary Mercantilism from the Financial Perspective   263

Bibliography   299

Index   315

ABOUT THE AUTHOR

 **John Smithin** is Professor of Economics in the Department of Economics and the Schulich School of Business, York University, Toronto, Canada. He holds a PhD from McMaster University, and has previously taught at the University of Calgary and Lanchester Polytechnic (now Coventry University) in England. His main research interests are in the fields of monetary theory and the philosophy of money and finance. He is the author/editor (co-author/co-editor) of *Keynes and Public Policy after Fifty Years* (1988), *Macroeconomics after Thatcher and Reagan* (1990), *Economic Integration between Unequl Partners* (1994), *Macroeconomic Policy and the Future of Capitalism* (1996), *Money, Financial Institutions and Macroeconomics* (1997), *What is Money?* (2000), *Globalization and Economic Growth* (2002), *Controversies in Monetary Economics* (1994, 2003), *Fundamentals of Economics for Business* (2006, 2009), and *Money, Enterprise and Income Distribution* (2009).

INTRODUCTORY REMARKS

I have called this book *Essays in the Fundamental Theory of Monetary Economics and Macroeconomics*. It consists of eight extended essays in the form of chapters on the topics about which I have lectured in the graduate course *Advanced Monetary Economics* (ECON 5500) in the Faculty of Graduate Studies, York University, Toronto for close to 20 years. Previously the course was taught by my colleague, the late Professor Meyer Burstein. So there has been considerable continuity in the subjects that have been addressed, for a period of decades. Professor Burstein and I fully agreed on what are the main issues in dispute in monetary economics, and what they have always been (see the list in Chapter 2). However, we probably took opposite substantive positions on each of them. There is another table in Chapter 2 that provides a graphical illustration of what the various intellectual options are.

From my own point of view, I now realize that this work continues the themes that I first addressed more than 30 years ago in my PhD thesis entitled *The Incidence and Economic Effects of the Financing of Unemployment Insurance* (Smithin, 1982). This took an entirely monetary/macroeconomic approach to public finance and included the concepts of endogenous money and credit creation. Work on these and on related issues, again, essentially the list in Chapter 2, has continued and (I hope) advanced and developed, through both editions of my *Controversies in Monetary Economics* (1994, 2003), and more recently in my *Money, Enterprise and Income Distribution* (2009a). In Chapter 7, there is a further progression, which I think moves on from what I wrote in Chapter 10 of MEI. What I there called the "demand for inflation" (DI) schedule now slopes upwards instead of downwards, in what seems to me (as I now think about it) to be a thoroughly "Keynesian" manner. The key to the change is a more detailed discussion of the transmission mechanism of monetary policy, together with the realization that, in principle, there is a negative relationship between the inflation rate and the real interest rate on loans from the commercial banks. The reasons for this are explained in several of the essays, including Chapters 4, 6, 7 and 8. In MEI there was a positive relationship between interest rates and inflation, and hence a negative relationship between interest rates and growth based on the artificially imposed *contra*-inflation preferences of central banks. This was influenced by the inflation-targeting literature of the early 21st century.

In lecturing to graduate students at York, I have tried hard *not* to present the material in a cut-and-dried "textbook" fashion. I have not hesitated, either to present original material, or to fully discuss the various controversies that exist in the field. This is reflected in the structure of the present work, and I think it fair to say that there are original contributions in each chapter.

The mathematical methods used are those that are accessible to beginning graduate students. I remember when that I was in graduate school, in the mid-1970s, I was much disappointed by the seemingly exclusive emphasis on mathematics, at a time when it seemed to me that there were urgent actual economic issues that needed to be discussed. As everyone knows, things have not changed much (if at all) in the interim. On the contrary, the interest in purely mathematical and statistical theory has increased. If, in some sort of time warp, I had to re-enter graduate school again today I would surely have much the same reaction, except that real-world economic problems have greatly intensified.

Nonetheless, in hindsight, I am grateful to my graduate teachers of all those years ago for having forced me to "do the math". I remember that there was a textbook in the mathematics course entitled *Fundamentals Methods of Mathematical Economics* (1974) by Alpa C. Chiang, which was a very clear exposition, and although I initially resented having to spend time on such material, instead of being (*e.g.*) introduced to the classic works in monetary theory, I quickly realized that just by working through it, I was *also* covering the material in all the other courses at the same time (macroeconomics, microeconomics, *etc.*). Each was taught with a highly mathematical approach. In practice this meant that just by learning the math I did save some time that I could spend by reading some of the more interesting literature. I remember being particularly impressed by Hicks's *Critical Essay in Monetary Theory* (2005/1967) which was one of many things that was not on graduate school reading lists in the 1970s, but should have been. As for the mathematics itself, in this book I have frequently referred to the fourth edition (2005) of the previously mentioned text, *Fundamental Methods ...* , now by Chiang and Wainwright. My students tell me that *"plus ca change, plus c'est la meme chose"* as far as mathematical methods in economics are concerned.

But *why* am I grateful for having been forced to do something I did not want to do? I still do not think that grinding through the math contributes much to "monetary science" (Mendoza España, 2012) as such. Anyone who is interested in the substantive issues in that complex field surely has to go far beyond anything on offer in mainstream academic economics. So what is the point? The answer is that I now see the role of the mathematics, *not* as being able to prove anything to anyone (even those who do have the theoretical training) but as a sort of check on one's own theoretical instincts. Is it possible to come up with a mathematical framework that replicates or, somehow conforms to, one's own theoretical insights? This sort of perspective has been ultimately been useful to me in checking that I do know what I think I know. This has been particularly true in the last three years or so, as I have been developing the *Alternative Monetary Model* (AMM) of Chapter 7. I do not think I would go as far as the 19th century economist Alfred Marshall and "burn the mathematics" (Gronewegen, 1995; Keynes, 1933), as otherwise there would be hardly be any point in writing this book. However, there is certainly at stage at which, when the issues *have* been understood, it is time to move on. Marshall himself did not keep to own *dictum.* His motto *natura non facit saltum* (nature does not make leaps) was designed expressly to justify/facilitate the use of differential calculus in economics. However, whether *natura* itself *facit saltum*, or not, the slogan has no real relevance to economics, which is supposedly a social science dealing with entirely different material. As I have argued elsewhere, in the social world there do most certainly occur "... revolutions in human behaviour at certain intervals in which everything changes as well as periods of relative stability. The propensity for sudden change requires ... an explanation quite as much as the periods of relative stability ... " (Smithin, 2009a). To see how this might be do-able, while still using some fairly simple mathematics, see Chapter 7.

As for substance of the mathematical methods used, I fully agree with authors as diverse as Paul Krugman (2012) and John King (2012) that notions of "inter-temporal optimization by representative agents", "the representative agent with rational expectations", the "micro-foundations of macroeconomics" and "dynamic stochastic general equilibrium models" should *not* be at the "heart" of macroeconomics (as Krugman puts it).

Monetary theory *itself* is what should be central. I have, nonetheless, included several examples of representative agent optimization models in what follows, as certainly students should be able to understand what is entailed, at least for the purposes of demystification. Most of the technical models used in what follows are "deterministic", strictly speaking. I have not used so-called "stochastic calculus" except in a couple of places where it is absolutely unavoidable. There are a number of reasons for this. Firstly, from the student's point of view these sorts of techniques are more than adequately covered in several of the other courses they have to take. Moreover, they can use these techniques (if they wish) in either their theoretical or empirical term papers. More fundamentally, from the point of view of "high" theory (Shackle, 1967), I think that it is a definite error to assume that agents living in a non-ergodic environment can be modeled as if they actually believe that the environment is ergodic (Keynes, 1937, 1939; Davidson, 2009, 2011). As I have pointed out elsewhere (Smithin, 2004c, 2009a), Keynes's method of dealing with fundamental uncertainty was to use a deterministic mathematical model for heuristic purposes, while making perfectly clear that at any time changes in expectations, or market sentiment, quite broadly defined, can immediately change the whole picture. The two points at which I have had to resort to the standard probabilistic notation, are (1) in the discussion of rational expectations in Chapter 3 (for obvious reasons), and (2) in the bank optimization model in Chapter 4 based on Kam and Smithin (2012), for the reasons explained there. Otherwise, of course, so-called "perfect foresight" models in the neoclassical tradition are just a special case of rational expectations. Therefore, if it is possible to show monetary non-neutrality in that context, it is possible to show it anywhere.

I would like to thank the following people who over the years have helped me to come to grips, in one way or another, with this difficult material. In alphabetical order, T. G. Albrecht, Constantine Angrydis, Philip Arestis, Sonmez Atesoglu, Syed Ahmad, Dave Barrows, John Beare, the late Stanley Bober, John Burbidge, the late Meyer Burstein, Tom Cate, Victoria Chick, Shin-Hwan Chiang, Kam Hon Chu, David Colander, Avi Cohen, Trevor Coombes, Eugenia Correa, the late Gilles Dostaler, Paul Davidson, Bob Dimand, Alexander Dow, Sheila Dow, Kevin Dowd, Nick Falvo, Tom Ferguson, David Fields, Duncan Foley, Guiseppe Fontana, Mat Forstater, the late Milton Friedman, Noemi Levy-Orlik, John Henry, Omar Hamouda, Harald Hagemann, Geoff Harcourt, the late Sir John Hicks, Geoff Hodgson, Ric Holt, Thomas Humphrey, Geoff Ingham, Tae-Hee Jo, Mundia Kabinga,

Eric Kam, Jong-Chul Kim, Jan Kregel, John King, Kayenat Kabir, Stephanie Kelton (Bell), Alain Parguez, the late Chris Paraskevopolous, Mark Peacock, the late John Pheby, Heiner Ganssman, Claude Gnos, John Grieve-Smith, Brian McLean, Tassos Malliaris, Andre Marques, Markus Marterbauer, Pijus Mitra, Allan Meltzer, D'Ansi Mendoza, Gary Mongiovi, Basil Moore, Warren Mosler, Tracy Mott, Jesus Munoz, Tony Myatt, Jonathan Nitzan, Tom Palley, the late Don Patinkin, John Paschakis, Steve Pressman, Marc Lavoie, David Laidler, Jeff Lau, Janet Landa, Joelle LeClair, Fred Lee, Duncan Li, Yongming Liu, Teresa Lopez-Gonzales, Jean-Guy Loranger, Tony Lawson, Ed Nell, Yogesh Oza, Ingrid Rima, Sylvie Rivot, Les Robb, Gordon Roberts, Louis-Phillipe Rochon, Colin Rogers, Eduardo Rojas, the late T. K. Rymes, Kh. Asad Saeed, the late Otto Steiger, Aqeela Tabassum, Claudio Sardoni, Malcolm Sawyer, Bill Scarth, Mario Seccareccia, Mark Setterfield, Anwar Sheik, Alexander Shoumarov, Barry Smith, Peter Spahn, Gary Sran, the late Lorie Tarshis, Hans-Michael Trautwein, the late James Tobin, Pavlina Tcherneva, Pierre Tu, Mun Tham, Brenda Spotton-Visano, Harvey Schwartz, Mezbah Uddin, Matias Vernengo, Klaus Weiermair, Randy Wray, Bernie Wolf, Frederick Zhou. I am sure there are omissions from this list that should not have been, and I hope anyone who notices this will forgive me.

I owe a real debt (which, contrary to my assertions here, cannot be expressed in purely monetary terms) to my publishers at World Scientific, who have nurtured this project from the beginning. I would like to mention by name Pui Yee Lum, who originally commissioned the manuscript, Yvonne Tan Hiu Ling, who was the first editor, and Sandhya Venkatesh who took over from Yvonne and has seen the project through to completion. Dipasri Sardar has patiently and expertly guided me through the production process.

My wife, Hana Smithin must have the final word of thanks as always, and who else should have it?

CHAPTER 1

MONEY, DEBT AND CREDIT IN THE ENTERPRISE ECONOMY

Introduction

This essay is the first in a collection with the overall title *Essays in the Fundamental Theory of Monetary Economics and Macroeconomics*, and the choice of words immediately raises the question of whether, or not, there is any essential difference between the two fields. In my opinion there really should not be any distinction, in spite of the numerous attempts that have been made (for at least two-and-a-half centuries since Adam Smith) to construct macroeconomic theories that ignore monetary and financial issues.

From a commonsense point of view, economy activity in a capitalist-type system is *all* about money (Smithin, 2000, p. 1). We continually speak and write about "making money", "losing money", "spending money", "saving money", and so forth. Yet, as I have remarked elsewhere (Smithin, 2010, p. 49), it is a curious fact that many of the social science and business disciplines studying economic activity, pay far less attention to this "most important institution in capitalist society" (Ingham, 2004, p. 195) than it seems to deserve. There are many existing theories about what money *does*, such as economic theories about money and inflation, political theories about money and power, sociological theories about money's cultural significance, *etc.* What is missing, however, is any detailed discussion of what a philosopher would call the *ontology* of money (Searle, 2005, p. 1, 2010, p. 5; Mendoza España, 2012). This means thinking about what money actually is, how it comes into being, and what is its nature. In business disciplines like accounting and finance, for example, it is taken for granted that sums of money are the proper subject for discussion, without much further inquiry. In economics, one of the most influential approaches in today's academic mainstream, that is the modern (now highly mathematical) version of the original "neoclassical" approach, has often taught that money itself is *not*

1

fundamentally important, and that what is really going on when economic activity occurs is a barter exchange of goods and services.

The Idea that Money is "Just Another Commodity"

For many centuries, well into the modern era, the ruling idea was that the value of money derives from its own intrinsic worth as a commodity. Classic examples were the precious metals like gold and silver, either as coins or ingots. Such objects were believed to have become money because market forces had made one or other of them the most acceptable or "exchange-worthy" item in trade in a given society. This gave rise to the misleading concept of money as the *medium of exchange*, which still appears prominently in the textbooks to this day. It suggests that the role of money is merely to simplify, make easier, or "lubricate" as the common metaphor would have it, trades that would somehow be taking place anyway. The idea is misleading, because the very notion of an actual physical medium "changing hands" implies that the characteristic transaction is a simple "spot" exchange of one thing for another on the spur of the moment (Hicks, 1989, p. 41). This is not so in any real money-using economy. Particularly for the larger more important transactions it is usually required that some sort of agreement must be reached (some kind of formal or informal contract must be made) before trade takes place. Moreover, it is not possible to be dogmatic about the timing of payment. The contract or agreement always comes first. However, sometimes the buyer must pay "in advance" before delivery of the item, while at other times payment is made later "in arrears". Spot payment is therefore only a special case of one of three possible types of contract (Hicks, 1989, p. 42). In all three cases, it is also implicit that money, the thing offered in *payment* (as opposed to mere exchange), is in a different *category* altogether from the particular good or service being sold. Money is something that, when tendered, definitively seals the bargain. Otherwise, when simply trading an apple for an orange, why not call *either* of them (or both) the medium of exchange?

It is a major weakness of traditional economic thinking that the only attempt made to understand the trading process beyond a simple act of barter was this assumption that market forces will "naturally select" one, or a limited number, of actual physical objects to serve as the money of exchange. Even during historical periods when money was obviously *not* a substantial physical object, for example, when it was a piece of paper or a book entry, it continued to be held that these representations were only symbolic of some more "intrinsically valuable" commodity underlying the whole transaction. However, the idea that the value of money could be guaranteed in this way, for example, by adherence to a commodity standard such as a gold standard or other metallic standard, was always extremely dubious (Innes, 2004/1913, p. 15). In today's world when the physical form of money may be nothing more than electronic impulses in a computer network, the idea that money is *intrinsically* any specific commodity is impossible to sustain. The flickering numbers on the screen do *not* represent any specific good, they are only a generalized unspecific claim to a partial share of the total of goods and services, and the claim exists only because it is socially recognized as such. This part of the claim is what is usually called the "purchasing power" of some particular sum of money. Moreover, purchasing power itself, though it is something that all economic actors must possess to be able to participate in economic activity at all, is subject to continual fluctuation as money prices change.

On the other hand, even if it is true that modern money is (almost) entirely physically *in*substantial (the computer networks themselves do have to exist) it should equally well be noted that the advent of computers, the internet, and so forth, has *not* actually led to the *disappearance* of money. This is contrary to what was frequently claimed would be the "wave of the future" by pundits of the late 20th century (roughly when these sorts of purely technological innovations made their first appearance). Money, in fact, retains the same importance in social life that it has always had, and it is actually quite striking how the contemporary financial problems that have preoccupied the business press in recent years do continue to be discussed in very much the same sort of terms as they always would have been throughout the 20th, 19th and 18th centuries, and earlier, regardless of the state of the technology.

To use some terms from economic sociology, there are really two separate issues that need to be identified in determining the composition of the mysterious entity called money. The first is the question of its "formal validity". What it is that makes money "money" in the sense of simply *qualifying* as 1 dollar, 20 dollars, or 100 dollars, and when tendered is "counted as" being able to settle debts in these amounts (and thereby complete contracts). The second is the "substantive validity" of money, which must mean something like the value of its purchasing power compared to the volume of goods and services available. Monetary theory eventually has to deal with both, but they are very frequently confused right from the start. This simple problem has been the source of much misapprehension and dispute on monetary matters over many centuries. In effect, the notion of intrinsically valuable money was supposed to solve both issues at once. However, the two are indeed separate and therefore the idea of commodity money has actually made very little contribution to understanding what money really is as a set of social relationships, and how the twin problems of the formal and substantive validity of money might be solved.

What is Money?

What, then, *is* money? The main alternative to a commodity theory of money is a "credit" or "claim" theory of money (Schumpeter, 1994/1954; Ingham, 2004, p. 6). Money is not thought of as (primarily) a physical object but as an entry in a ledger, a system of accounts, or a balance sheet. Debts are incurred and paid off by various balance sheet/accounting operations. As mentioned, it then becomes a key issue for the analyst to decide exactly *what* it is in any given system that "counts as" making payments or discharging debt in the circumstances.

The idea of credit money, or debt money, is sometimes expressed by statements to the effect "all money is credit" or "all money is debt", and so forth. For example, the Nobel Prize winning economist, Sir John Hicks, wrote to me in 1988 (the year before his death) as follows[1]:

> You are still at the stage I was at the time of my *Critical Essays* (2005/1967) making hard money and credit money as parallel alternatives. I now maintain that the evolution of money is better understood if one starts with *credit*! (original emphasis)

Meanwhile, Geoffrey Ingham, in his influential book, the *Nature of Money* (2004, p. 198), explicitly states that "all money is debt ..." , and at the same time refers throughout the work to the system of "capitalist credit money".

These positions are obviously far more realistic, both in terms of the historical development of a distinctive system of capitalism, and in thinking about current affairs, than the idea that the origins of money lie merely in the offer of one or another physical item in exchange for some other physical thing. Adam Smith (1981/1776, p. 65) talked about "an early and rude state of society" in which he *imagined* this sort of thing taking place, but as Searle (2010, p. 62) has astutely remarked "*there is no such thing as a state of nature*" (emphasis added) as far as human social institutions, including commerce, are concerned.

However, once we do start talking about social accounting and thereby use terms like "credit money" and "debt money", there is one obvious pitfall that needs to be pointed out and dealt with straight-away. This is simply that in any banking or financial system, credit and debt are just the mirror images of each other. For every debt there is a credit and *vice versa.* If, for example, a commercial bank extends a loan to an individual or a firm, then that would correctly be described as the granting of *credit,* and the loan is an earning *asset* to the bank. On the other hand, if somebody makes a deposit *in* a bank then, from the bank's point of view, that is a *debt* or *liability.* Confusion arises because, by definition, assets must be *equal* to liabilities in a balance sheet. Therefore, when a bank or similar financial institution does extends credit, its asset portfolio increases, but at the same time the liabilities side of the balance sheet must necessarily be rising also. In the simplest case, the person or firm receiving the loan just deposits the funds back with the same bank. Moreover, even if all of the funds are paid away to another financial institution the assets and liabilities of the system *as a whole* rise to exactly the same extent. So, there is always both credit creation and money creation at the same time. Conversely, when the loans are paid back this must amount to the "destruction" of money and credit. We need to be clear, therefore, in discussing these balance sheet operations, about *which* side of the balance sheet contains the entries we actually think of as *money.* The correct answer is that it is the funds (deposits) on the *liabilities* side of bank balance sheets that are the money, precisely to the extent that they can be transferred from one party to another, and therefore used to pay off other debts.

This corresponds to the definition of money given by Hicks in his last book, the posthumously published *Market Theory of Money* (Hicks, 1989, p. 42):

> Money is paid for a discharge of debt when that debt has been expressed in terms of money.

Also relevant is the complete version of Ingham's definition of the same phenomenon (already cited). The completed quotation from Ingham (2004, p. 198) is:

> All money is debt in so far as issuers promise to accept their own money for *any* debt payment by *any* bearer of the money. (original emphasis)

I would say that taken together, these two definitions already cover the historical special case of precious metal coins (and for that matter token coins also) as well as debt money. To make the pieces of metal "money", the issuer or guarantor of coins would always have agree to accept them back in payment of obligations to itself. It was this "acceptability" feature that was the key to the coins being money, not the physical properties of the bits of metal themselves (Ingham, 2004, p. 198). On this account it still needs to be explained *why* the issuers of money are in a position in which other actors have incurred binding obligations to them. If this can be done, then the formal validity of money is explained. Some of the answers that have been given to this question will be discussed in the section on "the hierarchy of money" below. The question of the substantive validity of money is still another matter.

Note that the statement that debts are "expressed in terms of money", immediately introduces the notion of a "money of account", which Keynes said was "the primary concept of a theory of money" (Keynes, 1971a/1930, p. 3). Modern textbooks similarly list one of the functions of money as providing the *unit of account*, meaning by this the abstract concept of a "dollar", a "yen", or a "peso", and so on. This is the unit in which prices are expressed, accounts are recorded and profit is calculated. Unlike Keynes, however, the textbook writers apparently do not think that this function is all that important. This is a mistake, because if there were no such function, it would be impossible to conduct business on a rational basis, or to engage at all in such activities as quoting prices, keeping accounts, or obtaining finance.

It is true that the concept of a unit of account, by itself, is not enough to establish the existence of a "monetary economy". There must also be a *means of payment* recognized as actually constituting the correct number of units of account when transferred. Keynes (1971a/1930, p. 3) explained that the money of account was the "*description* [of the thing]" and money itself was "the *thing* that answers to the description". The description, for example, may be "a dollar" and the "thing" answering the description could be a coin, a note, or an entry in the accounts of a bank. It has already been sufficiently stressed that the means of payment need not be a substantial physical object, but can easily be a book entry or computer transfer, as seen every day. All that is necessary is that what is transferred counts as the required sum in the particular social context (the formal validity of money once again). There is, in fact, no real problem in understanding why such things as the liabilities of banks and other financial institutions can quite easily play this role.

It will have been noticed that a number of the standard textbook functions of money have already been mentioned in the discussion. Sometimes, the textbooks say that money is "a unit of account, a *medium of exchange* and a store of value", whereas in other treatments, the functions are given as "a unit of account, a *means of payment* and store of value". We have stressed that the idea of the unit of account is more important than is usually allowed for in textbooks. Also, that a medium of exchange and a means of payment are *not* the same thing, even though these terms are often used interchangeably, and that the idea of a *means of payment* is by far the more useful concept in an actual money-using capitalist economy.

What, though, of the third function of money, money as a *store of value*? In academic theories of "portfolio choice" or the "demand for money", this is usually treated as a major issue, sometimes *the* major issue. Again, however, the emphasis seems all wrong. It is true that if money is to constitute "purchasing power" it must retain value, to at least to some extent, from one period to the next. Also someone, somewhere, must be willing to hold the money (that is, primarily, must be willing to hold bank deposits) correspondingly. However, money is obviously not the only, nor necessarily the best, possible store of value. A diamond ring, a house, a stock market portfolio, or a painting by a famous artist, can serve the same purpose — sometimes much better (for example, when money prices are rising). In spite of this, it has been noticed in history that money has frequently continued to be held and performed the unit of account and means of payment functions through out periods of inflation, and often for long after inflation rates have reached hyperinflationary levels. Therefore, it seems that these other two functions are what *really* matters (Hicks, 1989, p. 42).

This statement is by no means to deny that money might be more useful in capitalism if its "real value" could be kept more stable. In context, real value means the stability of purchasing power, as measured by an index of the average level of prices. To use the traditional notation, if M is an amount of money in dollars, and P is an index for the average (or aggregate) level of prices, then M/P will be the level of "real money balances" held. In terms of the formal and substantive validity of money, if we can decide what should be included in the calculation of M, this will define the formal validity of money. If we can then work out the value of M/P, this would represent money's substantive validity. However, the ability to preserve the value of real money balances (the substantive validity of money) in terms of its purchasing power does *not* necessarily mean that the rate of inflation — the *percentage rate of change* of the price level — must itself always be zero. This is frequently the conclusion reached in orthodox approaches to monetary economics. However, this same stability could also be achieved if, for example, the interest rate *paid* on nominal money balances, M, were to keep pace with the inflation rate. This is a point I have long argued (Smithin, 1994, 2003, 2010, p. 51).

Money as a Social Relation

It frequently bothers people to learn, as has just been suggested, that money is created when financial institutions make loans or purchase other assets, and effectively "destroyed" when the loans are called in. The idea that it is all done "with the stroke of a pen" (today, more likely a keystroke) is somehow disquieting. However, which is a point certainly not widely understood by either economists (Searle, 2010, pp. 200–201) or political pundits, is that just because something is not defined by its physical properties this does *not* mean it is not "real" (in the commonsense meaning of the term) or it cannot have causal effects in the physical/material world.[2] In fact, this is a characteristic property of all social institutions, social relations, or social facts (Ingham, 2005/1996; Mendoza España, 2012; Searle, 1995, 1998, 2005, 2010; Smithin, 2009a, 2010). They are in a different category from the so-called "brute facts", physical facts or the laws of nature, and money is a prime example of the general principle (Searle, 1998, pp. 126–128).

A "social fact" is what it is, not by the laws of nature, but because it is widely accepted as such by convention. To use some technical terms from social philosophy, it will involve such things as "collective intentionality", the "assignment of status function", and the adherence to "rules and norms" of behaviour (Searle, 2005, p. 19, 2010, pp. 40–43). A classic *non-economic* example would be something like a "line drawn in the sand" (Smithin, 2009a, p. 51) that serves as a boundary between two warring factions, or just two quarrelsome individuals on a beach. If both parties respect the boundary, it *does* keep the peace, not by virtue of its physical properties (nothing actually prevents anyone from stepping over the line), but only because it is respected as such. It can be *effective*, and has a definite impact in the world, as long as its conditions of existence are in place. As long as this is so, it continues to count as a barrier to the parties involved and they behave accordingly.

It seems to me that there are obvious parallels to be drawn with many of the most important economic institutions, including money itself, and all such things as titles to property, firms, banks, mortgages, pension plans, *etc.* All rely on the same sort of conditions of existence as the boundary line, and are just as real and "binding" on the individuals participating in them. The example of the boundary line, however, also illustrates how very easily a social consensus can evaporate. The boundary may seem, at one moment, to represent a solid barrier and an unbreakable taboo. At the next, if someone steps over it and no retaliation follows, it simply crumbles. There seems to be a clear correspondence between this and a typical sequence of events in the financial world (*e.g.*) in times of crisis.

For many people, the difficulty in grasping the analogy apparently lies not only in an instinctive rejection of idealist metaphysics so far as the brute facts are concerned, but rather in an inability to recognize that there exists *another* whole category of facts in the real world, social facts, which are not defined by their physical properties but nonetheless have definite causal effects. To again resort to some philosophical jargon these sorts of realities can be described as "ontologically subjective" but "epistemologically objective" (Searle, 1998, pp. 111–117). Although they may only exist in the form of human convention (essentially in people's minds) they do "matter". They have a real impact on behaviour and motivations, and *via* these routes on the material world. From this point of view (once the notion has been grasped) it is rather the longstanding tradition in economics to the effect that "money does not matter", "money is a veil", "money is an illusion", "money is neutral", and so forth that is strange and unrealistic. No-one would say that the boundary line does not matter, or any other binding social convention, so why should monetary, financial, and debt relationships be any different?

Money and "Enterprise"

If there has been confusion about the concept of money in mainstream economics, it has to be said that much the same is true even about the idea of an "economy" itself. The term, economy, is usually taken to refer generically to all possible methods of obtaining provisions. On this reasoning, the 17th century fictional character, Robinson Crusoe, for example, alone on a deserted island, is supposed to be as much engaged in "economic activity" as anyone else. In fact, the fictional *Crusoe Economy* is often a favourite starting point for a conventional economic analysis (Robbins, 1998; Robertson, 1940; Rothbard, 1998). The choices that Crusoe has to make are often presented as the paradigmatic example of the economic problem of "resource allocation". In spite of its continuing popularity, however, this discussion actually makes no sense at all as *social science*. By definition, the decisions the lonely Crusoe makes are not relevant to anyone but himself. Crusoe may well decide to "build a shelter" today rather than "go out fishing" or *vice versa*, and these decisions may make perfect sense to him, and be said to represent an "optimal allocation of resources" in this artificially narrow context. However, Crusoe does *not* have to worry about competition in the market for new housing, what amount of *money* the fish will bring when offered for sale, the availability of credit financing, the cost of health care, or indeed about the vast majority of the things that are of concern to people in a real economy. He is actually not participating in an economy in any meaningful sense.

Once we move beyond the isolated individual, and therefore have to "make provision" for more than one person, there are really only four other basic frameworks that have been identified in political economy and economic sociology, *potentially* capable of achieving this. The first of these might conveniently be labeled as a *traditional economy*, of which there have been countless variations in historical practice, such as hunting and gathering or traditional agriculture, for example. Whatever the details of how subsistence is achieved, the central organizing principle of a traditional economy is simply that what work should be done, when, by whom, and how the proceeds are to be shared, is settled precisely by custom or tradition.

The next broad generic type of economic framework would be that of a *command economy*. In this case, someone simply gives orders about what should be done, and how the produce should be divided, and the others obey. The notion of a command economy clearly also covers many historical and practical variants. It is the method of armies, for example, and of the various state socialisms of the 20th century, but also that of outright slavery, and physical and mental coercion of all kinds.

A third *potential* method (and here the emphasis should be particularly noted) is the notion of voluntary exchange in a free market. This is usually put forward as a normative ideal (rather a historical case study) by (*e.g.*) libertarians, free market economists and others. It is regarded as a much superior alternative to either custom or command, both because of the material benefits that may supposedly be achieved, and the absence of any form of coercion. The basic notion is that individuals offering items for trade will have either have made them by their own hands, or have otherwise acquired *undisputed* property rights in the goods and services offered, and that everything is done on a voluntary basis. Therefore, the goal of individual liberty is maximized. The difficulty with the argument is not with this "moral" standpoint, but because the concept of the market employed is purely abstract. It seems to lack any of the social structure that is necessary for actual markets to exist. For example, the decisive point in the present context, this type of system is frequently portrayed or modeled as ideally functioning *without* the need for money or financial accommodation of any kind (and possibly without even an abstract unit of account). The most rhetorically persuasive theoretical accounts are of such a system of exchange *lacking* all the financial and monetary paraphernalia of any real market system.

According to the theory, even if one of the commodities is chosen as simply a monetary *numeraire*, or somehow becomes the "medium of exchange" for convenience, as discussed earlier, this is supposed to make no difference at all to the way in which the system operates. Lack of attention to actual social structures means that it can hardly be correct to identify the abstract "pure exchange system" as resembling anything called capitalism, although it is unfortunately true that terms like "the market economy", "the free market", and "capitalism" are often very carelessly used as synonyms in both academic and political debates. Any system designated as capitalism must, of course, include the sale of goods (for *money*) in the market-place. However, even as far the discussion of money has taken us to this point, it can be seen that it necessarily involves much more than this in terms of social structure (Smithin, 2009a, pp. 20–22, 2009b, 2011). Therefore, following Keynes (1973), the hypothesized pure exchange system should have its own separate label and be defined as the *barter exchange economy*. Given that the idea is primarily a "thought experiment" about what might happen under hypothesized conditions, the system is also actually in a similar epistemological category to the fictional Crusoe example. They both differ from the alternatives of either command or custom, as *only* the latter have ever existed in historical actuality as *practical* methods of provisioning various societies.

Finally, there is the method of producing and delivery goods and services originally identified by the sociologist Max Weber (2003/1927, pp. 275–278), as part of his effort to decipher "the meanings and presuppositions of *modern capitalism*" (emphasis added). This, therefore, is a system which was certainly supposed to correspond to historical reality and, by implication, had reached something like its full maturity during Weber's own lifetime in the late 19th and early 20th centuries. It is defined as follows (Collins, 1986, pp. 21–22):

> (T)he provision of human needs by the *method of enterprise*, which is to say by private businesses seeking profit. (emphasis added)

It is interesting that this definition, quite sensibly, avoids entirely the problem of trying to pin down the vague, ambiguous, and ultimately vacuous, concept of "capital" itself (Smithin, 2009a, p. 2). At the same time, however, the use of the term modern in the previously cited quotation also indicates that, from one point of view, the author has cast his analytical net too narrowly. The point is that the method of enterprise, as defined above, and "commercial society" in general, would surely have been also recognizable as such in a much wide variety of temporal, geographical, and cultural *mileux* long before Weber was writing. Moreover, a hundred years later, we can see that this profit motive as evidently still a *main* or *underlying* principle of most of the extant economic systems today, in all parts of the globe. This statement remains valid, even though in *all* cases in the real world, both past and present, there clearly has never been a pure unmixed version of the enterprise economy. In all cases substantial "command" elements have been, or have remained, in place. There have always been such things as government bureaucracy and regulation, the police and armed forces, nationalized industries, and so forth, to a greater or lesser extent. So, in principle, what we should really mean by the enterprise economy is any system in which the profit motive plays a significant or leading role. As in cases of the command economy and the traditional economy, it can be readily conceded that there have been a number of historical variants.

It is highly significant, however, that of the (altogether) five potential alternative methods for obtaining provisions, mainstream economics in the academic world has seemed determined to focus exclusively on the two that are essentially hypothetical, conjectural or fictional (Dillard, 1988; Robbins, 1998), namely the Crusoe economy and the barter exchange economy. To that extent the economics profession can reasonably be accused of having badly misdirected its efforts.

To make such a statement is *not* to say that no-one has ever been stranded on a deserted island, or that it has never happened that barter exchange has occurred between (say) different nomadic tribes, foreign explorers and native peoples, or individuals in special situations such as the famous example of the POW (prisoner of war) camp during World War II (Radford, 2005/1945). Obviously, it is always *possible* for any two parties that come into contact to strike up any sort of "bargain" that they can reach an *ad-hoc* basis. Such parties can range from individuals, to social groups, to corporations, to the state. It is also possible for an individual to suddenly be placed in an extreme existential situation by accident, like Crusoe. However, *unlike* tradition, command or enterprise, what *is* in grave doubt is the idea that either of the other two modes of conduct has ever been the *main principle* by which any society has achieved its basic subsistence. That notion is entirely fanciful.

Discussions of the hypothetical existence of a fully-fledged barter exchange economy without money have occurred regularly throughout the history of economic thought, but there have never been descriptions of any historical reality. They have usually been mere thought experiments about the labour theory of value, or some other value theory. In the era of classical economics, this was true of both Adam's Smith's (1981/1776, pp. 65–66) discussion of isolated hunter-gathers (improbably) regularly exchanging "one beaver . . . for . . . two deer" (*op. cit.*), and also of Ricardo's (2004/1817, pp. 134–136) exposition of the principle of comparative advantage, with a hypothetical "England" and a hypothetical "Portugal" trading *physical* quantities of cloth for wine (in reality, England bought wine for *money* and Portugal bought cloth for *money*). Similar remarks could really be made about *all* such discussions, ranging from Aristotle (2006) in the 4th century BCE, to the likes of Marx (1970/1859, 1976/1867) and Menger (1892) in the 19th century (writers supposedly on opposite sides of the *political* spectrum, but sharing common Aristotalian roots on the subject of money), then on through 20th century authors like Robertson (1948/1922, 1940) and Robbins (1998), up to and including 21st century textbooks.[3]

Two main issues seem to arise in considering Weber's more realistic idea of the method of enterprise. Firstly, just by delineating this one particular method of providing for human needs compared to the others, it immediately highlights this question about *which* of them the social scientist concerned with economic issues should be studying. In spite of the obsession with barter exchange by its practitioners, it is notable that economic analysis *in itself as a specialized field of study*, has arisen only in connection with the rise of modern commercial society in the last few hundred years at most (Heilbroner, 1992, 1999; Heilbroner and Milberg, 1995; Smithin, 2009a, pp. 2–4). It therefore seems to be a straightforward argument that it is the method of enterprise which economists *should* be studying, rather than "institution free" mathematical theories of resource allocation (Lau and Smithin, 2002, pp. 6–7).[4] Second, and crucially, what is this "profit" that provides the incentive for private firms to act? Most obviously it is a sum of *money*, implying that the system could not function in its absence, and ruling out the possibility of achieving the same results through non-monetary methods.

The last point concerns the very feasibility of a system of production that entails taking a long position in goods and services, and functions *via* the generation and realization of monetary profits. To pursue this issue, and in spite of the original author's hostility to the profit motive, it is useful to go all the way back to Marx's exposition (Marx, 1976/1867) of what was later called the "monetary circuit" (Graziani, 2003; Parguez and Seccareccia, 2000, p. 101). In symbols the circuit goes as follows:

$$M - C - C' - M'. \tag{1.1}$$

This suggest that entrepreneurs first acquire money, M (by borrowing, issuing shares, or retaining previous earnings), with which they then acquire commodities, C, that are used in a production process to make more commodities, C'. Therefore, term $C' - C$ (C' minus C) is supposed to be the "real value-added" created as a result of the production process. The newly produced commodities, C', are then finally sold for more money, M'. The difference between M' and M is the money profit, without which, in the specific social setting, there would be no incentive for production to take place at all, because there would be no possibility of actually "realizing" the value-added that has presumably been created in the form of purchasing power.

Marx did not think the profit motive was legitimate, but nonetheless the single most important question to ask, in attempting to understand how the method of enterprise actually works is how it can even be *possible* for M' to be greater than M ($M' > M$) and thereby for money profits to exist, in the aggregate and on average across all enterprises? There is really only one viable answer (although it is not clear that either Marx, or Weber, or Keynes, for that matter, would have responded in this way). This is simply that, during the circuit, *both* credit and money creation must have taken place. Note that the orthodox economic concept of an increase in the "velocity of circulation" (of a fixed amount of money) is not relevant here. For example, in the case of paper money, a \$20 bill may pass from hand to hand and, in doing so appear to generate as much as \$100, \$200, or \$300 worth of business over some given period of time. However, still nobody can end up with any more than \$20 in their pocket, or to show to their accountant. This is an essential point.

For a more concrete example, imagine a hypothetical world that already has some familiar social structure in it (banks, for example), but initially has only one entrepreneur, who wants to make money by manufacturing a product called "widgets". The entrepreneur goes to a bank and takes out a loan of (say) $1,000,000 to spend on wages and raw materials. This appears on the asset side of the bank balance sheet, and, as described, will also create $1,000,000 worth of money in bank deposits on the liabilities side. Suppose further that after this event nothing else occurs in the financial sphere. No other entities are willing to take on loans or to make deposits, other than the original entrepreneur and the original workers/suppliers of materials. Meanwhile, the widgets are produced and offered for sale. It is actually *impossible* for the entrepreneur to make a profit in these circumstances. There is only $1,000,000 of money (that is, $1,000,000 in bank deposits, now in the accounts of the workers and suppliers), in existence. Therefore, even if the widget workers and suppliers are willing to spend *all* of their incomes on widgets and do no saving, there is *still* not enough money in the world for the entrepreneur even to pay interest to the bank, let alone make a profit.

How can this situation be resolved? The answer has to be that some other person or institution must also be willing to go into debt in order to accrue profits to the first mover. There are basically only three possibilities (or four, if we distinguish between domestic and foreign consumers). First, other entrepreneurs might be willing to take the same sort of chance. If a producer of another product "super widgets" also borrows $1,000,000 at the same time as the original widget maker, but the new product takes longer to make, when the original widgets come on the market there will be a total of $2,000,000 in existence. It will then be at least possible for the original widget-maker to make profits and repay interest and principal. This will depend on whether enough of the deposit-holders decide to buy widgets. Note, however, if this happens, and the first loan is paid off, the money supply declines, meaning that the maker of "super widgets" now, in turn, depends on some third party becoming indebted in order to have a chance to also make a profit. There would have to be, for example, a manufacturer of "extra super widgets" with a still longer production period, also willing to borrow, and so on. This is the reason why Keynes (1964/1936, p. 161) said that there would be trouble if the "animal spirits" of entrepreneurs ever faltered.

The second possibility is that consumers themselves (domestic or foreign) are willing to become indebted in terms of domestic currency to buy the widgets. In this case, there would be an issue of how a consumer-led boom can keep going if the consumers have trouble paying their debts.

Thirdly, the state itself could go into debt. It could run a budget deficit, and create monetary demand in that way. This was extremely important historically in the actual genesis of capitalism (Ingham, 2004; Kim, 2011), and there is no question of the state ever going bankrupt as it is the issuer of the money.[5] There could still be problems, however, due to the reaction of those politicians who *are* concerned about this sort of thing as is confirmed in real world politics every day. There might be calls to return to a "balanced budget", "sound finance", "fiscal responsibility", "austerity", *etc.*, thereby threatening, in effect, to shut everything down. Those in the society who already do have some money holdings (bank deposits) in place, of course, might also point to the opposite danger, that the budget deficit might become be too large, too *much* money (from their point of view) might be created and *existing* wealth devalued through inflation.

The last statement brings up the completely general point that for the money profits to be "real" (using this term now in the sense of "not inflationary") $M' > M$ must stimulate production in "value" or "volume" terms, that is $C' > C$, to the same extent. If the volume of commodities, C, stays constant there is no actual value-added production and $M' > M$ will only mean a rise in money prices. Credit creation is therefore a necessary, but not sufficient, condition for the existence of real profit. Presumably, it is this sort of thing that those who complain about "excessive" credit creation, propose to strictly limit the quantity of money, or worry about the "deficit" must be thinking. However, this way of looking at the problem is misguided. A binding restriction on the size of the money supply would only lead to more economic problems. There is no incentive for production to place at all (no incentive for anyone to take action to expand the value of commodities to C'), unless there *are* indeed some money profits to be made. Rather, it makes intuitive sense that the goal of policy should be to allow "just enough" credit creation to make $M' > M$ roughly correspond to $C' > C$ and not be channeled primarily into raising either the nominal prices of goods and services or the nominal prices of assets. The real difficulty that faces policy-makers and politicians along the political spectrum, is that this is far easier "said than done".

It certainly *cannot* be done simply by adherence to any (up-dated) version of the ancient "real bills doctrine" for the regulation of credit creation. This is the set of ideas which dominated the policy of the US Federal Reserve System for a long time after its founding in 1913 (Humphrey, 1993a; Meltzer, 2003, 2009a, 2009b; Smithin, 2003, pp. 88–92), and there are many modern proposals of the same general type. The real bills doctrine would seek to make sure that $M' > M$ always corresponds to $C' > C$ by either formal or informal (legal) regulation of the norms for banking behaviour. The idea of a "real bill" is a term that goes all the way back to Adam Smith in 1776 (Smithin, 2003, p. 88), and was supposedly a security which genuinely financed goods in process, as opposed to financial speculation. The 20th century version of this was an argument to the effect that if the commercial banks were to restrict themselves to short-term lending to finance "genuine" current production, all would be well. Unfortunately, these arguments, and each of its variants, are, and always have been, fallacious. In practice, any number of promises to pay can be issued in connection with the forward delivery of the same set of goods (that is the same goods can be re-sold any number of times). Also, the money value of any goods (or assets in some versions) serving to "back the bills" must necessarily contain a price as well as a quantity component. What does it mean to say that some piece of collateral is worth say $10,000, $20,000 or $30,000? If the higher figure is quoted, that will justify the creation of money of exactly the right amount to make the nominal valuation come true. The point is that, in the aggregate, no real bills-like criterion can provide an effective check on inflation, because any arbitrary increases in the money prices of the goods concerned will automatically be validated by subsequent endogenous increases in the nominal money supply (Humphrey, 1993a, pp. 22–23; Smithin, 2003, pp. 89–90). The upshot of this argument is that there has to be some other type of policy management, specifically *macroeconomic* policy management, to include both monetary policy (interest rate policy) and fiscal policy (the management of government spending and taxation), if indeed we are to ensure that "$M' > M$" does not greatly outstrip "$C' > C$". Regulation of the real bills type will not be enough.[6]

The need for $M' > M$ also brings out the important point that, although any single firm or individual may believe that they can "finance" their activities *without* the need for money creation, and still be profitable, this cannot be true for the economy as whole. As mentioned, the individual firm does indeed perceive all sorts of different financing choices available to it, as in a hypothetical "case in finance" in business school (issue bonds, issue equities, use retained earnings, *etc.*). However, all of these methods just transfer money from one use to another. They do not create any *new* money. So, although, in such circumstances (if these are the only methods of financing available) it still would be possible for a single firm to make a profit (at the expense of another firm elsewhere in the system), the economy *as a whole* cannot monetarily realize profits unless there is credit creation and money creation exactly as described.

On the subject of the different sources of finance there are also very often statements in the literature, such as that by Burstein (1995, p. 8), writing in this case about Wicksell, that "(h)e [Wicksell] much exaggerates the importance of banking in finance". What seems to be meant by statements like this (and there are many more recent examples) is, again, that at particular point in time the total amount of equities, bonds, and other types of financial securities issued may bear a greater or lesser proportion to the total of bank loans outstanding. Therefore, wherever, the proportion of "banking" in the overall total seems to be in decline, there are discussions in the financial literature about "disintermediation", "securitization", and so on, whatever terms are currently in vogue. As already seen, however, from the point of view of a *logical* understanding of how the system functions, what money is and "where it is that profits come from" (Collins, 1986, pp. 122–123; Schumpeter, 1983/1934), it is impossible to exaggerate the importance of the *basic* phenomenon of credit and money creation in the underlying structure of the enterprise economy.

Hierarchical Notions of Money

In an important paper, Bell (2005/2001, p. 505) argues that as money is indeed a social relation involving indebtedness, there will always be a hierarchy of money, depending on the issuer. Debts are of different quality from the point of view of the creditor (Hicks, 1989, p. 48), and therefore some types of money are more acceptable than others. However (strangely), this point is often obscured in textbooks on money, making it difficult for readers to understand why, for example, central banks can usually conduct monetary policy by manipulating interest rates, or what is actually happening in a financial crisis.

Any individual or institution can issue promises to pay (IOUs) denominated in the unit of account, on whatever terms. The question is, rather, how reliably those promises will be kept? To illustrate this point, Bell (2005/2001, pp. 505–508) envisages a simplified four-tier inverted "debt pyramid" ranking groups of debtors roughly in descending order of the acceptability of their promises. Generally speaking, households will tend to be on the fourth tier (actually the top of the inverted pyramid) business firms on the third, banks and other financial institutions on the second, and the state or government at the base. A stylized version of the debt pyramid is illustrated in Fig. 1.1.

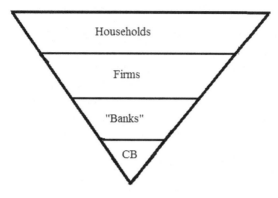

Fig. 1.1.   The debt pyramid.

A promise to pay by a household or a firm in the "higher" (less accept-able) tiers pyramid is not necessarily accepted at face value. This is simply because it may not be reliable. To deliver the required number of units of account, a firm would have to make profits correctly denominated in the unit of account, and in an acceptable form, a household would have to make wages correctly denominated, and so on. There must always be some doubt about their ability to do so, and this is *essentially* the meaning of the much abused term "risk" in the financial context.[2] Securities (IOUs) offered by those in the third and fourth tiers may therefore have to trade at a discount, or offer a higher rate of interest as a "risk premium" (Bell, 2005/2001, p. 506), in order to be accepted at all. Another way of making some higher tier IOUs more acceptable might be a promise of "conversion" into the debt of an entity further down in the pyramid. For example, obli-gations of some banks and other financial institutions in the second tier might be acceptable "at face value" because they are, in principle, con-vertible into first tier obligations (lower in the diagram) essentially those of the state central bank. This notion of "convertibility" was, in fact, also the basis of the old-fashioned gold standard of the 19th and early 20th centuries. At that time bank notes, including those of central banks, were convertible into gold coins. In the modern world, however, the liabilities of the second tier commercial banks are just convertible into the liabilities of the state central bank (CB). The liabilities of the CB itself are at the base of the pyramid, and do not need to be converted into anything else.

In the most general terms, the liabilities of the central bank are usu-ally defined as "currency in the hands of the non-bank public", CU, plus "bank reserves", R. Bank reserves, in turn, comprise the *remaining* cash outstanding in the vaults and tills, and automatic teller machines (ATMs), of the commercial banks, *plus* the deposits that are held by the commercial banks with the state central bank. These are assets to the commercial banks, but are liabilities to the state central bank. In the USA, these sorts of deposits are called "federal funds" which is actually a good description, but the terminology is not in use everywhere. The *total* of central bank liabilities is often called the "monetary base", or alternatively "high powered money". This last expression is not now a very accurate term as it is a holdover from the days of monetarism and the concept of the quantitative money multiplier. Nonetheless, we can conveniently use the symbol H, (at least) to stand for the base to sharply distinguish it from the overall money supply, M. The algebraic expression for the monetary base will therefore be:

$$H = CU + R. \tag{1.2}$$

It would clearly be possible in some future state of the world to imagine a system in which there are no actual bits of paper or coins and everything is done by computer. H and R would then simply be deposits on the liabilities side of the central bank balance sheet and nothing more than computer entries. In either state of the world, with cash or without, the total of H actually in existence at any point in time can easily be a very low figure compared to the total amount of deposits in the commercial banks. Its importance is conceptual rather than quantitative.

But, *why*, in fact, is there no need to convert the liabilities of the state central bank into anything else? The most plausible explanation for this is that given by the "chartalist" and "neo-chartalist" schools (Knapp, 1973; Wray, 1998, 2000; Goodhart, 2005). This is the argument that the most obvious characteristic of the state, as a whole, is that it has the formidable power to levy taxes. However, to give its money any sort of "currency" the state must accept back its own liabilities in payment of those same taxes. Taxation, therefore, is what gives rise to the initial demand for state-issued base money. It is needed in the first instance for the purpose of paying taxes, but then for convenience may be used for various private transactions also, including cash transactions and also for the clearing of settlement balances between private financial institutions who themselves have taken on obligations denominated in the unit of account.

Recall that the *general* principle set out earlier was that money is a social relation, or social institution, and that therefore the choice of the "ultimate" form of payment rests on the collective acceptance of whatever it is that finally discharges a debt. What the chartalists have added, to this basic notion, is that the specific social relation, decisive in practice, is the power of the state to levy taxes.

To avoid a misunderstanding about this point, prevalent ever since the original publication of Knapp's *State Theory of Money* in 1905, it should be emphasized, again, that what is at stake here is simply establishing the *formal* validity of money as defined earlier. At this stage of the argument the question of the *substantive* validity of money (for example, the determination of the price level) is not yet addressed. Nor is the argument simply that the state creates *fiat* money *ex-nihlio*, or is able to pass laws about "legal tender". The chartalist view is rather, based squarely on a definite position about social ontology as previously stated. This ability of the state to impose taxation is a clear example of a social relationship, or social fact. The money is not created "out of nothing" but as a result of a concrete set of social/power relationships. This discussion, of course, relates primarily to sovereign states with their own separate currency (as mentioned earlier). Although the existence of common currencies between different political jurisdictions does not contradict the "state theory of money", it nonetheless does imply that states which are members of a common currency area, such as the Euro-zone of the early 21st century have essentially provincial status from the monetary point of view.

It is important to note that the modern state will also typically accept the liabilities of certain "second-tier" financial institutions *directly* in payment of taxes (Bell, 2005/2001, pp. 506–507). That is they will accept cheques drawn on some commercial banks and other financial institutions in the second tier, that are correctly denominated in the unit of account, as discharging tax bills. All current taxpayers know this as a matter of common experience. The acceptance by the state of certain commercial bank liabilities in discharging tax debt then validates such obligations as money over and above any convertibility feature.

To summarize, the overall supply of money, M, may be said to consist of some subset of the total deposit liabilities, D, of certain financial institutions in the second tier (validated by the tax/money nexus) plus (again) currency in the hands of the public, CU. Therefore,

$$M = CU + D. \tag{1.3}$$

The money supply M, and the monetary base H, have only one term in common. Also, H in the modern world is also insignificant numerically compared to M. This does not mean that base money H is unimportant. Its existence is what ultimately allows the central bank its leverage over monetary (interest rate) policy. However, M best corresponds to what is meant by the overall "supply of money" in most textbook theories about the impact of money on the economy.

In fact, if we look at the website of any real world central bank we will see data for several *different* versions of M. These will have labels such as $M1$, $M2$, $M3$, and so on. In Canada, there are even such magnitudes as "$M1+$" and "$M2++$". This is due to the debate over *which* specific types of deposit, in precisely *which* financial institutions should be included. The central banks thus hedge their bets, so to speak, by reporting on a number of different magnitudes. For the purposes of theoretical discussion, however, we assume that both of the terms D and M are defined as broadly/inclusively as necessary.

It is a truism that the central bank can only *directly* affect the supply of the (smaller) monetary base H (its own liabilities) essentially *via* balance sheet operations. However, most schools of thought in monetary economics have also usually argued that (one way or another) they can attempt to control the total volume of bank lending, and hence M, indirectly how sarcasted that control can be is a matter of intense debate. Importantly, as the central bank is the "monopolist" in base money it can indeed control the rate of interest on loans of base money, using a variety of financial techniques. Notice, however, that if the bank does chose *to* set this interest rate at a definite level the actual quantity of H wide have to be left to find its own level. The interest rate on loans of base money is often a very short-term interest rate (perhaps an overnight rate). The precise institutional details of how the central bank sets this interest rates will differ from country to country, and have differed over time within each country as the institutions change and evolve. In the USA, the policy rate is currently identified as the so-called "federal funds rate". It is called the "overnight rate" in Canada, the "main refinancing rate" in the Euro zone, the "overnight call rate", in Japan, and so on. In earlier times, in the 19th and early 20th centuries, there was more emphasis on what was then called either the "bank rate" or the "discount rate" the rates at which central banks would lend directly to the other financial institutions. (These last two expressions frequently occur in the classic monetary literature.) In this set of essays, we will usually refer to the interest rate on loans of central bank liabilities simply as the *policy rate*.

When the central bank changes the policy rate, this is clearly also intended at least to influence the interest rates both charged and received by the commercial banking system for their *own* lending and deposit taking *via* the so-called "transmissions mechanism" of monetary policy. This works because the commercial banks do need central bank base money to settle claims among themselves, and also because no individual commercial bank can afford to get too far "out of step" with its rivals in the composition of its portfolio (Keynes, 1971a/1930, p. 23). Therefore, *reductions* in the policy rate of the central bank are usually intended to reduce interest rates in general, and thereby increase commercial bank lending (and ultimately *increase* the overall money supply *via* this route). Similarly, *increases* in the policy rate are intended to have the opposite effect. They are supposed to increase interest rates in general, reduce bank lending, and ultimately *reduce* the overall money supply. This interest rate channel is, therefore, one of the main ways in which the central bank can be thought to have any influence over the broader money supply. However, there is unlikely to be any precise quantitative relationship between H and M along the lines of what the older generation of textbooks called the "money multiplier". (This now somewhat outdated concept is further discussed in Chapter 3.) The point has already been made that in the modern world the actual amount of H in existence at any one time may actually be a very low figure. Most payments, including those for taxes, can comfortably be made using M.

To sum up, it can reasonably be argued that because of its irreducibly hierarchical nature money, in practice, is likely to be a "creature of the state" (Lerner, 2005/1947, p. 467). This therefore explains why central banks seem inevitably to play a leading role (Dow and Smithin, 1999; Smithin, 1994, 2003, 2009a). It is important to realize, however, that to make this sort of point is not, in principle, to argue strongly in favour of "government control of the economy", of or socialism. If the government were completely in control, the resulting economy would be an example of a "command" economy, it would not be the "method of enterprise". The argument rather simply entails a recognition of "social reality" (Searle, 1995, 2010), in the sense of what *sort* of institutions are needed for the method of enterprise even to exist. The possibilities of success for the market economy or capitalism do, in fact, seem to depend on a particular *type* of relationship between the state and the private sector, and therefore (very much so) on the sensible use of such monetary and fiscal policy instruments as are available to government.

Monetary Policy and Real Interest Rates

Because of the complex relationship that exists between the power of the state to levy taxes and the phenomenon of money and credit creation, the main control exercised by the central bank, not itself the taxing authority, is over the policy rate of interest. Indirectly, therefore, *via* the monetary policy transmission mechanism, the central bank can thereby also hope to have some influence or control over interest rates in general.

It should now be stressed that what matters is always the "real" rather the "nominal" rate of interest. A *nominal* interest rate is simply the percentage number quoted in the financial press for loans of money. This might be 1%, 3.25% or 5.5%, for example. A *real* rate, however, is the nominal rate *less* the generally expected rate of inflation. If expected inflation is (*e.g.*) 2%, the real rates, corresponding to the nominal rates just quoted, will therefore be -1.0%, 1.25%, and 3.5%, respectively. In general, for any type of interest rate (policy rate or otherwise) let r stand for the real rate, i for the nominal rate, and p^e for the expected inflation rate (lower case p is the percentage rate of change of the aggregate price level P). In this notation, the *expected real interest rate* will be, by definition:

$$r = i - p^e. \tag{1.4}$$

The expected real rate of interest is therefore equal to the nominal rate of interest minus expected inflation.

The expected inflation rate is, of course, not known for certain, and therefore the expected real interest rate is not known for certain. For some purposes, however, a reasonable "proxy" (Taylor, 1993, p. 195) or educated guess, for what "most people think" the real interest rate might be at any point in time is the *inflation-adjusted real interest rate*. This can be defined as simply a nominal interest rate less the currently observed inflation rate. We can therefore often say something like:

$$r = i - p \quad (approx.). \tag{1.5}$$

Now, use the specific symbol i_B to stand for the *nominal policy rate* itself, the effective nominal interest rate on loans of *base money*. (The subscript "B" has the connotation of the classic/historical term "bank rate", and serves to distinguish it from other interest rates in the system.) Given the logic from Eq. (4), which applies to all interest rates, the "*expected real policy rate*", r_B the expected real cost of borrowing base money, will therefore be:

$$r_B = i_B - p^e. \tag{1.6}$$

The notation r'_B (with the prime symbol) will be reserved specifically to mean the *inflation-adjusted real policy rate*, so that:

$$r'_B = i_B - p. \tag{1.7}$$

The inflation-adjusted real policy rate r'_B therefore has a specific meaning, and, note that, in principle, it is actually a definite policy choice, even if the central bank authorities are not consciously aware of making it. It would always be *possible* to adjust i_B whenever the observed inflation rate changes and thereby stabilize r'_B at any desired figure. Therefore, the actual level of r'_B is, clearly, in that sense, a choice. To illustrate, if we look at the website of any central bank, such as the Bank of Canada, on any particular day, and the target for the policy rate is reported as 1.0% while consumer price inflation is reported as 3.1%, we could say that the inflation-adjusted real policy rate using that particular measure of inflation, is −2.1%. The Bank of Canada must be "comfortable with" that figure, and thereby has "chosen" it, as the number could easily have be made otherwise if desired.[8]

What then, will be the effect of a change in monetary policy that causes a change in the inflation-adjusted real policy rate, r'_B, either deliberate or accidental? In subsequent essays many of the differing economic theories on these matters will be discussed in detail, but here the objective is to just give a rough sketch of what seems most likely to happen.

If real policy rates are increased, for example, this also increases the perceived real financing costs for the rest of commercial banking system, because of the role of base money in inter-bank settlements. Therefore commercial banks may be induced to pass on these costs to their own customers in their own real lending rates. This, in turn, will tend to discourage borrowing by the private sector from the banks. So, if the real policy rate is "high" this is intended to reduce bank lending, and reduce the rate of growth of the money supply. Most economic theory suggests that this will help to reduce inflation, but it may possibly also cause an economic slowdown. If the real policy rate seems "low" on the other hand, the same mechanisms (in reverse), will tend to encourage lending, increase the money supply and help to stimulate the economy (but may also cause the inflation rate to increase).

There needs to be some discussion about what will happen if the real rate policy rate, and *a fortiori* real interest rates in general, are so low as to become *negative* (as is the case in our real world example from the Bank of Canada). If the real policy rate is negative, this must also "encourage borrowing". However, there may now be outright inflationary instability. There would be an unlimited incentive to borrow at the source, and this may eventually spread throughout the system. Those currently holding money (bank deposits) may also be getting a negative real return, and will try to spend their money as quickly as possible.

The first scenario, a high real policy rate, would certainly enhance the store of value aspect of money (the "rich would become richer"), but will progressively discourage new economic activity and *new* wealth creation, as it spreads through the system. A low real policy rate, on the other hand, will provide some of the stimulus for credit creation and productive economic activity that we have seen to be essential and, as long as real rates on bank deposits do not become negative, financial holdings still retain *their* real value. Money will be performing the store of value function "as well as can be expected". There may be higher inflation, but it is not likely to "take off" in an uncontrollable manner. Negative real interest rates will provide still further stimulus to economic activity, but will also lead to inflationary instability if maintained for any length of time. By, putting these three ideas together, we arrive at the conclusion that the real policy rate, and therefore real interest rates in general, should preferably be stable at *low* levels. To achieve this the real policy rate should be "low but still positive" (Smithin, 1994, 2003, 2007a, p. 114).

From a practical policy point of view it should be noted that a policy of attempting to stabilize *real* interest rates in this way (by simply stabilizing the inflation-adjusted real policy rate) would still require relatively frequent changes to *nominal* policy rates, whenever the chosen measure of the inflation rate changes. Interestingly enough, therefore, the actual day-to-day conduct of monetary policy under a "real interest rate rule" (Smithin, 2007a) might not at first sight appear very different than when the authorities are pursuing other objectives. It would not seem like too much of a break with the way that monetary authorities have conducted themselves in the past. However, the policy would avoid the excessive swings in real rates that *do* occur under other regimes and have certainly seemed to play a major role in destabilizing both the financial and real sectors of the economy in many historical episodes.

Traditionally the idea of a "cheap money policy" was usually that *nominal* interest rates should be kept low (Howson, 1989). However, following the line of argument already set out, a policy of keeping the nominal policy rate itself at a constant level (actually at whatever level, no matter how high or low, will lead to instability as soon as there is any change in inflationary expectations. If the nominal rate is held constant, and something else touches off an inflation (from either the demand or cost side), the real interest rate must fall. This will encourage more borrowing, and more inflation, and the real rate might eventually become negative, with the consequences already noted. If, alternatively, a deflationary tendency (falling prices) sets in, again with the nominal rate constant, the real rate continually rises causing still further *de*flationary pressure.

What is arguably the worst case scenario will occur if the nominal interest rate is already zero, and *then* deflation sets in. The real rate will be rising inexorably even though the nominal interest rate is as low as it can possibly be. The result must be a recession or depression. In these circumstances, monetary policy relying on nominal interest rate changes becomes useless. This is the so-called "zero bound" of monetary policy. In principle, it would be necessary to try to cut real interest rates in this situation, but this *cannot* be done since it is not possible for the *nominal* policy rate to fall below zero. In effect, this is an up-dated example of Keynes's (1964/1936, p. 207) "liquidity trap". Some other alternative must be found to boost the economy. For example, there could be an expansionary fiscal policy. The government, in the sense of the Ministry of Finance or the Treasury, could increase spending, cut taxes, or *both*. The central bank itself might, alternatively, attempt what in recent years has come to known as "quantitative easing". This would involve the central bank buying up the bonds of its own government at the longer maturities on the open market, thereby directly affecting interest rates other than the policy rate (and as a side effect, injecting more base money into the system in that way).

To return to the discussion of conventional monetary policy, it remains to be explained how changes in a very short-term interest rate, the policy rate, can feed through to affect other interest rates in the system. The best answer to this is to combine the "horizontalist" theory of the determination of the nominal policy rate, put forward by economists such as Kaldor (1982), Moore (1988) and Lavoie (1992) in the 1980s,[7] with the earlier "expectations theory" of the term structure of interest rates worked out by Hicks (1946/1939, pp. 258–264). The horizontalist theory simply stated that the nominal policy rate is determined by the central bank (as we are already assuming), whereas the expectations theory held that "long rates" are logically the geometric average of expected future short rates (with some adjustment for "risk", the longer the time horizon).[9] Putting these two theories together then determines the nominal long rate. The "real" long rate would then simply be this numberless inflation expectations or some proxy for them as already discussed. Such an explanation would by no means preclude such episodes as long rates rising when short rates are falling (an inverted yield curve), and so on, and such things are very often noted and remarked upon in the financial press. However, *if* a consistent policy is pursued at the short end in either nominal or real terms (and through time), long rates (nominal or real) must eventually come into line. Attempts to refute the horizontalist theory have usually entailed interpreting any *temporary* changes in either expectations, or in the neoclassical risk premium, as being *permanent*, thus reversing the implicit causality between short rates and long rates. However, there is no logical justification for this in a monetary economy, provided that the monetary authority itself pursues a consistent policy (Smithin, 2009a, pp. 78–80).[10] Of course, it is quite reasonable to argue that central banks often do *not* purse a consistent policy in practice. Hence, there is likely to be continuing discussion about the behaviour of the yield curve and its vagaries

Mention of the concept of quantitative easing, just discussed, on the other hand, raises the question of whether the central bank could actually set interest rates at *all* maturities, simply by buying up all the bonds at a given maturity at a given price. In theoretical principle, there seems to be no reason why this could not be done. Moreover, this question of "debt management" has at least been discussed in policy circles from time to time, notably by Keynes in the 1940s (Tilley, 2005, 2010) and perhaps on two or three occasions since then. However, the intellectual, administrative, political and financial efforts that would be involved, and the sheer scale of what would be required makes it unlikely that real world central bankers have ever actually had anything like this in mind when putting forward proposals for so-called quantitative easing.

International Monetary Relations

Up to now the discussion has assumed the existence of a self-contained monetary network arranged in a hierarchical manner, dominated by a single state central bank, whose liabilities represent the money of account and ultimate means of payment. In reality, however, there is more than one such network in the world, and the international economy can therefore be seen, from this point of view, as the result of the *interaction* of the competing monetary networks. These networks are often (but not necessarily) identified with the boundaries of political nation states.

The exchange rate between any two of the different currencies can be "floating" (flexible) or fixed. In the first case, the *nominal exchange rate* between two currencies (which is defined in these essays as the *foreign currency price of one unit of domestic currency*) changes every day on the international markets. In the case of a fixed rate regime, central banks themselves intervene directly in international financial markets (buying and selling their own currencies as required) to keep the nominal exchange rate at a certain level. Although many people do think that this is highly desirable in order to stabilize international trade, it should be recognized that in reality the nominal exchange rate is actually only one of a great many factors determining international competitiveness. To assess the true competitive position it would be necessary also to consider price levels (themselves dependent on a number of factors) in the different countries, and therefore work out a *real effective exchange rate.*

For example, let E stand for the nominal or "spot" exchange rate, that is, today's foreign currency price of one unit of domestic currency, and P, as before, stand for the index of the average level of prices in the domestic country. Then P^* can stand for the average price index in the foreign country or rest of the world. The *real exchange rate, Q,* is therefore:

$$Q = EP/P^*. \tag{1.8}$$

If Q goes up, this would be called a *real exchange rate appreciation,* which means that exports from the domestic economy become relatively more expensive and therefore less "competitive" in foreign markets. A falling Q, or a *real depreciation,* would make domestic goods relatively cheaper and improve export sales. Therefore the real exchange rate, like the real interest rate, is a vitally important indicator of how successful the domestic economy is likely to be.

As was the case within a domestic economy, something like a hierarchical debt pyramid is also likely to emerge in the international arena, but based now on the acceptability to foreign wealth-holders of the different international currencies (Bougrine and Seccareccia, 2008, pp. 5–7). At a certain stage, the currency of one particular issuer may become the international *reserve currency* at the base of the international debt pyramid as happened historically, for example with the British pound in the 19th century, or the US dollar in the 20th century. This then gives a great degree of "hegemonic" power to the nation concerned, and its financial policies influence the whole world economy.

As there is no world government, there cannot any be any such clear-cut explanation (as there was in the national case) as to *why* a particular currency emerges as the most powerful internationally at any point in time. It is all a question of global politics and history. However, if the global system *does* have an inherent tendency to concentrate financial power, then in this international sphere in which questions of political legitimacy are far more difficult to resolve than locally, this raises intractable political difficulties. Some may therefore argue that there should be a "world government", and it is the case in history that there have been many attempts to set up various types of supra-national monetary standard and institutions. Examples would be the international gold standard of the 19th century, the Bretton Woods system of the mid-20th century and the associated international institutions. (These have lingered on to the present day, long after the system itself became defunct.) The same is true of the single currency in Europe in the 21st century (the Euro), on a more limited regional basis. However, in the time honored phrase, "power corrupts and absolute power corrupts absolutely", and therefore I have previously argued that it is more sensible to *diffuse* this potential economic and financial power as much as possible (Smithin, 1994, 1995, 2003, 2009a). This turns into an argument in favour of a flexible or floating exchange rate system (for nominal exchange rates), which would then allow the policy-makers in each country to pursue an independent course. It would make *both* the real interest rate in the domestic economy and the real exchange rate responsive to policy decisions by the *domestic* monetary authorities. The same idea about the diffusion of power is, of course, an argument *against* fixed exchange rates, "dollarization", currency boards, or a common currency between different jurisdictions, all of which (nonetheless) have their strong advocates in the modern world.

Conclusion

Money is a social relation, social institution, or "social fact", rather than a commodity, but it is nonetheless entirely "real" and has important causal effects in our lives. Money and credit creation are continuously necessary in order for firms to realize the profits, and for workers to receive the wages, on which the method of enterprise (capitalism) depends. Orthodox economics seems to have made a major error by ignoring this, and by treating economy activity mainly as a question of barter exchange. There is, specifically, a failure to understand that *both* the inflation-adjusted real interest rate (the nominal rate of interest adjusted for observed inflation), and, in international economic relations, the real exchange rate (the rate of exchange between currencies adjusted for price levels), are important *monetary* variables. Both of these variables, though they are certainly "real variables" and, in effect, "relative prices", in the standard economic sense, are determined *primarily* in the money and financial markets.

This is significant not only for an understanding of how the system works, but also what advice should be given about such matters as monetary, financial, fiscal, and trade policy. The first of the two variables, the real rate of interest, is what matters when it comes to making decisions about borrowing, lending, and investment. The second, the real exchange rate, is important in determining international competiveness and international trade flows. Views on how they are determined are therefore crucial in shaping the way in which economic changes are and will be interpreted, in both the domestic and international arenas.

Notes

1. Personal communication to the author dated October 4, 1988.
2. Keeping track of the different usages of the term "real" is a big problem in reading the mainstream economics literature. On the one hand, there is the idea of a dollar sum adjusted for the price level, or for inflation. On the other hand, there is the standard usage of real *versus* fictional. Nonetheless it is important to keep these things straight, and this important question will be taken up and discussed further in later essays.
3. Even if some of their authors may never have heard of the labour theory of value.
4. See also Heinsohn and Steiger (2000, p. 71) who quote the economist Harold Demsetz as pointedly asking: "What has mainstream economics been doing for the last 200 years if it has not been studying capitalism?" The answer is (mainly) studying either barter exchange, or the thought processes of Robinson Crusoe, in recent times greatly embellished with mathematics and statistics.
5. That is, in terms of the formal validity of money. No statement is made about its substantive validity (*e.g.*, how high the inflation rate

will be). It is crucially important, in interpreting this question, to be clear about the difference between a sovereign government with its own currency, such as the federal governments of the USA or Canada, and the situation of a provincial government, or an individual US state such as California. A provincial government could certainly become insolvent. Note that countries in the contemporary Euro zone, such as Greece, Ireland, Spain or Italy, essentially have provincial status from the monetary point of view. We return to this issue later in the text of the present chapter.

6. This statement is not, of course, meant to imply that there does not have to be stable legal framework for banking, or that other types of prudential financial regulation may not also be advisable.

7. It should be stated, for the record, that these heterodox economists understood the importance of the policy rate of interest well before these ideas entered the mainstream economic literature (which was not until the late 1990s).

8. There is always, of course, the problem of choosing which, of the many, alternative measures of inflation should be followed. Should it be the CPI (consumer price index) or some other measure? The Bank of Canada itself also reports an alternative "operational guide" for inflation, (known as "core CPI") which may be lower than the CPI. The question of choosing the "correct" index is, however, strictly speaking a matter of statistical technique rather than monetary theory *per se*. What is important from the theoretical point of view is that one measure is chosen, on more-or-less plausible statistical grounds, and that it is used consistently. In any event, clearly the real policy rate in Canada was *negative* in our example.

9. The term "risk" is in quotes because of the hopeless confusion that prevails everywhere about this topic. This arises from the inability to distinguish the theorems of statistical probability theory from the concept of fundamental uncertainty. See Davidson (2009).

10. There remains the issue of reconciling the horizontalist theory with the idea of "liquidity preference" (see Chapter 7).

CHAPTER 2

THE RECURRING DEBATES IN MONETARY ECONOMICS

Introduction

This is the second essay in the form of chapter in a collection with the overall title *Essays in the Fundamental Theory of Monetary Economics and Macroeconomics*, and it is convenient to start with a quote from a prominent historian of economic thought (Humphrey, 1998, p. 1), writing a decade and a half ago.

> Economists typically view their discipline as a progressive science in which superior ideas relentlessly supplant inferior ones in a Darwinian struggle toward the truth ... (but) ... every doctrinal historian knows ... that much of what passes for novelty and originality in monetary theory and policy is really ancient teaching dressed up in modern guises.

That passage is then followed by a couple of statements which, frankly, seem much more dubious at the present time of writing:

> To be sure, the increasing application of mathematical modeling has given these concepts greater rigor and precision. (*sic*)

And, then, particularly:

> Likewise, better data and more powerful empirical techniques have improved our statistical estimates of the relevant quantitative magnitudes. (*sic*)

I would say that probably a more accurate comment on both of the last two points is the statement attributed to Paul Krugman, in a lecture given at the London School of Economics, and widely quoted in the financial press in 2009[1]:

> "most macroeconomics of the past thirty years was spectacularly useless at best and positively harmful at worst."

Professor Krugman is, of course, a very prominent public intellectual whose own views in the public policy debate in the USA are widely known (Krugman, 2009), but the purpose of using this quote is not to enter directly into that debate. Simply as a statement about the "scientific" value of many of the narrowly technical mathematical and statistical exercises that have filled the academic journals in recent decades, however, the only quibble that seems possible would be about the length of time over which the statement might hold true. Davidson (2003/2004, pp. 256–257) dates the beginning of the malaise back to the late 1960s, and asserts that, after about 1970, articles expressing heterodox or dissenting views were systematically excluded from the most "prestigious" journals.[2] The same writer (Davidson, 2009, pp. 29–43) has also recently provided another powerful critique of the idea that the statistical theory and practice that has been useful in the natural sciences can be usefully applied to the realms of money and finance. These fields obviously relate primarily to human motivations and the social world.

In any event, in the original paper, Humphrey (1998, p. 1) finally goes on to say:

> Still, the basic ideas themselves often remain much the same. Thus instead of a steady progression of new paradigms, one sees repeated cycles of existing ones... (b)y itself the recycling of established ideas need be no cause for alarm. Theories may survive because experience... (shows)... that they possess a... degree of validity, and because no better theories have been found. The trouble is, however, that sound theories are not the only ones to survive. Unsound theories may co-exist with sound ones.

I certainly agree with this part of the general argument, though (no doubt) would differ from the author about which specific parts of inherited theory are sound or unsound, and should be retained or discarded. In both editions of my *Controversies in Monetary Economics* (Smithin, 1994, pp. 5–7, 2003, pp. 7–11), I also pointed to a number of what I called "standard themes", or debating points, that appear to have been present throughout most of the discussions in monetary economics, both historically and continuing in the modern era. In this essay, it will be useful to explicitly identify what each of these debates is.

There seem to be five main themes in all, each of which is discussed in detail in the upcoming sections. Also, I do not think it is correct to be as pessimistic as Humphrey seems to be about the possibility of deriving *new* theory that improves on the ideas of the past and will also be "sound". In the conclusion to the chapter, therefore, I will set out some of the characteristics that I think a desirable theory of the monetary economy should have.

The Ontology of Money — Its Nature and Functions

The first theme of our five themes is really the basic question that already ran through much of the discussion of Chapter 1. That is, how did the social constructs of money and credit come into existence in the first place, and how they are reproduced and maintained? The prospective monetary theorist, in short, must consciously or unconsciously take up a definite position on the ontology of money. As argued in Chapter 1, this is bound up with the entire logical/historical question of how the capitalist institutions, and in particular the concept of production for sale in the market, specifically for monetary reward, came to exert such a dominating influence in our social life. Unfortunately, the answers to these questions have tended to be either ignored or taken for granted in the orthodox economics literature. Either stance implies tacit acceptance of one version, or another, of the view that the "market" itself is the primary concept. Money must emerge *from* the market, it is thought, which then leads on inexorably to an underlying commodity theory of money that is anachronistic at best. In Chapter 1, however, it was shown that another view is possible. Namely, that money itself, the very idea or concept of money, is the starting point. Rather than money emerging from the market, *the market emerges from money*. In this case money is seen as a social relation and as a key piece of social technology, and therefore actually as a pre-condition for market exchange and "monetary production" to take place at all (Ingham, 2005/1996, 2000). The further implication is that there should be an underlying credit or "claim" theory of money, which would subsume any actual historical examples of commodity money as special case. On this point, see Graziani (2003) who quotes Keynes's famous remark about the old Indian rupee being "a note printed on silver".

Most of the theoretical and policy questions in dispute in macroeconomics ultimately come down to the positions that are explicitly or implicitly taken in this logically prior debate, about what money actually *is*. Smithin (2003, p. 8), for example, has quoted Bougrine and Seccareccia (2001) who have stated unequivocally that "the... policy divide in macroeconomics is provided by competing *conceptions* of money". (emphasis added)

How Does Money Get into the Economy?
How is it Created and Destroyed?

In another work Bougrine and Seccareccia (2010, pp. 33–34) have also raised one of the most important of the subsequent *analytical* questions, when they ask how money gets into the economic process. As they put it, "how is it [money] created and destroyed?". This is a reference to the ongoing debate over whether money should be treated as an "exogenous" or an "endogenous" variable. These are terms taken originally from mathematics or engineering. An *exogenous variable* is something that is determined outside the system being studied, whereas an *endogenous variable* is determined within the system. The final value of an endogenous variable (in the case of economic variables either in nominal or real terms) is part of the *solution* to the system, and is *not* a given data. As far as money is concerned, the main question is whether the quantity of money (the number of dollars, yen, or euros available) should be treated as a fixed amount (with a clear implication that five dollars handed to you is five dollars *not* available to me), or rather, as capable of expanding and contracting, rising and falling, as the economy itself expands and contracts.

The discussion of bank lending and credit creation in Chapter 1 strongly suggested that the endogenous money approach is by far the closest to reality. However, unfortunately it also has to be said that a great deal of formal economic theory (perhaps most of it over the years) has made the opposite assumption that the money supply is fixed. In those circumstances, if more money needs to be made available, this would have to be a conscious decision on the part of the monetary authorities.

What Determines the Real Rate of Interest
on Loans of Money?

An equally important issue is how the *real* rate of interest on loans of *money* is determined. As explained in Chapter 1, a real rate of interest is, formally speaking, the quoted interest rate adjusted for expected inflation. As discussed, if the symbol, i, stands for a nominal interest rate, r for the corresponding real interest rate, and p^e for expected inflation, the expected real interest rate is defined as:

$$r = i - p^e. \tag{2.1}$$

As previously mentioned, a reasonable proxy (or guess) for value of the expected real interest rate might simply be the nominal interest rate less than the currently reported inflation rate (lower case p itself). Repeating Eq. (1.5) from Chapter 1, what we there called the inflation-adjusted real interest rate, is therefore:

$$r' = i - p. \tag{2.2}$$

By far the most popular assumption about the determination of real interest rates of interest among professional economists, and perhaps not only for purely scientific reasons, has been that the real interest rate is determined fundamentally by forces *outside* of the monetary system (Fletcher, 2000, 2007; Smithin, 2002b, 2009d). It is exogenous to that system. If this is so, the actual determinants of the real interest rate would have to do only with the various motives for barter exchange. They would involve such things as the demand for physical capital goods and machinery, on the one hand, and the rate of time preference on the part of "savers", on the other. These savers, moreover, are thought of as (in principle) actually storing up physical goods, rather than not spending money.

It is somewhat confusing that these notions of "productivity and thrift" are also so often called "real" economic forces in the same sense as we talked earlier (in Chapter 1) about the brute facts or physical facts. This is actually a different *concept* of real from that of a real economic variable merely in the sense of an inflation-adjusted magnitude using index numbers. Unfortunately, the language that is employed does lead on naturally (in the absence of any genuine investigation into the nature of money) to the idea that therefore a "real variable" must be determined by "real forces" in something like a purely materialistic sense.

In dealing with this problem we will find the terminology of Burstein (1995, p. 1), who distinguishes between "a monetary theory of the real rate of interest" and "a real theory of the real rate of interest", very useful. In Burstein's terms, the barter exchange theory of interest, and the doctrine of the natural rate of interest, which have appeared in one guise or another throughout the whole history of discussion of monetary topics (Humphrey, 1993b), is a *real theory of the real rate of interest*. Moreover, once such an assumption is made it is clear that this immediately forecloses any debate about whether, or not, monetary changes can have any lasting significance for the rest of the (real) economy. By *definition*, they will *not*. It might still be accepted by economists taking this view that monetary policy changes can affect the nominal interest rate, i. However, if the opinion is that no action on the part of the central bank or in the money markets can *ever* affect the real interest rate, the real rate must be a "natural rate".

In terms of Eqs. (2.1) and (2.2), the argument would be that even if i might be controlled, there is no way to pin down inflation expectations, p^e. Therefore, the overall value of r must eventually conform to some external standard set (*e.g.*) by the rate of time preference or the somewhat mythical "marginal productivity of capital" (MPK). If so, there really can be no question of any long-lasting impact of monetary changes on any of the other important real economic variables. Similar sorts of idea could also be applied to the concept of the real exchange rate. The counterpart in international economics to a real theory of the real rate of interest, would be a "real theory of the real exchange rate", also assumed to be determined by non-monetary influences such as the barter terms of trade.

An alternative to the natural rate doctrine however, would be, in Burstein's terminology, a *monetary theory of the real rate of interest*. How might this idea be interpreted in terms of Eqs. (2.1) and (2.2)? The first step is simply the recognition that the inflation-adjusted real rate of interest r' in itself is *definitely* a monetary or financial phenomenon. Next, it would have to be argued that the formally defined expected real rate of interest, r, must eventually conform to r' and not the other way around. (This could happen, for example, because of the impact that a consistent policy on r' would have on inflation expectations). In such a case, the rest of the economy, including things like the subjective rate of time preference and everything else, must adjust to the real interest rate established in the monetary system, under the influence of the central bank, rather than the reverse. Now, the outcome of the debate over monetary policy would no longer be a foregone conclusion.

The inflation-adjusted real rate of interest, r'; must *indeed* be admitted to be a monetary phenomenon as soon as it is admitted that the central bank *can* indeed influence nominal interest rates. This is usually conceded on all sides (except in the case where a *cut* is required and the nominal interest rate is already at zero). It can then hardly be denied that the central bank can set r'_B, the inflation-adjusted real policy rate, as all they have to do is to adjust the nominal rate when the observed inflation rate changes, and therefore can influence r' *via* the transmission mechanism. To put this in another way it can be argued that r'_B *does in fact*, change every time the actual inflation rate changes, if the central bank authorities *fail* to respond by adjusting i_B. In that sense, they are *always* responsible for whatever the value of r'_B is (except, again, in the zero bound case when a cut in i would be needed).

The real question in adjudicating between monetary and real theories of the real rate of interest, is not whether the central bank can influence r', but whether or not there is also some other separate principle (the natural rate idea) that sets r independently of r'. A real theory of the real rate of interest argues (wrongly) that this is so (r is one thing, r' is another, and r is, in some sense, more basic). This has usually been the conventional view. A monetary theory of the real rate of interest asserts that there is *no* natural rate principle and that therefore, r, and everything else, must eventually adjust to r'.

In the case of a monetary theory of the real rate of interest (just mentioned) one of the variables that would also have to adjust would be the real exchange rate between the domestic economy and the rest of the world. If it is argued that the real rate of interest is a *monetary variable* the real exchange rate must be a *monetary variable* also.

What is the Main Monetary Policy Instrument that Can be Employed by the Central Bank to Determine the Pace of Money and Credit Creation?

The discussion of real interest rate determination above is obviously relevant to, and necessarily touched upon, another of the main continuing themes. This is the long running debate about the appropriate "monetary control variable" or monetary policy *instrument* (Lavoie, 2010; Lavoie and Seccareccia, 2004; Taylor, 1993; Walsh, 1998, 2009).

This is not (quite) the same issue as what determines real interest rates, and therefore needs some separate discussion. The question now is whether control of the money must necessarily be exercised indirectly, for example, *via* the manipulation of nominal interest rates (as was certainly implied in the argument of the previous section). Or, can the nominal "quantity of money" be controlled *directly* by the central bank.

The issue arises because in textbooks of the previous generation, it *was* frequently argued that the central bank can (or should be able to) quantitatively control the level (or the rate of growth) of its own liabilities, the monetary base, which was traditionally given the symbol, H. It was further argued that the central bank can also directly control either the level (or the rate of growth) of M, the money supply itself, because of a stable numerical relationship between H and M known as the "money multiplier". Some introductory textbooks in fact, to this day, still retain the concept of the money multiplier. The most "basic" of them go even further, and just *assume* that there is a unique *level* of M controlled (somehow) by the central bank,[3] which itself is the exogenous monetary policy variable.

In either of these cases, the implication is that the total number of dollars in circulation in the economy is fixed unless some deliberate decision is made to change it.

As implied in the discussion so far, however, in reality the actual monetary control instrument typically employed by central banks, throughout the 18th, 19th, much of the 20th centuries, and now into the 21st century, has usually been a short-term nominal interest rate of some kind (Goodhart, 2002). This is the interest rate referred to in Chapter 1 as the *policy rate*. This means, essentially, the interest rate on loans of central bank base money. In this case, with the policy rate as the instrument, *both* the monetary base and the overall money supply become endogenous variables, and there would not now be a set numerical relationship between H and M. It would still be the case (at the level of principle) that it is the central bank's *monopoly* over base money that ultimately gives it influence over interest rates, and hence over the total of bank lending, and thereby the overall money supply. However, this control works through an interest rate channel rather any direct quantitative relationship between the monetary base and the overall effective money supply.

As well as debunking the notion of a strict money multiplier, however, it is also important to note that when the bank is setting interest rates, and thereby also allowing endogenous changes in both the monetary base and the money supply, monetary policy itself can never be the *only* economic variable affecting money supply growth. With the money supply is endogenous, more or less anything which can "change", and have an impact either on the cost or demand side of the economy can affect the total of bank lending, and hence the money supply.

Although it has always been much more realistic to think of the monetary policy instrument as being an interest rate, this has not necessarily been the chosen point of view of the pure economic theorist. This is because there are a number of awkward problems in trying to reconcile this position with what has usually been the accepted (micro)economic doctrine of how interest rates get determined. It is difficult to reconcile the facts of the matter with various deeply held preconceptions of how real interest rates would *theoretically* be determined in a barter exchange economy.

If the analyst has already decided that the "true" or "natural" rate of interest (as it was called above) is determined otherwise than by central bank policy, but *then* has to admit that there may be another rate that *is* set by the central bank, it becomes necessary to sharply differentiate between the two. Ultimately, it has to be argued that the outcome of economic policy decisions hinges on any discrepancy between the two interest rates. This type of argument has, in fact, frequently been made in the history of economic thought (including much quite recent orthodox theory of the early 21st century). However, it is uncomfortable for the theorist to do this. It would be much easier just to say that the money supply "is what it is", *the* rate of interest "is what it is" (determined by "real" economic forces), and that there is no connection between the two. Many theorists in the past, usually known as "quantity theorists", have, therefore, indeed taken that way out.

How Do Monetary Changes Affect Other Economic Variables?

The last of the recurring monetary themes must evidently be the clash of views about the impact (if any) of changes in the monetary variables on the other important economic variables, and particularly on the so-called real variables. Whether or not monetary changes are defined as changes in interest rates, or as changes in the money supply, how do such changes affect things like the level of real output (real GDP), or its rate of growth. How do they affect the level of employment, real wages, the real exchange rate, and so on? Real GDP means real gross domestic product and it is the usual measure in macroeconomics of the total volume of output, or real value-added, produced by a nation's economy during a given accounting period such as a quarter or a year. It is actually the dollar value of the output divided by some suitable price index. The so-called "expenditure breakdown" of *real* GDP is as follows:

$$Y = C + I + G + (EX - IM), \qquad (2.3)$$

where Y stands for real GDP, C is real consumption spending, I is real investment spending (investment in capital equipment plus inventories), G is real government spending on goods and services, and $EX - IM$ is real net exports (exports minus imports).

One of the main questions being asked, therefore, is whether monetary policy changes can affect a real variable like the total flow of output Y over a given period, or its rate of growth, y (where $y = [Y - Y_{-1}]/Y_{-1})$? Or, do these changes only affect nominal variables such as the aggregate price index, P, and/or (again) its rate of change, the rate of inflation p, [where $p = [(P - P_{-1})/P_{-1}]$. If "money" cannot affect the level of output or any other real economic variable, and *only* affects the price level or some other nominal variable it is generally said to be *neutral*. If it *can* affect real variables it is said to be *non-neutral*. In a similar manner, it would also be possible to talk about the neutrality or non-neutrality of fiscal policy, that is changes in government spending and taxation, and how these affect real and nominal variables.

As usual in economics the term "real" is a bit misleading. It conjures up an (almost) purely physical image of an agglomeration of tangible objects which have come off various production lines. But, in fact, the definition of GDP is not that sort of thing at all. It is meant to be, basically, the total sum spent on final goods *and* services over an accounting period, such as a quarter or a year, reduced to a common denominator. Real GDP therefore cannot be directly observed. The numbers have to be worked out. This may be done by, first, noting the dollar or money sum spent on the total of final goods/services (which, in principle, *can* be counted) and then coming up with a suitable index number for the aggregate price level. The figure for real GDP is obtained by dividing the dollar sum by the aggregate price index. In effect, it is a measure of the total amount spent on final goods and services relative to the purchasing power of money. In short:

$$PY = \text{nominal GDP} \qquad\qquad (2.4)$$

and:

$$Y = PY/P = \text{real GDP.} \qquad\qquad (2.5)$$

Note that by including the concept of services we already admit that value need not, actually, reside in any tangible object at all. Many tangible things produced do have values and those that do we included in GDP. However, some tangible things do not have values and some intangibles do and the definition excludes exchanges of existing assets, and also tries not to double-count the value of intermediate goods (goods used up in the production process of the final good or service).

The main dividing line on the issue of monetary neutrality or non-neutrality arises from disagreements about whether or not monetary factors can *permanently* affect real variables, as opposed to having some "short run" or fleeting impact. It has quite often been conceded that both monetary and fiscal policy can have a temporary effect and are therefore capable of non-neutrality in the "short run". However, this pragmatic approach on the part of some economists almost always remains compatible with the much more deeply-held belief that money is *always* neutral in the "long run". The vast

majority of economists have been taught to believe that there can be no
permanent economic effects of monetary changes on real economic variables
changes. While allowing for short-run effects, the conventional wisdom is
that such changes can only ultimately affect price levels or the inflation rate.
The nuances of individual opinions held on these issues naturally depends
to some extent, on each of the underlying debates already discussed, that is,
views about the nature and functions of money, whether money is exogenous
or endogenous, whether or not there is a natural rate of interest, and what
is the monetary policy instrument.

If the orthodox view has almost always been to assert long-run neutrality there nonetheless remains a large difficulty with this in explaining *why*
it is that monetary issues and problems have so often been at the forefront
of real world political debate. In the real world, arguments over money go
on all the time, not only in the context of the relationship between money
and inflation, and not only during the immediate aftermath of a financial
crisis.

Having now introduced each of the five main recurring themes in the
field of monetary economics, the next few sections of the chapter go on to
briefly discuss opinions on these matters in some of the main schools in the
history of economic thought.

Classical Monetary Economics

The classical economists were the original theorists of the industrial revolution in Britain, during the second half of the 18th century and the first half
of the 19th centuries. For the purposes of discussing monetary theory, the
list would have to include such figures as (*e.g.*) Hume (1987/1752), Smith
(1981/1776), Ricardo (2004/1817) and Mill (1987/1848). It has even been
suggested that Marx, writing a few decades later, might be included with
this group (Ingham, 2004, pp. 61–63) at least far as money is concerned.

The views of the classical economists on our five main debating
themes were straightforward and highly influential for later generations
of economists. Firstly, the classics did believe that the origin of money was
in physical commodities, particularly the precious metals such as gold or
silver. Some writers held that this would imply a cost of production theory
of the price level. The relative price of gold, for example, versus that of
other commodities, would depend solely on the effort made in digging the
gold out of the ground. A more widely accepted theory of prices, however,
which gained ground as the classical theory developed, was the previously

mentioned "quantity principle" or the quantity theory of money. The idea was that once gold (or some other commodity) has become money, there will be a demand in its monetary uses that overshadows the previous demand as a "use value". Moreover, for an item like gold, the stock of which has been slowly accumulated over the centuries, realistically the amount of it already in existence is far greater than the amount that could be added in a typical year by new mining (Keynes, 1971b/1930, p. 259). From the theoretical point of view, and as far as the world economy as a whole is concerned, the amount of gold (money) in existence might therefore in normal circumstances reasonably be treated as a fixed quantity. There would be, in effect, a fixed supply of money. The average world price level at any point in time would be determined by the quantity of gold relative to the demand for it as money.

If there *did* happen to be an unusual increase in the quantity of gold available to the money-using sectors of the global economy at a particular time (as occurred in the 16th century after the Spanish conquest of Mexico and Central and South America, and after the gold "strikes" or gold "rushes" in North America and South Africa in the 19th century), this would cause a general increase in prices. The same would be true in an *individual* country in any year if its gold stocks were to rise (fall) temporarily because of a balance of payments surplus (deficit). This would tend to push prices up (down) in the individual country while the surplus (deficit) is occurring. In equilibrium, however, it was believed that eventually the price level for all the nations on a gold standard must conform to the global average.

On the topic of interest rate determination, classical economists were adamant that the real rate of interest on loans of money is determined by real (non-monetary) economic forces, typically identified as the "productivity of capital" and the "rate of time preference". The classical economists therefore accepted the doctrine of the natural rate of interest. Actual interest rates observed in the marketplace were supposed to simply *reflect* the natural rate, and therefore ultimately could *never* be permanently changed or manipulated by monetary policy.

The main principle of monetary policy was, supposed rather to be that of maintaining the convertibility of the central bank's banknotes into gold. In the debates leading up to the passage of the (in)famous Bank Act of 1844 in Britain, this was labeled the "currency principle". The idea was that the note issue of the central bank (the monetary base of those days), should in principle be backed by gold reserves. Moreover, ideally, each note should be exchangeable at *par* and on demand for the equivalent in gold coins. Therefore, the preferred monetary policy instrument was thereby the monetary base itself. It should be rigidly tied to the gold reserves.[4]

It perhaps goes without saying that the classical economists were among those who thought that monetary changes could not have any long lasting or permanent impact on the real economy or the level of employment. The main argument on policy was simply that if the currency principle was *not* maintained, and too much paper money was printed, the result would be inflation. If the currency principle *was* maintained, and even if the gold stock did not grow, the real economy itself could continue to grow at its own "natural rate" without any problem. In this case there would simply be deflation, falling prices, but nobody (apparently) would be bothered by this. None of the classics seemed to grasp (or even consider), the point made in Chapter 1 about the need for the realization of aggregate *monetary* profits if capitalism is to work.[5]

To the classical economists, then, money was definitely *neutral* in the sense that it was not believed to have any lasting, or long run, impact on the real economy. For the sake of realism, allowance was sometimes made for monetary non-neutrality in the short run, and this was true as far back as Hume's (1987/1752) celebrated statement in the mid-18th century. Hume assumed some temporary "rigidity" or "stickiness" of nominal prices, and/or nominal wages (to use modern terminology). From Hume himself onward, however, all classical economists believed that any such temporary effects would soon disappear (Laidler, 1996), and that money was neutral in the long run.[6]

Monetarism

Monetarism was the name given to the much publicized revival of the quantity theory of money, in the second half of the 20th century. This was a movement associated, in particular, with the work of Professor Milton Friedman of the University of Chicago. A main difference from the older classical theory was that the updated version of the quantity theory was *not* restricted to the idea of money as gold or any other commodity. Its advantage was that it could be applied to paper money, bank money, computer entries or anything at all that was being accepted as money in a particular society at a particular time. Paradoxically, however, the advantage of monetarism in this respect may also be counted as one of its weakest points *theoretically*. The basis of the eclecticism was, actually, a distinct *lack* of attention to the all-important questions of the ontology of money. Friedman and his colleagues wanted to recast the quantity theory simply as a generic "theory of the demand for money" that could be "made formally identical with that of the demand for a consumption service" (Friedman, 1956, p. 4). Their argument was that if a conventional micro-economist wants to analyze the demand for refrigerators, for example, not very much attention need to be paid to what it is that refrigerators actually *do* for the consumer (except in the vaguest possible terms about preserving food). It can just be taken for granted that there is a desire to possess the item called a refrigerator, and then the analyst can try to identify all the factors that might affect the demand for units of this good. These would involve such things as the climate, the prices of refrigerators themselves, the prices of substitutes such as iceboxes, and the wealth and incomes of the potential consumers. There is no need to explain in detail how a refrigerator works, what are the engineering principles behind it, and so on. The monetarists (wrongly) thought that this same methodology could be applied to money and, hence, that they could avoid any awkward questions about exactly what money *is*, or the precise role that it plays in capitalism. As with the refrigerator, it could just be taken for granted that there is a thing called "money" and that people have a demand for its services, whatever they are.[7]

However, this strategy cannot possibly work for money. As already discussed extensively in Chapter 1, money as a social institution plays a far more crucial role in the social structure of capitalism than does any individual consumer or "capital" good. There is, therefore, no escape from the need to decide what money is and what it does, if there is ever to be any genuine attempt at an explanation of how the system of enterprise is able to function.

If the monetarist theory of the demand for money was an attempt at drastic simplification, the theory of the supply of money was also equally straightforward. In monetarist models the supply of money supply, M, was taken to be an exogenous variable, directly under the control of the central bank. Therefore, an expansionary monetary policy would entail an increase in the total quantity of dollars that make up M, whereas a "contractionary" (restrictive) monetary policy would mean a decrease in the amount of dollars. There was fairly minimal discussion of the issue of money creation by the banking system, which would usually be limited to some discussion of the money multiplier process. It was suggested that there was a fairly tight link between the monetary base and the money supply, a position already criticized, so that control of the monetary base, the liabilities of the central bank could be assumed to imply control of the overall money supply itself.

At the theoretical level money frequently was treated literally as *fiat* paper money, as in Friedman's famous metaphor of a "helicopter drop". When the money supply was to be increased the hypothetical helicopter would simply shower banknotes across the land. When the money supply was to be decreased, the helicopter would simply vacuum them up again with a suction pump. This was *all* part of a general opinion that monetary issues could be strictly separated from "the subject of finance" (McCallum, 1989, p. v), in a way that would be literally impossible in a proper endogenous money theory.

Monetarism accepted the classical view that the real rate of interest rate is determined by the natural rate and that, therefore, monetary policy can have no permanent impact on real interest rates (Friedman, 1968). The interest rates observed in the market place were believed to quickly reflect changes in the putative natural rate. According to the monetarists the monetary policy instrument should not be a rate of interest but the level or the growth rate of the monetary base itself. The only sort of impact that monetary policy could have on interest rates would be on nominal rates, *via* the inflation rate. The ultimate effect of a monetary policy expansion for example, would be to cause nominal interest rates to rise rather than fall. This occurs because, if the real interest rate is indeed determined by forces outside the monetary system, and then an increase in the rate of monetary growth occurs to cause an increase in inflation, the nominal interest rate must eventually rise.

Finally, monetarists held, as the classics had done, the view that money is both neutral and *super-neutral* in the long run. As already explained, neutral money means that an increase in the level of the nominal money supply only causes an increase in the aggregate price level and does not affect any real economic variables. The term "super-neutral" is an extension of this, which implies that an increase in the *rate of growth* of the money supply will only affect the *rate of inflation*, and not any real variables.

For the sake of realism, and as was also the case with some of the classical economists, monetarism did allow that monetary changes might have some (explicitly temporary) effects on real GDP in the short run. It was accepted that money could be non-neutral or non-super-neutral in the short run (where this "short run" could actually be a year or more in duration, the sort of time horizon of the business cycle). The explanation for this, again, would be such things as temporary wage or price rigidities, or mistaken expectations. In retrospect, for example, monetarism explained the Great Depression of the 1930s by a large fall in the money supply in the USA at the time (Friedman and Schwartz, 1963, 1982; Friedman and Friedman 1980, pp. 79–80). Even in that extreme case, however, there was still the underlying idea that equilibrium would eventually be restored. For a monetarist, money is always neutral and super-neutral in the long run.

Keynes

John Maynard Keynes, writing before the era of monetarism between the two World Wars of the 20th century, may well have been the most famous monetary economist of all time. He claimed to have decisively refuted the classical theory only for the monetarists, and others, later to claim to have decisively refuted Keynes. What position did Keynes take on each of our five main themes or debating points in monetary economics? The answer to this question is something of mixed bag.

On the ontology of money there are, in fact, three chapters on the topic at the beginning of the first volume of the *Treatise on Money* (Keynes, 1971a/1930), where Keynes does present a detailed view of the nature and functions of money, which seems to run very much along creditist and chartalist lines. There is also the evidence of the "missing" draft chapter (Keynes, 1973) of the *General Theory of Employment Interest and Money* (Keynes, 1964/1936), in which Keynes makes clear the difference between a monetary or "entrepreneur" economy and a barter exchange economy, and stated that his *General Theory* is intended to apply to the former (Asimakopolous, 1988; Dillard, 1988; Smithin, 2009a). However, this crucial chapter was *not* included in the final published version of the book. On the contrary, for the *General Theory*, a decision was made to let "technical monetary detail [fall] into the background" (Keynes, 1964/1936, p. vii). This was an error in retrospect. Had the chapter been kept in, or some reference made back to the discussion of "representative money" (Keynes, 1971a/1930, pp. 5–6) in the *Treatise*, it might well have been easier for his audience to understand the argument being made in the second book.

Another difference in presentation between the *Treatise* and the *General Theory* is that in the former there is already a fairly extensive discussion of banking, central banking, credit and money creation and so on, and hence of endogenous money. However, by the time of the *General Theory* the money supply, M, was treated as an exogenous variable. It became a "given" at any point in time, which only could be changed by a deliberate act of policy. This made the entire discussion of the money supply difficult to distinguish from that in later monetarism. The same point also explains why even the Keynesian theory of the *demand* for money was basically similar to the monetarist one (Leeson, 2003a, 2003b; Smithin, 2004a). Throughout the initial stages of the so-called "monetarist versus Keynesian" debates in the mid-20th century much of the discussion was unfortunately only about empirical nuances such as the "interest elasticity of the demand for money", and not at all about more fundamental theoretical matters. This was possible because the competing frameworks that were advertised as monetarist versus Keynesian in the textbooks were actually not as different as might have been supposed from the apparent ferocity of the academic debate. From a later "Post Keynesian" point of view the assumed exogeneity of the supply of money in the *General Theory* would also cause difficulties for any attempt to put forward an alternative explanation of inflation. Logically, it would be difficult to bring in wage-push or cost-push theories of inflation, for example.

On the other hand in spite of ending up with fairly "standard" notions of money supply and demand, Keynes clearly did *intend* to break with orthodoxy quite radically on the question of interest rate determination. There is no doubt at all that he did try to provide a "monetary theory of the real rate of interest", *via* the so-called "liquidity preference" theory of interest rates. The concept of liquidity preference was *not* just a question of providing a new name for the theory of the demand for money, as Tobin's (1958) famous article seemed to imply, nor of simply inserting an interest rate argument into the demand for money function. According to Keynes's own statements it was a definite attempt to provide an alternative theory of interest determination based ultimately on speculation in the financial markets. However, in the form that Keynes presented it in the *General Theory*, the liquidity preference theory unfortunately does not actually *succeed* in providing an alternative theory of interest rates. Again, this failure was a result of the assumption of a fixed nominal supply of money. This makes the theory vulnerable to the argument that with a sufficiently large deflation (a sufficiently large fall in prices), the *real* supply of money M/P can always increase enough to satisfy any conceivable degree of "liquidity preference". This is the "Pigou effect" or "real balance effect" originally discussed by such economists as Pigou (1943) and Patinkin (1948). As the dates of these publications indicate, this idea was very quickly picked up by orthodox economists, enabling them to *dismiss* the Keynesian interest rate theory on theoretical grounds. To point out the vulnerability of Keynes's *GT* argument on this score is *not* to argue that the overall concept of liquidity preference is unimportant, as eventually did Leijonhufvud (1981b) for example, (on somewhat different grounds). On the contrary, liquidity preference, properly reinterpreted, does indeed turn out to have a vital role to play in explaining many features of the business cycle and of financial crises. It must be kept in the model. However, in the specific historical situation it was *not* the vital clue, which Keynes thought would be, to an alternative, non-materialistic, fundamental explanation of interest. (This immediately raises the question of where such an explanation is to be found, and the answer must be at the level of social ontology, as already discussed in Chapter 1, and earlier in the present chapter.

Returning to Keynes, in the *Treatise* the policy rate of the central bank was correctly identified as the main monetary policy instrument. This was called "bank rate" in the terminology of the 19th and early 20th centuries (Keynes, 1971a/1930, pp. 166–179). However, by the time of the *General Theory*, a few years later than the *Treatise*, and in keeping with the absence of "technical monetary detail" in the later book, there is much less discussion about bank rate. Now, it seems that changes in the money supply itself (changes in M) represent changes in monetary policy. This is another shift of focus between Keynes's two major books that tends to weaken, not strengthen, the overall argument (Rymes and Rogers, 2000, pp. 267–268).

On the fundamental question of monetary neutrality *versus* non-neutrality there seems little doubt that in the *General Theory* Keynes did at least have the *intention* to demonstrate that both monetary and fiscal policy (changes in government spending and taxation) were non-neutral. Moreover, that they were non-neutral in *both* the short run and the long run. However, it would be difficult to argue that he ever really succeeded in persuading the rest of the economics profession that he had achieved this goal (Salant, 1985; Meltzer, 1988; Smithin, 2003, 2004b, 2009a). The most usual interpretation of Keynes's heroic intellectual effort was that he had only provided the same sort of argument as some of the classical economists and the later monetarists (Laidler, 1999). That is, although he *claimed* to have shown that an economy could be permanently depressed most people thought that he had simply re-cycled the age-old argument that temporary wage rigidities, or the like, can cause temporary unemployment.

One of the reasons for this failure of communication, I think, is that, seemingly for the first time in the *General Theory*, and even though the topic was macroeconomics and money, Keynes nonetheless wanted to couch his arguments in terms of standard "Marshallian" microeconomics. This meant using marginalist mathematics, at least to the limit of his personal technical range, and also, even more importantly, assuming that conditions of so-called *perfect competition* prevail in all markets. These dubious features were presumably included to prove his *bona fides* to the rest of the economics profession in this important work. Why was it necessary to do this? I suppose that everyone who has spent any time at all studying economics in graduate school will be familiar with the sort of peer pressure that might lead someone go down this route (King, 2012), but it is nonetheless profoundly discouraging to think that even a great figure as Keynes apparently felt it necessary to do this. In any event, it was bound to lead to mistakes.

As already hinted, probably the more crucial of these two points in the present context is about the assumption of perfect competition rather than the issue of marginalism. This is because among the conditions defining a state of perfect competition is the idea that each firm in each industry is so small in relation to the market that it simply *believes* it can sell all the output it wants to at the "going price". However, if firms do believe this, and act on it, then it is already be quite clear that there is no theory that could ever be devised that will make changes in the aggregate demand for goods and services permanently alter a firm's behaviour. The only escape from such a conclusion would be, once again, by such devices nominal wage or price rigidities that serve to "throw a spanner in the works" (Leijonhufvud, 1968, 1981a, pp. 4–6), and temporarily prevent some actors from carrying out their plans, but only *temporarily*.

Making the assumption of a perfect competition clearly says nothing *at all* about what markets conditions are actually like in the real world. The idea of perfect competition in all markets is self-evidently a theoretical abstraction, although this seems not always to be apparent to many of the theorists themselves. Nonetheless, it is precisely this abstraction that makes it impossible to give any coherent theoretical account of how aggregate demand changes might ever have anything more than a transitory effect.

Compared to this basic theoretical point the use of marginalism, as such, might actually have been regarded as something of a side issue were it not such a sticking point for the "experts" (Kaldor, 1983, 1985). In fact, marginalism is neither a necessary nor a sufficient condition to arrive at a macroeconomic theory that ignores the demand side (Smithin, 2004a, 2009a, 2009b). It is important mainly to budding mathematical economists, in order to prove their own *bona fides,* to demonstrate to their colleagues that they can "do the math" (*i.e.*, solve optimization problems). It is true that for historical reasons, so-called marginalist methods did come to be closely associated with the first subjectivist theories of value that emerged in the late 19th century. Nonetheless, it would be logically possible to subscribe to a subjectivist theory of value with or without marginalism. It can also be shown that under *imperfect competition* (rather than perfect competition) real monetary demand does "matter", again, with or without marginalism.

If both statements are true, however, apart from careerist motives, the analyst may as well simply abandon marginalism for (most) practical rather than rhetorical purposes. It is not, after all, anything like a realistic description of the way in which decisions are actually made. Moreover, from what has just been said, it does not bring much else that is useful to the table, excepting perhaps whatever intellectual pleasure is to be gained from working out problems in differential calculus. One caveat to this position could be made in the case of some types of firm behaviour, particularly that of financial and banking firms. This is because, given the economic sociology of the system, such firms may be constrained to behave in a certain way (that is, to maximize profits) if they are to succeed on their own terms of reference in the existing environment. No comparable case can be made, however, that it makes any real sense to describe the behaviour of households, individual consumers, or workers in this way.

Wicksell

The fourth main strand of existing monetary theory is that usually associated with the name of Knut Wicksell (1965/1898, 1969/1958, 1907). However, it is important to note that exactly the *same* theory was available to Thornton (1991/1802) a hundred years earlier and that it once again became textbook orthodoxy, a hundred years *after* Wicksell's time, in the early years of the 21st century. By this time it had a variety of various new labels such as "the new consensus model" (NCM), "modern monetary economics",[8] "modern macroeconomics", *etc.* (Fontana and Setterfield, 2009; Taylor, 2007; Cecchetti, 2006). In this guise, it is the theory that had developed to replace monetarism in the years immediately before and after the millennium, following the publication of the famous paper by Taylor (1993). Related papers, notably by Taylor (2000) and Romer (2000), solidified the form in which the model made its way into the textbooks.

One of the criticisms that is often made about Wicksell's original work (although not, usually, in quite these terms) is that he does *not* pay much attention to ontological issues concerning money and the banking system. In effect, he just takes the whole set of institutions, central banks, commercial banks, firms and so on for granted. There is no real attempt at any explanation of *why* any of these are needed, or what role they play in capitalism. In a colourful phrase Burstein (1995, p. 7), for example, writes that "Wicksell's eccentric bank cartel makes loans of money elastically at bank rate". Later, he goes on to say that "his system is inexplicable unless his cartel or dominant public bank is a proxy for a central bank like the American Federal Reserve System" (Burstein, 1995, p. 67).[9] I would say that very similar sorts of problems existed with the "modern macroeconomics" model in the early years of the 21st century. The need for realism forced economists developing the new consensus to accept the idea that the monetary policy instrument will be the central bank policy rate. Therefore, they were also forced into extensive discussion of "interest rate operating procedures" and relationships between the central bank and commercial banks in inter-bank money markets (Dofinger and Debes, 2010; Lavoie and Seccareccia, 2004; Lavoie, 2010; Smithin, 2004b, pp. 57–58; Kam and Smithin, 2012). However, once again there was no *real* attempt to explain why these sorts of institutions should be vital to the operation of a system of decentralized market exchange, or why they should even be in existence (according to the tenets of the orthodox microeconomic theory). One of the main, and seemingly intractable, academic research problems of the time (the early 21st century) was to actually try to model the "micro-foundations" of such an institutional environment in the usual mathematical form (Woodford, 2003; Rogers, 2006; Tcherneva, 2009; King, 2012).

The strong point of Wicksell-type theory is the clear recognition that money is indeed endogenous, and that there is therefore *always* both credit creation and money creation (and destruction) *via* the banking system as the economic process unfolds. However, neither Wicksell, nor the more recent new consensus economists, seemed ever to recognize that as soon as money is allowed to be endogenous in this way, this must also open field for several alternative theories of inflation such as cost-push and/or conflict theories. Instead, in Wicksellian theory, the explanation of inflation is made to revolve narrowly around discrepancies between the policy rate of interest (the rate set by the central bank) and the so-called natural rate (Smithin, 2012). This retention of a natural rate concept however, is, in turn, the weakest point of the theory. Even though there now is a story about the central bank policy rate and the overall role of the commercial banking system and bank lending, there remains an underlying commitment to a "real theory of the real rate of interest". Wicksellians *still* want to think of interest rates as being ultimately determined by non-monetary factors, even though there is not, and never has been, any convincing explanation of how this can be so when developed systems of banking and finance in existence, not just barter. Here is how Wicksell (1965/1898, p. xxv) defines the supposed natural rate:

> This natural rate is roughly the same thing as the real rate of actual business. A more accurate though abstract, criterion is obtained by thinking it as the rate which would be determined by supply and demand if real capital were lent in kind without the intervention of money.

Once again, at the source, this is an example of the continual reference back to a hypothetical state of barter, and an *explicit* assumption that the introduction of a completely different type of social system, with money, banks and so on, makes no difference. Unlike in monetarist theory or classical monetary theory it is (at least) admitted that the interest rates actually observed in reality differ from the supposed natural rate. Therefore, the monetary policy *instrument* in Wicksellian theory is evidently the policy rate of the central bank.[10] Indeed, the basic theory is that a discrepancy between the two types of rates of interest is at the root of the trouble. If the policy rate is less than the natural rate it is thought that this causes prices to rise, whereas a high policy rate relative to the natural rate is believed to cause *deflation*.

Wicksell himself was actually somewhat confused about the question of real versus nominal interest rates, as were the vast majority of economists (interestingly enough excepting Thornton), until relatively late on in the 20th century (Meltzer, 2003). The new consensus economists, writing at the very end of the 20th century and the beginning of the 21st, eventually *did* seem to catch on to the idea that in effect we should be comparing the "real" policy rate to the "real" natural rate (on the presumption that this does exist), but nothing more is done with this insight except to assert the desirability of inflation targeting. They had taken over the real/nominal distinction from monetarism. Moreover, even this element of apparent continuity in the academic arena caused theoretical problems. It was certainly *not* always understood by modern economists that for both of the earlier schools (monetarist and classical), the assumption was that the interest rates *actually observed* in the marketplace were dictated by natural rate. This is *not* so in Wicksellian theory. In fact, the biggest difficulty with the overall argument is that once the theory of interest rates is *dissociated* from any observable phenomena there is no reason at all to suppose that the presumed natural rate of interest actually exists.

It can be shown that in any system there does exist a particular value of the *inflation-adjusted real policy rate* that is consistent with zero inflation, given the other economic parameters (Barrows and Smithin, 2009; Smithin, 2009a, 2009c). However, this is not really a "natural rate", in any of the other multiple senses in which Wicksell used the term. In particular, there is no reason for it to correspond with the hypothetical interest rate concept that might (or might not) exist in a barter economy (that does not itself exist). Moreover, the setting of the real policy rate that would achieve zero inflation in a real system is *not* necessarily the "optimal" interest rate for the economy from other points of view, such as that of promoting economic growth or achieving full employment (Smithin, 2009a, 2009c). We can let Keynes (1964/1936, pp. 242–243) have the last word on the subject of the mythical natural rate of interest. He wrote of his own previous work in the *Treatise on Money*:

> ... it was a mistake to speak of the natural rate of interest or to suggest that the ... definition [in the *Treatise*] would yield a unique value for the rate of interest irrespective of the level of employment. ... I am no longer of the opinion that the concept of a "natural" rate of interest has anything very useful or significant to contribute to our analysis.

To return to Wicksell, what, finally, was his attitude on the issue of the neutrality or non-neutrality of money? The answer is straightforward. For Wicksell, money was neutral in *both* the long run and the short run. Discrepancies between the policy rate and the natural rate are supposed to lead only to changes in prices (albeit continuous changes in prices), for as long as the interest differential persists. This is the famous "cumulative process" (Wicksell, 1965/1898, pp. 94–95). For the 20th/21st century new consensus, apart from the issue of recognizing that monetary policy is conducted *via* changes in interest rates (and, a strange *lack* of interest in the question of money demand), their positions on basic macroeconomic theory were more-or-less identical to those of monetarism. The argument, once again, again was that due to nominal rigidities, mistaken expectations and so forth, monetary and fiscal policy changes could be non-neutral in the short run but were always neutral in the long run.

Conclusion

The earlier-mentioned discussion of the attitudes taken by leading monetary theorists to each of the five major debating points in the fundamental theory of monetary economics, has identified some of their successes as well as their mistakes and confusions. This naturally leads on to the question as to what a preferred theory of monetary economics and/or macroeconomics might look like. By way of a conclusion to this chapter I will suggest what seem to me to be the desirable features of such a theory (Smithin, 1994, 2003, 2009a).

1. Firstly, the preferred theory should map out an explicit ontology of money, along the lines of the first few sections of this essay and of the discussion in Chapter 1. It must explain, for example, that money is a fundamentally a social institution not a commodity, and why, nonetheless, this "social relation" can have substantial causal effects in the material world. It must explain how credit creation, and its residue in money creation, are absolutely *needed* in order to generate any sort of profit, and why there is a hierarchy of money. It should made be clear above all that the establishment of this set of institutions is a necessary condition for capitalism (that is, the method of enterprise) to exist in the first place. It must also, therefore, clarify the role of the constitutional state (as opposed to a "confiscatory" or totalitarian state),[11] in sustaining the types of monetary and financial institutions that are necessary for the system of enterprise to function.

2. Secondly, the preferred theory should include both of the concepts of endogenous money and the money circuit, treated as an integral part of the economic process, and must fully explain their roles. The supply of money is not fixed. An important insight deriving from this point is that, therefore, the theory of inflation, on the one hand, and the theory of economic growth and employment, on the other, are in principle two quite separate things. They are linked *only* because of the dual role of banking and credit. However, once this point *is* grasped, it should then be possible to explain *all* of the different combinations of inflation and growth that have indeed occurred in reality (Smithin, 2002a, p. 584). It would be possible to also allow for all the possible sources of inflation, such as cost-push inflation, conflict inflation, and demand-pull inflation, as well as for the effects of both monetary and fiscal policy on inflation (Smithin, 1994, 2003, 2009a). Taking these points together the theory should therefore be less vulnerable to the "empirical problems" (Smithin,

1990) that frequently do arise with economic orthodoxy whenever something occurs that is at odds with the textbooks. There have been serious problems with the textbook narrative in *each* of the last four decades, when confronted, for example, with "stagflation" in 1970s, high unemployment in the 1980s, the "tech boom" of the 1990s, or the financial crisis in the first decade of the 21st century.

Precisely because it is possible to separate out the theory of inflation from the theory of economic growth, in this way, the preferred theory would not simply be "inflationist" for the sake of it. It was admitted earlier that it would be a good thing from the point of view of incentives under capitalism if the "value of money" was more stable. However, what does this mean? Does it really mean that there should literally be *zero* inflation that is, no price changes at all on average? This actually seems quite incompatible with the basic spirit of capitalism. On the other hand if the value of money holdings at least keeps pace with inflation (which means, in the modern world, that the real interest rate *received* on bank deposits is non-negative), this would still mean that the "value of money" would be stable, as stable as it is ever likely to be.

3. Thirdly, there must be a *monetary* theory of the *real* rate of interest. If fundamentally money is a social relation, the real rate of interest on money must also be a social relation, involving money. This in itself is sufficient to explain why, at the end of the day, the central bank usually has power over interest rate determination. The bank is the social institution at the heart of the "government/money complex",[12] and the resulting real rate of interest on money loans is very much part of the social fabric itself. We are then faced squarely with the (essentially ethical) question of what the real rate of interest rate *should* be. This has to do ultimately with questions of income distribution, power, and the political settlement. In this connection, it is very important to clearly distinguish interest from *profit* (Smithin, 2009c). As will be shown in later chapters, the basic trade-off in income distribution is between profit, real wages, real interest and the tax burden. Disputes over the "interest burden" are therefore fundamentally similar to disputes about taxation.

As suggested earlier, the counterpart in international economics to a monetary theory of the real rate of interest is a monetary theory of the real exchange rate. The real exchange rate should *also* be thought of as an endogenous variable, rather than being assumed to be fixed by non-monetary factors such as the hypothetical barter terms of trade.

4. Fourthly, it should clearly be recognized that the main monetary policy instrument is indeed usually a nominal interest rate, the policy rate of the central bank. This brings us back to the question of how the sorts of real interest rate changes, discussed earlier, can actually be achieved. As previously argued, simply adjusting the nominal policy rate for changes in reported inflation will stabilize the inflation-adjusted real policy rate. It is important, however, also to remember that if the nominal interest instrument is to be employed successfully to change real rates there may *have* to be at least some inflation in the system in order to have a room to maneuver on real rates. As already discussed if, for example, the nominal rate has fallen to zero and then there is deflation, it would not then be possible to change the real rate just by changing the nominal policy rate.

The above is one of a number of factors leading to the suggestion that rather than of policy targeting either the inflation rate or the price level itself, the desirable monetary policy would be a *real* interest rate rule, that does stabilize the *inflation-adjusted* real policy rate (Smithin, 1994, 2003, 2007a, 2009a). Unfortunately, the alternative interest rate policy, that of "pegging" a nominal rate interest rate at whatever level, would only lead to instability of *either* an inflationary or deflationary character.

5. Finally, it should be recognized that both monetary and fiscal policy changes are inevitably non-neutral in both the short run and the long run. They affect not only the ups and downs of the business cycle, but also the average growth rate of the economy itself. According to the preferred theory, it would therefore be a good thing if the notion of "functional finance", originally due to Lerner (1943) could be revived (Nell and Forstater, 2003). This means simply that changes in government spending and taxation would then be judged by the impact that they actually have on the economy, and not on arbitrary financial rules such as the size of the government budget deficit, or the size national debt relative to GDP (nor because of any perceived need to "balance the budget"). This sort of statement, in spite of appearances to the contrary, does not really impinge in any way on the ideological debate about the scope or size of government in relation to the overall economy. It does not necessarily support a "tax and spend" agenda, for example. The real issue, which was well-understood by Keynes, is rather the extent to

which, when there is government spending, this is "loan expenditure" (Keynes, 1964/1936, pp. 128–130) instead of increasing taxes to pay for it. In short, it is all about the "optimal" size of the budget deficit relative to GDP. Similar sorts of policy judgments and considerations to those arising in functional finance apply also to monetary policy, and specifically to the decision about what the optimal level of the *real* rate of interest on money loans should be.

Notes

1. See Kane (2009).
2. See also King (2012).
3. Including, it must be said, Barrows and Smithin (2009, pp. 211–212). That book does, however, clearly discuss the issue of what the monetary policy instrument is in *reality*.
4. In practice in 19th century Britain, there was also a fixed "fiduciary issue" of notes over and above the amount backed by gold. Moreover, over time and really as a matter of necessity, changes in bank rate (the policy rate of the day) did eventually come to be recognized as one of the main financial techniques by which control over the gold reserve might actually be exercised in practice (Keynes, 1971a/1930, pp. 167–168).
5. Which, to be fair, has been true of the majority mainstream economists ever since.
6. This example, of the demand for refrigerators, was actually used at one stage in the monetarist literature of several decades ago, but I cannot now place the reference.
7. See also, Smithin (2009a, pp. 87–89, 2004a).
8. Not to be confused with the "modern money theory" (MMT) of Wray (2012).
9. This is an anachronism on Burstein's part, as the Federal Reserve did not exist for a full decade-and-a-half after the publication of Wicksell's book. Presumably, Wicksell was thinking about something like the Swedish Riksbank or the Bank of England.
10. Wicksell himself (misleading) called this the "market rate", but what he seemed to mean by this that was the interest rates actually *seen* in the financial market places are those that are dictated, or at least influenced, by monetary policy.

11. It is very important to stress this distinction. Note also that there will be a detailed discussion of the roles of taxation and government spending, in later chapters in the form of essays. The matter has already been touched on in Chapter 1.

12. This is a pun on US President Eisenhower's 1950s concept of the "military/industrial complex".

CHAPTER 3

VARIATIONS ON THE THEME OF THE QUANTITY THEORY OF MONEY

Introduction

The purpose of this third chapter in the series *Essays in the Fundamental Theory of Monetary Economics and Macroeconomics* is to discuss the revival of the ancient quantity theory of money that took place in the second half of the 20th century under the name of "monetarism". The quantity theory has been one of the main alternative approaches to monetary economics that have been competing for allegiance for as long as theories of political economy have existed. Its main competitors have usually been Keynesian/mercantilist-type theory, on the one hand, and Wicksell-type theory, on the other.

The point of discussing the 20th century version is that, by then, it had reached its most sophisticated and mathematically-orientated incarnation.[1] Therefore, in studying this relatively recent episode in the history thought, it is possible to cover most of the issues that arise in the quantity theory framework in a definitive way. This chapter provides a synthesis of material previously discussed in Barrows and Smithin (2006, 2009) and Smithin (1993, 1994, 2003), with the addition of a more detailed mathematical treatment.

The time horizon studied is between Friedman's (1956) "restatement" of the quantity theory of money in 1956 and the appearance of a brief quote in an article by McCallum (1986a, p. 1) 30 years later, noting "the *recent downturn in popularity* of the Lucas–Barro theory of cyclical fluctuations induced by monetary misperceptions" (emphasis added). Tobin (1981) had earlier called Friedman's (1968) views on monetary policy "Monetarism Mark I", and labeled the more "high-tech" theory, associated with Barro (1984), Lucas (1981), and Sargent (1979), which was sometimes also called either "rational expectations theory" or "new-classical theory", as "Monetarism Mark II". Both versions are discussed here.

On a number of occasions (*e.g.*, Friedman, 1974a, 1989; Friedman and Schwartz, 1982) Friedman and his collaborators have dealt explicitly with the relationship between the monetarist restatement of the quantity theory and earlier versions, including Irving Fisher's (1911) "transactions equation", and the "Cambridge cash-balances approach" (Keynes, 1923; Marshall, 2003/1923). By the mid-1950s, however, Friedman was complaining about "the atrophied and rigid caricature" that the quantity theory had by then become (Smithin, 2003, p. 42). Nonetheless, it will be convenient to begin our analysis here with just such a caricature. This will illustrate the main issues that Friedman must have felt he had to address in developing a more flexible and "up-to-date" version of the theory.

A "Caricature" Version of the Quantity Theory of Money

The simplest "caricature" version of the quantity theory, using familiar notation, would be:

$$MV = PY, \tag{3.1}$$

where M stands for the nominal money supply, V is the "velocity of circulation", P is the aggregate price level, and Y is real GDP. The term on the right-hand side of Eq. (3.1) PY, is nominal GDP (or nominal income). Therefore, in Friedman's (1989) terminology, Eq. (3.1) would be the "income form" of the quantity theory, and V is the "income velocity" of circulation. In Chapter 1 and elsewhere (*e.g.*, Smithin, 2010, pp. 54–55), I have argued that the whole notion of the velocity of circulation is actually somewhat bogus. It is supposed to have the connotation of how rapidly money change hands. However for a given supply of dollars, V will turn out to be a greater or lesser number depending simply on the length of the time period considered. Conceptually, also, (in terms of understanding how the economic process functions and how profits are generated), it is reminiscent of the children's party game "pass the parcel". If we have one 20 dollar bill and pass it from hand to hand in a room more or less quickly during a half-hour period, we can *claim* that we are doing 800 dollars worth of business, 600 dollars worth of business, 1000 dollars worth of business, or any other attainable number. Still no-one can end up with more than 20 dollars in their pocket. In spite of these problems, unfortunately the idea of the velocity of circulation has always played a key role in academic discussion of the quantity theory, and for that reason it must be one of the main concepts dealt with here.

As it stands, Eq. (3.1) is a tautology (true by definition) rather than a theory. It is always possible from published statistics to come up with the dollar figure for the flow of national income, PY, over a given accounting period (such as a quarter or a year). Also, it is easy to obtain a dollar value for the average level of (some) measure of the money stock, M, over the same period. Their ratio, V, can then be residually determined as $V = PY/M$. However, this calculation would not be an informative exercise. What would turn the quantity *equation* into a more meaningful quantity *theory* are the various assumptions made about the behaviour of the individual components (Smithin, 2003, p. 42).

To derive the simplest (caricature) version of the quantity theory, the specific assumptions required are (i) that real income, Y, is determined independently of any monetary influence; (ii) that the nominal money supply, M, is exogenously determined by the monetary authorities, and (iii) that velocity, V, is a constant. In technical language the assumptions are *neutral money*, *exogenous money*, and *constant velocity*.

The quantity theory then becomes a very simple theory of price level determination. A change in the money supply will lead to an equal proportionate change in the price level in the same direction. A doubling of the money supply will cause a doubling of prices, for example, whereas if the money supply falls by 25%, prices will fall by 25%. This is most easily shown if the level output, Y, is not growing (the same flow of output is repeated every accounting period). Then we can write $dY = 0$ and $dV = 0$ by assumption. Then, totally differentiate Eq. (3.1) to yield:

$$VdM = YdP, \qquad (3.2)$$

and, because $V = PY/M$:

$$dP/P = dM/M. \qquad (3.3)$$

For completeness of the argument, it should be noted that according to "supply-side economics" even if money *is* neutral, output can *still* be growing (obviously not from demand growth but "under its own steam", so to speak). It was argued, in Chapter 1, that this is not at all a good model for a *real* capitalist economy because of the need for firms to realize monetary profit.[3] Nonetheless, the idea that "supply creates its own demand" (that growth can occur purely from supply side factors, such as the accumulation of physical plant and equipment, the growth of the labour force, and technological change), has always been extremely influential within the economics profession. As so many people do argue this way, the simple mathematics of this case should be worked out for the sake of argument. Therefore, take logarithms (logs) of (3.1), and differentiate with respect to time:

$$(1/M)(dM/dt) + (1/V)(dV/dt) = (1/P)(dP/dt) + (1/Y)(dY/dt).$$

$$(3.4)$$

Even though output *is* now allowed to grow, we are still assuming that $dV/dt = 0$. Therefore, (3.4) can be rearranged to simply give:

$$(1/P)(dP/dt) = (1/M)(dM/dt) - (1/Y)(dY/dt). \qquad (3.5)$$

So, with the economy supposedly growing at a rate determined independently of the monetary system, the percentage rate of change of the price level (the inflation rate) is equal to the percentage rate of growth of the money supply, less the supply-driven economic growth rate. As the symbol $\dot{P}$ (P dot) is often used to stand for dP/dt, the time derivative of the price level (and $\dot{Y}$ for dY/dt, etc.), Eq. (3.5) can also be written as:

$$\dot{P}/P = \dot{M}/M - \dot{Y}/Y. \qquad (3.6)$$

Still further simplifying the notation, we can let lower case p stand for the rate of inflation, as in previous chapter, also lower case m for the rate of growth of the money supply and lower case y for the economic growth rate. Therefore, $p = (1/P)(dP/dt) = \dot{P}/P$, $m = (1/M)(dM/dt) = \dot{M}/M$, $y = (1/Y)(dY/dt) = \dot{Y}/Y$ Eqs. (3.5) and (3.6) are identical to:

$$p = m - y. \qquad (3.7)$$

Each of Eqs. (3.4), (3.5) and (3.6) thus expresses the most basic insight of the quantity theory, which is that the inflation rate will be (roughly) equal to the rate of monetary growth less the economic growth rate. If the economic growth rate is 2.5% a year and money supply growth if 10%, then a quantity theorist would expect the inflation rate to be (about) 7.5%. To achieve zero inflation (stable money prices), money supply growth would have to be reduced to around 2.5%, to match the supply-determined economic growth rate. Nobody, presumably (even working with the very simplest version of the theory) would have expected these numbers to work out exactly in the real world, but this is the general idea.

Potential Criticisms of the Quantity Theory

The simplistic version of the quantity theory set out previously is potentially open to attack on three separate grounds, which correspond to each of the original assumptions made. First, the level of real income, Y, may indeed be affected by monetary factors, and therefore some of any change in the money supply may be reflected in a change in output, rather than prices. Second, the money supply, M, may not be a given quantity but could be an endogenous variable responsive to changes in other variables, *via* bank credit creation for example. Third, velocity, V, may not be a constant but also a variable, and in this case some (or all) of the effect of any money supply change might be absorbed in a change in velocity.

In short, money may not be neutral, the money supply may be endogenous, and velocity may not be stable. Therefore, the caricature version of the quantity theory can hardly be regarded secure if it could be rebutted by even just mentioning any one of these points. Friedman's attempt revive the quantity theory in the mid-1950s might well therefore have been understood in terms of an effort to meet each of these potential objections head on, thus generating a "more subtle and relevant" (Friedman, 1956, p. 3) version of the theory, which would be immune to these criticisms. For the monetarists, the idea that increases in money supply growth lead to inflation *was* an important idea, and was believed to be "true" at some basic level. Friedman and others would therefore have perceived their task as providing more sophisticated arguments that would be able to establish this point and disarm the critics.

Responses to Criticism

The neutrality of money?

Friedman's solution to the problem of the effect of money on real income was similar to that of the earliest writers on the quantity theory, such as Hume (1987/1752) centuries before. Essentially, the strategy was to concede the impact of money on output for the short run, but *not* for the long run. It was held that monetary changes can be non-neutral in the short run, but are always neutral (and super-neutral) in the long run.[4] With this argument, monetarism was thereby able to retain the basic proposition about the long-run relationship between money and inflation, while at the same time providing a viable explanation for business cycle fluctuations. In fact, the blame for both types of problem could be laid firmly at the door of the central bank.

As mentioned, the monetarists believed that the economy converges to a long-run equilibrium growth rate that is (ultimately) independent of any monetary influence, and reflects only the real forces of "productivity and thrift" (Friedman, 1974b). The real interest rate was also thought to depend only on real factors, and so, for monetary analysis, could be treated more-or-less as a constant. These assumptions are consistent with the neoclassical growth model of the mid-20th century (Blanchard and Fischer, 1989; Jones, 1998), but they also to some extent reflect earlier traditional teaching at the University of Chicago (Burstein, 1963; Friedman, 1974a; Leijonhufvud, 1981b). The monetarists believed, in fact, that there are natural rates of both economic growth *and* the real rate of interest. These concepts are closely connected with another "natural rate" popularized by Friedman, the "natural rate of unemployment" (Friedman, 1968).

Short-run non-neutrality on money, on the other hand, might arise because at least some economic actors (such as labour) are either slow to realize the implications or monetary growth, or are unable to react quickly enough to it (perhaps because they have already signed contracts, for example). So, there will usually be either mistaken expectations, or nominal rigidities, or both, in the short run and either will be enough to account for short-run non-neutrality (Friedman, 1968, 1989; Friedman and Friedman, 1980). It is somewhat ironic that, in retrospect, there now seems to be little difference between this type of argument and what was (wrongly) called the "Keynesian" model in textbooks at the time.[2] The main point to notice is probably that monetarists did stress the idea that the various non-neutralities are explicitly temporary and relatively short-lived. Eventually expectations will catch up, and/or nominal wages and prices will adjust, and any real effects from monetary changes will eventually dissipate (Friedman, 1968).

As the monetarist version of the quantity theory was able to allow for short-run non-neutrality, and hence booms and downturns in the economy, while also retaining the traditional long-run relationship between money and prices, this was an important factor in enhancing the plausibility and acceptability of the theory. It meant that the theory could no longer be accused of bankruptcy in the face of historical episodes like the Great Depression of the 1930s (Friedman, 1974b). And, yet, this position was still consistent with the view that in the long-run changes in the money supply would only affect prices and, given enough time, the real economy would always bounce back.

The basic argument about short-run non-neutrality is best illustrated by considering *first* a hypothetical world in which the economy is not growing. Suppose, rather, there is a unique equilibrium level of output, which could be called the natural *level* of output, or Y^N. To see how this is determined, let there be a total demand function for labour of the form $N^D = G(W/P)$, with $G'(W/P) < 0$, and, also a supply function, $N^S = J(W/P)$, with $J'(W/P) > 0$.[3] If "market forces" ensure that labour demand equals labour supply then we have:

$$G(W/P) = J(W/P). \tag{3.8}$$

This is usually described as the case of "perfect wage and price flexibility", because both nominal wages and prices must adjust to achieve any given level of the real wage rate (W/P). The operation of the labour market therefore yields a unique equilibrium real wage $(W/P)^N$, and a unique level of employment N^N, as shown in Fig. 3.1.

Next suppose that the aggregate production function is of the traditional form:

$$Y = F(N), \quad F'(N) > 0, \quad F''(N) < 0. \tag{3.9}$$

Given the equilibrium level of employment there will be a corresponding unique natural level of output, Y^N, shown in Fig. 3.2. This natural level of output is also (very confusingly) sometimes called the "full employment"

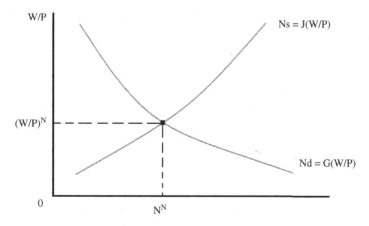

Fig. 3.1. Labour market equilibrium with perfect wage and price flexibility.

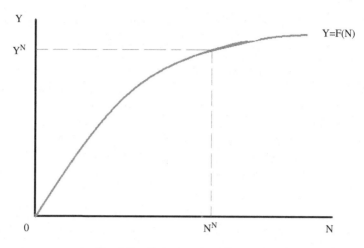

Fig. 3.2. Output and employment.

level of output in textbooks. (It is confusing because even the textbook writes themselves admit that, in reality, the level of employment can be more, or less, than this.) The main idea, however, is that Y^N is a level of output to which the market will "settle down", and that any deviations will be short-lived. This is the maintained hypothesis of the quantity theory of money and (really) of all orthodox theory. If the unique natural level of output does exist, then by definition it should *not* be responsive to any changes in the average level of prices, P. If, for example, prices were to *rise*, nominal wages should *increase* by the same amount to keep the real wage constant, and *vice versa* if prices were to fall.

Therefore, the aggregate supply "curve" (as it is called) for the hypothetical equilibrium economy will simply be a vertical straight line. This is also sometimes labeled the "classical aggregate supply curve", or the "long-run aggregate supply curve" (LRAS) as in Fig. 3.3. In addition to penciling in the LRAS, the original quantity equation itself can be re-arranged to become effectively an "aggregate demand" (AD) function to go with it as in:

$$P = MV/Y. \tag{3.10}$$

Figure 3.3 is therefore nothing else than a graphical illustration of the quantity theory of money. An outward shift of the AD function caused by an increase in the quantity of money from M to M', will only increase the price level from P to P', and have no other effects. It is also worth noting that *only* a change in the money supply (or possibly an arbitrary change in

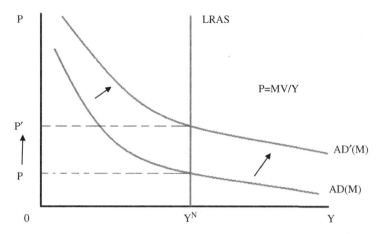

Fig. 3.3.   The quantity theory of money illustrated in graphical form.

the velocity of circulation V, ruled out by assumption here), is capable of having any effect on aggregate demand.

This version of the quantity theory therefore prevents a Keynesian-type fiscal policy "stimulus", for example, from having any impact at all on the economy (not even on prices in this extreme case). By way of an example, for a closed economy (one that does not trade with the rest of the world) the nominal national income identity is:

$$MV = PC + PI + PG. \qquad (3.11)$$

Therefore, if neither M nor V changes total demand, MV, must stay constant. Therefore, it has to be argued that any dollar increase in government spending, PG, will be totally offset (*e.g.*) by a decrease in private investment spending, PI, of the same amount. This is the origin of the idea that private investment spending is "crowded out" by government spending. Note, however, there is no substantive economic reasoning behind this claim, even though it has certainly has been influential politically. It depends solely on assumptions about the behaviour of M and V.

Thus far, the discussion has done nothing more than to reinforce the notion of monetary neutrality. The real question, though (as explained) is whether or not the argument can be modified so that it does not appear to be an extreme position to potential critics. What the 20th century monetarists *really* wanted to be able to do is to allow for some short non-neutrality in the short run, and so explain why central bank activity often does have a discernable impact on real GDP in reality, and yet, at the same time, preserve the basic long-run spirit of the quantity theory.

One of the easiest ways to do this is simply to suggest that the average level of money wages, W, tends to get "stuck" temporarily at some given level, perhaps due to the current state of labour relations, or to the various contracts and other commitments that employers and employees have entered into. Suppose that the average level of the index number for the money wage is currently W_2, and compared to the price level P_2, this combination is consistent with the equilibrium real wage rate, $W_2/P_2 = (W/P)^N$. What happens, though, if the price level starts to fall below P_2, say to P_1 or P_0, and the average level of money wages does *not* immediately change? If money wages are "sticky" in this way then as prices fall, *real* wages *rise*, and firms will employ less labour. In Fig. 3.4, N_1 is a lower level of employment than N^N, for example, N_0 is a lower level than N_1, and so on. If on the other hand prices were to *rise*, to P_3 or P_4, with wages still at W_2, real wages will *fall*. Now firms will want to hire more labour.

The levels of employment can be translated into levels of output *via* the production function of Fig. 3.2. Then comparing these results to the price levels themselves, we obtain a temporary upward-sloping *short-run aggregate supply curve* (SRAS) as illustrated in Fig. 3.5.

This will stay in place for as long as the average level of money wages is "stuck" at W_2. The quantity theory will not *fully* hold over this period of time, because any increase in the supply of money that increases demand (shifts out the AD curve) will temporarily increase the level of output as well

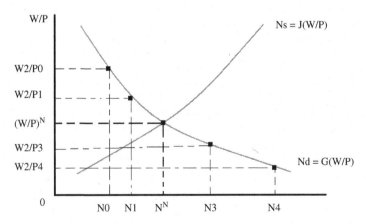

Fig. 3.4. A labour market with "sticky" nominal wages.

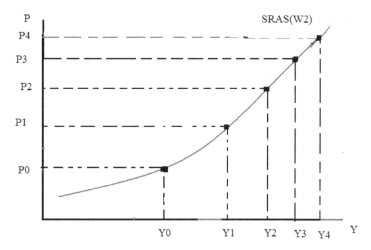

Fig. 3.5.   The short-run aggregate supply curve.

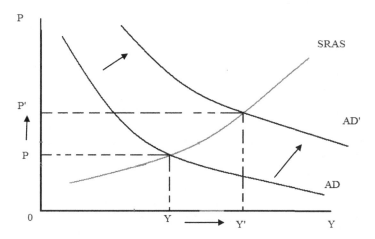

Fig. 3.6.   With "sticky" nominal wages money can be non-neutral in the short run.

as causing some increase in prices. Money is non-neutral in the short run, as shown in Fig. 3.6.

There must be a whole family of SRAS curves similar to the one in Fig. 3.4, a different SRAS curve for each possible level of the average nominal wage rate. If the money wage increases from W_2 to W_3, this shifts the SRAS curve *back* and to the left (reducing supply at each level of prices). Conversely, if the average level of money wages falls, say from

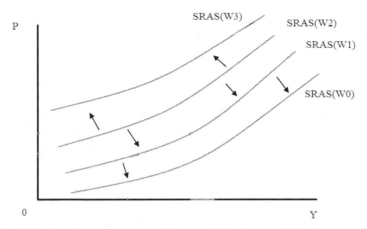

Fig. 3.7.   The short-run aggregate supply curve shifts when nominal wage rates change.

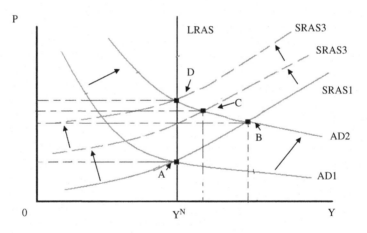

Fig. 3.8.   An increase in the money supply.

W_2 to W_1 to W_0, this will shift the SRAS curve out and to the right, increasing supply at each level of prices. A sample of SRAS curves is illustrated in Fig. 3.7.

We are now in a position to consider the whole sequence of events (supposed) to occur whenever there is a change in the money supply. Assume that the economy illustrated in Fig. 3.8 starts in equilibrium at point "A".

At this stage output is at its natural level Y^N, real wages are also at their natural (or equilibrium) level, and the average level of nominal wages is consistent with the price level at that point. Then let there be an increase in the money supply, shifting the aggregate demand curve outwards. For as long as the average level of money wages does not change, the original SRAS curve remains relevant. There will be boom conditions in the economy which, in context, means a higher level of output and a somewhat higher price level, at point "B". However, after some time, or so the argument goes, the very experience of the boom itself will cause things to change. Economic actors will begin to ask for higher wages, to build higher prices into contract demands, and so on. The average level of money wages will rise, and the SRAS curve will start shifting back, in the first instance to the position containing the new temporary equilibrium point at "C". The boom is already beginning to fade away due to the upward pressure on wages and costs. Eventually the boom disappears entirely, and the final position is at point "D". At this point there is no difference in output from what it was initially, there are only higher prices. Therefore, if we are comparing only the situation at the starting point "A" to the final outcome at "D", all that has happened is that the increase in the money supply has caused an increase in prices, as the quantity theory predicts.

In the long run the quantity theory holds and money is neutral. Along the way, however, there has been a temporary stimulus to output and employment, money is non-neutral in the short run. The time horizon over which this is all supposed to happen is about the length of the typical business cycle. Maybe a year, 18 months, or 2 years for the expansionary phase (Friedman, 1983). From the point of view of political economy, the message that seems to be delivered is that it was not worthwhile "stimulating" the economy in the first place.

Figure 3.9 then shows the opposite case of a reduction in the supply of money. Suppose central bank feels, for some reason, that the average level of prices at the initial starting point "A" is "too high". It therefore decides to reduce prices permanently by reducing the supply of money. Aggregate demand falls, but with sticky nominal wages the initial impact of this is as much on real GDP as on prices. Therefore, there is a recession, and the economy slides *backwards* along the original SRAS curve to point "B" in the first instance. Prices do fall somewhat, but wages do not follow at once, they stay at their original nominal level for a least some period of time. Real wages are therefore rising, profits are getting squeezed, and this is why there is an economic downturn. However, once a recession has been going on for some time, the experiences of falling output and unemployment will themselves cause economic actors to begin to revise their demands downward. They will settle for lower wages in new contracts, and perhaps

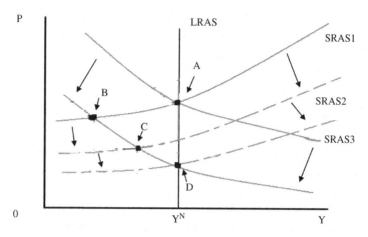

Fig. 3.9.   A decrease in the money supply.

agree to "rollbacks" of existing contracts. The SRAS curve will begin to shift down and to the right, for example to the position that contains a new temporary equilibrium at point "C". Employment and output begin to increase again, as workers and others price themselves back into the market. Eventually it is hoped that the process will work itself out and the recession will be over. The initial level of output will be restored, and the only lasting effect will be lower prices all round as at point "D". It can once again be argued the quantity theory of money will hold in the long run, and that the recession is only temporary.

There is another way of looking at this process though, which is that, in effect, the central bank is *deliberately* creating unemployment in order to force the various economic actors to scale back their wage demands. This could be a sensitive issue politically, if the people affected ever came to understand what is going on. Therefore, in these sorts of circumstances central banks are at great pains to stress how, in their view, the temporary sacrifice is "well worth it". The slogan "short-term pain for long-term gain" expresses this point of view exactly, even though it is doubtful, in practice, how short-lived is the "pain", and how lasting the "gain", respectively.[5]

The exogeneity of money?

A second problem with the basic (or caricature) version of the quantity theory is the question of whether or not the money supply can reasonably be thought of as exogenous variable. How can this be true in an economy with a developed banking and financial system? Within the framework of monetarism the issue was addressed by the concept of the "money multiplier" (Friedman, 1960, 1989). The monetarists did have to accept the argument that in a credit economy money is "created" whenever commercial banks extend loans, and "destroyed" when the loans are repaid (as explained in Chapter 1). However, in response, they argued that in order to exercise this money-creating power, the commercial banks must always hold sufficient reserves of the base money of the system (the liabilities of the central bank) in order to satisfy any of their depositors who happen to ask for payment in "cash". As the monetary base consists of central bank liabilities, it can be argued the authorities should at least be able to control *this* quantity by balance sheet operations. Hence, if the money multiplier exists, *via* this route exercise some control over the overall money supply also.

One difficulty that arises in this context is the problem of actually defining the overall money supply (as opposed to the base) for this purpose. Which liabilities of *which* commercial financial institutions should be included? It was argued in Chapter 1 that is best to define the money supply as broadly as possible and many monetarist economists would have completely agreed with this. However, this does reinforce the point that the vast bulk of the money supply consists *not* just of items in the balance sheet of the central bank, but also the deposit liabilities of many and various other financial institutions. However it is defined statistically, therefore, the broader notion of the money supply is not, in principle, a fixed quantity. Can it be made to appear so for the purposes of the monetarist argument?

As previously discussed in Chapter 1 and following Friedman (1960, 1989), let CU stand for currency in the hands of the public, D for those bank deposits that are included in the relevant definition of the money supply, and R for bank reserves. The generic definition of the money supply is then:

$$M = CU + D. \tag{3.12}$$

With this notation the definition of monetary base, the liabilities of the central bank (also known as "high-powered money"), is:

$$H = CU + R. \tag{3.13}$$

Next, multiply Eq. (3.13) by M/M, and substitute in from Eq. (3.12) to obtain:

$$H = [(CU + R)/(CU + D)]M. \tag{3.14}$$

Finally divide both the numerator and denominator on the right-hand side by D, and re-arrange, to arrive at:

$$M = [(1 + CU/D)/(CU/D + R/D)]H. \qquad (3.15)$$

Equation (3.15) says that there is a numerical ratio between the liabilities of the central bank, H, and the overall money supply, M, that depends on the "banking ratios". These are the "cash to deposits" ratio, CU/D, and the "reserves to deposits" ratio, R/D. The first of these is determined by the behaviour of the public, in literally deciding how much cash they would like to keep "in their pockets". The second is determined by the banks themselves, who make the decision about what reserve to deposit ratio is prudent.[5] Equation (3.15) therefore (potentially) provides the basis for a monetarist answer to the difficulties posed by the existence of a credit economy. The argument is that *if* the CU/D and R/D ratios are reasonably stable, and *if* the central bank can control the size of its own balance sheet (hence control H) the money supply, M, will also be under control. Totally differentiating, we obtain:

$$dM/dH = (1 + CU/D)/(CU/D + R/D). \qquad (3.16)$$

This is the so-called money multiplier relationship. If the monetary base increases or decreases by (say) one dollar the equation suggests that the money supply itself will increase or decrease in the ratio $[(1 + CU/D)/(CU/D + R/D)]$. If CU/D is 0.04, for example, and R/D is 0.01 (and both of these numbers are stable and do not change) the overall money supply will increase or decrease by around \$21, for each dollar of base money injected or withdrawn from the economy.

This was felt by the monetarists to be an adequate answer to the problem of monetary control, but there are some obvious counter-arguments. Suppose that the banking ratios are *not* stable. The money supply may get out of control in that way, and this type of argument is often brought up in the literature on "financial fragility", for example. Even more significantly, if the central bank uses changes in a nominal rate of interest (the "policy rate") as the monetary policy instrument rather than a quantitative rule, the monetary base H, *itself* becomes endogenous. Control over the final money supply, M, must then be exercised *indirectly* by the central bank's "interest rate operating rocedures" (Smithin, 2004b). The money supply itself becomes an endogenous variable. In that case, there is unlikely to be any set numerical relationship between M and H (Lavoie, 2010; Kam and Smithin, 2012).

The velocity of circulation and money demand

The third problem for the simple quantity theory is the question of how the velocity of circulation might behave. It is a fairly obvious point to make that it surely will *not* be the case that velocity is a strict constant in practice. However, for changes in velocity really to do very much to upset the underlying logic of the quantity theory, they would either have to be *totally* unpredictable, or (the opposite case) would have to change *exactly* in the reverse direction from changes in M. On the other hand, if it is allowed that velocity *can* change, but always does so in a fairly predictable manner, and never by enough to totally offset changes in M, then this could be allowed for in working out the precise quantitative relationship between M and P (and between m and p). It would not affect the basic causal chain. Quantity theorists are not aware of the weaknesses of the concept of velocity from the point of view of the viability of the monetary production economy, so this was not a concern.

Therefore, in early days of the monetarist controversy, one of the main preoccupations of monetarist economists in their studies was the issue of whether or not the demand for money was a "stable and predictable" relationship, empirically. If the demand for money were to be predictable the implication is that velocity would also behave predictably. Velocity is, in some sense, the inverse of the concept of money demand. But *why* was there an exclusive focus on money demand and velocity rather than on other issues? This is because Friedman and his collaborators seemed to believe that the main point of the "Keynesian revolution" had been the assertion that velocity was highly unstable (Friedman, 1974a, 1989; Friedman and Schwartz, 1982). There was stress on the special case of Keynes's supposed notion of "absolute liquidity preference" (Friedman, 1974a, p. 21), the "liquidity trap" of the textbooks. This view of what Keynesian theory was all about is highly questionable (Patinkin, 1974), but the point here is what the monetarists themselves believed the Keynesian "challenge" to be. Friedman, apparently saw one of his main tasks as reformulating the quantity theory as a theory of the demand for money, in which money demand (and hence velocity) could be expressed as "a stable function of a limited number of variables" (Friedman, 1956, p. 16). What would be achieved by such a reformulation is for the quantity theorist to escape from the restrictive assumption of constant velocity. Nonetheless velocity remains determinate and it can be argued that it will respond in *predictable* ways to changes in variables that affect the demand for money.

Many writers have suggested that Friedman's approach to money demand was not really new in 1956. It could even be regarded as a development of the Keynesian theory of money demand *itself* (Patinkin, 1974; Leeson, 2003a, 2003b; Smithin, 2004a), or alternatively, that of Hicks (1982b). For a quantity theorist, however, the value of the approach would have been in rescuing the theory from its most obviously restrictive assumptions.

To see the argument, write down the theory of money demand that was common to both "Keynesians" and "monetarists" in the version that appeared in 20th century textbooks:

$$(M/P)^D = L(Y, i), \qquad L_Y > 0, \ L_i < 0. \tag{3.17}$$

Equation (3.17) states that the demand for real money balances depends *positively* on real national income Y, and *negatively* on i, the nominal rate of interest. The first argument is what survives of Keynes's "transactions demand for money" (Keynes, 1964/1936, p. 170), when translated into the "income version" of the quantity theory. The second is the opportunity cost of holding money, when money itself does not bear interest.[6] This demand for money function leads directly to the "variable velocity" version of the quantity theory, which is:

$$MV(i) = PY, \qquad V_i > 0. \tag{3.18}$$

Equation (3.18) is just a specific functional form of (3.17). Next recall the relationship between the nominal interest rate, i, and the real interest rate, r:

$$i = r + p^e, \tag{3.19}$$

where p^e stands for the expected inflation rate. Using this in the variable velocity quantity theory we arrive at:

$$MV(r + p^e) = PY. \tag{3.20}$$

Putting things in this way allows for an argument that the quantity theory will still hold in equilibrium (also called the "steady-state") even though, when out of the steady-state velocity can be changing.

Note that if the model does converge to a steady-state equilibrium, expected and actual inflation will be equal at that point, $p^e = p$. Also, by definition, the inflation rate itself must then have settled down to *its* equilibrium value (whether this is high or low), implying that $dp/dt = 0$. Finally recall that, according to monetarist theory, the *real* rate of interest is supposed to be fundamentally determined outside the money markets, by the "natural rate". Therefore, in the steady-state $r = r^N$ and $dr^N/dt = 0$. Putting all these ideas together, we have:

$$V = V(r^N + p) \tag{3.21}$$

and, differentiating with respect to time:

$$\dot{V} = dV/dt = V_i(di/dt) = Vi(dr^N/dt + dp/dt) = 0. \tag{3.22}$$

Totally differentiating Eq. (3.20) using (3.21) and re-arranging, we therefore get back to:

$$p = m - y. \tag{3.23}$$

This is simply the most basic version of the quantity theory, once again. The theory still holds in "steady-state" equilibrium.

Stability/Convergence in the Monetarist Model

The result just described above depends on the assumption that the model eventually does converge to the steady-state. A further step that has to be taken, therefore, is to show that this will indeed be the case. Why does the inflation rate not continue rising (or falling) forever? In order to answer this question, and putting the point in mathematical language, it is necessary to consider the *stability* properties of the model. To do this note that if the velocity of circulation *is* changing, then instead of (3.22), the inflation rate will be given by:

$$p = m + (1/V)/(dV/dt) - y. \tag{3.24}$$

To focus on the relationship between inflation and changes in velocity, assume, for the time being, that there are no changes in the two exogenous variables (M and Y). Therefore, both monetary growth and economic growth can be set to zero, $m = 0$ and $y = 0$. Equation (3.24) reduces to:

$$p = \dot{V}/V = (1/V)(dV/dt). \tag{3.25}$$

It is not possible just to set dV/dt also equal to zero as before, because we are now explicitly looking at the behaviour of the model out of the steady-state. Instead, from the expression for velocity in Eq. (3.21), we can write:

$$dV/dt = V_i(dr^N/dt + dp^e/dt).$$ (3.26)

Substituting this result back into (3.25), with $dr^N/dt = 0$, we obtain:

$$p = (V_i/V)dp^e/dt.$$ (3.27)

Equation (3.27) shows how the inflation rate is changing over time during the transition process. From Eq. (3.18), it can be seen that the expression for the "interest elasticity" of the demand for real money balances, η, will also involve the term V_i/V, that is:

$$\eta = -[d(M/P)/di][i/(M/P)] = i(V_i/V).$$ (3.28)

Substituting back into Eq. (3.25) we can therefore write:

$$p = (\eta/i)(dp^e/dt).$$ (3.29)

Out of the equilibrium state, the inflation rate depends on (i) the interest elasticity of money demand, (ii) the nominal interest rate, and (iii) the time derivative of inflation expectations.

At this stage, it becomes necessary to inquire in more detail about how inflationary expectations are formed. During the monetarist era, the most popular assumption was that of "adaptive expectations", such as the scheme in Eq. (3.30):

$$dp^e/dt = \lambda(p - p^e).$$ (3.30)

This says that inflation expectations will change by some fraction, λ, of the error in expectations that economic actors have already made, on average. For example, if the current inflation rate turns out to be 10 percentage points more than was originally expected beforehand (if $p > p^e$ by 10 percentage points) expectations for the future will adjust, but not by the full amount of the error. They might only be adjusted upwards by (say) 5 or 6 percentage points (λ would be 0.5 or 0.6). In other words, people in the economy are "adapting" their expectations as they go along, but in a somewhat conservative way.

Notice that Eq. (3.30) can be substituted into (3.29) to eliminate the term p. This gives an expression that involves only the expected inflation rate and its time derivative:

$$dp^e/dt = \lambda[(\eta/i)dp^e/dt - p^e].$$ (3.31)

This can be re-arranged to yield a *differential equation* in inflation expectations. In more straightforward language, this is an equation that explains how inflationary expectations adjust over time:

$$dp^e/dt = \{-1/[1 - (\lambda\eta/i))]\}p^e. \tag{3.32}$$

As shown by Chiang and Wainwright (2005, pp. 481–483) a general property of difference equations is that for eventual convergence to equilibrium the coefficient in an equation like (3.32) must be negative (<0). In this particular case, therefore, the basic condition for the convergence of inflation expectations is $(\lambda\eta/i) < 1$.

The above inequality is an expression involving: (a) the adjustment coefficient in the adaptive expectations equation, (b) the interest elasticity of money demand, and (c) the nominal interest rate. Scarth (1996, pp. 59–61) calls this "Cagan's convergence requirement" after the paper on hyperinflation by Cagan (1956). As all the terms are in fractions or percentages, one interesting point to notice that the *higher* is the rate of inflation and hence the higher is the nominal interest rate, the *more* likely is the convergence requirement to be satisfied. Notice, therefore, that by the term equilibrium we do *not* mean to say that the inflation rate has to be low in the steady-state. In the above mathematical exercise (for convenience), the stability condition was derived on the assumption that the equilibrium inflation rate is zero. However, it makes no difference what the steady-state inflation rate is to start with, or eventually turn out to be. The only requirement is for actual and expected inflation to converge to *some* constant rate. This could be 1%, 10%, 100%, 1000%, 100,000%, or any number. What *is* fundamental to the quantity theory of money, however, is that the inflation rate in equilibrium, whether high or low, is dictated mainly by the underlying rate of monetary growth.

The Monetarist Adjustment Mechanism

Once it has been decided that the monetarist model with adaptive expectations is quite likely to converge to steady-state equilibrium, the remaining issue to be dealt with is how the economy will actually behave in the *transition* from one equilibrium state to another.

For example, suppose that the rate of monetary growth is 5%, and, to take the simplest case, the real economy has a natural *level* of output that is not growing over time $(y = 0)$. Then the quantity theory tells us that the equilibrium inflation rate will also be 5%. We also know from the quantity

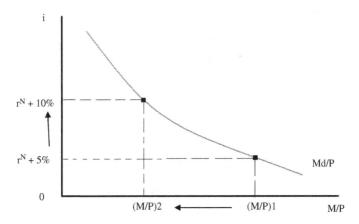

Fig. 3.10.   Money demand and inflation.

theory that if there is an increase in the rate of monetary growth to 10%
this must *eventually* also cause the inflation rate to increase to 10% in the
new equilibrium. The question that must now be asked, however, is how
the inflation rate will behave during the transition period from one steady-
state equilibrium to another. Consideration of the graphical version of the
money demand relationship in Fig. 3.10 suggests that the answer may not
be straightforward.

As seen in Fig. 3.10, an increase in the equilibrium inflation rate (in
our example, an increase from 5% to 10%) causes an increase in the nominal interest rate by the same amount. Therefore given the original money
demand equation in (3.17), and as shown in the diagram, there must be a
reduction in the demand for holdings of real money balances (M/P) in the
new equilibrium. But how can a reduction in M/P ever be achieved in practice? The cause of the higher inflation rate is originally an *increase* in the
rate of growth of nominal money balances. Moreover, in the final equilibrium both m and p must be growing at the *same* rate to keep the ratio M/P
at its new, Lower, level. The only possible answer is that the inflation rate
must have been rising *faster* than the underlying rate of monetary growth,
at some point during the transition period. This is the only way holdings of
real money balances can be reduced to the desired level. This process gives
a good example of the common economic phenomenon of "overshooting",
as shown in the next diagram in Fig. 3.11.

In Fig. 3.11, what is happening is that we imagine the economy has been
at its natural level of output for some time (the economy is not growing),

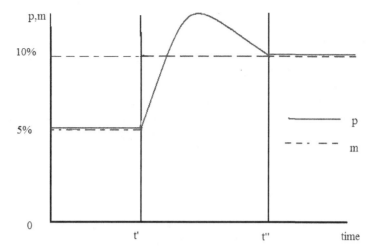

Fig. 3.11.   Adjustment of the inflation rate to the steady-state.

whereas money supply growth has been at $m = 5\%$ the whole time. Therefore the inflation rate has also been $p = 5\%$. Then, at time t', let there be
a once-for-all increase (jump) in the rate of growth of the money supply
to $m = 10\%$. Thereafter the money supply continues growing at the new
higher rate. We know from the quantity theory that the new equilibrium
inflation rate will eventually be $p = 10\%$, and the system reaches that state
at time t''.

What happens in the meantime, however? As can be seen, there is, first,
a period when the inflation is increasing at a slower rate than the rate of
monetary growth. Later, there is an episode when it is increasing at a much
faster rate. The initial phase reflects the admitted short run non-neutrality
of money, when the new higher rate of money growth affects mainly output
rather than prices. Soon, however, according to the monetarist model, the
boom will fade away and inflation will set in. The inflation rate then rises
back up to the same level as the rate of monetary growth, but afterwards
goes up beyond it for some time. People are now aware of the inflation, and
are trying to get rid of their money (spend it) as fast as possible. However,
the rapid rate of spending makes prices still faster.

Just this sort of behaviour has been observed in reality particularly
in hyperinflationary situations. Eventually, when the public have got rid
of their excess money holdings, that is, reduced their real money balances
to the new preferred lower level, the extra spending pressure dies down.

The inflation rate will eventually settle down to the *new* equilibrium level, $p = 10\%$ which nonetheless is still higher than the starting level (5%).

The term "overshooting" is used here to refer to the inflation rate rising faster than the underlying rate of change of monetary growth for some time during the transition. Note, however that similar phenomena can arise in many other situations in financial economics, such as the behaviour of exchange rates and stock prices, for example. There can also be "undershooting", when the variable concerned is declining.

As inflation adjusts, in a complicated way, to changes in the rate of monetary growth, from a monetarist point of view the same must also be true of nominal interest rates. For the monetarist the behaviour of nominal interest rates simply reflects that of inflation. Figure 3.12 therefore depicts the same situation as in Fig. 3.11, but now shows the time path of the nominal interest rate. When the inflation rate was steady at 5%, the nominal interest rate was also steady at 7% (we assume a real "natural" rate of 2%). At time t', when the rate of monetary growth increases from 5% to 10%, the nominal interest rate initially falls *below* the 7% level. This must imply that even the real rate is *temporarily* falling (below 2%), as the inflation rate does not fall.

This period of falling interest rates (both real and nominal) corresponds to the short-lived boom that monetarists argue will occur in the initial phase of a monetary expansion. Identifying this stage of the process of interest rate dynamics was actually quite important to the monetarist model for

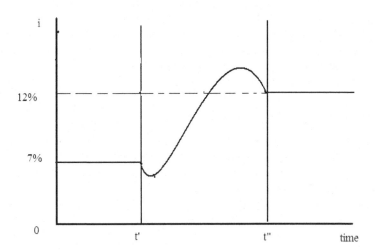

Fig. 3.12.   Adjustment of nominal interest rates.

public relations (PR) purposes, because most people in the real world do (correctly) identify lower interest rates with monetary expansion, at least in the first instance. Therefore, if monetarist economists wanted to credibly comment on financial markets, they could hardly ignore this phenomenon. Friedman (1989) calls this the "liquidity effect" on interest rates. However, because nominal interest rates must follow the same pattern as inflation, it could also be argued that they will quickly bounce back to the original level (7% in this case), and then will even go much higher for a time reflecting the overshooting of inflation, before settling back to a equilibrium level of 12%.

The assumed behaviour of nominal interest rates was important rhetorically in arguments against *any* attempt to lower interest rates as a matter of public policy. It could always be argued that any policy designed to reduce interest rates may seem to succeed at first, but eventually must fail, and will lead to even *higher* interest rates in the long term. This debating point transparently relies on *not* making clear the distinction between nominal and real interest rates, and also on the *assumption* that real interest rates can never be permanently changed, but nonetheless could be persuasive in debates with non-specialists.

The Lucas Supply Curve

As mentioned earlier, when during the 1970s and 1980s the model of "monetary misperceptions with rational expectations", became fashionable for a time, this seemed for many readers to be a natural extension of the quantity theory/monetarism, perhaps with the addition of somewhat more sophisticated mathematics. The model revolved around the famous "Lucas supply curve", named after Lucas (1981), and Eq. (3.33) below is a dynamic version of this due to Smithin (2003, p. 69). The expression "dynamic" here means that the equation deals with relationships between the growth rate and the inflation rate (rather simply between levels of output and the price level) and it is therefore more "realistic", at least to that extent.

$$y = y^N + (1/\beta)(p - p^e). \tag{3.33}$$

This expression states that if the inflation rate, in the current period, turns out to be greater than was expected at the time when contracts were being made and nominal wages were being set, this will provide an incentive for entrepreneurs to take actions that increase the growth rate of real GDP.

It is the expectations error itself that provides the incentive for the growth rate to rise above or fall below the supposed natural rate. In an upswing, for example, entrepreneurs may see the rate of change of prices in their own markets rising, but do not know that this is happening everywhere. Nor do they perceive it in their cost structure, because of the general expectation that inflation would be lower than it actually is. It just seems that profits are rising, and they cannot yet see that this will turn out to be illusory at the macroeconomic level. The opposite happens in the downturn. This is the "monetary misperceptions" theory of the business cycle. It essentially provides a somewhat more mathematically formal argument than the original monetarist theory.

Connection with the Phillips Curve

The Lucas supply curve, as discussed above, is closely related to the equally famous concept of the "Phillips curve" named for Phillips (1958), or rather, to its later "expectations-augmented" version (Laidler, 1996; Leeson, 2002).

The original Phillips curve was an empirical relationship between the rate of change of money (nominal) wages and the unemployment rate in Britain from 1861–1957. It was literally a downward sloping *curve*. As there is always a close association between wage inflation and price inflation, the idea of a similar price inflation/unemployment trade-off seemed to follow, and this concept was then taken up and propagated by economists all over the world. During the 1960s, it was widely believed that there existed a permanent and stable negative "trade-off" between inflation and unemployment which could be exploited for policy purposes. This was the opposite view to the monetarist position, and it was therefore important for monetarist economists to be able to comment on it and argue against it.

For simplicity, a 1960s era price-inflation Phillips "curve" (reduced here to a straight line rather than an actual curve) can be represented by an equation such as:

$$p = \alpha(u^N - u), \qquad \alpha > 0 \qquad (3.34)$$

where u^N is Friedman's "natural rate" of unemployment. Figure 3.13 illustrates this relationship in a graphical form.

The implication of Fig. 3.13 is that the unemployment rate can be permanently held down *below* the natural level, as long as the actual inflation rate is high enough. Monetarists of *both* the Mark I and Mark II varieties

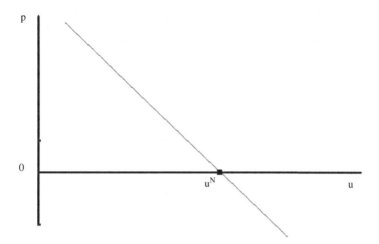

Fig. 3.13.   The original Phillips "curve" in a linear version.

would have wanted to avoid this conclusion, and therefore argued that the short-run or "expectations-augmented" Phillips curve (SRPC) must shift bodily whenever inflationary expectations change. An "expectations-augmented" version of the Phillips curve would be:

$$p = \alpha(u^N - u) + p^e. \tag{3.35}$$

Equation (3.35) differs from (3.34) by stating that there are actually *two* potential reasons for the inflation rate to increase, rather than just one. Inflation will still increase if unemployment is very low, and *vice versa*, as in the original Phillips curve logic. However, even if unemployment *is* at the natural rate, and there is no labour market disequilibrium, it is now argued the observed inflation rate will also increase if inflation is simply *expected* to increase. This happens because the various economic actors take action to preserve their *relative* economic positions. If this is a reasonable argument, it makes a big difference to the interpretation of the Phillips curve. This implication is now that when actual and expected inflation are equal $(p^e = p)$ unemployment must always be at its "natural" rate $(u = u^N)$. There is therefore no permanent trade-off between inflation and unemployment, and the long-run Phillips curve (LRPC) must be vertical. The set of short-run Phillips curve trades-off exists only when actual and expected inflation rates are *not* the same. This is the situation illustrated in Fig. 3.14.

To see the connection between the Phillips curve and the Lucas supply curve note that there must also be a relationship between the

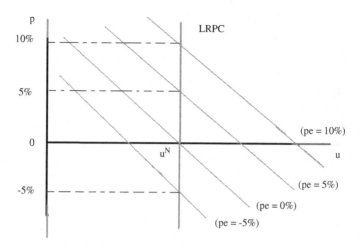

Fig. 3.14.   Expectations-augmented Phillips curves.

"unemployment gap" and the "growth gap" along the lines of Okun's law, named for Okun (1962). As with the Phillips curve, the original Okun's "law" was actually an empirical finding. In this case, it was an investigation about how much the economic growth rate would have to increase before it makes an appreciable impact on the unemployment rate. The original findings were for a particular time and place (the USA post-WWII), and the details do not matter now. However, the general idea was that for the unemployment rate to fall by (say) 1% the economic growth rate usually has to increase by twice that or *more*, say by 2% or 2.5%. In Eq. (3.35), the coefficient β/α would be a positive fraction (such as 0.5 or 0.4)

$$(u - u^N) = (\beta/\alpha)(y^N - y), \qquad 0 < \beta/\alpha < 1. \tag{3.36}$$

Next substitute (3.36) back into (3.35) to obtain:

$$y = y^N + (1/\beta)(p - p^e), \quad 1/\beta > 0. \tag{3.37}$$

This is exactly the same as the version of the Lucas supply curve set out in Eq. (3.33) earlier.

"Rational" Versus Adaptive Expectations

We can now write down a complete three-equation macroeconomic model that summarizes the views on the (age-old) issue of monetary neutrality versus non-neutrality as these had evolved within mainstream economics by the last two decades of the 20th century. The reference should really be to "super-neutrality" versus "non-super-neutrality", because in what follows the assumed monetary policy "instrument" is a change in the *rate of growth* of the money supply (rather than its level). The core equations of the model are:

$$p = m - y \qquad \text{(aggregate demand)}, \qquad (3.38)$$

$$p = \beta(y - y^N) + p^e \qquad \text{(aggregate supply)}, \qquad (3.39)$$

$$m = x + \varepsilon \qquad \text{(money supply rule)}. \qquad (3.40)$$

Equation (3.38) reverts to the simplest version of the quantity theory of money involving rates of change. This now becomes a linear "aggregate demand function" relating inflation to demand growth. Equation (3.37) rearranges the Lucas supply curve to show inflation on the vertical axis rather than on the horizontal axis. Finally, Eq. (3.38) is a very simple version of a "money supply rule", which specifies the rate of growth of the money supply decided by the central bank. The rule contains a deterministic element, x, relating to deliberate policy, but also introduces a random error term, ε. This is inspired by the statistical theory of probability that was heavily favoured by economic theorists at the time (and still is today). The error term is assumed to be a normally distributed "random variable" with a mean (average) of zero. The rule therefore says that the central bank is *trying* to achieve some particular percentage rate of money growth, whether this is 2%, 3%, or 5%, but in practice will make random errors in doing so. If the authorities are trying to achieve, say, a 3% money growth rate each year, sometimes this might turn out be 2.8% or 2.95%, sometimes it might be 3.1%, and so on. However, the average error over time is zero. In these circumstances, a *systematic* monetary policy change would be a decision to either increase or decrease the x term *permanently*. The term Δx, the *deliberate change* in x, would then be non-zero, either positive or negative, for just one period. However, there is also an unsystematic component to monetary policy, random errors that cannot be controlled, or be made subject to deliberate policy decision in any single period (although they will average out to zero in the long-run).

As "expectations" now play a key role in the model, the next question is to ask exactly how will these expectations be formed? During the 1970s and 1980s, this was a matter of intense debate between economists who would otherwise have been on the same side of the fence ideologically. This was the period known as the "rational expectations revolution". It would always have been possible, just to pick an adaptive expectations scheme, similar to that in Eq. (3.28) above. However, an alternative method that became available to mathematical economists at the time was instead to assume so-called "rational expectations".

An adaptive scheme that would fit into the model in Eqs. (3.38) to (3.40) is:

$$(p^e - p^e_{-1}) = \lambda(p_{-1} - p^e_{-1}), \qquad 0 < \lambda < 1. \tag{3.41}$$

A simpler version could even set $\lambda = 1$. Then, the expected inflation rate reduces to:

$$p^e = p_{-1}. \tag{3.42}$$

In this case, economic actors are supposed to "adapt" to previous experience just by assuming that the inflation rate in the current period will be the same as it was in previous period.

On this assumption, use (3.42) in (3.39), and solve the system for the growth rate of real GDP (y). This gives:

$$y = [1/(1 + \beta)]y_{-1} + [1/(1 + \beta)]y^N + [\beta/(1 + \beta)][\Delta x + \Delta \varepsilon]. \tag{3.43}$$

Equation (3.41) is therefore a difference equation[7] in economic growth. In effect, it is a description of the business cycle in this model, where $\Delta x = x - x_{-1}$ and $\Delta \varepsilon = \varepsilon - \varepsilon_{-1}$. Under adaptive expectations, therefore, output growth in the short run depends not only on the "random shocks", but also on the deliberate changes that the central bank is trying to make (the systematic part of monetary policy, Δx). A deliberate increase in money supply growth will, in the first instance, cause a business cycle upswing. A deliberate reduction in monetary growth causes a fall in the real GDP growth rate, or even a recession. Therefore, it seems that monetary policy does "matter" under *adaptive* expectations, at least in the short-run. Consistent with the general results of monetarism, however, if the systematic component of monetary policy undergoes no further changes, and that in future $\Delta x = 0$, the system will eventually converge to a long-run equilibrium growth rate, subject only to random fluctuations due to the error term. That is:

$$y = y^N + \Delta \varepsilon. \tag{3.44}$$

Again, here is the result that even if money is non-neutral (actually non-super-neutral) in the short run, it is neutral (actually super-neutral) in the long run. The quantity theory still holds "on average" over time. It is

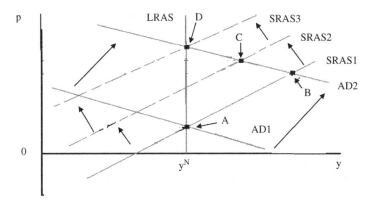

Fig. 3.15.   Dynamic adjustment to an increase in money supply growth.

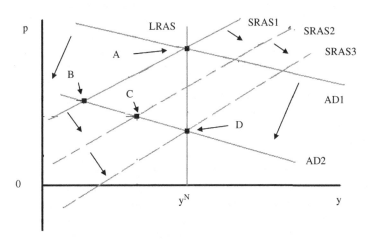

Fig. 3.16.   Dynamic adjustment to a reduction in money supply growth.

clear that this argument, also illustrated graphically in Figs. 3.15 and 3.16, really just consists of some mathematical refinement of the basic monetarist arguments, already discussed in detail earlier but now translated into inflation/growth space.

A problem does arise, however, because these results can change if we consider other possible models of expectations formation such as rational expectations: Under rational expectations the basic idea is that expectation of the inflation rate should be given literally by its *statistical expected value* generated by the equations of the model itself. If for example, $E(p)$ is the "expectations operator", the *rationally* expected inflation rate is not that shown in Eq. (3.42), or any other number derived from an adaptive scheme, but, rather:

$$p^e = E(p). \tag{3.45}$$

This mathematical/statistical interpretation of human behaviour is of very great appeal to those academic economists who strongly believe that economic methodology should replicate that of the natural sciences. On this view, the only rational decision-making procedure available to atomistic economic actors embedded in a quasi-naturalistic mathematical system is "optimization subject to constraints" (Smithin, 2004c; King, 2012). Within this type of framework, it actually becomes *inadmissible* to argue that some players might form expectations adaptively, or by some other rule of thumb, or have any other type of thought process that is not statistically based. This in spite of the fact that it is human behaviour we are talking about, and, in reality, human beings can, and presumably do, decide to do whatever they want.

The rational expectations argument is that if the actors do not form expectations using statistical methods, if they are not statisticians, or if they do not consume the products of statistical research, then they are not "optimizing" their activities, not be using all the information that is available to them, *etc.* (They would not be keeping to the "rules of the game".) It might seem hardly necessary to point out the weaknesses of these sorts of arguments from a common-sense perspective, but it is important to realize that they have always been very attractive to mathematically-trained academic economists. This was *particularly so* during the time period under discussion.

To continue with the exercise for the current model, we know from the quantity theory of money that $p = m - y$. Therefore, the "rational expectation" of the inflation rate must be simply:

$$p^e = E(p) = E(m) - E(y) = E(x) + E(\varepsilon) - E(y). \tag{3.46}$$

And, because the expected value of the error term is zero, this will reduce to:

$$p^e = x - y^N. \tag{3.47}$$

Then, using (3.47) in instead of (3.42) we obtain a different solution for the growth rate of real GDP:

$$y = y^N + [1/(1 - \beta)]\varepsilon. \tag{3.48}$$

The upshot is that under rational expectations the short run has "disappeared". Real GDP growth is *always* at its natural rate, except for unpredictable fluctuations due to the random or unsystematic component of the policy process. This sort of result, when first articulated, was very appealing, not only for mathematicians, but also for all those economists who are generally suspicious of what they call "government interference" in the economy. The reason is that it seems to show that the *deliberate* use of monetary policy has no impact whatsoever on the economy (except on the inflation rate). It does not affect the growth rate or unemployment rate. Ironically only the random policy *errors* (which, by definition, are not planned) can have any impact. Although our model deals explicitly only with monetary policy, it is also clear that in a (somewhat different) model a similar kind of argument might be applied to fiscal policy interventions, involving taxes and government spending.

From the perspective of political economy this so-called *policy irrelevance* result had a powerful ideological charge. Government policy-makers can *mistake* and have a negative impact on the economy, but they can do nothing to systematically improve it. They can make things worse, but cannot make things better. Therefore, the argument is that the government should simply get out of the way. This would certainly suit a political argument in favour of "small government".

However, also notice that for the more traditional monetarists (*e.g.*, of the mid-20th century) who were also (generally) believers in *laissez-faire*, this more extreme position had its downside. Originally, the idea was to allow for *some* short-run impact of monetary changes for the sake of realism, but to keep the neutral money argument for the long run. However, using rational rather than adaptive expectations seems to wreck this argument. From the traditional monetarist point of view therefore *complete* policy irrelevance might seem to be too much of a "good thing". In many ways it was a return to the "caricature-type" theory they had been trying to avoid.

A Cash-In-Advance Macro Model

Another of the main methodological *obiter dicta* of mainstream academic economics in the late 20th century, in addition to the notion of rational expectations and the use of statistical theory, was the insistence that no economic proposition, even at the macroeconomic level, could be regarded as valid unless it could be derived from a mathematical theory of individual choice, specifically dynamic optimization subject to constraints (Sargent, 1979; Lucas, 1987; Blanchard and Fischer, 1989; Turnovsky, 2000). In the macroeconomic context, this was described as providing the so-called "micro-foundations of macroeconomics" (Smithin, 2004c; King 2012). A critique of this way of thinking was provided in Chapter 1, in the context of the distinction between "brute facts" (physical facts) and social facts, and that argument need not be repeated here. The purpose of this section is rather, for the sake of argument, to inquire whether or not it is *possible* to "rigorously" derive something like the propositions of the quantity theory using the micro-foundations approach.

It turns out that it is fairly easy to provide micro-foundations for the quantity theory, (even if doing so actually provides no further information about it). It is possible, for example, to use the so-called "cash-in-advance" (CIA) macroeconomic model. The CIA method is one of a number of the devices that are found in graduate textbooks (Blanchard and Fischer, 1989; Walsh, 1998; Turnovsky, 2000) in attempts to introduce monetary factors into neoclassical economic models which otherwise would reduce to barter exchange. The following exercise also employs the device of the "infinitely lived representative agent", whereby the choices of the agent are supposed to mirror those of the average of all the agents in the economy, and thereby are thought to be relevant at the macroeconomic level.[8]

In the mathematical optimization problem, a representative consumer/worker "maximizes utility" over an infinite time horizon by trading-off the utility gained from consumption, C, with the disutility of work, N. The optimization problem in discrete time is:

$$\text{Max}: \sum_{t=0}^{\infty} \beta^t U(C_t, N_t), \qquad U'(C) > 0, \ U'(N) < 0 \qquad (3.49)$$

subject to the followings constraints[9]:

$$B = B_{-1} + WN + i_{-1}B_{-1} - PC - M, \qquad (3.50)$$

$$M \geq PC. \qquad (3.51)$$

Equation (3.50) is a standard budget constraint. The idea is that the consumer/worker enters the current period with some interesting-bearing financial assets ("bills" or "bonds") on hand, in the amount B_{-1}, then receives income consisting of the predetermined nominal interest payments on those holdings $i_{-1}B_{-1}$ (at the nominal interest rate prevailing last period) plus wages WN earned in the current period from any new work done. Some of the income is spent on consumption goods PC, and some is saved. The amount of interest bearing securities carried forward to next period, B, is the difference between income and spending, minus any of the assets converted into non-interesting bearing money, M.

The second constraint faced by the worker/consumer is the inequality in (3.50). This is the CIA constraint. The implication is that the consumer must pay CIA for any consumption goods, PC, that are purchased, and this is the reason why some of the financial assets have to be converted into M before any transactions can take place. It has already been explained (in Chapter 1, for example) that this sort of thing does *not* really make much sense as a description of a real world economy. In the real world money is a "means of payment" rather than a "medium of exchange", and, in principle, all types of contract settlement involving money should be allowed, paying in advance, paying on the spot, or paying in arrears. The CIA constraint is therefore simply an artifice, one of a number of devices used in neoclassical economics for getting "M" into a model in which it might not otherwise be there. What follows, therefore, is in no sense a defense of the procedure. The purpose is merely to see how it works out mathematically.

The term β in the original problem is known as the "discount factor", meaning that future receipts of "utility" are discounted at the rate of time preference of the representative worker/consumer. Therefore:

$$\beta = 1/(1 + \theta). \tag{3.52}$$

The next step is to introduce two co-state variables, α and λ, into the model (one for each of the constraints),[10] and the optimization problem becomes:

$$\text{Max: } \sum_{t=0}^{\infty} \beta^t \; \{U(C_t, N_t) + \lambda_t[B_{t-1} + W_t N_t + i_{t-1} B_{t-1} - M_t - P_t C_t - B_t] $$
$$+ a_t(P_t C_t - M_t)\}. \tag{3.53}$$

The "first-order conditions" for a solution to the problem can be found by differentiating with respect to each of the "choice variables" C, N, M and B, and setting the results equal to zero.[11] This gives the following expressions:

$$U'(C) - \lambda P + \alpha P = 0, \tag{3.54}$$
$$U'(N) + \lambda W = 0, \tag{3.55}$$

$$-\lambda - \alpha = 0, \tag{3.56}$$

$$\beta\lambda_{+1}(1 + i) - \lambda = 0. \tag{3.57}$$

Then, substituting (3.56) into (3.54) and using (3.57) we arrive at two "Euler equations"[12]:

$$[\beta U'(C)]/P = [U'(C_{+1})/P_{+1}](1 + i), \tag{3.58}$$

$$-[2U'(N)/U'(C)] = W/P. \tag{3.59}$$

It can be seen that these expressions correspond in some ways to the familiar "IS curve" and "labour supply function" that appear in intermediate level textbooks. However, the mathematical optimization procedure is supposed to be a more "rigorous" method of deriving these sorts of relationships.

The model can finally be closed (solved) by adding some more economic structure. It is possible, for example, to bring in the production function · from Eq. (3.11), and also rely on the standard neoclassical idea that "profit-maximizing competitive firms" produce up to the point where the marginal product of labour is equal to the real wage rate. This gives:

$$Y = F(N), \quad F'(N) > 0, \quad F''(N) < 0, \tag{3.60}$$

$$W/P = F'(N). \tag{3.61}$$

There is actually no physical capital in the model (it is set up so that there are only financial vehicles for savings). Therefore all of the physical output must be consumed, and:

$$Y = C. \tag{3.62}$$

To solve the model implicit in Eqs. (3.58)–(3.62). Let N^N stand for the equilibrium level of employment (the "natural" level of employment), and Y^N for the corresponding equilibrium level of output (the "natural" level of output). A solution to the model exists in the steady-state (when $C_{+1} = C = C_{-1}$, etc.), and can be written as:

$$\beta/P = (1 + i)/P_{+1}, \tag{3.63}$$

$$-[2U'(N^N)/U'(F(N^N))] = (F'(N^N)), \tag{3.64}$$

$$Y^N = F(N^N), \tag{3.65}$$

$$M/P = Y^N. \tag{3.66}$$

In principle Eq. (3.64) may be solved for the equilibrium level of employment N^N, which, in turn, will yield the equilibrium level of output Y^N, via (3.60). Next take logs of Eqs. (3.63) and (3.64) and differentiate with respect to time. The steady-state solution reduces to:

$$r^N = \theta, \tag{3.67}$$

$$Y = Y^N, \tag{3.68}$$

$$p = m. \tag{3.69}$$

This turns out to be the quantity theory of money *par excellence*. Output is always at its natural or equilibrium level, and there is also a "natural rate" of interest, determined by the rate of time preference of the representative worker/consumer. Meanwhile, the inflation rate is equal to the rate of monetary growth. In effect, the model with the CIA constraint has turned out simply to be the quantity theory of money with $V = 1$. Therefore, it is actually fairly straightforward to provide micro-foundations for the quantity theory of money.

Unfortunately, however, the exercise seems once again to show that the greater the degree of "rigour" (Sargent, 1979, p. xiii) employed in deriving the results, the closer we come to getting back to the original "caricature" version of the quantity theory. This occurred in the previous section, assuming rational expectations, and has now happened again using the method of "dynamic optimization with a representative agent". Recall, however, that the original complaint about the caricature version of the quantity theory was that it was *not* rhetorically convincing to potential opponents. So, the argument seems to have come full circle.

Global Monetarism

In this final section, the objective is to briefly inquire how monetarist ideas can be applied to the international economy. From the current perspective, the most significant feature of this is the existence of different national and supranational currencies. Recall from Chapter 1 that the real exchange rate between two different currencies is given by:

$$Q = EP/P^*, \tag{3.70}$$

where Q is the real exchange rate, E is the nominal exchange rate (defined as the foreign currency price of one unit of domestic currency), P is the domestic price level, and P^* is the foreign or "world" price level. In the monetarist/quantity theory view, the main point is that Q is *not* a monetary variable, but is thought to be determined by the barter terms of trade. In a theoretical treatment, this idea can be simulated by the "law of one price", which makes $Q = 1$ for simplicity. Then:

$$EP = P^*. \tag{3.71}$$

There are *two* possible scenarios for extending the ideas of the quantity theory to the open economy. First, nominal exchange rates might be *fixed*. In this case, the national central bank must continually intervene in the foreign exchange markets, buying and selling their own currency as required in order to fix the nominal exchange rate. If this is the policy, then the result is that domestic inflation rate will be dictated by the inflation rate in the rest of the world. When the central bank buys foreign exchange (sells its own currency), on standard quantity theory principles this is supposed to increase the domestic money supply *via* the money multiplier process and increase the domestic price level. When the central bank sells foreign exchange (buys it own currency) this tends to reduce the domestic money supply and reduce the price level. In this way, both the money supply and the domestic inflation rate are supposed to respond primarily to the external balance of payments situation and the inflation rate must eventually conform to whatever is going on in the rest of the world. To see this simply take logs of (3.71), and differentiate with respect to time (holding E constant). This shows that:

$$p = p^*. \tag{3.72}$$

A fixed exchange rate policy might therefore commend itself to "conservative" economists if the inflation rate in the rest of the world is low, and can be trusted to remain so. In effect, the policy "ties the hands" of the domestic central bank or government. They would not be able to pursue an independently inflationary policy.

A second scenario is when the exchange is flexible or "floating". The domestic central bank does not intervene in the foreign exchange markets, and, therefore, given the monetarist understanding of the money supply process, it is able to retain control over the rate of growth of the domestic money supply. It can thus inflate or deflate at its own whim. Letting the exchange rate float would commend itself to conservative economists if the "rest of the world" was actually pursuing an inflationary policy. Domestic conservatives could then legitimately urge their own central bank not to do the same.

Under floating exchange rates, Eq. (3.71) actually becomes a simple theory of exchange rate determination:

$$E = P^*/P. \tag{3.73}$$

This is known as the "purchasing power parity" (PPP) theory of exchange rates. Taking logs and again differentiating with respect to time:

$$\dot{E}/E = p^* - p. \tag{3.74}$$

The nominal exchange rate will be appreciating (rising) if the domestic inflation rate is lower than that in the rest of world, but will be depreciating (falling) if the domestic inflation rate is higher than elsewhere. Another way of expressing this result by going back to the "caricature" version of the theory of money demand (for both the domestic economy and the "rest of the world"), is as follows:

$$\dot{E}/E = (m^* - m) - (y^* - y). \tag{3.75}$$

This says that the nominal exchange rate will be appreciating when the rate of growth of the domestic money supply is lower than in the rest of the world, and/or, if the domestic economy is growing faster than in the rest of the world (and *vice versa*).

In addition to the PPP condition, which derives from the assumption that the *real* exchange rate is a "real" and not a "monetary" variable, both monetarists and the later new-classical economists also held that several international *interest parity* (arbitrage) conditions are relevant. The point of this was to extend the concept of the natural rate of interest to the whole global economy. The underlying idea is that the global "capital market" will (supposedly) ensure that real interest rates are the same everywhere, *even* when exchange rates *are* floating. The first such interest arbitrage condition is the "covered interest parity" (CIP) condition, stated as:

$$i - i^* = (E - F)/E, \tag{3.76}$$

where i is the domestic nominal interest rate, i^* is the foreign nominal interest rate, and F is the forward exchange rate (the foreign currency price of one unit of domestic currency, delivered one period in the future). The CIP condition asserts that nominal rates of return in different international centres must be equalized by arbitrage when covered by a forward contract.

A somewhat stronger condition would be "uncovered interest parity" (UIP):

$$i - i^* = [E - E_{+1}]/E. \tag{3.77}$$

Here E_{+1} is expected value of the *future* "spot" exchange rate. This condition goes further than CIP and implies that nominal (expected) rates of return in different international centres are equalized by arbitrage, even when *not* covered by a forward contract.

If both CIP and UIP hold, the implication must be:

$$F = E_{+1}. \tag{3.78}$$

In these circumstances the forward exchange rate is literally equal to the statistical expected value of the future spot rate. This is a quintessential "rational expectations" or "efficient markets" result. Finally, if all of PPP, CIP and UIP hold, then:

$$r = r^*. \tag{3.79}$$

This would be called "real interest rate parity" (RIP) meaning that the domestic real interest rate is the same as that in the rest of the world. The upshot of the argument is therefore to reinforce the established view of classical, monetarist, and new-classical economists, and many others, that monetary policy can do nothing to affect domestic real rates of interest.

There are serious weaknesses in this argument from the point of view of political economy, which will be taken up and discussed in more detail in later chapters. (In particular, it is a big step to go from the CIP condition to the UIP condition. The first involves a completely "risk-less" transaction, while the second certainly does not.) Moreover, the crucial idea that the real exchange rate must conform to the barter terms of trade (rather than the other way around) is effectively asserted rather than proved (just as the idea that there is a natural rate of interest is always asserted rather than proved). The point of the exercise here, however, has been simply to show how quantity theoretic ideas work out mathematically in the open economy setting.

Conclusion

Strangely enough, the outstanding characteristic of all almost all variations on the theme of the quantity theory of money, including the various versions of 20th century monetarism, is that they only provide a *real* theory of the enterprise economy rather than a *monetary* theory of this type of economy (Burstein, 1995; Schumpeter, 1994/1954; Smithin, 2003, 2009a).

In spite of its name, monetarism was really only an elaboration of, and slight modification to, the theory of the barter exchange economy. It describes a world in which the institution of money as such is not really essential. Indeed in many ways in this type of discourse it seems that the existence of money only causes problems, such as the possibility of inflation itself, or that the very fact that there are such things as *money* prices and wages to be "sticky" in the first place. The theory supposes that all important *relative* prices, such as the real rate of interest, and the real exchange rate, are finally determined by non-monetary forces and that there are "natural rates" of both economic growth and unemployment to which the economy always returns. Therefore, the only lasting impact of any monetary changes can only be on inflation. It has already been already argued, in Chapters 1 and 2, that this type of argument can by no means capture the essential role of money and credit in the institutional framework of the "enterprise economy". The quantity theory is one of the many theories that completely neglect the need for the generation and realization of money profit if real economic activity is to occur at all. Later chapters in the form of essays in this book will examine other approaches to monetary economics, and will use similar criteria to evaluate them.

However, there is a final point that does need to be made on the other side of the ledger and should not be overlooked. This is that (really all), theories of inflation, not only monetarism, and particularly considered in isolation from theories of growth or employment, do rely on at least some sort of *correlation* between the pace of monetary growth (however defined) and inflation. It is important also to draw attention to this. The issues in dispute are not really about the obvious point that "too much money", in some general sense, may be associated with inflation. Mostly they are about questions of causation. What are the *underlying* social forces or policy initiatives (not just those of the central bank) that are causing inflationary pressures *via* the medium of the monetary and financial system? Moreover, is there, in fact, any connection to be discovered between the forces that do determine growth and employment, and those that determine inflation. If so, what is it?

Notes

1. I do not mean to imply that these are necessarily the same thing.
2. As in the various neoclassical theories of economic growth. See, for example, Jones (1998) or the first two or three chapters of any standard textbook.
3. If money is said to be *neutral*, this usually means that a change in the *level* of the money supply only affects the price level. If money is *super-neutral* it means that a change in the *rate of growth* of the money supply only affects the *inflation rate* (and none of the real variables).

4. In this instance (and elsewhere) the G' (and J') notation stands for the first partial derivatives of the relevant functions. Later we will also use an alternative subscript notation for first partial derivatives when convenient.

5. This can obviously be a very low figure in today's electronic world.

6. It was generally assumed in this literature that none of the deposits included in the definition of "money" would earn interest. This would be an anachronism today.

7. A difference equation is equivalent to the idea of a differential equation, already discussed, but applies in discrete time rather than continuous time.

8. King (2012) says that the representative agent in the "dynamic stochastic general equilibrium model" (DSGE) of modern mainstream economics is a RARE individual. (This is an acronym for a "representative agent with rational expectations".) The model below is non-stochastic, so the agent in this case must, I suppose, be RAPF (a meaningless acronym), a "representative agent with perfect foresight".

9. In the notation that follows, variables at time $t = 0$ have no subscript (*e.g.*, X) and variables at time $t = 1$ will be denoted as X_{+1}, *etc.*

10. Note that α and λ do not now have the same meanings assigned to them earlier in this chapter. The same is true of the symbol β in the optimization problem. (There are a limited numbers of letters in the Greek alphabet available to be used in mathematical exercises.)

11. Notice that in (3.56) the CIA constraint is now assumed to hold with equality.

12. Named after the 18th century Swiss mathematician.

CHAPTER 4

WICKSELLIAN AND NEO-WICKSELLIAN
MODELS OF MONETARY ECONOMICS

Introduction

The subject of this chapter, the fourth in the series *Essays in the Fundamental Theory of Monetary Economics and Macroeconomics*, will be one of the main approaches to monetary theory *other* than those of the quantity theory of money on the one hand, and broadly Keynesian ideas on the other. This is the idea that the price level or inflation rate will depend primarily on interest rate *differentials*, for example on the difference between the average interest rate charged by the banking system and the rate of return to be earned by the use of borrowed funds. The basic argument has been associated historically with the name of Knut Wicksell (1965/1898, 1969/1958, 1907). However, it is also important to note that essentially the same theory was already available to Thornton (1991/1802) a hundred years earlier, and that it once again became textbook orthodoxy a hundred years *after* Wicksell's time in the early years of the 21st century. By this time, it had a variety of new labels such as "the new consensus model" (NCM), "modern monetary economics",[1] "modern macroeconomics", *etc.* (Fontana and Setterfield, 2009; Taylor, 2007; Cecchetti, 2006). In its most recent guise, it is the theory that developed to replace monetarism in the years immediately before and after the millennium, following the publication of the famous short paper on "interest rate rules" by Taylor (1993). Two related papers by Romer (2000) and Taylor (2000) were widely read, and solidified the form in which the model made its way into the textbooks. Somewhat later, an advanced work on monetary theory was published (Woodford, 2003), which actually had a very similar title to that of Wicksell's (1969/1898) volume *Interest* and *Prices*.

Interest Rates and Inflation

In an environment in which the money supply consists primarily of claims on the liabilities side of bank balance sheets, it is actually not surprising that many authors have identified the interest rates charged by the banking system as being an important factor determining the demand for bank credit, and therefore of how rapidly *both* sides of bank balance sheets will expand. In a system with an inconvertible currency and a state central bank, the liabilities of the central bank themselves are the primary reserves for other financial institutions. Therefore, the interest rate effectively charged by the central bank for loans of these reserves, which was historically called something like the "bank rate" or "discount rate", is the "lynch-pin" of the entire system (Keynes, 1971a/1930, pp. 138–139). There have been many different institutional mechanisms at different times and places, for making bank rate "effective" (Keynes, 1971a/1930, p. 179). In recent practice in the USA, for example, the inter-bank "federal funds rate" has been regarded as one of the main monetary policy instruments (Atesoglu and Smithin, 2008). Whatever the precise institutional details, it is clear that central bank monopoly supply over the ultimate monetary base gives it power over what we will generically call the "policy rate" (Friedman, 2000; IMF, 2001). The fundamental Wicksellian argument is that the level of the policy rate *relative* to the rate of return which can be earned by using borrowed funds determines the nominal rate of expansion of the system as a whole. Hence, the interest differential also determines the level of money prices and/or the inflation rate, as the money supply itself adjusts endogenously to the incentives provided by interest rate changes.

Usually, Wicksell-type arguments have confined themselves to the impact on either the price level or the inflation rate. Only very occasionally have there been forays into thinking about the real effects of changes in interest rates. Ironically, in the light of later developments, the Keynes of the *Treatise on Money* (1971a/1930) was actually in the first camp, whereas the Hayek of *Prices and Production* (1967/1935) was one of the few in the latter. As Hicks (2005/1967, p. 204) neatly put this point: "... Wicksell plus Hayek said one thing, Wicksell plus Keynes said quite another". As already remarked in Chapter 2, Keynes later changed his mind about interest rates in the *General Theory* (1964/1936). The "Austrian" theory of the business cycle in the 1930s (Hayek, 1967/1935, 1994), was unique in actually making interest rate discrepancies responsible for booms and depressions in the *real* economy, although, at the time, also strongly supported the argument that not much could be done about unemployment by "activist" public policy. The traditional Wicksellian argument was that if the interest rate charged by the banking system is *less* than the return to be had on projects employing the borrowed funds, there will be a continuing expansion of the money supply, as a result a "cumulative" increase in prices (Wicksell, 1965/1898, p. 95). If the interest rate charged by the banking system is *higher* than the rate of return elsewhere there would be deflation. Thornton (1991/1802, p. 254) had stated much earlier that everything depends "principally on a comparison of the rate of interest taken at the bank with the current rate of mercantile profit". In his own discussion, nearly a century later, Wicksell made the same analysis hinge on the difference between what he called "market rate" of interest (meaning the rate current in *money* markets and therefore largely influenced by central bank policy) and the "natural rate" of interest (Leijonhufvud, 1989, p. 268).

A key point that has recurred in most of the discussions on this issue, historically and up to the present, is that whatever corresponds to the natural rate is assumed to be determined *outside the monetary system*, as if in the hypothetical barter capital market, in which borrowing and lending can take place without the intermediation of money. It is regarded as a real phenomenon determined by the ubiquitous forces of "productivity and thrift", or, by something like the "pure theory of capital" (Hayek, 1941) that would supposedly apply under barter exchange. It cannot be altered any by purely *monetary* forces. This concept of a natural rate of interest, impervious to monetary manipulation, has been a doggedly persistent theme in political economy for the past two and a half centuries. From point of view of monetary analysis the implication is that the real interest rate can be treated essentially as a constant (although the natural rate itself may change, for example, due to changes in productivity, but not for monetary reasons). The conclusion is, usually drawn that if the "monetary" interest rate (the rate that can be affected by the policy of the central bank) does not conform to the barter rate, there will be trouble.

Bank Loans and the Endogenous Supply of Money

In what follows let r^N stand for the "natural rate", the rate supposedly, determined by demand and supply in physical capital markets (a real rate determined by "real" economic phenomena), and i for the "market rate" or "money rate" (a nominal rate determined in the money markets, ultimately by monetary policy). (As already suggested it is better to call this the "policy rate"). However, we will not use a separate subscript notation for this, at least until the last section of the present chapter, because both the traditional Wicksellian and modern neo-Wicksellian literature have tended to assume that the issue of the "transmission mechanism" between the interest rate (set by the central bank) and the prime lending rate of commercial banks is unproblematic. For theoretical purposes they simply posit one "monetary" interest rate that is ruling in the "money market", but is ultimately determined by central bank policy. This is to be compared to the non-monetary natural rate. A baseline version of generic Wicksell-type interest rate theories, therefore, corresponding to the equally simple "caricature version" of the quantity theory in Chapter 3, might have the rate of increase of the money value of bank loans responding to the *gap* between i and r^N.[2] That is:

$$(1/L)(dL/dt) = \alpha(r^N - i), \quad \alpha > 0 \tag{4.1}$$

where L stands for the money value of bank loans. Equation (4.1) says that the *greater* is the difference between the natural rate and the policy rate the *faster* will the public be willing to take on bank loans. On the other side of bank balance sheets (the liabilities side), it must also follow that the monetary residue, M, of the loans, is increasing at the same rate, so that:

$$(1/M)(dM/dt) = \alpha(r^N - i). \tag{4.2}$$

In the notation of previous chapters, with m standing for the *rate of growth* of the money supply, this could also be written:

$$m = \alpha(r^N - i). \tag{4.3}$$

Both Eqs. (4.2) and (4.3) state that if the policy rate or "monetary" rate is less than the natural rate, this increases the incentives for borrowing from the banking system, and hence increases the rate of money supply growth (on the other side of bank balance sheets).

The Theory of Inflation

Next, recall that, from the most basic version quantity theory, the inflation rate p will be roughly equal to the rate of growth of the money supply, m, less the rate of growth of the real economy, or y. For simplicity, we will continue to use this straightforward theory of money demand in the present discussion. Therefore:

$$p = m - y. \tag{4.4}$$

Substituting (4.4) into (4.3), this gives a theory of inflation:

$$p = \alpha(r^N - i) - y. \tag{4.5}$$

We will return to this expression below. Next however, also assume, for the time being, that the economy is not growing, and that there is a unique "full employment" level of output, so that $y = (1/Y)(dY/dt) = 0$. The theory of inflation in (4.5) then reduces to:

$$p = \alpha(r^N - i). \tag{4.6}$$

In this most basic version of the Wicksellian theory, if the rate of interest set by the banking system is below the natural rate $(i < r^N)$ the result will be inflation $(p > 0)$. If the policy rate is above the natural rate $(i > r^N)$, there will be deflation $(p < 0)$. To achieve stable prices, or zero inflation, $(p = 0)$ the authorities would have to set the nominal policy rate equal to the natural rate $(i = r^N)$. In effect, they have to make the policy rate conform to the natural rate.

Supporters of this type of argument do not need to represent themselves as having "overturned" the quantity theory of money, but simply as having provided a more "realistic" version of the theory, appropriate for an economy with a developed credit system (Laidler, 1999). Setting the policy rate different from the natural rate explains the mechanics of how additional credit money gets into circulation in a banking system, but, in other respects, much of the familiar quantity theory world-view can remain intact.

The Real Policy Rate Versus the Real Natural Rate

Although Eqs. (4.4) and (4.5) are enough to give the flavour of generic Wicksell-type theories there are a number of problems with their interpretation, mainly reflecting the fact that historical discussions of the approach rarely made an explicit distinction between the (so-called) real and nominal rate of interest in the manner that is widely accepted today.

In modern terminology, a nominal rate of interest is simply the percentage rate actually quoted for a loan of money, whereas the real rate is (technically) the nominal rate adjusted for expected inflation. Of course, expected inflation is not actually known to anyone other than the actor holding the expectation, and this simple fact has caused endless problems for formal mathematical economic theorizing. Nonetheless, everyone agrees that it must be a real rate, (in some sense), rather than the nominal rate that is important for economic decision-making. It is usual to attribute the first formal recognition of the distinction between real and nominal interest rates to Irving Fisher (1896),[3] but the full acceptance of this idea by the economics profession did not really occur until, (perhaps), as late as the inflationary period of the 1970s. When economists of previous eras used terms like "real" or "money" interest rates therefore, as did Wicksell, this was not necessarily in their present day meanings.

A lack of attention to the Fisherian distinction between real and nominal interest rates, however, does make the formulation in Eqs. (4.5) and (4.6) very difficult to interpret. The natural rate, r^N, must be a real rate both in the modern sense of the "nominal rate less expected inflation", and also because it is thought to be determined by "real" (non-monetary) economic forces. The natural rate theory of interest must be "a real theory of the real rate of interest". On the other hand, the policy rate or money rate must in the first instance be a nominal rate determined in the monetary sphere by administrative decision.

In spite of this, and as already discussed, it is certainly possible to distinguish between the *nominal* policy rate and the *real* policy rate, actually in two senses. The real rate can be used strictly in the sense of the nominal policy rate less the *expected* inflation. Also, however, given that the nominal policy rate is essentially a matter of administrative decision, we can speak of the "inflation-adjusted real policy rate". This would be simply the policy rate less the currently observed inflation rate. In an inflationary equilibrium the two senses of the "real" policy rate must coincide. Moreover, in a neoclassical *general* equilibrium the real policy must be equal to the supposed natural rate. But, what is the causality, and what is the basis of the assumption that it is the variable r^N which is immutably fixed? Note that, the inflation-adjusted real rate is the *only* "real" interest rate that can actually be *observed*. Also, by definition, any explanation of this inflation-adjusted real policy rate which *differs* from how the natural rate is supposed to be determined must by definition be what we have called "a monetary theory of a real rate of interest".

As the observed inflation rate is known and the central bank certainly does deliberately changes the nominal policy rate from time to time they are automatically changing the inflation-adjusted real rate, whether or not that was the intention. It is therefore, at least *possible* to stabilize the inflation-adjusted real rate, whether or not any central bank has ever attempted to do this in practice. This could be done by adjusting the nominal policy rate whenever the observed inflation rate changes. This particular "real" interest rate variable is always determined by monetary policy, either consciously or unconsciously,

One of the several problems that follow from the various confusions about real and nominal interest rates is that if an economist wants to hold a theory involving *both* neoclassical general equilibrium concepts *and* something like a Wicksellian approach to the inflation question, then the traditional idea of economic equilibrium seems to require a *deflation* when nominal interest rates are set too low rather than inflation as in Wicksell (McCallum, 1986b). To see this, suppose that the nominal interest rate is permanently set by policy at the level, i, and the natural rate, r^N, is interpreted as a real rate. In this case (abstracting from population growth and depreciation, *etc.*) neoclassical equilibrium "at the margin" will ultimately require that the real rate charged by banks, r, be equal to the natural rate, r^N:

$$r = r^N. \tag{4.7}$$

But, as mentioned, the technical definition of r, involving inflation expectations, is:

$$r = i - p^e. \tag{4.8}$$

Also, in full equilibrium it will be true that $p^e = p$. So we must have:

$$r = i - p, \tag{4.9}$$

which implies:

$$p = i - r^N. \tag{4.10}$$

This would be a big problem from the point of view of an orthodox economist who becomes interested in Wicksellian ideas because Eq. (4.10) seems to suggest that a setting of the *nominal* policy rate below the natural rate must cause inflation to fall, not rise. Higher nominal interest rates would imply inflation not deflation. Such a positive association of nominal interest rates and inflation would have been perfectly acceptable in the monetarist model (see Chapter 3), with an exogenously determined rate of monetary growth, and a constant real interest rate. However, it is the opposite of the relationship suggested in the Wicksellian tradition, when a nominal interest rate is the policy instrument.

This contradiction, therefore, did become something of a "puzzle" debated in the academic world in the late 20th century, at a time when many specialists in monetary economics were in the process of having to make the transition from broadly monetarist to broadly Wicksellian ideas. There is a detailed discussion of this in McCallum (*op. cit.*, 1986b), for example.[4] The solution is to realize that neoclassical equilibrium cannot in fact, be achieved in the case when the nominal interest rate is just arbitrarily set at some given level Smithin (2003, 2007a, 2009a). In principle, the Wicksellian argument is essentially a *disequilibrium* rather than equilibrium theory, at least as far as interest rates are concerned.

This is also the point in the discussion at which thinking about the precise relationship between the theoretical notion of a real interest rate and the (observable) inflation-adjusted real rate becomes essential. As mentioned, the definition of a real interest rate including expectations is:

$$i = r + p^e. \tag{4.11}$$

Substituting this back into Eq. (4.5) we therefore find:

$$p = \alpha[r^N - (r + p^e)]. \tag{4.12}$$

Next, note that if either observed inflation is used as a proxy (guess) for expected inflation (which is an argument that neoclassical economists have conceded to be reasonable in the policy context)[5], or in a model assuming rational expectations/perfect foresight, we would have $p^e = p$. In either case, we can obtain the expression:

$$p = \alpha[r^N - (r + p)]. \tag{4.13}$$

Solving for the inflation rate:

$$p = [\alpha/(1 + \alpha)](r^N - r). \tag{4.14}$$

Equation (4.14) therefore recasts the basic neo-Wicksellian theory in terms of discrepancies between two different *real* interest rates. The argument now is that if monetary policy is such that the *real inflation-adjusted policy rate*, set by the central bank, is less than the *real* natural rate, the result is inflation. The opposite would occur if the real policy rate is set higher than the real natural rate. One consequence of this shift in focus is that the goal in monetary policy now comes to be seen as achieving a policy-related *real* rate which exactly mirrors the supposed real natural rate. The aim is to achieve, by luck or judgment (although, interestingly, *not* by any supposedly automatic equilibrating mechanism inherent in the market system) the ultimate desired state of:

$$r = r^N. \tag{4.15}$$

In this case, according to Eq. (4.14), there will be no inflation. It continues to be assumed that the real natural rate, r^N, is given. No thought is given to the possibility that the natural rate itself could change (in response to changes in r), nor to the idea that the natural rate is not directly observable out of equilibrium.

The difference between the theory of the type just discussed, and either monetarism or the earlier classical theory, is that, in monetarism or classical theory, it was assumed that the real interest rates *actually observed* in the marketplace are always determined by the natural rates. This is the only assumption that could make the relationship between nominal interest and inflation shown in Eq. (4.10) plausible.[5] The Wicksell-type theories, on the other hand, are implicitly assuming that there are *two* real interest rates to be taken into account. These are the natural rate which exists "off stage" so to speak, and the real policy rate. Moreover, the only interest rate phenomenon that can be observed is the inflation-adjusted real policy rate. Therefore, according to neo-Wicksellians, the only means by which *all* of the real rate concepts can be made to line up with the (given) natural rate must involve adjustments in the inflation-adjusted real policy rate *via* the instrument of the nominal policy rate.

In terms of the evolution of thinking about monetary policy, I would argue that the next step should be simply to drop the idea of the unobservable natural rate altogether (Smithin, 1994, 2003, 2007a, 2009a). It would then be necessary to take very seriously the idea of a "monetary theory of the real rate of interest". This was also the view of Keynes (1964/1936, pp. 242–243). However, this route was definitely *not* taken by any of the genuine Wicksellians or neo-Wicksellians, in either the 19th, 20th or 21st centuries.

Zero Inflation in a Growing Economy?

Up to now the discussion has been mainly about an economy which is not growing, and whose rate of output is therefore steady at the "full employment level". As mentioned in previous chapters, however, another recurring theme of classical and neoclassical economics has always been that (in addition to the natural rate of interest) there is also a natural rate of *growth* in the economy. This is determined essentially by supply-side rather than demand-side factors.[6] In order to complete the discussion of the generic Wicksellian models, therefore, let the symbol y^N stand for this "natural rate of growth", and go on to assume (as a Wicksellian presumably would do) that the economy is growing at that rate. Then refer back to Eq. (4.5), which can now be written:

$$p = \alpha[r^N - (r + p)] - y^N. \tag{4.16}$$

The solution for the inflation rate is therefore:

$$p = [\alpha/(1 + \alpha)](r^N - r) - [1/(1 + \alpha)]y^N. \tag{4.17}$$

The inflation rate will increase if the real inflation-adjusted policy rate is set below the natural rate, but will fall if the "natural rate" of growth increases (*e.g.*, due to technological innovation).

Suppose now that the monetary authorities have the objective of zero inflation or stable prices, $p = 0$. If so, clearly they must set the inflation-adjusted policy rate as follows:

$$r = r^N - (1/\alpha)y^N. \tag{4.18}$$

In order to achieve zero inflation in these circumstances, the real policy rate must be *increased* one-for-one if the natural rate of interest increases, and *reduced* by a factor of $(1/\alpha)$ if the natural rate of growth increases.

This a proto-typical example of a so-called "interest rate rule", for the central bank, and although it is not suggested that this version is realistic,[7] it well illustrates the *type* of argument that must be made if monetary policy is to be conducted in this way. Wicksellian-type interest rate rules somewhat more complicated than this were certainly taken very seriously by policy-makers at the end of the 20th and into the 21st century. The next section goes on to explore this question in more detail.

Interest Rate Rules in the Late 20th Century

About a hundred years after Wicksell was writing, towards the end of 20th century, there had actually been for some time a relative *lack* of attention to the interest rate instrument of monetary policy on the part of academic theorists. Initially, from the publication of the first modern textbooks in the late 1940s and up to the early 1970s, (so-called) "Keynesian" models were the order of the day. These models stressed the importance of aggregate demand, but assumed a fixed money supply. Then, from roughly the late 1970s to the early 1990s, the standard textbook fare was based on monetarism, the 20th century version of the quantity theory of money. As we have seen the policy advice that came from this quarter was to directly control the growth of the money supply, and not worry about interest rates.

The lack of attention to interest rates, however, turned out to be something of an embarrassment after the collapse of the "monetary targeting" experiments of the early 1980s. This did eventually force the central banks to revert to a pragmatic interest rate and/or exchange rate focus (Smithin, 1990, 1994, 2003). Then, from roughly the mid-1990s onwards, at least up until the financial crises of the early 21st century, a new textbook orthodoxy developed in the form of a simple three-equation neo-Wicksellian model. This was the NCM approach mentioned above. The most salient features of the new textbook approach were (a) it was now recognized that the monetary policy instrument *is* a nominal interest rate (the policy rate) and (b) the supply of money and credit is endogenous. It became impossible for textbooks to go on making statements to the effect that the central bank "cannot control interest rates" and so forth, at a time when the central banks themselves were saying and doing the *opposite*, and moreover interest rate policy had become a favourite topic for discussion in the financial press. By the beginning of the 21st century, the new situation was widely acknowledged. According to Friedman (2000), for example:

> ... (in the late 1960s) ... the Federal Reserve, like most central banks at that time, made monetary policy by setting interest rates. The same is once again true today. In retrospect, much of the intervening experience proved to be a historical detour.

However, it was the Wicksellian element in the new orthodoxy that was meant to be the "face saver". There was still supposed to be another interest rate, a natural rate, somewhere in the model that eludes control of the central bank and exerts a decisive influence behind the scenes. As in Wicksell, economic outcomes were made to hinge on any discrepancy between the policy rate and the natural rate.

Consider, for example, the exposition by Lewis and Mizen (2000, pp. 248–250) of the concept of a "central bank reaction function". They suggest that the following monetary policy reaction function, which is a version of the "Taylor rule", after Taylor (1993), was a fair characterization of the way in which central banks were formulating rules for setting interest rates around the turn of the 20th and 21st centuries:

$$i = r^N + \theta_1(p - p^*) + \theta_2(Y - Y^N) + p. \qquad (4.19)$$

This rule would have the central bank raise the nominal policy rate, i, whenever the natural rate itself increases (although it *still* not clear how they would know this). The central bank should also increase the nominal policy rate if the *observed* inflation rate p increases, and, even more so, if the observed inflation rate happens to be greater than some chosen "target" level, p^*. In a recession, on the other hand, if the level of output Y seems to be falling below its own "natural" level Y^N, the central bank would cut the policy rate. The coefficients θ_1 and θ_2 are the weights that the central bank is applying to the different policy objectives. If, for example, they give equal weight to inflation being to inflation being "too high" and output being "too low" (unemployment being "too high"), we would have $\theta_1 = \theta_2 = 0.5$ (Wicksell himself would have put no weight on unemployment, of course).

As the last term on the right hand side of Eq. (4.19) is the observed inflation rate, p, this *does* suggests that the rule the central bank is following is couched in terms of the real inflation-adjusted policy rate with observed inflation explicitly serving as a "proxy" for expected inflation (Taylor 1993). Moving the term p over to the left hand side of the equation, we can write:

$$r = r^N + \theta_1(p - p^*) + \theta_2(Y - Y^N). \qquad (4.20)$$

When the rule is expressed in this way, the suggestion is that the central bank should raise the real (inflation-adjusted) policy rate if inflation is seen to exceed the arbitrary target p^*, but should reduce the real policy rate in a recession.

If the intercept, in both Eqs. (4.19) and (4.20), is interpreted as the "equilibrium real interest rate" (Lewis and Mizen, 2000, p. 249), the natural rate, the Wicksellian pedigree of the discussion is obvious. *If* the inflation target is achieved, and output is also happens to be at its natural rate, we have $p = p^*$ and $Y = Y^N$, and, therefore:

$$r = r^N. \qquad (4.21)$$

This, once again, is the Wicksellian equilibrium condition. In these circumstances, the monetary authorities have succeeded in setting the real policy rate equal to the supposed natural rate, output is at its supposed natural level, and inflation is "on target". This makes the "Wicksell connection" (Leijonhufvud, 1981b, p. 131) obvious. However, it does not yet prove that attainment of the result in (4.21) is actually *possible* merely by following the rule in (4.20).

The "New Consensus Model" (NCM)

Following on from the above remarks, the purpose of this section is to present a relatively simple version of the complete NCM of the early 21st century. Note, however, that what is presented here is modified/revised from the textbook's approach in at least one important respect. The textbooks typically used diagrams and equations relating the *level* of output to the inflation *rate*. This was an advance over the aggregate demand and supply (AD/AS) model of the mid-20th century which only related the *level* of output to the price *level*. However, following Barrows and Smithin (2006, pp. 191–198, 2009, pp. 251–259) and Smithin (2009b, pp. 256–265), the exposition here goes one step further, and relates the economic *growth* rate to the inflation *rate*.

The difference can be important if the objective is eventually to comment on the real world policy debate. Research reports on the economy (*e.g.*, from banks, financial institutions, brokerage houses, government agencies etc.) do *not* refer to the behaviour of either the price level or the level of output, but rather, to the inflation rate and to the rate of economic growth. A forecast will say something like "growth will pick up in the next quarter (or year)", or "inflationary pressures are rising". Therefore, any textbook model (or more advanced model) must be unrealistic if it works in levels of output, rather than rates of growth. (This is also true of several of the models presented throughout these chapters, primarily for technical/mathematical reasons.) In the case of the NCM however, it is fairly easy to recast the discussion entirely in dynamic terms (this means putting it in terms familiar to "market watchers" in the real world) and this is the premise of what follows.

To call any theoretical framework a "consensus" must run the risk of exaggeration. It means the approach to macroeconomics and monetary theory that was widely accepted in academia, central banks, finance ministries, and research institutes for policy-making and theoretical discussion around the beginning of the 21st century. It should go without saying that even if there is a consensus on a topic at any time, this does not necessarily imply that it is "true", scientifically accurate, or not subject to rational criticism. It simply means that the approach has majority support within the relevant peer group.

In terms of basic principles and policy commitments, and in spite of the advertised break with monetarism, the new consensus was not, in fact, all that much different from its predecessor nor from most of the traditional lineage of classical and neoclassical economic thinking. It was simply the latest development of this current of thought. As in the past, pride of place was given to low inflation, "sound money", fiscal prudence and so on, over other possible economic objectives. As in classical thought, economic growth was thought to depend entirely on "supply side" factors that determine the "natural rate" of real GDP growth. It might be admitted that this natural rate itself could be changed, or improved on. However, this could *only* be as a result of such things as technical change or improvements in productivity. Specifically, it *cannot* occur from any change on the demand side. Demand side changes might be allowed to have some strictly temporary effects on the business cycle, but are nonetheless confidently believed to have *no* lasting impact on the underlying growth rate itself.

All of this is by now very familiar. The main difference from traditional ideas was really only the Wicksellian twist of recognizing that central banks conduct monetary policy *via* changes in interest rates. The basic idea is that the central bank sets the policy rate, and the money supply then adjusts endogenously as a result of the subsequent lending and borrowing activities of the commercial banks and the public. This may not have been much of a "revelation" to experienced players in the financial markets, or to some heterodox economists such as the Post Keynesian school, but it probably did require some painful adjustment for many economists to what, by the time the 20th century drew to a close, had been the conventional academic economic thinking for many years. In particular, the new consensus seemed to require the construction of an economic model that made no reference to some deeply ingrained traditional concepts, such as the LM (liquidity/money), curve, the velocity of circulation of money, the demand curve for a *fixed* supply of money, and so on.

For economists with a conventional academic training a major problem with the idea that an interest rate, as such, can be a *policy* variable, is that according to the usual way of looking at things, interest rates should be determined in a "market" just like any other price (in this case, the market for "loanable funds"). If, on the contrary, it is argued that the central bank *sets* the interest rate on loans of its own liabilities there is no guarantee that their choice will conform to the theoretical market equilibrium. Usually it will be either lower or higher than this hypothetical benchmark. In the former case, what must be happening is that the central bank is directly or indirectly making additional funds available by credit creation to satisfy the demand for finance at that level, regardless of the amount of current saving. This is bound to cause theoretical difficulties for economists with a conventional academic training. In reality, it is simply the central banks' monopoly supply of its own liabilities (base money), that allows it to set the rate. However, for many centuries, it had been a basic tenet of orthodox economics to deny that any such thing was possible (Humphrey, 1993c, pp. 35–44). Nonetheless, by the late 20th and early 21st centuries, in order to subscribe to the new consensus, economists would reluctantly have to accept something like this analysis. I think that this was the main reason why it was *also* deemed necessary to bring back the Wicksellian concept of natural rate of interest (in spite of the additional confusion that this causes). The idea is to salvage at least *something* of the notion of a market-determined interest rate.

There are some other possible caveats to the idea that the central bank can decisively control the overall level of money rates. It is true, for example, that traditionally the central bank only controls one specific interest rate, and a very short dated one at that. Therefore, for monetary policy to be the decisive factor it must be argued that there is some well-defined "transmissions mechanism" for monetary policy whereby changes in the specific policy rate eventually feed through to the other interest rates in the system.[8] Also it can always be claimed (and often is claimed), by the central banks themselves, that they only follow rather than lead the market, when changing interest rates. As against both of these arguments, however, in the modern world even a brief glance at the business news will soon reveal headlines about the central bank "hiking" (increasing) or "cutting" (decreasing) interest rates, apparently of their own accord. There are even headlines when central banks simply leave interest rates unchanged. (This is also apparently newsworthy.)

Once the doctrinal difficulties have been overcome, the basic framework for policy analysis in the NCM (our version of it) consists of just three straightforward macroeconomic relationships with the issue of the transmission mechanism treated as unproblematic. First, there is a "demand function" resembling a traditional IS (investment/savings) curve, namely;

$$y = d - \varepsilon r, \qquad \varepsilon > 0. \tag{4.22}$$

Equation (4.22) states that output growth depends positively on a demand parameter, d, "total net autonomous demand" as a percentage of GDP, and negatively on the real rate of interest. The second key relationship is a short run "supply function" that is essentially a short-run Phillips curve (SRPC), or rather (because it actually relates inflation to output growth rather than unemployment) an "accelerationist" aggregate supply equation.

$$p - p_{-1} = \beta(y_{-1} - y^N), \qquad \beta > 1. \tag{4.23}$$

The third and final element of the NCM is a central bank "reaction function", of the type discussed in the previous section, such as:

$$r = r^N + \gamma(p - p^*), \qquad 0 < \gamma < 1. \tag{4.24}$$

To briefly see how the (ultimately simple) expression in Eq. (4.22) is derived, start with the usual GDP breakdown for a closed economy:

$$Y = C + I + G, \tag{4.25}$$

where $Y =$ real GDP, $C =$ real consumption spending, $I =$ real investment spending and $G =$ real government spending. Then, add a "Keynesian-type" consumption function of the form:

$$C = cY_{-1} - T, \qquad 0 < c < 1, \tag{4.26}$$

which suggests that consumers plan to purchase to consumer goods equal to some fraction c (the propensity to consume) of the level of real GDP experienced in the previous period. (They are therefore sticking to their perceived "budget" in that sense.) However, they also have to reduce their current demands by the full amount of the real tax burden, T.[9] Substituting (4.26) into (4.25), and dividing through by Y_{-1}, gives:

$$Y/Y_{-1} = c + (Y/Y_{-1})(I/Y) + (Y/Y_{-1})(G/Y) - (Y/Y_{-1})(T/Y). \tag{4.27}$$

Use the notation that $x = I/Y$, $g = G/Y$, $t = T/Y$ and $c = 1 - s$, (s is the propensity to save). Recall also that the growth rate of real GDP is $y = [(Y - Y_{-1})/Y_{-1}]$. Using (4.27) and rearranging:

$$(1 + y)(1 - x - g + t) = 1 - s, \qquad (4.28)$$

and, taking logs:

$$y = x + g - s - t. \qquad (4.29)$$

According to (4.29), the growth rate of real GDP is equal to investment spending as a percentage of GDP, plus government spending as a percentage of GDP, minus the propensity to save, and minus the average tax rate. Next, specify an investment function that makes investment as a percentage of GDP depend on the real interest rate, such as:

$$x = x_0 - \varepsilon r, \qquad \varepsilon > 0 \qquad (4.30)$$

substituting (4.30) into (4.29) we arrive at:

$$y = (x_0 + g - s - t) - \varepsilon r. \qquad (4.31)$$

The term d in Eq. (4.22) is a *portmanteau* demand parameter, including fiscal policy variables, the "animal spirits" (Keynes, 1964/1936) of the entrepreneurs (embedded in the term x_0), and the savings propensity. In short, $d = x_0 + g - s - t$.

The version of the accelerationist principle employed in Eq. (4.23) states that inflation in the current period will tend to increase if the rate of GDP growth in the previous period was greater than the supposed natural rate of growth. This will continue to happen for as long as the discrepancy is maintained. Equation (4.23) explicitly relates inflation to growth, rather than the level of output. It is therefore directly comparable to the expression explaining demand growth in Eq. (4.22). A technical point to notice about (4.23) is that, as current inflation depends only on past events, the short-run supply curve (SRAS) actually comes out flat. This gives the model at least some "Keynesian" properties, but only in the short run. The SRAS does not stay in place in subsequent periods, however, and therefore, any Keynesian features disappear eventually, when the actual rate of growth settles down to the natural rate ($y = y^N$).

The central bank reaction function, in Eq. (4.24), is a simplified version of Eq. (4.20). It states that the central bank will raise the *real* policy rate if the natural rate of interest rises, and also if the inflation rate is higher than some arbitrary target level, p^* (and *vice versa*). The monetary policy is one of *inflation targeting*. However, the policy *instrument* used to try to hit the target must be a nominal interest rate. In practice, therefore, "increasing the *real* policy rate" must mean increasing the nominal policy instrument by *more* than one-for-one, whenever there is an increase in observed inflation. This aggressive, and pre-emptive, stance towards inflation has been called the "Taylor principle" (as opposed to Taylor rule), in much of the literature (Mankiw, 2001, 2003; Davig and Leeper, 2007, 2010; Farmer *et al.*, 2010; Woodford, 2010). In fact, the willingness to actually *increase* real rates when deemed necessary (rather than simply respond to inflation) has played a crucially important role in the political economy of the new consensus.

Now substitute (4.24) into (4.22), re-arrange (4.23), and write down the equilibrium condition. It is then possible to construct a simple "aggregate demand and supply" model in inflation-growth space as follows:

$$p = [(1/\varepsilon\gamma)d + p^* - (1/\gamma)r^N] - (1/\varepsilon\gamma)y \quad \text{(AD)}, \qquad (4.32)$$

$$p = p_{-1} + \beta(y - y^N) \qquad \text{(SRAS)}, \qquad (4.33)$$

$$y = y^N \qquad \text{(LRAS)}. \qquad (4.34)$$

The model consists of an aggregate demand relationship (AD), a flat short-run supply function (SRAS), and a vertical long-run supply function (LRAS), the equilibrium condition.

The derived demand relationship in (4.32) shows the downward sloping demand-side relation in inflation/growth (p, y) space, obtained by substituting the monetary policy reaction function into the "dynamic" IS curve. It is important to realize that the negative relation between growth and inflation is due *solely* to the assumed response of monetary policy. It occurs because whenever (*e.g.*) inflation increases the central bank *deliberately* raises real interest rates, and thereby reduces demand. Moreover, *without* this policy response, the demand-side of the model would actually "collapse" (Coombes, 2009, 2010). This is a significant theoretical weakness of the NCM.

There are two potential shift variables for the constructed demand function in Eq. (4.32). First, there is the composite demand parameter, d, which, as we have seen, includes a number of things, including fiscal policy changes. An increase in d represents an increase in overall demand growth. Second, there is the inflation target itself, p^*. A lower (more stringent) inflation target reduces demand, because the central bank will need to raise real interest rates in the attempt to achieve it (and *vice versa*). The inflation target is therefore the primary indicator of the stance of monetary policy.

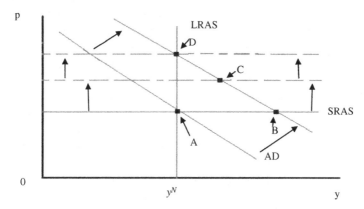

Fig. 4.1. The effects of a demand expansion.

As an illustration of how demand changes work out in the new consensus framework, Fig. 4.1 shows graphically the impact of an increase in the demand parameter. The figure itself actually looks altogether similar to those that have been used in the textbook analysis of fiscal policy for many decades now (ever since the first academic reaction *against* Keynesian ideas, dating from the late 1970s). This is not surprising, as the basic/underlying economic philosophy remains unchanged from the era of monetarism. The main difference in the late 20th century and early 21st century was really only in the interpretation of what is occurring behind the scenes, as far as monetary policy is concerned. In particular, it is now clear that some part of the response to a demand expansion is *deliberately* caused by the monetary policy reaction, rather than just by "market forces".

The basic argument remains that although a demand expansion may cause an initial boom in the economy, shown here by an outward shift of the demand function and a move from point "A" to point "B", this will inevitably fade away over time, leaving only higher inflation as the end result. The SRAS curve will gradually shift upwards, and with each shift the growth rate will fall back, and the inflation rate will rise. For example, this occurs at point "C". The process will continue until the new steady-state equilibrium is reached at point "D", by which time any effect on the growth rate has faded away. There is only higher inflation. In terms of political economy, it is apparent that the point of this argument is to suggest that there should be no attempt to stimulate the economy in the first place.

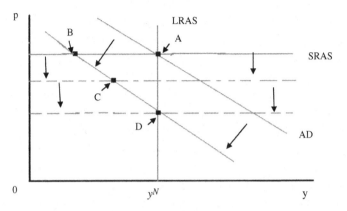

Fig. 4.2.   A lower inflation target.

A second graphical example, in Fig. 4.2, shows what occurs in the new consensus framework when the inflation target itself is revised (in this case in a downward direction). The idea of an "inflation targeting" policy was one of the main policy recommendations of the new consensus. In this case, the change represents a shift to a "tighter", or more "stringent" policy. The central bank will need to raise the real policy rate of interest in the attempt to hit the new lower inflation target. In Fig. 4.2, the demand schedule moves back and to the left. Starting from point "A", there will first be a monetary policy-induced recession at point "B". This accounts for the concerns that *both* business and labour always feel when such a policy is announced. However, soon, according to the new consensus, a downward adjustment of expectations must take place. The SRAS will begin to shift downward, inflation will fall, and the central bank will "feel able" to reduce interest rates once again. Thereafter, growth is supposed to begin to increase again from its low point. There will be a series of ever more favourable "temporary equilibria", such as that at point "C". The NCM economists argue that the process will continue until the new long-run equilibrium is reached at point "D". The end result will be a lower actual rate of inflation, and there need to be no *permanent* reduction in economic growth. If all this happens, it would vindicate an inflation targeting policy, at least in the most general terms. The inflation rate is made lower, and the growth rate eventually gets back to "normal".

We can summarize the basic results of the NCM as follows. In the long run, the growth rate will always conform to the natural rate. That is:

$$y = y^N, \tag{4.35}$$

meanwhile, the equilibrium inflation rate will be determined by:

$$p = (1/\varepsilon\gamma)d - (1/\gamma)r^N + p^* - (1/\varepsilon\gamma)y^N. \tag{4.36}$$

One interesting point to note about this, however, is that the new inflation target itself is *never* actually achieved. A lower target rate does reduce the equilibrium inflation rate, but the target *itself* will be elusive. From Eq. (4.36) it is clear that the final equilibrium rate of inflation, although lower than before (e.g., in Fig. 4.2), still does not conform to the target. In spite of this, the political economy behind the inflation targeting narrative is to convince the public that inflation targeting is a desirable policy objective regardless of the initially depressing impact on jobs and employment.

Our model also determines the level of the real rate of interest that will prevail in the market-place in growth equilibrium. This will *differ* from the natural rate if the inflation rate is non-zero. Although the economic growth rate does supposedly conform to *its* natural equilibrium level, nonetheless, Wicksellian theory still rests on "disequilibrium" as far as interest rates are concerned. The steady-state real rate of interest is actually given by:

$$r = (1/\varepsilon)(d - y^N). \tag{4.37}$$

Therefore, a demand increase always tends to *raise* real interest rates. This makes the result consistent with very some traditional arguments in neo-classical economics, for example, about the "crowding out" effect. However, there is a paradox here because the mechanism by which this occurs is not a question of "market forces" (as would have been argued in more traditional theory). Rather what causes interest rates to rise is the *deliberate* monetary policy response of the central bank. There would be no increase in the real rate of interest if the central bank did not "make it so". What is going here, therefore, is that in some sense, the behaviour of the central bank is now supposed to validate or confirm the traditional arguments of neoclassical economics, whether or not those arguments were correct in the first place.

The other main determinant of the steady-state real rate of interest in Eq. (4.37) is the natural rate of growth itself. If an increase in the natural rate of growth y^N does occur, this will reduce the equilibrium real interest rate. Strangely enough, a more traditional argument would probably have been that a higher natural growth rate would justify a *higher* interest rate, but the opposite occurs here. This is because an increase in growth actually reduces inflation, and hence "allows" the central bank to reduce interest rates. The overall impression to be gained from these remarks is that to some extent traditional views on economic policy are supported in the neo-Wicksellian NCM. However, the central bank, in particular, has to work *hard* to make this happen.

A final question to ask in this framework is what would actually be required to achieve a *zero* inflation rate, stable prices? It is not good enough just to set a "target" of zero, because from (4.36) the target will not be hit. It can be seen that not only must $p^* = 0$, but also the *intercept term* in the monetary policy rule must continuously be adjusted to reflect or offset any changes than might occur to the demand parameter, and the natural rate of growth. Notice that this sort of adjustment would, in fact, be impossible if the intercept really is the Wicksellian natural rate of interest r^N (as most of the textbooks argue). In that case, the intercept could never be changed by monetary policy. It is now clear, therefore, that the standard textbook interpretation of "interest rate rules" does not take into account practical reality. Even granted its existence (which I do not), there is no way for central banks to know before-hand what the hypothetical natural rate should be. In any empirical application the intercept term can only be some number that is *chosen* by the central bank on the basis of experience, "rules of thumb", political expediency, or similar. As such, it can always be changed, and if we index the different possible values of this term by the notation r_j ($j = 0, 1, 2, \ldots, n$), it becomes just another indicator of the overall monetary policy stance. Equation (4.24) must be re-written as:

$$r = r_j + \gamma(p - p^*), \qquad 0 < \gamma < 1. \tag{4.38}$$

Similarly, Eq. (4.36) must become:

$$p = (1/\varepsilon\gamma)d - (1/\varepsilon)r_j + p^* - (1/\varepsilon\gamma)y^N. \tag{4.39}$$

To achieve zero inflation in these circumstances, (in addition to a target of $p^* = 0$) it is clear that the actual value of r_j must be continuously adjusted until we arrive at something like:

$$r_j = (1/\gamma)(d - y^N). \tag{4.40}$$

Comparing (4.40) and (4.37), the implication is that finally the intercept term and the equilibrium interest rate must be *made* equal if price stability is to be achieved. It is this sense *only* that the *final* value of the r_j term in Eq. (4.40) could be called a "natural rate". It is a natural rate only if we *define* the natural rate as "the value of the intercept that is consistent with zero inflation". However, it cannot be a natural rate in the other main sense of the term, that of a rate somehow uniquely determined *outside* of the monetary model *via* barter exchange. The most that can be said is that when r_j and r do coincide, and also the inflation target is zero, then the equilibrium inflation rate will be zero. However, there is nothing inherent in the system that prevents either the equilibrium interest rate, or the equilibrium inflation rate, from taking on quite different values at any time.

A "Wicksellian" Model with a Representative Agent

As mentioned in previous chapters, one of the long-standing methodological principles of mainstream academics economics which has been the norm for several decades now, is the objective of attempting to provide the so-called "micro-foundations" of macroeconomics. This is the idea of trying to derive macro-level propositions, not from investigations into social ontology, but by working out hypothetical mathematical dynamic optimization problems facing individual "representative" economic agents on the assumption that the results derived also do provide some information about aggregative processes. This procedure is not defensible on general scientific grounds (King, 2012), but it is something, that graduate students, in particular, must grapple with because of intense peer pressure. So, the question naturally arises (in the context of this overall intellectual framework) whether or not "micro-foundations" can be provided in the case of Wicksell-type monetary economics. No claim is made that much will be added to our previous discussion by the exercise, but it is necessary at least to address to issue.

Therefore, in this section the micro-foundations issue is investigated using a straightforward dynamic optimization model. A convenient starting point for the discussion is the commentary on, and critique of, the work of Woodford (1998, 2003), by Rogers (2006). Woodford has been one of the leading contributors to the mainstream literature, although note that the mathematical formulation used in what follows is necessarily at a much simpler level than in the original debate. It is nonetheless still possible to follow Rogers' main argument, which was that the relevant mainstream literature tended to confuse, or blur, three issues, all apparently connected to institutional change occurring in the monetary system, but that are actually quite distinct.

The three issues are the following:

First, the question of whether or not it is theoretically possible to write down a mathematical system of an economic process without money, that is a pure "accounting system of exchange" (McCallum, 1985).

Second, the observation of specific technological changes occurring at the time, such as the switch over to an electronic payments system, which are the most obvious surface phenomena as the system evolves.

Third, the standard Wicksellian theme of the conduct of monetary policy by changes in interest rates.

In truth, the first of these questions has already been answered long ago, and should have been a non-issue theoretically. There have always been such things as general equilibrium models, real business cycle models, real growth models, and so forth, that deal only with relative prices and barter exchange, and purport to explain economic affairs entirely on that basis. The problem with such models is not really their further mathematical/theoretical development, but their relationship with reality.

Classical and neoclassical economists were always able to construct models that "do without money" (Woodford, 1998; Rogers, 2006). The problem is that in the actual world money does exist, has always existed, and continues to exist, computerized or not. Both before and after the advent of computers, various theoretical devices have been tried, presumably for the sake of realism, to introduce money into neoclassical models that would otherwise work perfectly well, theoretically, on the assumption of barter exchange. Examples of this (dating from well before computerization) are such things as "cash-in-advance" (CIA) models, "overlapping generations" (OLG) models, models with "money in the utility function" (MIU) and several others (Walsh, 1998; Smithin, 2003). The difficulty with all of them, however, is that they generally turn out to have the property that money is "inessential" to the results obtained (Hahn, 1983). Rogers claim was that the work of Woodford and others in the same field continued to exhibit this property.

The second point is that, in the modern context, although the institutional/technological changes having to do with electronic money, the computerization of the payments system, and so on, *seem* to involve fundamental questions of principle, this is really only a valid interpretation if beforehand the basic understanding of money had been that of a "commodity" and a "medium of exchange". On the other hand, if money is, and has always been, understood as basically a social relation, involving the incurring and repayment of debt, and the delineation of the abstract unit of account, there is no fundamental change. The physical form of the money whether involving electronic methods, book entries, pieces of paper or notches in a medieval tally stick (Wray, 1990) would be irrelevant.

Therefore the only issue remaining that is of any intellectual substance is the third, the Wicksellian theme of whether monetary policy is conducted *via* base control or by changes in interest rates. This, really has nothing to do with the existence or non-existence of money itself. The very idea of an interest rate on "loans of money" clearly presupposes that there is indeed something called money in the system.

Given these preliminary remarks, how might it be possible (nonetheless) to construct a Wicksell-type model using the methodology of dynamic optimization by a representative agent? Consider, for example, the following optimization problem, of an infinitely-lived representative worker/consumer with an objective function and budget constraint:

$$\max \sum_{0}^{\infty} \beta^t U(C_t, N_t), \qquad U'(C_t) > 0, \ U'(N_t) < 0 \qquad (4.41)$$

subject to:

$$B - B_{-1} = WN + i_{-1}B_{-1} - PC. \qquad (4.42)$$

This a model in which production involves only labour inputs, N, and in which all the output produced in a given period is consumed (as consumption C) within that period. The good produced might be perishable, for example. There is also, however, a financial asset B (say "bills" or "bonds") of fixed nominal value, denominated in the unit of account, holdings of which attract a nominal interest rate i. In a Wicksellian framework, it is assumed that the financial and banking structure is such that this nominal interest rate is determined primarily by the policy of the central bank. For our purposes it *is* the policy rate. Finally, note that the notation in Eq. (4.41) is such that variables current at time $t = 0$ have no time subscript (*e.g.*, B), and that variables current at an earlier time, such as $t - 1$ (*etc.*) are denoted (*e.g.*, B_{-1}).

It is an interesting question whether or not this construct can actually be called a "monetary model" in the usual sense in which this term is employed in neoclassical economics. Is this one of the many "models without money" featured in the mainstream literature around the turn of the 21st century? In terms of the ontology of money, however, there is certainly a strong case to be made, to the contrary, that this *is* a monetary model, even though there is no explicit "transactions technology" or "medium of exchange". There is a unit of account, and as the consumption good is perishable, the "financial asset" is the only vehicle by which to accumulate "wealth" over time. The model "simulates" a situation in which more alternatives to hold wealth (*e.g.*, some capital goods) do exist, but, nonetheless, "money" is the ultimate or final means of discharging a debt. In our case, the only means of preserving wealth, discharging debt, or getting paid, are the bills/bonds.

In what follows, the rate of time preference of the worker/consumer will be denoted by the symbol, θ. The discount factor in the original optimization problem is therefore $\beta = [1/(1 + \theta)]$. Substituting (4.42) into (4.41), the dynamic optimization problem becomes:

$$\max \sum_{0}^{\infty} \beta^t \{U(C_t, N_t) + \lambda_t[W_t N_t + (1 + i_{t-1})B_{t-1} - P_t C_t - B_t\}, \quad (4.43)$$

where λ is a co-state variable. Differentiating with respect to the choice variables C, N, and B, the first-order conditions for the solution of the problem are:

$$U'(C) - \lambda P = 0, \quad (4.44)$$
$$U'(N) + \lambda W = 0, \quad (4.45)$$
$$(1 + i)\lambda = \lambda_{+1}, \quad (4.46)$$

and the "Euler equations" are therefore:

$$U'(C)/P = \beta U'(C_{+1})/[P_{+1}(1 + i)], \quad (4.47)$$
$$-U'(N) = [U'(C)](W/P). \quad (4.48)$$

As in the previous optimization problem studied in an earlier chapter, the model may be closed by specifying a standard production function with the real wage equal to the marginal product of labour. Therefore, as all current output is consumed:

$$Y = F(N), \qquad F'(N) > 0, \ F''(N) < 0, \quad (4.49)$$
$$W/P = F'(N), \quad (4.50)$$
$$Y = C. \quad (4.51)$$

Using Eq. (4.47) through Eq. (4.51) and imposing the equilibrium condition $C_{+1} = C = C_{-1}$, *etc.*, the whole system reduces to:

$$P_{+1}(1 + i) = \beta P_t, \tag{4.52}$$

$$-U'(N^N) = U'[F(N^N)][F'(N^N)]. \tag{4.53}$$

Now, let the equilibrium level of employment be denoted N^N (the "natural" level of employment). Then, as $Y^N = F(N^N)$, $\beta = [1/(1 + \theta)]$, and $r = i - [(P_{+1} - P)/P]$, the solution finally boils down to:

$$r = \theta, \tag{4.54}$$

$$Y = Y^N. \tag{4.55}$$

The solution is that in equilibrium the level of output is at its "natural" rate, and the real rate of interest is equal to the rate of time preference (it "natural rate").

Even though a "socially constructed" monetary/financial asset, B, has been introduced into the problem, these results just repeat the conclusions of non-monetary neoclassical economics as already seen in previous chapters. It would not quite be accurate (semantically) to say that money is "inessential" in this particular model. Without money, there would be no opportunity to exercise "time preference" of any kind. Also, and as already stressed, there is an implicit payments structure, in the model, with firms paying wages, consumer buying goods and so on. This would not exist in a plausible model of a reality "without money". It is still true, nonetheless, that the ultimate equilibrium of the real economy, Y^N, does not turn out any differently than would have been in the case in a Crusoe-style microeconomic model of labour/leisure choice. The point is, therefore, that even after having worked out the supposed micro-foundations, we are still faced with the original problem of how to explain inflation in this framework.

Also, how will it to possible to characterize the conduct of monetary policy? The only thing to do is to insert some form of interest rate rule for monetary policy, similar to those introduced in the discussion of the NCM above. This is a similar criticism to that which Rogers (2006) made of the existing literature. The explanation of how the inflation rate, or price level, is determined does not emerge from the exercise of working through the "micro-foundations". It is still necessary to add an interest rate rule with what are thought to be the desired properties, to an otherwise standard neoclassical model.

There is still another problem with Eq. (4.54) which reprises the problem of how interest rates and the inflation rate will be correlated, as previously discussed. The definition of the real interest rate in a perfect foresight model is:

$$r = i - p. \tag{4.56}$$

Now suppose that the policy rate of interest is just set arbitrarily at a given nominal level, i. From (4.54) and (4.56) we would get:

$$p = i - \theta. \tag{4.57}$$

Therefore, if the equilibrium exists, the implication from Eq. (4.57) is that an *increase* in the nominal interest rate *increases* the inflation rate. This is not a Wicksellian-type result at all. It would not have been a problem for an old-fashioned monetarist perspective, nor the model in MacKinnon and Smithin (1993), where a positive correlation between inflation and nominal interest rates was rationalized by the fact that interest rate policy was non-neutral. However, neither of these explainations is going to work for the model under consideration here.

One possibility (from the discussion in the previous section) is to try to add a more complicated central bank reaction function to determine the nominal interest rate. For example, suppose we posit a central bank reaction function which adjusts nominal interest rates according to the formula:

$$i = i_j + \gamma p, \qquad 0 < \gamma < 1. \tag{4.58}$$

Unfortunately, however, the Wicksellian argument still does not work. Substituting Eq. (4.58) into the definition of the real rate of interest, and using the equality in (4.54), we obtain:

$$i_j + \gamma p - p = \theta. \tag{4.59}$$

Solving for inflation:

$$p = [1/(1 - \gamma)](i_j - \theta). \tag{4.60}$$

As the expression $[1/(1 - \gamma)]$ is positive, the result is still that an increase in the nominal interest rate (meaning, in this case, the intercept term in the interest rate rule, i_j) will increase the inflation rate, and a decrease in the rate will decrease the inflation. This is not what Wicksell said at all.

Interestingly enough, at this point, to solve the situation, it is necessary once again to invoke the "Taylor Principle". This is the idea that the authorities should always try to raise the nominal rate by *more* than one-for-one with observed inflation. This can be written as:

$$i = i_j + (1 + \gamma)p. \tag{4.61}$$

More concisely:

$$i = r_j + \gamma p. \tag{4.62}$$

Substituting (4.62) back into (4.42):

$$r_j + \gamma p - p = \theta. \tag{4.63}$$

The solution for inflation will now be:

$$p = [1/(1 - \gamma)](\theta - r_j). \tag{4.64}$$

This is more "Wicksellian" in spirit. Equation (4.64) says is that if the real "base rate" for monetary policy (the *real* intercept in central bank reaction function, r_j) is consistently less than the "natural rate" there will be inflation. I suspect that this is actually where the notion of the "Taylor Principle" (an aggressive anti-inflation policy raising *real* interest rates sharply whenever inflation emerges) originally comes from, disastrous though the principle has been in practice.

In summary, the Wicksell-type model just constructed finally comes down to:

$$Y = Y^N, \tag{4.65}$$

$$p = [1/(1 - \gamma)](\theta - r_j). \tag{4.66}$$

The conclusion in the level of output is always at its natural rate (the same level that would prevail in a barter exchange economy) and if the base real policy rate is too low relative to the rate of time preference (essentially Wicksell's natural rate), there will be inflation. The exercise of working through the micro-foundations has not therefore really added anything new to what are, by now, familiar theoretical propositions.

The historically-minded reader will note that the model in (4.65)–(4.66) is only a marginal advance from position already reached by Keynes (1971a/1930, pp. 121–144), in Chapter 10 of his *Treatise on Money*. This does not seem to be much to show for nine decades of intensive mathematical research in academia.

A Simple Theory of Banking and the Relationship between the Central Bank and Commercial Banks

It was mentioned earlier that once we do start to think of the central bank as conducting monetary policy by changing interest rates, there really ought to be some account of the "transmissions mechanism" whereby changes in the interest rate directly under the control of the central bank feed through to other interest rates in the system. However, this was not a main focus in either the Wicksellian or neo-Wicksellian literature. In the macro-theoretical development of this approach, there was a tendency to treat the interest rate in the monetary policy rule and the rate relevant to business firms, as one and the same. At the very least, it was assumed that there is a direct one-for-one connection between them. Therefore, the purpose of the next few sections is to try to fill this gap to some extent.

A simple theory of banking is presented to explain the relationship between those commercial banks that have "direct clearing" facilities with the central bank (this is Canadian terminology) and the central bank itself. This helps to elaborate a version of the transmissions mechanism in a stylized institutional setting. The argument follows that of Kam and Smithin (2012) and is influenced by the *critique* of the neoclassical theory of banking due to Rymes (1998) and Rymes and Rogers (2000), and the discussion of the theory of "free banking" put forward by White (1984) some years ago. The issues involved have previously been briefly discussed, briefly, by MacKinnon and Smithin (1993, pp. 774–775) and, in somewhat more detail, by Tabassum (2007) in a doctoral thesis proposal.

Profit maximization is assumed although, as already explained, in other areas of the macro model the application of optimal choice theory, or a "utility maximization" methodology, could reasonably be criticized on the grounds that these are not, realistic descriptions of the way in which decisions are actually made. For some types of *firm* behaviour, however, and particularly those of financial and banking firms, there may be a genuine caveat to this that justifies a *profit maximization* methodology. This is along the lines that, given the economic sociology of the system, such firms are constrained to behave in a certain way (such as maximizing profits) if they are to succeed *on their own terms of reference*, in the existing environment. This could be defended, even if the same sort of case could not reasonably be made about consumers, or workers, behaviour, for example.

The Commercial Bank Balance Sheet

Table 4.1 is a stylized/simplified balance sheet of a commercial bank which makes loans L at a competitive interest rate i_L, and accept deposits, D, on which it also pays a competitive deposit rate i_D. It may choose to hold reserves, R, consisting of the (assumed) non-interest bearing liabilities of the central bank, but there are no formal reserve requirements. It is not a crucial requirement that the interest rate on reserves be equal to zero. However, it is crucial that the central bank has the monopoly power to effectively determine this interest rate, whatever it is. In that case, we can say that the rate of interest on reserves is "set at zero".

In the assumed institutional environment, clearing with the other commercial banks is conducted *via* the central bank and if, at the end of a designated accounting period, a commercial bank finds itself with a negative settlement balance S at the central bank, the rules require that they must borrow to make good this deficiency at an interest rate, i_B, decided by the central bank itself. In context, therefore, this can be identified with what we have been calling the "policy rate" of the central bank. It is not suggested that this assumed institutional environment exactly replicates the existing framework in any real world jurisdiction. The i_B term is a "proxy" for policy rates in the real world, which might (historically) have been "bank rates" or "discount" rates or the like. In the contemporary financial environment the policy rate is often an overnight intra-bank lending rate of some kind, constrained by a fixed "band" between the central bank's own lending and deposit rates, and pushed closer to either the upper or lower bound by various financial techniques (Atesoglu and Smithin, 2008; Lavoie, 2010).

The Optimization Problem for Bankers

The optimization problem for the commercial bank is therefore:

$$\max: \Pi = i_L L - i_D D - i_B \int_0^\infty f(x) dx (\mathrm{S} - R) - \mu L. \tag{4.67}$$

Table 4.1.   The commercial bank balance sheet.

Assets		Liabilities	
Reserves	R	Deposits	D
Loans	$\underline{L}$	Settlement balances	$\underline{S}$
	$R + L$		$D + S$

The sum $\int_0^\infty f(x)dx$ can be interpreted as the subjective cumulative probability distribution (in the view of the bankers themselves) of the likelihood of the commercial ending up with a negative settlement balance that needs to be financed. For example, if (a big *if*) the bank was operating in an ergodic environment (Davidson, 2009, pp. 37–38) *and* also the probability distribution was known to be "normal", the figure would be 0.5. However, I would say that neither of these conditions is likely to hold in reality, and therefore the number the bankers put in simply "is what it is", so to speak. It is the bankers' *own* subjective estimate of what the risks are. Some of the empirical evidence actually suggests a typical pass-through coefficient that is less than one but much larger than 0.5 (Atesoglu, 2003/2004; Uddin *et al.*, 2011; Sran, 2012). Therefore, simplify the notation by introducing the term σ, where:

$$\sigma = \int_0^\infty f(x)dx, \qquad 0 < \sigma < 1. \tag{4.68}$$

It is tempting to interpret the term μ as the average cost "per dollar" of making bank loans, and perhaps this would not be unreasonable. A difficulty here, though, is that it difficult to conceive of any precise analogue to a textbook physical "production function" in the nebulous case of banking (Dow and Smithin, 1999). It is probably safer to say that μ must be high enough to cover costs and earn the normal rate of return for banks *given* existing institutional arrangements, market structure, current banking legislation and regulation, *etc.* It would then be ultimately determined by these four sets of conditions.

Substituting in from the bank balance sheet, the optimization problem becomes:

$$\text{max:} \; \Pi = i_L L - i_D(L + R - S) - i_B\sigma(S - R) - \mu L. \tag{4.69}$$

The choice variables for the bank are the volume of loans granted and the quantity of precautionary reserves they choose to hold. The implication of this is that there will be no fixed numerical "money multiplier" or "deposit multiplier" relationship between these two variables. They are both endogenous. First-order conditions for the problem are obtained by differentiating (4.69) with respect to L and R and setting the results equal to zero. This yields:

$$i_L - i_D = \mu, \tag{4.70}$$

$$i_D = \sigma i_B. \tag{4.71}$$

The mark-up between commercial bank lending rates and deposit rates is equal to the coefficient μ, and the deposit rate is actually a "mark-down" from the central bank's setting of the policy rate. The degree of this mark-down depends on the subjective assessment of the "risk" (as this is called in neoclassical economics) for a commercial bank that does not "keep in step" (Keynes, 1971a/1930, p. 23) with its rivals. In the previous literature a similar sort of result has sometimes been called the "two-for-one" rule (Rymes and Rogers, 2000, p. 259), but again that would depend on the assumptions of ergodicity and a normal distribution which, as already argued, cannot be justified in practice.

Combining Eqs. (4.70) and (4.71), there is linear relationship between the policy rate and the commercial bank lending rate as in Eq. (4.72) below. This therefore provides an explanation of the monetary policy transmission mechanism, whereby increases in the nominal central bank policy rate are passed through to nominal interest rates in general. The relationship is:

$$i_L = \mu + \sigma i_B. \qquad (4.72)$$

A further useful step is then to subtract the observed inflation rate, p, from both sides of equation. This gives:

$$i_L - p = \mu + \sigma r'_B - (1 - \sigma)p. \qquad (4.73)$$

In this new expression, r'_B is the inflation-adjusted real policy rate, that is, the nominal policy rate adjusted for the currently observed inflation rate ($r'_B = i_B - p$.) This definition therefore gives some insight into what was entailed in previous discussions (Smithin, 2003, 2007a, 2009a, 2009b) that have suggested a "real interest rate rule" for monetary policy. As a purely practical matter, such a rule would have to involve a target for the inflation-adjusted policy rate rather than the policy rate less *expected* inflation, as the true "expected" inflation rate is not known. The interesting question, then, is whether the similar "inflation-adjusted" commercial bank lending rate in Eq. (4.73) can also be taken as a proxy for the real lending rate itself. If so, and in the absence of any other reliable indicator on which borrowers can base their estimates, Eq. (4.73) might be re-written as:

$$r = \mu + \sigma r_B - (1 - \sigma)p. \qquad (4.74)$$

The upshot of this exercise is that if the term r in Eq. (4.74) does stand for the "real interest rate" involved in economic decision-making (for example, the interest rate in an investment function, or in an IS curve in a macro model), then the equation shows how central bank activities can have an influence over this rate. Working through the details of the transmissions mechanism has suggested a mechanism whereby a "real interest rate rule" on the part of the central bank can also influence the real interest rate perceived by commercial banks and their borrowers, and hence may have an effect on the either the real economy or the inflation rate by this route.

A final point to notice in this case is that there is likely to be a *negative* relationship between the inflation-adjusted real lending rate and the rate of inflation itself. This is a significant result at the level of theoretical principle. The reader is reminded, however, that in a world where the central bank is following some other sort of rule that entails frequent *changes* in the real policy rate, this underlying theoretical relationship may be obscured. In that case the central bank would then be *deliberately* raising, or lowering, the real policy rate whenever inflation rises or falls. Similarly in a crisis or panic situation, such as the last few years, when the central bank is desperately holding the nominal policy rate close to zero, the real rate changes whether the central bank wants it to or not.

Conclusion

It can be argued that Wicksellian and neo-Wicksellian models do represent "progress" in monetary economics to some extent, over (say) the simple quantity theory. However, this is mainly because they take it for granted that the money supply is endogenous, and therefore do have to deal with the key issue of credit creation and money creation (and destruction) in a developed banking system. They have to accept that the main monetary policy instrument employed by the central bank is a nominal interest rate.

At the same time, however, the Wicksellian approach clings to idea that the real rate of interest *on money* is a not specifically a monetary phenomenon. There remains the idea that somewhere in the system, there must exist a non-monetary "natural rate" of interest that is not observable, but (nonetheless) is supposed to exert a decisive influence. This is not a "progressive" idea and one that, ultimately, is even less convincing than the classical notion that interest rates in the marketplace *directly* reflect non-monetary concepts, such as time preference or a purely materialistic/physical return to "capital". The next step in monetary theory should be to do without the notion of a natural rate of interest altogether, primarily on the grounds that money is essentially a social relationship and that therefore the rate of interest must also be a social relationship. We still need, however, the notion of the "real rate of interest" in the strictly inflation-adjusted sense.

It is not necessary to extend this particular chapter which is in the form of an essay to take into account the implications of the open economy and exchange rates, for Wicksell-type models. The relevant formulas for the relationship between foreign and domestic interest rates, and between interest rates and exchange rates have already been discussed in Chapter 3. The main point that needs to be made here is (once again) that if a national central bank wants to pursue an interest rate policy different to the rest of the world (rest of the world) there will have to be a floating exchange rate. If on the other hand the international financial policy is to fix the nominal exchange rate, then the interest rate policy must be directed solely to that end, and the national economy must accept the inflation rate prevalent elsewhere.

Notes

1. Not to be confused with the modern money thereby (MMT) of Wray (2012).
2. This general specification stresses a direct link between the inflation rate and the interest differential. This is in order to link up the argument with some of the more modern theories discussed below. Wicksell himself, however, in common with other historical writers, would likely have simply postulated a relationship between the *volume* of loans and the interest rate differential. See Humphrey (1993d, p. 304).
3. This, however, is not quite accurate. Humphrey (1993a, pp. 68–69) suggests that Thornton (1991/1802), for example, also had a clear grasp of the concept.
4. See also the paper by Howitt (1992).
5. In that case the nominal rate would have to adjust to inflation, as it does in monetarism.
6. Recall that we have earlier questioned whether any such thing actually exists in a real money-using capitalist that relies on the "method of enterprise".
7. I am not aware that any rule along these specific lines has actually been discussed in the current economics literature. However, it would be the logical consequence of a belief that there is both a natural rate of interest and a natural rate of growth.

8. This important issue is discussed in more detail later in this chapter, and was also touched on earlier in Chapter 1.
9. The precise explanation of why this is an appropriate specification will be taken up again in Chapter 7.

CHAPTER 5

KEYNES, SAMUELSON, HICKS AND THE FATE
OF KEYNESIAN ECONOMICS

Introduction

The title of a paper by Blanchard (2000), which was an attempt to sum up progress in the field of monetary economics and macroeconomics during the 20th century, was as follows: "What do we know about macroeconomics that Fisher and Wicksell did not?" As seen in previous chapters, it does make perfect sense to link Fisher and Wicksell to late 20th century mainstream macroeconomics. Fisher (1911) can be certainly regarded as a precursor of the "monetarism" of Friedman (1956, 1968), that was mainstream orthodoxy down to the mid-1980s. Similarly, the "new consensus" on interest rate policy that subsequently developed in the late 20th and early 21st century owes a great deal to Wicksell (1965/1898). However, in terms of the overall intellectual history of the 20th century, putting matters in this way leaves a big gap in the middle, where the economic theory and social philosophy of Keynes (1923, 1964/1936, 1971a/1930, 1971b/1930) ought to be.

The purpose of this chapter, therefore, the fifth in a series with the title *Essays in the Fundamental Theory of Monetary Economics*, is to discuss the work of Keynes, particularly that of the *General Theory* (1964/1936). Another objective is to re-examine the way in which Keynes's theory was initially presented to the public by his best-known interpreters. A third is to inquire into what, finally, became of "Keynesian economics"?

There has always been a current of thought in orthodox/mainstream economics, which claims that Keynes's work was either "... quite wrong... (or)... nothing new". Keynes himself (1964/1936, p. v) had *predicted* that this would be case. When these attitudes are examined in more detail, however, the first claim (that it is wrong) seems to boil down simply to assertions about the (false) equivalence of barter and monetary exchange, rather than any engagement with the specifics of the theory of monetary production (Asimakopolous, 1988; Dillard, 1988; Graziani, 1990, 2003; Rochon, 1999; Smithin, 2009a; King, 2012). The second claim (that it is nothing new) requires an interpretation of Keynesian theory that makes it rely on nominal wage and price "stickiness" or "rigidity" of some form and, thereby, renders it indistinguishable from later monetarism (Laidler, 1996, 1999; Leeson, 2003a, 2003b; Smithin, 1996a, 2004a). For that matter, Keynesian economics would be made indistinguishable from much of 18th and 19th centuries' *classical* economics.

These sorts of conclusion must also ignore Keynes's own, quite specific, claim to have brought about a revolution in economic thinking. In a letter to George Bernard Shaw dated January 1, 1935,[1] for example, Keynes confidently wrote as follows:

> ... to understand my state of mind... you have to know that I believe myself to be writing a book on economic theory which will largely revolutionize — not, I suppose, at once but in the course of the next 10 years — the way the world thinks about economic problems. When my new theory has been duly assimilated and mixed with politics and feelings and passions, I can't predict what the final upshot will be in its effects on action and affairs. But there will be a great change, and, in particular, the Ricardian foundations of Marxism will be knocked away... I can't expect you, or anyone else, to believe this at the present stage. But for myself I don't merely hope what I say — in my own mind I'm quite sure....

While it is certainly possible to argue that Keynes did *not* actually achieve this goal of revolutionizing economics (and that the theory presented was deficient in some way that accounts for this) it is quite *un*reasonable to think that the author of this passage could himself have believed that he would have been able to set off a "revolution" just by asserting the existence of nominal wage and price rigidities. Moreover, it is also true that in the 10 years of real time following the publication of the *General Theory*, and then for most of the *next* 30 years or so down to the mid-1970s, there were plenty of economists and policy-makers who, took Keynes precisely at his word. Therefore, the turn away from Keynes, and the return to views resembling those of either Fisher or Wicksell, does seem to be a clear-cut example of the "long swings in economic understanding" identified by Leijonhufvud (2004).

What, exactly, were the ideas that were lost in the ultimately wholesale rejection of Keynesian thought by the end of the 20th century? First and foremost, the *theory of effective demand* itself, more generally the very idea that demand conditions matter, in an essential way, for the determination of real economic outcomes. Whether or not he actually succeeded, Keynes tried to present this as a fundamental part of literally "a more general theory" of a monetary economy, and not just a question of confronting changes in nominal aggregate demand with sticky nominal wages or prices (Keynes, 1964/1936, p. 27). The idea was clearly *meant* to be part of a new theory of monetary production, not just a caveat to the existing theory of barter exchange. Second, the anti-Keynesian reaction threatened the very methodology of monetary macroeconomics itself. The explicit aim of the orthodox "micro-foundations" project in the last quarter of the 20th century was to eliminate macroeconomic methods altogether (King, 2012; Lucas, 1987, pp. 107–108; Smithin, 2004b, 2009a, pp. 41–42) and roll up all of economic theory under the heading of *microeconomics*. This would be a problem not just for Keynesian theory, but even for some of the most important of the anti-Keynesian *macroeconomic* theories, and for any coherent non-reductionist way of looking at the problems of the social world. Milton Friedman (1974b, p. 134), for example, certainly did not accept that Keynes's theory was accurate, but nonetheless wrote as follows:

> ... Keynes was ... [not] ... seeking an abstract system of all embracing simultaneous equations ... Keynes's theory is the *right kind of theory* in its simplicity, its concentration on a few key magnitudes, its potential fruitfulness. I have been led to reject it, not on these grounds, but because I believe that it has been contradicted by evidence ... (emphasis added)

Such a stance would, at least, mean that debate could be about substantive issues rather than, as so often in the academic literature, over whether or not a theoretical claim conforms to some approved/official methodology. Hayek (1994, p. 60), on the other side of this issue, explains his unwillingness to being drawn into the debate over the specifics of Keynes's *General Theory* by his "taking issue with the whole macrodynamic approach". He also says of Milton Friedman (Hayek, 1994, p. 145) that:

> "[although] ... one of the things I often have publicly said is that one of the things I most regret is not having returned to a criticism of Keynes's *Treatise* ... it is as much true of not having criticized Milton's *Positive Economics*, which in its way is quite as dangerous a book.

Although the comparison between the two books is strained, and even though Friedman's (1953) own explicitly stated methodological views are not, in themselves, defensible against Hayek, this statement does suffice to illustrate the seriousness of the matters at stake.

The main issue highlighted by these references taken together, is whether or not it is reasonable (as Hayek and others would insist) to attempt to derive propositions valid at the macroeconomic level simply by analogy to the microeconomics of what is after all only a *hypothetical* system of barter exchange between atomistic agents. The point that Hayek seems to be missing, as do many of the more recent writers deprecating macroeconomics as such, is that the concept of money itself, the need for credit creation to generate monetary profits, and the imperative under capitalism to reduce everything to valuation/calculation in monetary terms, are precisely what provides the element of "organic unity" to the system. This is what *necessitates* (let alone justifies) the basic approach of monetary macroeconomics (Fletcher, 1987, 2000, 2007; Simmel, 2005; Ingham, 2004). These methodological questions have been discussed in more detail in Smithin (2002b, 2004b, 2009a, 2011), and in Chapter 1 of this series.

As for Keynes's own theory, Ingrid Rima (1996, p. 495) rightly describes the Keynes/Post Keynesian model of aggregate demand and supply, drawn in *Z&D N* space, as representing "Keynes's aggregate demand and supply schedules". This is correct even though Keynes himself did not offer a graphical exposition. The graphs were due to the work of the later Post Keynesian writers, such as Davidson and Smolenksy (1964) and Weintraub (1961). There are also similar graphical and algebraic expositions of Keynes's theory in Chick (1983, pp. 62–81), Davidson (1994, pp. 18–29, 2011) and Patinkin (1976, pp. 83–94, 1982, pp. 123–153). Arguably the fields of macroeconomics and monetary economics would be much further ahead had this basic framework been more widely accepted as authoritative (Smithin, 2007b). Unfortunately, however, aggregate demand and supply (AD/AS) concepts have since evolved considerably and in divergent directions. The following argument therefore takes a more-or-less chronological approach starting with the original Keynesian model. It is shown that the issues first arising in that context have carried through to all the subsequent debates.

The Theory of "Effective Demand" (Keynes, 1936)

The monetary theory put forward in Keynes's best known work is often called the theory of "effective demand", and Chick (1983, p. 65) has made it clear that there is a distinction to be made between effective demand, as such, and aggregate demand. She writes, *"effective* demand, in contrast to aggregate demand, is not a schedule — it is the *point* on the schedule... which is 'made effective' by firms' production decisions". This means that the principle of effective demand is *missing* from the standard presentations of AD/AS analysis in most textbooks. Such constructs do have a (downward sloping) aggregate demand schedule, derived in its most basic form simply by re-arranging the equation of exchange from the quantity theory, $MV = PY$. However, in these models demand ultimately plays no role in determining output. The level of real GDP depends only on supply-side factors involving technology and the labour market (Chick, 2000, p. 124). The demand side residually determines the price level, but that is all.

In contrast Keynes's original supply and demand functions are *both* described as *upward sloping* in *Z&D, N* space, where Z is the "aggregate supply price of the output from employing N men", and N is the level of employment. The supply price represents "the expectation of proceeds which will just make it worth the while of the entrepreneurs to give that employment" and the relationship between Z and N is known as the "aggregate supply function". There is similarly an aggregate demand function, D, defined as the "proceeds... entrepreneurs expect to receive from the employment of N men" (Keynes, 1964/1936, pp. 23–25). In equilibrium, Z and D are equal, thus determining the amount of employment.

In the graphical version in Fig. 5.1, with nominal GDP, Z and D (PY in modern notation) on the vertical axis, and employment, N, on

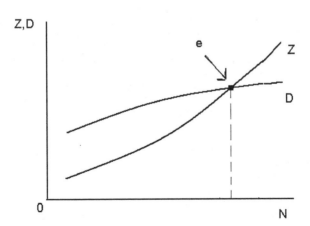

Fig. 5.1. The point of effective demand.

the horizontal axis, the Z function cuts the D function from below defining the point of effective demand at "e".

Inferences about the slopes of the demand and supply schedules can be re-constructed from the text of Chapter 3 of the *General Theory*, and on this basis, the underlying model may be written as follows:

$$D = D1 + D2, \qquad \text{(demand price)}, \qquad (5.1)$$

$$D1 = \chi(N), \quad 0 < \chi'(N) < 1, \qquad (D1 \text{ is a positive function}$$
$$\text{of employment)}, \qquad (5.2)$$

$$Z = PY, \qquad \text{(supply price)}, \qquad (5.3)$$

$$Y = Y(N), \quad Y'(N) > 0, \quad Y''(N) < 0, \quad \text{(production function)}, \quad (5.4)$$

$$W/P = Y'(N), \qquad \text{(real wage = marginal}$$
$$\text{product of labour)}, \qquad (5.5)$$

$$D = Z \qquad \text{(the point of effective}$$
$$\text{demand)}. \qquad (5.6)$$

As Davidson (1994, p. 33, 2011) points out, it is interesting that at this stage Keynes simply labeled the two demand categories $D1$ and $D2$, rather than the usual C and I for "consumption" and "investment" (purchases of physical capital equipment). This tends to suggest that the $D2$ category was important *primarily* because this was the portion of total demand that is *not* dependent on current employment or current income, rather than the idea that it might include "capital goods". Meanwhile $D1$ is simply the portion of demand that *is* dependent on current employment. All that Keynes really needed to do to break the classical "Say's Law" (that supply creates its own demand) is to assert the mere *existence* of the $D2$ category itself, regardless of what the spending in it is "for". From this point of view, it does not matter whether it is spent on physical capital equipment or anything else. Possibly the only reason that the first category, $D1$, became identified with consumption spending is simply an empirical judgment that, in fact, consumer spending is mainly dependent on current income. Meanwhile, investment spending, in the strict sense, is certainly a *candidate* to be one of the categories that might be determined by "something else", such as the "animal spirits" of the business community. However, the point is that it is not the *only* possible candidate.

Keynes was well aware that *any* type of additional spending would suffice as being part of $D2$ for the purposes of boosting aggregate demand.

For example, see the famous "banknotes in bottles" passage in the *GT* (1964/1936, pp. 129–130):

> It is curious how commonsense wriggling for escape from absurd conclusions, has been apt to reach for wholly "wasteful" forms of loan expenditure rather than for partly wasteful forms which ... tend to be judged on strict "business" principles ... the form of digging holes in the ground known as gold mining is the most acceptable of all solutions.
>
> If the Treasury were to fill old bottles with banknotes, bury them at suitable depths in disused coalmines ... and leave it to private enterprise on well tried principles of *laissez-faire* to dig the notes up again ... there need be no more unemployment and ... the real income of the community, and its capital wealth would probably become a good deal greater that it actually is. It would indeed be more sensible to build houses and the like; but if there are political or practical difficulties in the way of this, the above would be better than nothing.

Apart from this clear statement, however, unfortunately in both the *Treatise* and the *General Theory* there is also much (I would say far too much) discussion about the incentives for investment in physical capital goods and their relationship to an ill-defined concept of "saving". Keynes seems to forget that such categories would really only make sense in a Crusoe-type economy, where both savings and investments are literally quantities of physical goods. Keynes's "struggle to escape from old ideas" was incomplete in this sense, and did provide many openings for later reductionist and materialist critics. For now, however, we can simply note that if $D1$ is a function of N and $D2$ is not, then the overall *aggregate demand function* is similarly a function of N. Substituting (5.2) into (5.1):

$$D = f(N) = \chi(N) + D2. \qquad (5.7)$$

To derive the *aggregate supply function* consider Keynes's (1964/1936, p. 5) remarks that he accepts the "first postulate" of classical economics. This is the marginalist idea, that under competitive conditions, the real wage is equal to the marginal product of labour [Eq. (5.5)]. However he *rejects* the "second postulate" that the real wage is equal to the "marginal disutility of employment". The implication is that the level of employment determined by effective demand is a position *on* a conventional "labour demand" curve, but *off* the comparable conventional "labour supply curve" (Patinkin, 1982, pp. 133–137; Chick, 1983, pp. 72–74). Keynes also accepted the notion of the diminishing marginal productivity of labour [as in Eq. (5.4)]. Therefore, from Eqs. (5.3), (5.4) and (5.5), the Z or supply schedule emerges as an explicit function of N:

$$Z = PY = WY(N)/Y'(N). \tag{5.8}$$

Both the D and Z functions therefore, do have the positive slopes shown in Fig. 5.1. An increase in the autonomous component of aggregate demand, $D2$, will shift the D function, and the point of effective demand, to the right in the diagram, increasing the level of employment.

Aggregate Demand and Supply in "Wage Units"

The basic Keynesian theory can easily be expressed in real terms by deflating nominal values by the "wage unit" (Patinkin, 1982, pp. 129–130). The argument does *not* therefore depend on what mainstream economists would later call "money illusion". On the assumption of "homogenous labour" (Chick, 1983, pp. 68–69; Hicks, 2005/1967, p. 127), the wage unit can be identified with the nominal wage W. It is then possible to divide both the D and Z expressions through by the term W to determine real aggregate demand and supply in "wage units".

At this point Keynes does revert to the usual C and I notation (Keynes, 1964/1936, pp. 90, 115). This is therefore used in what follows (while, still keeping in mind the potentially misleading connotation of "investment"). Keynes also now makes real consumption C_W a direct function of Y_W (real income in wage units), rather than N. The total of real aggregate demand in wage units is therefore:

$$D_W = C(Y_W) + I_W. \tag{5.9}$$

Using Eqs. (5.3), (5.4) and (5.5), the Y_W term can be written as:

$$Y_W = Y(N)/Y'(N). \tag{5.10}$$

Therefore, the demand and supply (D_W and Z_W) functions, in wage units, are given by:

$$D_W = C(Y(N)/Y'(N)) + I_W, \tag{5.11}$$
$$Z_W = Y(N)/Y'(N). \tag{5.12}$$

To graphically illustrate the real demand and supply functions, it is convenient to use some (familiar) specific functional forms for the consumption and production function. For example, let $C(Y_W) = cY_W$, where c is the both the average and marginal "propensity to consume" ($0 < c < 1$), and

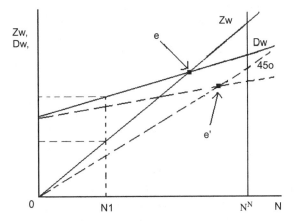

Fig. 5.2. Aggregate demand and supply in wage units.

let the production function (5.4) take the form $Y = A_0 N^\alpha$, with $0 < \alpha < 1$ (Patinkin, 1982, pp. 134–135). The slope of the supply function is then $1/\alpha$, which is greater than one and is also steeper than the slope of the demand function, c/α, as illustrated in Fig. 5.2.

Patinkin (1982, pp. 123–158) had three criticisms to make about the theory as reconstructed above, and although these are *not* the main issues that most earlier and later critics mainly focused on, it is worth elaborating on each of them here before the larger issues are discussed. The first of Patinkin's criticisms relates to Keynes's off-hand statement (1964/1936, p. 25) that, at the point of effective demand "the entrepreneur's expectation of profit will be maximized". As Patinkin correctly argues this is not literally true. There will be other positions in the diagram at which profit expectations are (absolutely) greater. Nonetheless, by analogy to the usual microeconomic supply/demand in textbooks, *e* is certainly the *market* equilibrium. Therefore, the incorrect wording of Keynes's passing statement does not invalidate the theory *per se*.

In a somewhat similar vein Patinkin (1982, pp. 144–150) also questions whether Keynes's published treatment is consistent with the marginalist approach to economic theory. This is because of the infamous footnote in which Keynes (1964/1936, p. 55) sets out the conditions for the supply curve to have a slope = 1. According to Patinkin, this shows that on at least one occasion Keynes identified supply "... not with the profit-maximizing supply curve ... but ... the $45°$ radius ... representing total variable costs" (Patinkin, 1982, p. 144). In Patinkin's view this apparent error in applying marginalist principles reflected a continuing influence of the method of Keynes's *Treatise on Money* (1930) on the exposition of the *General Theory*. This is probably fair comment from the point of view of doctrinal history. However, the issue of whether the macroeconomic supply curve is derived on marginal or average cost principles makes no difference, whatsoever, to the substance of the theory itself. If marginalism was "correctly" applied the equilibrium would simply be at (*e.g.*) e' rather than e. The issue does raise the question of whether or not Keynes made a serious *tactical* error in trying to introducing marginalist ideas into monetary macroeconomics in this way. It simply paved the way for exactly these types of discussion ever since, none of which, however, has any real meaning as far as actually providing an explanation of unemployment is concerned.

Patinkin's third criticism did involve what seems to be a more significant issue from the macroeconomic point of view. This is the question of whether the demand or the supply function should be regarded as genuinely embodying entrepreneurs' expectations. Keynes's definitions of D and Z above are ambiguous on this point. There are different views on this in the literature. Chick (1983, p. 63), for example, explicitly labels the D function as D^e (for expectations), whereas, according to Weintraub (1961, pp. 35–36) the demand function should represent "actual outlays", as opposed to the "expected outlays" shown along the supply function. Patinkin's (1982, pp. 126–127) argument was that there is a contradiction if (*e.g.*, at N_1), firms/entrepreneurs are held to simultaneously hold the two different "expectations of proceeds" suggested by the Z_W and D_W curves. His solution, like that of Weintraub, would be to take the supply function itself as genuinely embodying expectations, while the demand curve represents actual outcomes.

Patinkin concedes that each of these potential problems with Keynes's exposition could fairly easily be resolved by making the appropriate adjustments to the original narrative (Patinkin, 1982, p. 153). However, there still remain the two *main* points on which subsequent critics of Keynesian economics were led to dispute the theory.

The first of these has to do with the role (in the above set of equations, the *lack* of a role) for the rate of interest. There is a very revealing quote about this from Hayek (1995a, p. 162) in the course of a critique of Keynes's *Treatise on Money*. Hayek makes a remark to the effect that:

> I begin to wonder whether Mr. Keynes has ever reflected upon the function of rate of interest in a society in which there is no banking system.

An obvious retort to this is to similarly wonder whether Hayek, or other like-minded economists (then and now) have ever reflected on the function and meaning of the rate of interest *on money* in a system in which there is necessarily a banking system. However, Hayek's statement does clearly identify one of the two main issues in dispute.

By the time of the *General Theory* in fact, it is clear that Keynes intended to totally reject the classical/neoclassical theory of the determination of the real rate of interest (by the equality of real investment and real savings in a barter capital market), and to replace it with an entirely different monetary theory of the real rate of interest. From Keynes's point of view this would be a theory relevant to the *actual* capitalist system in which banking, money, and credit creation do play a decisive role. The issue of whether or not Keynes actually succeeded in doing this is a matter extensively discussed in other chapters.

In terms of the model of Eqs. (5.1)–(5.6) however, the strategy, was obviously to treat the term I_W as an exogenous magnitude in the first instance, and then to see how changes in this term would affect employment. At a later stage it would then be possible to discuss how interest rates themselves are determined and to add an explicit "investment function". Joan Robinson (1970) comments on Keynes's difficulty in getting his ideas across to the economics profession in the 1930s as follows: "(i)t would have been much simpler to start by assuming a constant rate of interest and a perfectly elastic supply of money". Remarkably, given Keynes's then status as "the most famous economist of our time" (Simons, 1936), the reason that this was *not* done (according to Robinson) was that "he had to make every possible concession to [the orthodox] point of view in order to get a hearing". Hicks (2005/1967, p. 133), in the famous IS/LM paper, did recognize the existence of what he called "Mr. Keynes's special theory", in which interest rates were determined otherwise than by the classical theory. Hicks even conceded that "a large part of the argument runs in terms of this system". Unfortunately however, he (Hicks) then obscured this vital point by his insistence (at the time) that the IS/LM system was the best description of the "general" as opposed to "special" Keynesian theory. It is reasonable to argue that Hicks, himself, in number of his later works (Hicks, 1982a, 1982c, 1989, 2005/1967) eventually accepted that this was misleading, but in the mid-1930s the damage was done. We return to a fuller discussion of the Hicksian IS/LM model later in the present essay. Finally, there is an interesting quote from Leijonhufvud (1981a, pp. 173–174) about the confusion over interest rates. According to Leijonhufvud debates about interest rate theory marked as a "critical fork in the road", for the economists who came after Keynes, and goes on to say that:

> ... Roberston turned back to a personal view ... Robinson and ... Kahn took the liquidity preference turn, soon to go beyond where Keynes left off ... the neoclassical Keynesians — going flat out in their brand new IS/LM machine ... failed to see any fork and ended up in the bog between the roads....

The reader of the present work will realize that this question has been identified throughout as one of the most important topics in monetary theory.

Aside from the interest rate issue, the other main threat to the credibility of Keynesian theory, in the eyes of orthodox economic theorists, was that as Keynes had admittedly introduced the "classical postulates" about the labour market, and also a general presumption that the economy studied operates under competitive conditions (Keynes, 1964/1936, pp. 5–7, 17–18), the question is bound to be asked why in effect one "postulate" is deemed to hold, and not the other. Keynes was quite happy to accept the first postulate (about the real wage being equal to the marginal productivity of labour), but rejected the second about the marginal (dis)utility of labour.

Therefore the critics could always argue, and always have argued, that Keynes's explanation for unemployment can only be some type of wage rigidity or stickiness that, in an economic downturn, prevents real wage adjustment as prices fall, and hence allows for so-called "involuntary unemployment" (Keynes, 1964/1936, p. 15). It has already been explained that this charge of an arbitrary assumption of rigid/sticky wages was exactly the grounds on which the Keynesian approach was dismissed as theoretically inadequate by textbooks later in the 20th century (Salant, 1985, p. 1180). It was the basis of the idea that there was "nothing new" in Keynes. Keynes certainly thought he was saying something new, but it also has to be said that the actual definition of *involuntary unemployment*[3] in Keynes (1964/1936, p. 15) does leave the distinct impression that failure of labour markets to "clear" is an important part of the explanation (Chick, 1983, pp. 72–74; Smithin, 1985, 2009a).

Keynes did simultaneously make the counter claim that "the ... character of the argument is precisely the same whether or not money-wages ... are liable to change" (Keynes, 1964/1936, p. 27) and contributed an entire chapter (Chapter 19 of the *General Theory*) on the effect of "changes

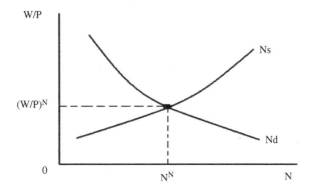

Fig. 5.3.   Equilibrium in the labour market in neoclassical economics.

in money wages" (Keynes, 1964/1936, pp. 257–279). However, turning to that chapter, it seems to do nothing more that bear out Patinkin's (1976, pp. 105–107) interpretation that it is a theory of sluggish adjustment/disequilibrium (Smithin, 1984, 1988). The whole terminology and set of concepts employed by Keynes were therefore unfortunate, because they seem to lead inexorably back to the baseline assumption in neoclassical economics of wage and price flexibility in perfect competition. If both of these assumptions hold, neoclassical economists would argue that the equilibrium level of employment and the real wage rate are determined *solely in the labour market*, as illustrated in Fig. 5.3,[4] and they cannot see how Keynes can escape this conclusion.

From this point of view, and translating the argument back into the $Z\&D$, N model, the point of effective demand can only be a "disequilibrium" situation. The ultimate equilibrium level of employment N^N (the "natural level" of employment) must be that pre-determined in the labour market. The argument be transferred into Z, N space just by drawing a vertical line at the level of employment N^N as in Fig. 5.4.

Figure 5.4 repeats the specific functional forms that were employed in Fig. 5.2, but now imposes the assumption of labour market "clearing" under competitive conditions. This picks out a unique level of employment along the Z curve at N^N ruling out any permanent influence from the principle of effective demand. On this view, if the economy ever does *temporarily* have a lower of level employment at the Keynesian point of effective demand e', this *by itself* will soon provoke the necessary adjustments (*e.g.*, falling wages) to quickly bring the economy back to N^N. Eventually the D curve

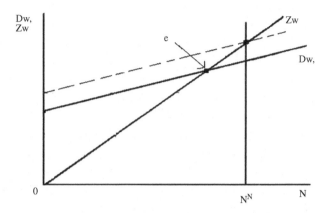

Fig. 5.4. The point of effective demand treated as a short-period disequilibrium.

would simply have to adjust to this given level of employment, as in "Say's Law", and as shown by the dotted line in Fig. 5.4.

Imperfect Competition

Kaldor (1983, pp. 11–15) argues that the key strategic error made by Keynes in all this was the attempt to combine the theory of effective demand with classical/neoclassical notion of perfect competition. Instead, the correct foundation for a theory of effective demand would be a generalized notion of *imperfect* competition at both the microeconomic and macroeconomic levels. According to Kaldor (1983, p. 14), "the acceptance of Marshallian microeconomics" on the part of Keynes was a mistake. This is because, in effect, the theory of perfect competition simply *assumes* that firms can sell all they like at the "going price". In Kaldor's view, on the contrary, "the very notion of production in the aggregate being limited by demand [should pre-suppose] a state of affairs in which the production of individual firms in industries of all kinds is limited by lack of orders and not by productive capacity... the individual producer faces a *limited* demand for his product — not an infinitely elastic demand... " (Kaldor, 1983, p. 11). Hence, the competitive marginalist condition should be replaced, either by:

$$P = [(\eta + 1)/\eta][W/Y'(N)], \tag{5.13}$$

or by a similar version involving average cost pricing. At the macro level, η is "the... [aggregate of] the elasticit[ies] of demand facing the individual producer[s]" (Kaldor, 1983, p. 17).

This idea of imperfect competition and limited demand at the individual firm level and the macro level does, in fact, turn out to be the crucial issue for the supply side of a "more general" theory of aggregate demand and supply. Although it seems astonishing that after the passage of so much time, and the publication of so much "scientific" economic research, the point is not more widely recognized, nonetheless it can be demonstrated that Keynes's theory of employment can, in this way, be rendered immune to the second of the two main charges traditionally levied against it.

If we can take it that the "representative" entrepreneur, or firm, perceives that it faces a downward-sloping demand curve at the microeconomic level, the same will be true at the macro level, by a simple process of summation (Kalecki, 1971a, pp. 44–49; Smithin, 2007b). Therefore, to derive the equivalent of Keynes's macroeconomic Z function in this context, first define the term k as:

$$k = [(\eta + 1)/\eta] \quad \text{(the mark-up)}. \tag{5.14}$$

The expression k is therefore effectively the average or aggregate mark-up over marginal cost. The next question to ask is how will this mark-up behave when overall level of aggregate demand increases? Suppose, for example, that:

$$k = k(Y), \quad k'(Y) < 0. \tag{5.15}$$

This suggests that if total aggregate demand does increase (as indexed by an increase in the level of GDP or Y) the representative producer expects to share in this. At the same time, however, as a result of the greater overall demand, the price elasticity of demand for each firm's own particular product would also be expected to increase. Therefore the mark-up k, both for the representative firm and in aggregate is expected to *fall*. The aggregate demand schedule continues to be determined by the same set of factors as before, but now the question is what will be the impact of the specification in (5.15) on Keynes's aggregate *supply* function.

The result is that there will be an upward-sloping relation between Y and N similar to Keynes's Z_W function, but, in this case, using the modern concept of real GDP. Note that from Eqs. (5.14) and (5.15):

$$W/P = Y'(N)/k(Y). \tag{5.16}$$

Then, invoke the inverse of what is usually called the labour supply function, such as $W/P = H(N)$, with $H'(N) > 0$. Note that this specification does not imply causality between labour supplied and the real wage (as in the usual discussion of the "second postulate"), but the opposite. The causality, goes from real wages to actual employment. Using this in (5.15) we obtain:

$$k(Y) = Y'(N)/H(N). \tag{5.17}$$

Totally differentiating:

$$dY/dN = [H(N)Y''(N) - Y'(N)H(N)]/[H(N)^2 k'(Y)] \quad (>0). \tag{5.18}$$

This is the slope of the supply (Z type) relationship between Y and N, which is again positive. However, now the upward slope does not depend *at all* on such things as labour market disequilibrium, rigid wages and so forth.

It remains now to bring back the aggregate demand function, but with the modern concept of real GDP rather than Keynes's D_W. This can be written simply as:

$$Y = C(Y) + I, \qquad C'(Y) > 0. \tag{5.19}$$

Substituting (5.5) into (5.19):

$$Y = C[F(N)] + I. \tag{5.20}$$

Then, totally differentiate this expression to find the slope:

$$dY/dN = C'[F(N)][F'(N)], \quad (>0). \tag{5.21}$$

The demand function is also a positively-sloped relation between Y and N. The reconstructed aggregate demand/supply model can then be graphed in Y, N space as shown in Fig. 5.5.

Just as Keynes said originally an increase in aggregate demand, shown as a shift outwards of the aggregate demand function will increase the level of employment. The equilibrium level of employment goes up from $N1$ to $N2$. However, this result cannot be overturned by the usual counter-arguments.

Looking at matters in this way, by stressing imperfect competition, would also rid the analysis of some of the obsolete concepts that Keynes did bring into the *General Theory* such as the distinction between "voluntary" and "involuntary" employment. This notion has caused endless difficulties of interpretation. However, in the case where the "representative firm" is facing a downward sloping demand curve, the distinction really has no concrete meaning. There is an expression superficially *resembling* a standard

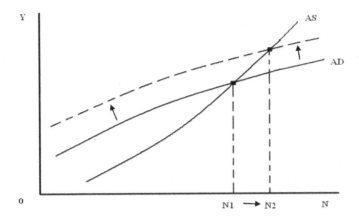

Fig. 5.5.   Reconstructed aggregate demand and supply functions in Y, N space.

labour supply function in the model, but it has been turned around to constitute a "wage curve", with the real wage rather than employment as the dependent variable (Smithin, 2009a, pp. 117–119, 2009c). Moreover, because of the binding demand constraint, the original level of employment could never have been claimed to be an "optimal" or preferred position.

Samuelson's "Keynesian Cross" (1948)

After Keynes, the next step in the evolution of AD/AS analysis was Samuelson's drastic over-simplification in the "Keynesian cross" diagram. This is "the familiar diagram which has served to translate the central message of the *General Theory* to generations of economics students" (Patinkin, 1982, p. 9). The aggregate demand function is still upward sloping, this time in E, Y (expenditure/income) space, and it can still be claimed that output is determined by effective demand. However, the role of aggregate supply is completely obscured. Keynes's aggregate supply function is replaced by the "45° line" illustrating the national income identity $E = Y$ (expenditure equals income). Therefore, the clear impression is given that *only* demand matters for the determination of output. Patinkin (1982, p. 152) does suggest that the 45° line *could* have been treated as a supply curve by assuming "... that every point... corresponds [on the 45° line] to a different real wage rate". However, he also goes on to say that "admittedly, it generally was not". The impact of Samuelson's work was therefore to severely simplify and weaken the Keynesian model by cutting out the supply-side entirely. In the context of a closed economy model, the expenditure side of the national accounts will come down to:

$$E = C + I + G. \tag{5.22}$$

Total spending E, is equal to consumption spending C, plus investment spending I, plus government spending, G. Also, the national income identity must hold by definition:

$$E = Y. \tag{5.23}$$

The next step in the construction of this elementary model is to add a consumption function along Keynesian lines that determines the level of consumption spending. Samuelson, in fact, made consumption depend upon "disposable income" $Y - T$ (income less taxes), which was not in Keynes. In this case, if the symbol c is allowed again to stand for the propensity to consume, the consumption function will be:

$$C = c(Y - T), \qquad 0 < c < 1. \tag{5.24}$$

Then, substitute Eqs. (5.24) and (5.23) into (5.22) to obtain:

$$Y = c(Y - T) + I + G. \tag{5.25}$$

The equilibrium solution for the level of real GDP is:

$$Y = [1/(1 - c)](I + G - cT). \tag{5.26}$$

Real GDP therefore depends positively on investment spending and government spending, and negatively on taxes. Figure 5.6 provides a graphical analysis of this theory of income determination. (This is the

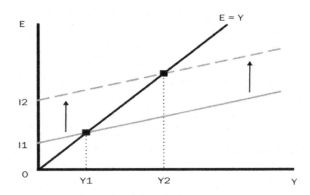

Fig. 5.6.   The "Keynesian cross" in a graphical version.

actual "Keynesian cross" diagram). The expenditure function is positively inclined, but with a slope less than one, and the 45° line has a slope equal to one. Output is determined by the intersection of the expenditure/demand function and the 45° line. If there is an increase in any one of the components of demand, such as an increase in government spending G, this will shift the expenditure function outward, and bring about an increase in real GDP (and presumably employment).

Another of the concepts that Samuelson took over from Keynes's *General Theory* was the notion of the "multiplier" that Keynes himself adapted from a famous article by Kahn (1931). This was the idea that a given increase of some component of demand, such as investment or government spending, would actually lead a larger increase in GDP than the original amount of spending, maybe several (multiple) times larger. The algebraic expressions for the investment multiplier, the government expenditure multiplier and the (negative) tax multiplier, in our version of Samuleson's model, are:

$$dY/dI = 1/(1-c), \quad > 0 \qquad (5.27)$$
$$dY/dG = 1/(1-c), \quad > 0 \qquad (5.28)$$
$$dY/dT = -c/(1-c), \quad < 0. \qquad (5.29)$$

Suppose, for example, that the propensity to consume out of disposable income is $c = 0.75$. This means that out of each dollar of disposable income 75c is spent, and 25c saved. In that case, the investment multiplier and the government expenditure multiplier would both be equal to four, and the (negative) tax multiplier, dY/dT, would be (-3). An increase in government of spending of one million dollars, for example, would supposedly increase GDP by four million dollars (a multiple of four), whereas a tax increase of one million dollars will *reduce* GDP by three millions.

As a word of caution note that the (so-called) multipliers in Eqs. (5.27)–(5.29) and thereafter in the entire textbook tradition following Samuelson, are "comparative static" concepts, whereas Kahn (1931) had originally envisaged something like a dynamic process analysis. However, this shift was inevitable given Keynes's own essentially static methodology.

One point that is obvious from looking at these "multiplier" results is that this version of Keynesian economics completely cuts across what was the conventional wisdom about the government budget (fiscal policy) before Keynes's time, and became so once again (following a hiatus of about 40 years), from the mid-1970s down to the present day. The traditional approach to "sound finance" is always to "balance" the government budget, to cover all government spending by taxation. A glance at the contemporary business and financial press in the modern era will immediately confirm that this is once again regarded as the norm or ideal (even if not always lived up to) today. However, the government spending multiplier and tax multiplier in Eqs. (5.28) and (5.29), taken separately or together, imply that this cherished conservative principle can be thrown out of the window. They seem to say both that an increase in government spending is a "good thing", and *also* that a cut in taxes is a "good thing". If the argument were widely accepted this might lead to both spending *increases* and tax *cuts* happening at the same time, and the figures for the public finances simply would not add up. In most periods of history, certainly including the present (and, ironically, even if the result was a booming economy) there would surely have been a "political outcry" about this.

In fact Samuelson, in 1948, was very well aware of the political ramifications of the multiplier analysis. This seems to be the reason he tried to go a step further than Keynes, in presenting the concept of the so-called "*balanced budget multiplier*". In retrospect this was nothing short of an attempt to justify an increase in government spending (and hence the size of government), *in and of itself* for its own sake, regardless of how the spending is financed, and the argument (which was *not* the original Keynesian argument), was in the long run to have disastrous consequences from both the political and the economic point of view.

The idea "floated" by Samuelson was that if an increase in government spending is financed dollar for dollar by an increase in taxation (so that the increment to the budget is balanced, in that sense) the positive effect of the increase in government spending is large enough to outweigh the negative effect of the increase in taxation, and will *still* cause the GDP to increase. To see the mathematical logic of Samuelson's argument, set $G = T$ in Eq. (5.26) to yield:

$$Y = [1/(1-c)](I + G - cG). \tag{5.30}$$

Then, work out the "multiplier" dY/dG again, on the balanced budget assumption. This is:

$$dY/dG = (1-c)/(1-c) = 1. \tag{5.31}$$

Therefore (in this particular example) the balanced budget multiplier is exactly equal to one. There is no actual "multiplying" effect, but nonetheless

(5.31) does still claim that an increase in government spending of $1,000,000 will "work" in the sense of increasing the GDP by the same amount (by $1,000,000). On this argument, "Keynesian economics" need *not* unbalance the budget, and what later came to be called a "tax and spend" strategy, while growing the overall size of government, will nonetheless reap benefits in terms of an increase in GDP. I have myself subscribed to this sort of proposition in the past (*e.g.*, Marterbauer and Smithin, 2000, 2003). However, later, in Smithin (2009a, pp. 184–188) I showed that the argument is *not* correct. This is because, as pointed out in Chapter 1, in order for profits to be "realized" and therefore for the economy to be able to grow at all, at least *one* of the economy's sectors *must* be running a deficit. There is no hint of this in Samuelson's balanced budget multiplier analysis. It is true that the sector in deficit does not *have* to be the government (in the closed economy case it could be private sector firms or domestic consumers, in the open economy the foreign sector). However, *if* the government itself is to have any positive impact on the economy it must also run a budget deficit.[4] A budget surplus would have a definite negative effect.

Would, therefore, *pace* Samuelson a balanced budget be simply neutral? Unfortunately, it would not. Samuelson's model completely ignores the supply side. When this is put back in and the effects of both spending and taxation on *each of* demand and supply are fully worked out, the balanced budget multiplier will actually come out *negative*. In terms of the history of economic thought the ultimate impact of Samuelson's interpretation was highly detrimental to the public understanding of what Keynesian economics was *really* all about. The implication was drawn by the public, and by the policy-makers themselves, that an outright "tax and spend" policy would always be beneficial for the economy. When this turns out not to be the case, the conclusion is drawn that it is somehow Keynes's analysis that is at fault. However, the original mistake was due to Samuelson. This issue is taken up in more detail and further discussed in Chapter 7.

The final question that seems reasonable to ask about Samuelson's model is how the "Keynesian cross" might be portrayed in an alternative "aggregate demand and supply diagram" in P, Y (price-output) space? The standard AD/AS presentation became an even more "familiar diagram to generations of students" over the years than the Keynesian cross itself.

In the Samuelson model in P, Y space the aggregate supply (AS) curve must be horizontal, at some "fixed" price level P_0. The aggregate demand (AD) curve, on the other hand, is simply a vertical line. AD does not

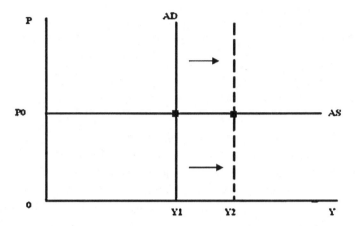

Fig. 5.7. Aggregate demand and supply in P, Y space in the simple Keynesian model.

depend on the price level at all, because real GDP is already determined solely on the demand side by Eq. (5.26). If something then occurs to cause real GDP to increase (an increase in investment spending or an increase government spending for example), this must be shown as a shift outwards of the vertical AD curve. A problem with putting things this way, however, is that it leaves the determination of prices and the inflation rate in the air.

In textbooks of the same genre as Samuelson this was usually covered by discussion of the so-called "inflationary gap" or "deflationary gap" that could be studied in the Keynesian cross diagram. However, this was never satisfactory, given that all discussion of supply side issues was eliminated from the analysis. It was left to the later post-Keynesians to add an account of what might actually determine the price level, and also what can cause it to change. These issues are taken up in more detail in the next section.

Cost-Push and Conflict Inflation

According to Joan Robinson (1979, p. xix) in addition to the theory of effective demand:

> "one of the most important insights of the Keynesian revolution was ... that the general level of prices in an industrial economy is determined by the general level of costs, and the main influence upon costs is to be found in the relation between the money-wage rate and the output per unit of employment".

So, this is what Robinson proposes that the missing theory of prices should be. The idea was to add a cost-push, or wage-push, theory of inflation to the idea that the level of demand determines output (Weintraub, 1958). To illustrate, suppose for simplicity that prices are a mark-up over average costs, both at the individual firm level, and in the aggregate. If wages are the most important cost factor, as implied in the quote from Robinson, this gives rise to the aggregative expression:

$$P = kWN/Y, \tag{5.32}$$

where P is the price level, k is the average/aggregate mark-up, WN is the nominal wage bill, and Y is the level of real GDP. Average labour productivity can then be defined as:

$$A = Y/N. \tag{5.33}$$

Substituting (5.32) into (5.33), taking logs and differentiating with respect to time:

$$\dot{P}/P = \dot{k}/k + \dot{W}/W - \dot{A}/A. \tag{5.34}$$

Although it was shown earlier that the mark-up is, in principle, an endogenous variable (it can change), in the cost-push literature its *rate of change* was taken to be zero, so that $\dot{k}/k = 0$ (presumably the mark-up is *not*, in fact, changing in every period at a constant rate). Equation (5.34) therefore reduces to:

$$\dot{P}/P = \dot{W}/W - \dot{A}/A. \tag{5.35}$$

So, the basic idea, according to wage push or cost-push theory, is that inflation is determined by the rate of change of nominal wages (the main cost factor) less the rate of growth of labour productivity. An important point that should now be made is that the whole notion of cost-push inflation relies heavily on the idea of endogenous money, identified earlier as one the key debating points in monetary economics. To see this, bring back the simple equation of exchange from the quantity theory of money, which in this context now reverts to a tautology:

$$MV = PY, \tag{5.36}$$

where M is the nominal supply of money, and V is the velocity of circulation. Taking logs and differentiating with respect to time:

$$\dot{M}/M + \dot{V}/V = \dot{P}/P + \dot{Y}/Y. \tag{5.37}$$

For simplicity set the rate of change of velocity at zero, so that $\dot{V}/V = 0$. Then combining Eqs. (5.37) and (5.37), we arrive at:

$$\dot{M}/M = \dot{W}/W + \dot{N}/N. \tag{5.38}$$

Equation (5.38) shows that the money supply is increasing endogenously at the same rate as the nominal wage bill. In the aggregate firms are (effectively) borrowing the nominal wage bill from the banking system. This simultaneously increases the supply of money on the liabilities side of commercial bank balance sheets, and then feeds through into the inflation rate.

However, there remains one loose end in the argument for the generic wage/cost-push model, concerning the motivation for the ongoing *nominal* wage push. It does not seem to be very convincing just to assume an exogenously given rate of increase in nominal wages. Surely workers are interested primarily in real wages? The motivation for asking for an increase in nominal wages must, at least, be the hope that this will be a lasting increase, *relative* to prices, and will not be completely offset by an increase in inflation as soon as it has occurred.

This sort of insight leads on to another version of the cost-push argument that has sometimes been called "conflict inflation" (Rowthorn, 1977; Lavoie, 1992, 2007; Smithin, 2009a, 2012). In this argument inflation is caused by, or is a spill-over from, conflict over real income shares. By way of illustration, suppose that wage bargainers have a target real wage in mind, and that they will therefore always ask for a nominal wage increase sufficient to compensate for price level increase in the previous period. In this case:

$$(W/P)_0 = W/P_{-1}. \tag{5.39}$$

If workers want to improve their relative position therefore, rather than just maintaining it, they must try to increase the value of the target wage $(W/P)_0$ itself. From (5.39) we can see that the nominal wage rate will then be given by:

$$W = [(W/P)_0]/P_{-1}. \tag{5.40}$$

Then using (5.40) and (5.33) in (5.32), and taking logs:

$$p = k + w_0 - a, \tag{5.41}$$

where $a = \ln A$, $p = \ln P - \ln P_{-1} = \dot{P}/P$, and $w_0 = \ln(W/P)_0$. The inflation rate, p, increases if either the mark-up or target real wage increases, and

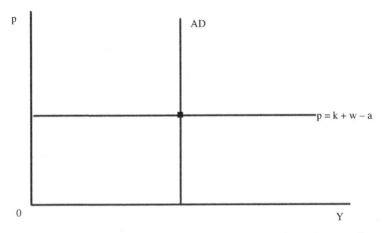

Fig. 5.8. Aggregate demand and supply in p, Y space for a "post-Keynesian" conflict inflation model.

falls if productivity increases. With this new inflation equation it becomes possible to graph the AD/AS model in inflation/output space rather than price/output space. The AD curve is still a vertical line, and the inflation rate is given simply by the horizontal line defined in Eq. (5.36).

An important point to notice about the conflict inflation analysis is that if firms want to increase the mark-up k now, or workers want to increase the target real wage w_0 now, and then simply *maintain* that same situation in the future, this will nonetheless lead to a permanent increase in inflation. The inflation will continue even if neither group aims for further increases in their real share but only want to maintain the new higher (relative) level. Essentially the *same* conflict over real incomes is repeated every period. Therefore, a once-for-all increase in either the mark-up or the profit share causes an increase in the inflation rate now and continuing in future. A once-for-all increase in average labour productivity will allow the inflation rate to fall, given the existing profit share and real wage rate, as in this situation, there are more goods available for all and therefore less reason for conflict.

Hicks's IS/LM Model (1937)

Hicks's famous paper interpreting Keynes was published in 1937, nine years before Samuelson's influential textbook, but during the years when the (sup-posedly) Keynesian influence was at its strongest in academia, it was usually dealt with from the student's point of view only *after* the Keynesian cross formulation. Hicks's model was regarded as the more "advanced" economics.

The main point of the IS/LM exercise was to discuss the other main issue about which Keynes had been criticized by mainstream economists, the theory of interest rates. Even though IS/LM was a more advanced treatment than the Keynesian cross in this sense, it still did *not* take up issues of inflation or the price level. In the form that it entered the public domain it relied heavily and explicitly on the "fix-price" assumption (as Hicks himself later called it). The original 1937 article actually held the nominal wage rate constant but, in practice, this amounts to much the same thing as holding the price level constant.[5] An underlying assumption of the generic IS/LM model is therefore, once again, that:

$$P = P_0. \tag{5.42}$$

The aggregate price level is taken to be fixed or "stuck" at the level P_0, and the model cannot explain how the price level or inflation rate in determined (except by bringing back some of the ideas about cost-push, discussed in the previous section).

As far the rate of interest itself is concerned, Hicks's idea of a "general theory" in 1937 was to somehow "reconcile" the classical investment/savings theory and the Keynesian liquidity preference theory. In hindsight, however, this attempted reconciliation turned out to be a highly confusing exercise. Rather than to attempt to integrate two incompatible (and ultimately unsuccessful) theories, it would have been better to replace *both* of them with a workable "monetary theory of the real rate of interest", that could take its proper place in the Keynesian scheme. It is true that Hicks could certainly point to material in the *General Theory*, which Keynes himself had written, that might provide justification for the attempt at a synthetic theory. The main source was the material in Chapter 15 of the GT (Keynes, 1964/1936, pp. 199–204). It is only fair to point out, however, that many years later, after having completed much more of his own highly innovative work in monetary theory, Hicks did finally come to see that something like what he had originally called Keynes's "special theory" might have been more to the point. As he put it, "(o)ne is driven back in the end (or what has so far has been the end) from Keynes to Wicksell" (Hicks, 1982a, p. 237). Even this statement, however, is slightly ambiguous. Wicksell did understand that monetary policy operates by the central bank setting the base level of interest rates. But, recall that there were always *two* interest rates in Wicksell that also had to be "reconciled", the policy rate and the natural rate. So, does Hicks mean to keep the idea of a "natural rate" of interest or not? It can be argued that Hicks was still "hedging his bets" to some extent, even with the above statement (Smithin, 1991).

At the time when the IS/LM model first appeared, the discussion was not so much about different types of interest rate, but more of a concern that the *same* interest rate had to do two jobs. The idea was that there should be a single equilibrium rate consistent with both "investment equals savings" in the real goods market and "money demand equals money supply" in the money market. What this rate has to be can be discovered by noticing that in each "market" there is a separate relationship between interest rates and income each of which must be satisfied. Putting the two schedules together, it can then be determined what the equilibrium level of the interest rate (the one that is "doing both jobs") must be.

The slope of the IS (investment/saving) curve[6] can be derived from the following three equations. The first of these is the national income identity:

$$Y = C + I + G. \tag{5.43}$$

Next, add a consumption function depending on disposable income, this time in a general functional form:

$$C = C(Y - T), \qquad 0 < C_Y < 1. \tag{5.44}$$

Finally specify an investment function which makes the level of investment depend negatively on the real rate of interest, such as:

$$I = I(r), \qquad I_r < 0. \tag{5.45}$$

Substituting (5.45) and (5.44) into (5.43) we have:

$$Y = C(Y - T) + I(r) + G. \tag{5.46}$$

Equation (5.46) is the basis of the IS relationship between interest rates and income (although it is usually graphed the other way round, with the real interest rate on the vertical axis and income on the horizontal). To obtain the slope of the IS curve totally differentiate (5.46) to yield:

$$dY = C_Y(dY - dT) + I_r dr + dG. \tag{5.47}$$

Then, the slope dr/dY can be worked out by setting changes in the exogenous variables to zero ($dG = dT = 0$):

$$dr/dY = (1 - C_Y)/I_r, \qquad < 0. \tag{5.48}$$

The IS curve is therefore negatively sloped.

The LM curve, meanwhile, will turn out to be positively sloped and the main reason for this is the assumption of a fixed (exogenous) supply of money. The money supply is "given" at the nominal level M, so that:

$$M^s = M. \tag{5.49}$$

Next, add the type of money demand function widely used by both "Keynesians" and "monetarists" in the mid-20th century (which Hicks had taken from Chapter 15 of the *General Theory*). This would be something like:

$$M^d/P = L(Y, i), \qquad L_y > 0, \; L_i < 0. \tag{5.50}$$

Equilibrium in the "money market" is given by:

$$M^d = M^s. \tag{5.51}$$

Then, from Eqs. (5.49), (5.50), and (5.51) the equation for the LM curve is simply:

$$M/P = L(Y, i). \tag{5.52}$$

In all of the mid-20th century literature, money was assumed to be non-interest-bearing and the i term is supposed to stand for the *nominal* interest rate. Therefore, as it stands, there would be a problem in reconciling the inverse IS curve in Eq. (5.46), which depends on the real interest rate, with the LM curve in Eq. (5.52) that depends on the nominal rate. Recall, however, that the price level in the IS/LM model is supposed to be fixed. Therefore, both the actual and the expected inflation rate must be zero. As $p^e = p = 0$ and $i = r + p^e$, then $i = r$, so the IS and LM curves *can* be reconciled. Equation (5.52) becomes:

$$M/P = L(Y, r). \tag{5.53}$$

Next, totally differentiate (5.53) with $dP = 0$ (and "normalizing" the price level itself at $P = 1$), to yield:

$$dM = L_Y dY + L_i dr. \tag{5.54}$$

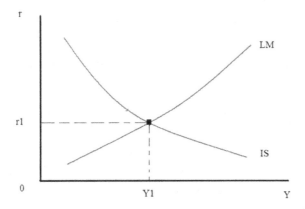

Fig. 5.9.   The IS/LM model in graphical form.

As the money supply is fixed, $dM = 0$ and the slope of LM curve is:

$$dr/dY = -L_Y/L_i. \tag{5.55}$$

The LM curve can therefore be represented as positively-sloped in r, Y space and confronted with the IS curve in a simple graphical model. It is this model that is supposed to determine both the real rate of interest and the level of income. Although this does give a solution with a unique interest rate consistent with equilibrium in both the goods market and the money market, notice that the deeper issues of interest rate theory, (particularly the vital question of whether there should be a "real theory of the real rate of interest" or a "monetary theory of the real rate of interest") are totally elided. The IS/LM model can be used to argue that *both* monetary and real factors are involved. This, confuses, rather than clarifies, one of the key issues in dispute in monetary economics. By the time of the early 21st century the IS/LM model itself was no longer fashionable, but it is fair to say that its legacy, to intensify the underlying confusion about the nature of interest rates, remains.

In the IS/LM context changes in the "equilibrium" levels of the real interest rate and output are explained by shift of either the IS curve or the LM curve. To see how changes in government policy variables, in particular, affect output and real interest rates in IS/LM, use (5.46) and (5.52) and totally differentiate to obtain:

$$(1 - C_Y)dY - I_r dr = dG - C_Y dT, \tag{5.56}$$

$$L_Y dY + L_i dr = dM. \tag{5.57}$$

In matrix form, the system can be written as:

$$\begin{vmatrix} (1 - C_Y) & -I_r \\ L_Y & L_i \end{vmatrix} \begin{vmatrix} dY \\ dr \end{vmatrix} = \begin{vmatrix} 1 & -C_Y & 0 \\ 0 & 0 & 1 \end{vmatrix} \begin{vmatrix} dG \\ dT \\ dM \end{vmatrix}. \tag{5.58}$$

Then solve using Cramer's Rule (Chiang and Wainwright, 2005, pp. 103–107). The results are:

$$dY/dG = I_r L_Y / [L_i(1 - C_Y) + I_r], \qquad > 0 \tag{5.59}$$

$$dr/dG = -L_Y / [L_i(1 - C_Y) + I_r], \qquad > 0 \tag{5.60}$$

$$dY/dT = -C_Y L_i / [L_i(1 - C_Y) + I_r], \qquad < 0 \tag{5.61}$$

$$dr/dT = C_Y L_Y / [L_i(1 - C_Y) + I_r], \qquad < 0 \tag{5.62}$$

$$dY/dM = I_r / [L_i(1 - C_Y) + I_r], \qquad > 0 \tag{5.63}$$

$$dr/dM = (1 - C_Y) / [L_i(1 - C_Y) + I_r], \qquad < 0. \tag{5.64}$$

These results make the claim that an increase in government spending will increase the level of output and at the same time increase the real rate of interest, but not by enough to cause so-called "complete crowding out". The same holds true for a cut in taxes. An increase in the nominal supply of money will increase real GDP, but reduce real interest rates. For a long time, in the mid-20th century, these were thought to be the "reasonable" assumptions about the effects of monetary and fiscal policy by mainstream economic opinion (and perhaps still are today in some quarters). However, it is clear that none of them are really secure, because of the fix-price assumption and the confusion that reigns about the theory of interest rates and of the supply of money.

A final question to ask about the closed economy IS/LM model is how this might be translated into the later (and more familiar) textbook AD/AS model in P, Y space, (as done was earlier with the Keynesian cross formulation). The AS curve will clearly again be a horizontal line at the price level P_0, as in all pseudo-Keynesian models operating on the fixed-price assumption. To discover what the aggregate demand curve looks like it is necessary to carry a "thought experiment" to see what might happen *if* prices were allowed to change, even though (as already said), they will *not* be allowed to change when the model is actually used.

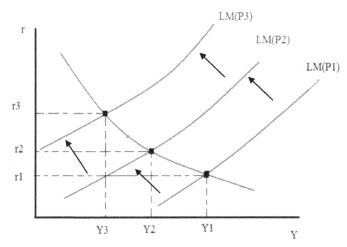

Fig. 5.10. A "thought experiment" in the IS/LM model considering different aggregate price levels.

Let there be a hypothetical increase in the price level. For example, what would be the consequences of letting the price level rise first to P_1, then to P_2, and then to P_3, in the diagram in Fig. 5.10? Each of these increases in P would reduce the real money supply, M/P, as the nominal money supply, M, is fixed. Therefore the LM curve shifts back and to the left, putting upward pressure on real interest rates. Increases in real interest rates then, in turn, reduce the demand for real goods and services at each price level.

Next graph the resulting combinations of price levels and interest rates as in Fig. 5.11. This traces out a notional aggregate demand curve downward-sloping in P, Y space. Following on from this the AD curve, just derived, can then be confronted with a horizontal line for the AS curve reflecting the (actual) assumption that price are fixed at $P = P_0$.

This step completes the translation of the overall Hicksian IS/LM model into the more familiar P, Y space of the intermediate level textbooks. In Fig. 5.12, anything that shifts the IS curve outwards will also shift the aggregate demand curve outwards, and *vice versa*. Similarly anything that shifts the LM curve outwards (inwards), also increases (decreases) aggregate demand. For example, the increase in output in Fig. 5.12 could be caused by any of an increase in government spending, a *reduction* in taxes, *or* an increase in the money supply.

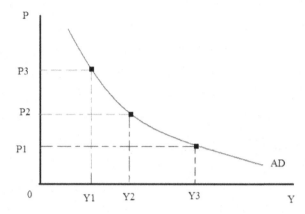

Fig. 5.11.   The aggregate demand curve as derived from the IS/LM model.

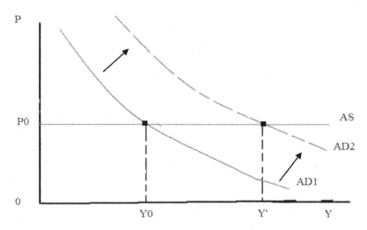

Fig. 5.12.   An aggregate demand and supply representation of the IS/LM model.

The Mundell–Fleming Model (1963)

The Mundell–Fleming model of the 1960s, named for Mundell (1963b) and
Fleming (1963) was simply an extension of the fixed-price IS/LM model to
the open economy. From what has been written so far it must be clear to
the reader that by this time (the 1960s) whatever was being called "Keynesian economics" in the academic mainstream had deviated very far from
anything to do with John Maynard Keynes. Nonetheless, the IS/LM framework *was* regarded as a "Keynesian" model by the orthodox academy, and

therefore the Mundell–Fleming model was similarly regarded as the application of Keynesian economics to the open economy.

Mundell and Fleming had both argued that in a small open economy, with "perfect capital mobility", interest rates would have always to revert to the "world" or "global" level. Otherwise, or so it was argued, there would be no hope that the domestic balance of payments (BOP) position could ever be in equilibrium. There would be massive capital inflow or capital outflow as soon as the domestic interest rate deviated slightly, either upwards or downwards. The impact of this assumption is to neatly remove the problem of interest rate determination from the open economy model. (Even though this had been as one of the *main* problems in the closed economy version of the IS/LM model.) The assumption is:

$$r = r^*, \tag{5.65}$$

where r^* is the "world" or "foreign" interest rate. Simply put, Eq. (5.61), which known as the "BOP curve", is just a horizontal line in r, Y space. Next, the IS curve itself must be modified in the international setting to take account the role of net exports in the breakdown of total aggregate demand. The GDP identity for the open economy is:

$$Y = C + I + G + NX, \tag{5.66}$$

where $NX = X - IM$ (net exports). The real exchange rate continues to be denoted by $Q = EP^*/P$, where E is the nominal exchange rate, (the domestic currency price of one unit of foreign exchange), P^* is the foreign price level, and P is the domestic price level.

A general functional form for the IS curve in an open economy might therefore be:

$$Y = C(Y - T) + I(r) + G + NX(Q), \qquad NX_Q < 0. \tag{5.67}$$

The last term in (5.67) states that a fall (rise) in the real exchange rate, Q, will tend to increase (decrease) net exports and increases (decreases) total aggregate demand for domestic goods. The depreciation (appreciation) makes domestic goods relatively cheaper (more expensive).

Having defined the BOP and IS curves for the open economy note that the LM curve would remain as previously derived in Eq. (5.49). The equilibrium of the three schedules IS, LM and BOP, can be then depicted graphically as in Fig. 5.13. The IS/LM/BOP construct shows possible combinations of "solutions" for the levels of interest rates and real GDP that

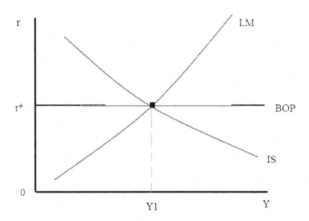

Fig. 5.13.   Equilibrium in the Mundell–Fleming model.

would ensure both "internal equilibrium" (investment/ savings balance) and "external equilibrium" (equilibrium in the balance of payments).

As in the original IS/LM model the Mundell–Fleming model continued (unrealistically) to assume fixed prices, now including both the foreign and domestic price levels, so both may be "normalized" at $P = P^* = 1$. In algebraic terms the Mundell–Fleming model therefore reduces to two equations only:

$$Y = C(Y - T) + I(r^*) + G + NX(E), \qquad (5.68)$$

$$M = L(Y, r^*). \qquad (5.69)$$

Totally differentiating:

$$dY = C_Y D_Y - C_Y dT + I_r dr^* + dG + NX_Q dE, \qquad (5.70)$$

$$dM = L_Y dY + I_r dr^*. \qquad (5.71)$$

If world interest rates themselves are not changing, this can be simplified further by writing $dr^* = 0$.

There have been a number of simplifying assumptions, so far, but in the open economy context there is also at least one one inevitable complexity that must be faced. This is that there are always at least two types of exchange rate "regime" to be considered. The nominal exchange rate may be "floating" (also known as a "flexible" exchange rate) in which case E is an endogenous variable. Or, it may be "fixed", in which case the assumption is that $dE = 0$. For the *flexible exchange rate* case, the model in matrix form is:

$$\begin{vmatrix} (1 - C_Y) & -NX_Q \\ L_Y & 0 \end{vmatrix} \begin{vmatrix} dY \\ dE \end{vmatrix} = \begin{vmatrix} 1 & -C_Y & 0 \\ 0 & 0 & 1 \end{vmatrix} \begin{vmatrix} dG \\ dT \\ dM \end{vmatrix}. \tag{5.72}$$

Solving by Cramer's rule, the results are:

$$dY/dG = 0, \tag{5.73}$$

$$dY/dT = 0, \tag{5.74}$$

$$dY/dM = NX_Q/NX_Q L_Y, \qquad > 0 \tag{5.75}$$

$$dE/dG = -1/NX_Q, \qquad > 0 \tag{5.76}$$

$$dE/dT = C_Y/NX_Q, \qquad < 0 \tag{5.77}$$

$$dE/dM = (1 - C_Y)/L_Y NX_Q, \quad < 0. \tag{5.78}$$

Under flexible exchange rates the government expenditure and tax multipliers are equal to zero, but an increase in the money supply will be "effective" in increasing real GDP (in the short run). While having no effect on output, an increase in government spending or a cut in taxes, will cause the nominal exchange rate to appreciate (with prices fixed this also means a *real* exchange rate appreciation) whereas an expansionary monetary policy will cause an exchange rate depreciation. Overall, these findings have been interpreted as showing that fiscal policy is *not* effective in changing output and employment in a regime with flexible exchange rates, but that monetary policy does seem to "work". So, the general impression that was created by professional economists (certainly at the time in the 1960s and 1970s) was that supposed "monetarists" should favour floating exchange rates, whereas so-called "Keynesians" should be against rates. It cannot be emphasized too strongly that this is *not* at all a valid interpretation, for reasons already explained in other chapters, and Chapter 8. However, such reasoning, essentially based only on the Mundell–Fleming model, has unfortunately been influential.

In a graphical interpretation of the flexible exchange rate case, the results for fiscal policy can be shown by an outward shift of the IS curve, starting from point "A" in Fig. 5.14. The IS shift puts upward pressure on interest rates (the central bank is paying attention only to the exchange rate, not the interest rate) thereby making the domestic interest rate temporarily/fleetingly higher than interest rates in the rest of the world, as at point "B". However, this is supposed, will cause immediate "capital

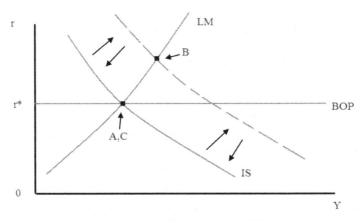

Fig. 5.14.   Fiscal policy "does not work" in the Mundell–Fleming model with flexible exchange rates and fixed prices.

inflow" to the domestic economy, and the situation at point "B" cannot be sustained. The currency will appreciate, the exports of the domestic economy will become "uncompetitive", and net exports will fall. The IS curve will shift back again, and the only stop to this process is when it has shifted all the way *back* to the original position at "A, C". The basic argument is that if the exchange rate is floating, any attempt to increase demand by fiscal policy will always be offset by an appreciating currency, and a fall in net exports.

The case of an expansionary monetary policy, again starting from point "A" is illustrated in Fig. 5.15. In this case, the increase in the money supply shifts the LM curve outwards to the right, and the effect is to temporarily *reduce* interest rates at point "B". The lower interest rates will cause capital outflow (funds will leave the country) and the nominal exchange rate falls (depreciates). With prices fixed both at home and abroad this is also a depreciation of the real exchange rate. Net exports will increase, meaning that total aggregate demand for domestic goods and services also increases, and the IS curve shifts in an outward direction, reinforcing the original LM shift. The process will only stop when interest rates have returned to "normal" (the world level, r^*) at point "C". Although interest rates have not finally changed there is a higher level of output than there was to start with. The monetary policy has "worked" by depreciating the currency.

In the *fixed exchange rate* case, by definition no depreciation of the currency will be allowed. The central bank will intervene in the foreign

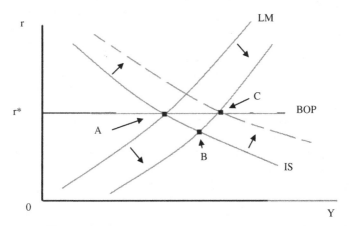

Fig. 5.15. Monetary policy "works" in the Mundell–Fleming model with flexible exchange rates and fixed prices.

exchange markets, buying and selling their own currency as required. According to the Mundell–Fleming model the implication of this is that the results just discussed will be entirely reversed. The model in matrix form becomes:

$$\begin{vmatrix} (1 - C_Y) & 0 \\ -L_Y & 1 \end{vmatrix} \begin{vmatrix} dY \\ dM \end{vmatrix} = \begin{vmatrix} 1 & -C_Y & NX_Q \\ 0 & 0 & 0 \end{vmatrix} \begin{vmatrix} dG \\ dT \\ dE \end{vmatrix}. \qquad (5.79)$$

The results are:

$$dY/dG = 1/(1 - C_Y), \qquad > 0 \qquad (5.80)$$
$$dY/dT = -C_Y/(1 - C_Y), \qquad < 0 \qquad (5.81)$$
$$dY/dE = NX_Q/(1 - C_Y), \qquad < 0 \qquad (5.82)$$
$$dM/dG = L_Y/(1 - C_Y), \qquad > 0 \qquad (5.83)$$
$$dM/dT = -C_Y L_Y(1 - C_Y), \qquad < 0 \qquad (5.84)$$
$$dM/dE = NX_Q L_Y/(1 - C_Y), \qquad < 0. \qquad (5.85)$$

The money supply is now an endogenous variable and the nominal exchange rate is exogenous (fixed). However, this does not mean that the construct involves a genuine endogenous *money* theory. In such a theory, the money supply would always have to be endogenous (rising and falling with the volume of bank loans) regardless of the exchange rate regime.

Even though the exchange rate is now fixed for most of the time, it, of course, remains possible for the monetary authorities to arbitrarily "devalue" or revalue" the currency at periodic intervals simply by policy choice. According to Eq. (5.82) therefore, in what would have been regarded as "heresy" at the time of classical economics, a devaluation of the exchange rate (a deliberate weakening of the currency) would actually be *good* for the economy. It would increase the money supply and increase the level of output and employment.

As compared with the flexible exchange rate regime the main lesson that was drawn from the second set of exercises is the (misguided) idea that, when the exchange rate is *fixed*, fiscal policy "works", and monetary policy "does not work". In reality, no policies "work" in the fixed rate case. The case of an expansionary fiscal policy, however, according to the theory, is shown again in Fig. 5.16. As before, the IS curve shifts out and to the right, temporarily putting upward temporary upward pressure on interest rates. This again causes capital inflow to the domestic economy, but, as the nominal exchange rate is now supposed to be held fixed, the currency cannot be allowed to appreciate. Instead, there will be an inflow of foreign exchanges reserves as the central bank will sell its own currency, to prevent the appreciation. As a result the domestic money supply will increase and the LM curve shifts out to the right. The final equilibrium will find the domestic economy with interest rates back at "world" levels, but with a higher level of output.

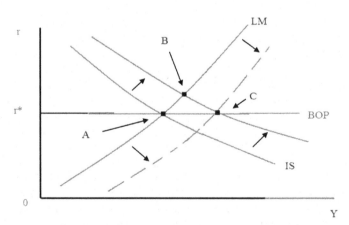

Fig. 5.16.   Fiscal policy "works" in the Mundell–Fleming model with fixed exchange rates and fixed prices.

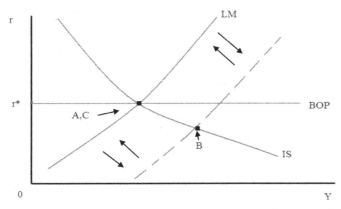

Fig. 5.17. Monetary policy "does not work" in the Mundell–Fleming model with fixed exchange rates.

Monetary policy however does not "work" in the fixed exchange rate case. As shown in Fig. 5.17, as expansionary policy, for example, intially tends to push interest rates down. But, as the exchange rate is not allowed to fall, the fall in interest rates means a sell-off of foreign exchange reserves, which forces the domestic money supply back down to its original level. The LM curve is pushed back to its original position, and no increase in output occurs.

The overall message conveyed by the Mundell–Fleming model was that fiscal policy (supposedly the characteristically Keynesian choice) could be used as a policy option when exchange rates are fixed, but could not under floating exchanges rates. The opposite was thought to be true for monetary policy. As already emphasized this fitted in to some extent with popular (mis)understandings of what "Keynesians" and "monetarists" were supposed to believe in the 1960s, 1970s and 1980s. In the final analysis, however, these results were of no *practical* use to economists of any ideological stripe, in thinking about exchange rate policy.

There are two problems with the theory which more than justify this statement. First, once again the treatment of interest rates is clearly deficient. It amounts to merely assuming that a "natural rate" exists once again, now at the global level. There is no discussion of the "currency risk premium" (Smithin, 2002/2003, 2003, pp. 165–169), that must apply to on domestic interest rates for any jurisdiction that has a *separate* national currency which could, in principle, change. Second, in the world of mainstream economics it should never, in any event, have been admitted that *either* monetary or fiscal policy could having any significant impact on the economy (regardless of the nature of the exchange rate regime). The only reason that either of them had any effect in the Mundell–Fleming model was the short-run fix-price assumption (wrongly taken as "Keynesian"). In principle, orthodox economists should have been arguing that all of macroeconomic policy is just supposed to boil down to (a) controlling the inflation rate and (b) balancing the budget. However, if those are indeed the objectives, it would be possible make a case (on those grounds) *either* for a flexible rate or a fixed exchange rate. To see this it is necessary only to remember the arguments that were actually made, rightly or wrongly, *in favour* of such arrangements as (*e.g.*) the gold standard in the 19th century or the European "single currency" in the 21st century.

A more common-sense attitude from a more genuinely Keynesian point of view, on the other hand, is surely to argue that to advocate *any* kind of activist policy, monetary or fiscal, does require the necessary "degrees of freedom" for the relevant authorities to be able to carry out their decisions (Smithin and Wolf, 1993; Smithin, 1994, 2003). Therefore, policy activism should imply flexible exchange rates. At the level of basic principle, fixing an exchange rate must definitively reduce the ability for any jurisdiction to pursue any type of policy (monetary or fiscal) that differs from their partners. (This is because it has already been decided, in effect, that everything must be focused on just the one objective of preserving the exchange rate.) If, on the contrary, it is argued or believed that any type of activist policy is possible, at all, a floating rate logically allows more scope for the pursuit of such polices. These important issues are taken up and discussed further in Chapter 8.

Conclusion

Davidson (2009, pp. 161–173) adds an Appendix to his recent book *The Keynes Solution* entitled: "Why Keynes's ideas were never taught in American universities". (Moreover, in the relevant period, if they were not taught in the US universities, they would not have been taught anywhere else either.) The above discussion has gone some way to explain why this was so.

Part of the blame does lie with Keynes's own exposition, but a great deal more with the way in which the ideas were interpreted by mainstream economists, and how they entered the textbooks. It was argued above that Keynes's exposition could, in fact, have been made immune to the idea that it depended solely on nominal wage or price rigidities. All that would have been required is to use the idea of imperfect competition rather than "perfect competition" as the background for macroeconomic analysis. In order to completely, reconstruct Keynes's theory completely along these lines, however, it would also have had to be recognized that *much* more work needed to be done on the theory of interest rates and the theory of endogenous money (as discussed in several other places in these chapters). This was more than many of the economists who described themselves as "Keynesians" were prepared to do. They would have to have undertaken something like a complete revision of the entire *corpus* of monetary economics.

In the Appendix to this chapter, there is more discussion on the topic of resurrecting the original Keynesian model. It is shown how a theory of inflation of the cost-push or conflict type can be appended to the "modified" Keynesian theory of employment.

Notes

1. A quotation from this letter appeared on the back cover of a widely distributed edition of the *General Theory*, published by Macmillan in 1964.
2. According to Keynes (1964/1936, p. 15):

   > Men are involuntarily unemployed if, in the event of a rise in price of wage goods relatively to the price of the money-wage, both the aggregate supply of labour willing to work for the current money-wage and the aggregate demand for it at that wage would be greater than the existing volume of employment.

   Smithin (1985, 2009a) has shown that this definition does imply that for unemployment to be "involuntary" (in this sense) the money wage must be fixed.
3. This model has already been discussed in more detail in Chapter 3.
4. Keynes, by the way, seemed to be well aware of this. In the *General Theory*, the fiscal policy advocated is "loan expenditure" defined as "a convenient expression for the net borrowing of the public authorities on all accounts whether on capital account or to meet a budgetary deficit" (Keynes, 1964/1936, pp. 128–129, Footnote 1).
5. Hicks's original lettering for the two schedules was also slightly different. Originally the diagram was labeled "IS/LL".
6. When there is a government sector in the economy the equilibrium condition must be $I + G = S + T$ or "injections equals withdrawals", rather than just "investment equals savings".

Appendix

One of the main conclusions of Chapter 5 was to show that the *basic* Keynesian theory that employment is determined by "effective demand" can (fairly easily) be resurrected in an economy in which there is generally imperfect competition. This is a better option than assuming perfect competition, which rules out demand considerations from the start. This version of the theory is not subject to criticism about reliance on rigid wages, money illusion *etc.* Figure A5.1 repeats Fig. 5.5 to illustrate. The solution for employment in Fig. A5.1 is self-contained, and derived purely in real terms.

However, this still leaves the problem of providing a theory of inflation to go along with the theory of employment. Therefore, suppose we were to graph the point of effective demand in inflation/employment space, to begin the task. The "ED curve" would simply be a vertical line at the point of effective demand. How can the inflation rate itself be determined? The most straightforward suggestion is to borrow from the discussion in Chapter 5 above about conflict and cost-push inflation. The "price equation" from the imperfectly competitive model (5.13) can be repeated as:

$$P = [k(Y)]W/Y'(N), \qquad k'(Y) < 0, \qquad (A5.1)$$

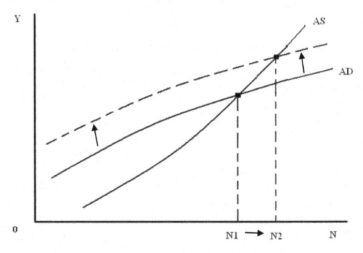

Fig. A5.1.   Keynesian effective demand in a model with imperfect competition.

where k is the mark-up or profit share. Then, add to this a "conflict" explanation of how the real wage is determined:

$$W/P_{-1} = (W/P)_0 = H(N), \qquad H'(N) > 0. \qquad (A5.2)$$

Substituting (A5.2) into (A5.1) and using the production function $Y = Y(N)$ gives:

$$P = \{k[Y(N)]P_{-1}H(N)\}/[Y'(N)]. \qquad (A5.3)$$

Divide through by P_{-1}:

$$P/P_{-1} = \{k[Y(N)]H(N)\}/Y'(N)]. \qquad (A5.4)$$

The inflation rate, $p = (P - P_{-1})/P_{-1}$, is given by:

$$p = \{k[Y(N)]H(N)\}/Y'(N)] - 1 \qquad (A5.5)$$

with a slope of:

$$dp/dN = \{Y'(N)\{k'Y'(N)H(N)$$
$$- k[Y(N)]H(N)Y''(N)\}/[Y'(N)]^2, \quad (> 0). \qquad (A5.6)$$

Therefore, the relation between employment and inflation is positively sloped. As employment increases, workers can push for higher real wages which spills over into inflation. The overall model can be graphed as in Fig. A5.2.

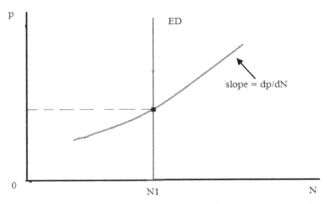

Fig. A5.2. A Keynesian model with imperfect competition, employment determined by effective demand, and conflict inflation.

The upward sloping relation between inflation and output in Fig. A5.2 is, however, by no means a "Phillips curve". There is no *causal* relation between inflation and output, as output is already determined in Fig. A5.1 with no reference to inflation. Nonetheless, the model includes both cost-push/conflict explanations of inflation and demand-pull theories of inflation, and both have the underlying premise of an endogenous theory of money.

Figure A5.3 illustrates a cost-push theory of inflation. An increase in real costs, from whatever source, shifts the positively-sloped infla-

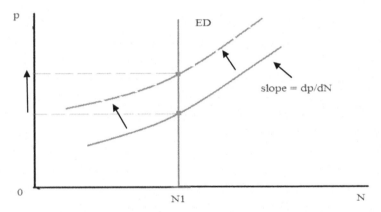

Fig. A5.3. Cost-push or "conflict" inflation.

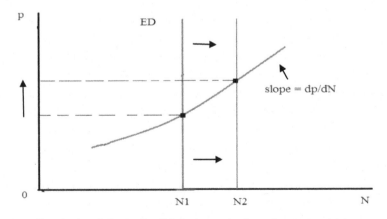

Fig. A5.4. A demand-pull inflation under imperfect competition.

tion/output relation up and to the left. This causes an increase in inflation, but (in this particular model) has no effect on the level of employment.

Figure A5.4 illustrates that demand-pull inflation is also a possibility. In this case, both inflation and employment increase.

CHAPTER 6

LONG-RUN MODELS OF MONETARY GROWTH, FORCED SAVING, WEALTH, TIME PREFERENCE, AND THE NEOCLASSICAL THEORY OF CAPITAL

Introduction

In this chapter, number six of eight, the topic is a concept which, in the history of economic thought, was usually called "forced savings" (Humphrey, 1993e, p. 257; Hayek, 1991, pp. 49–50; Caldwell, 1995, pp. 16–17). In the second half of the 20th century, the name somehow became changed to the "Mundell–Tobin effect" (Kam, 2000, 2005), after the contributions by Mundell (1963a) and Tobin (1965). Although this probably just reflects the "scientism" of academic economics in the latter period (naming some social phenomenon after its supposed discoverers as if it was a theorem in theoretical physics), it is true that modern graduate students often have difficulty with the original label. This is because, if the forced saving effect actually succeeds, the final result is supposedly to increase the physical "capital stock"[1] and therefore, ultimately, make possible *more* rather than less *consumption* in aggregate. Contemporary students probably do not keep clearly in mind, at least not until "they have become professor themselves" as Joan Robinson (1964, pp. 66–67) once said,[2] that in classical and neoclassical economics *both* savings and investment have usually been thought of as essentially physical quantities of goods. This is the essence of orthodox economics, no matter how counter-intuitive the idea may seem to be in an actual money-using economy.

On this view goods which are "saved" in the sense of "not being consumed" more-or-less *automatically* become investment goods. Saving is not just "equal to" investment it is essentially the same thing. This is why in the standard neoclassical growth model, for example, an increase in the savings propensity is a pre-requisite for a move to a higher growth path.

From the students' point of view a better term for "forced saving" would probably be "forced investment". In fact, in the so-called "Austrian" capital theory of the 1930s, associated particularly with the work of Hayek and von Mises (Caldwell, 1995), the term "over-investment" was actually used. In that case the modifier (over) was meant to imply that this "forced" investment could not be sustained. It would eventually have to be painfully undone in the course of a depression. This was the entire Austrian explanation of the business cycle.

In the era of classical economics, at an earlier stage in the history of economic thought, the notion of forced saving had usually been treated in a less dramatic fashion. It tended to be regarded as a theoretical anomaly, a sort of unavoidable "exception to the rule" of long-run monetary super-neutrality. It is anomalous because the cause of the forced saving and the subsequent additional investment, if it comes about, is actually inflation. So here is a case in which (except on the later Austrian account), if the investment is maintained, inflation seems to *permanently* increase the capital stock, output and employment. This has always gone against the grain for the vast majority of orthodox economists, to whom inflation is anathema.

The way the forced saving mechanism is thought to work, if it does work, is to reduce the incomes or wealth of anyone whose wages or other receipts are fixed in nominal terms, or who are holding assets denominated in nominal terms. It therefore causes these individuals to reduce their real consumption expenditure. The compulsory saving, however, releases resources for investment, and increases the capital stock, thereby causing an increase in output, employment and total consumption in the future. It is important to note that the forced saving effect is *not* just the usual argument about nominal rigidities causing *temporary* non-neutrality. It is something more than that. The argument is that even if all the relevant nominal adjustments *are* made in the future, the initial fall in real consumption spending has already occurred, and has therefore been "embodied" in an increased stock of capital goods. The effect persists into the future.

The term "forced" obviously carries a suggestion that this process is somehow morally wrong. In the typical economist's view, all would be well if people *decide* to save more physical goods of their own free will. In that case, the increase in the capital stock would represent their expressed wishes. In the forced saving case, however, even if the practical outcome is the same, the change has occurred by depriving some groups of people of their resources and arbitrarily allocating them to different purposes. This is what would be morally wrong from a classically liberal point of view.

In several of the macroeconomic models I have put forward over the years (*e.g.*, Smithin, 1994, 1997, 2003, 2005, 2009a), I have tried to show how, in reality, a similar result to the forced savings effect (that is, an increase in income or growth) could be achieved without there actually being any absolute losers (there would be more "pie" for everyone).[2] This would entail a policy of keeping the real interest rate on money "low but still positive" (Smithin, 1994, p. 187, 2003, p. 148). However, this is not the point to be discussed here and has been covered in several other chapters. Rather the main issue, at the moment, is to discuss how, in each generation, orthodox economists, classical, neoclassical and "Austrian", have reacted to the *possibility* of the forced saving effect.

As already suggested, a typical response in the history of economic thought has either been just be to accept the possibility of forced saving as an "unfortunate reality", and then to downplay its empirical significance, as, for example in McCallum (1991), in a 20th century contribution, or to focus on the moral issues. A somewhat more robust reaction on the part of a classical or neoclassical economist, however, would be simply to deny that "market forces" could ever let such a thing happen, and try to put forward some explanation of why they would not. According to Humphrey (1993e, p. 258) Ricardo was the most famous historical figure in this camp. The point of the following discussion is mainly to evaluate a number of the 20th century "neoclassical" attempts to make this same point.

As already stated the most spectacular critique of forced saving was that of the Austrian economists von Mises (1980/1934) and Hayek (1967/1935, 1995a, 1995b, 1995c) in the early 20th century. Here the argument was that forced "saving" as a result of inflation cannot be successful because will lead directly to the previously mentioned "over-investment", and will distort the structure of relative prices. Therefore, it will need to be undone in an extended period of recession or depression. Hayek's argument therefore came at a convenient time in history from the marketing point of view. However, I agree with Hicks (2005/1967) and Friedman (1974b) that the Austrian business cycle theory was very far from convincing as an explanation of real world episodes, such as the Great Depression of the 1930s. In fact, in the historical circumstances in which it was first presented, the narrative could have been (and frequently was) perceived as actually dangerous to the very *survival* of the capitalistic economic system of the day. It came across as a sort of economic "catch-22" the implication being that there were no policy actions, whatever, that could possibly be taken to alleviate a bad situation. From the present point of view, nonetheless, the theory remains a good example of a dramatic intellectual argument against any attempt to "stimulate" an economy by inflation.

A similar sort of argument in *neoclassical* theory would not have attempted to bring in the various arguments about timings, lags, the structure of production, and so forth, that are featured in Austrian theory. In any event, these arguments are literally impossible to state in precise terms (Hicks, 2005/1967, pp. 204–205). The neoclassical version would be rather simply to assert than the forced saving argument does not work *at all.* (The capital stock is *invariant* to the rate of inflation.) This position does not actually provide any sort of explanation of recessions, or economic downturns. However, in the neoclassical world this omission does not matter, as the point can easily be covered by assuming sticky prices or mistaken expectations. It does though make the same (deeper) theoretical point as the Austrians, that any attempt to stimulate the economy by inflation will not work. By the same token, the counter-argument that what in the 20th century was called the Mundell–Tobin effect, can work "in theory", would also be *prima facie* evidence against the Austrian concept of over-investment.

A "Long-Run" Model

In Smithin (1980), I argued that one particular model from that time period was useful in discussing the longstanding issues involved, in mathematical terms. This was the model put forward by Begg (1980), which fortunately was based on the simpler neoclassical theory of "capital" rather the more complex, and essentially incomprehensible Austrian theory. A version of Begg's model follows below:

$$Y = C(Y, W) + \dot{K} + \delta K, \qquad 0 < C_Y < 1, \ C_W > 1, \ 0 < \delta < 1 \quad (6.1)$$

$$M/P = L(Y, i), \qquad L_Y > 0, \ L_i < 0 \quad (6.2)$$

$$Y = F(K), \qquad F_K > 0, \ F_{KK} < 0 \quad (6.3)$$

$$W = K + M/P, \quad (6.4)$$

$$i = r + p^e, \quad (6.5)$$

$$r = F_K - \delta, \quad (6.6)$$

$$p^e = p, \tag{6.7}$$
$$\dot{M}/P = (M/P)(m - p). \tag{6.8}$$

In this model, Y is real GDP and is thought of as some sort of multi-purpose physical commodity (the famous "putty" of neoclassical capital theory) which can either be consumed or invested. The "consumption function" is given by $C(Y, W)$, and $\dot{K}$ is the time derivative of the capital stock (that is, net investment). The term δK is replacement investment, where δ is the depreciation rate, and total investment is therefore $\dot{K} + \delta K$. The "money" that exists in this model is assumed to be non-interest-bearing. However this would not be a crucial assumption in a more detailed model as long as the interest rate on base money is at least *controlled* by the central bank (Kam and Smithin, 2012), either at zero or some other figure. On the existing assumptions, holdings of real money balance are therefore given by the familiar M/P, where M is the nominal money supply, and P is the price level. The expression $L(Y, i)$ is the liquidity function, that is, the demand function for real money balances and it involves *nominal* interest rates precisely because of the assumption that money does *not* bear interest.

The production function $Y(K)$ has output depending only on the capital stock, and for simplicity there is no mention of labour input. This is the opposite assumption to the production functions suggested for macroeconomic analysis elsewhere in this work and is worth noting simply for that reason, the other chapters having usually put forward something like a (virtual) "labour theory of production" (Smithin, 2005, 2009a). However, it has already been shown that essentially the same macroeconomic analysis will go through in either case, so the change is not of fundamental significance. In each of the functional forms in Eqs. (6.1) to (6.3) a simple subscript notation is used to denote partial derivatives, and each of these is given a familiar sign.

A few additional points need to be made about this model by Begg, all relating to the date it was first published, more than 30 years ago.

Firstly, this was at the height of the monetarist influence in academic economics. Therefore, monetary policy in this model is thought of only in terms of the setting the rate of growth of the money supply (which then causes inflation). There is no discussion about interest rate policy or anything about the relationship between the central bank and the commercial banks. However, one of the things that will be shown further is that it is quite possible to recast the whole model in interest rate terms, and thereby bring it more "up-to-date", without changing the basic results on forced savings. Secondly, this period a generation ago was exactly when the issue of "rational expectations" was a popular topic in academic economics. There was therefore a large amount of discussion about this in the original paper, and also in a later volume by the same author (Begg, 1982). The model set out in Eqs. (6.1) to (6.3) is actually a non-stochastic model with perfect foresight, and the author correctly makes the point that this is simply a special case of rational expectations. It is the idea of rational expectations pushed to its logical conclusion. Thirdly, and for the purposes of the present discussion very importantly, the paper was published at a stage just *before* the idea of the "micro-foundations of macroeconomics" had gained such a stranglehold on the mainstream academic literature as happened later on (Smithin, 2004; King, 2012). The significance of this last point will become clearer as the discussion proceeds, the main point being that this omission could easily become an opening for *later* critics to discount some of the results. It will also be shown below, however, that this is *not* a generally valid argument.

To simplify the notation again following Begg (1980), introduce the symbol Z to stand for real money balances, that is $Z = M/P$.[3] Therefore:

$$Z = L(Y, i), \qquad (6.9)$$
$$\dot{Z}/Z = m - p. \qquad (6.10)$$

We can now simply ask the question whether or not money is "super-neutral" in this model in the steady-state? In the traditional terminology, recall that money is neutral if a change in the level of the money supply only affects the price level and none of the "real" economic variables. Money is *super-neutral* if a change in the *rate of growth* of the money supply only affects *inflation*. In this particular model, the most important question is about super-neutrality.

In the steady-state, it must be true by definition that:

$$\dot{K} = \dot{Z} = 0. \qquad (6.11)$$

The levels of the capital stock and holdings of real money balance must both settle down to their steady-state values. This further implies that:

$$p = m. \qquad (6.12)$$

Therefore, in the steady-state, the equilibrium inflation rate will be equal to the rate of monetary growth as in the basic quantity theory of money, but with a twist as we shall see. The solution for the steady-state capital stock can then be found by successive substitution of Eqs. (6.12), and (6.2) through (6.7), into (6.1). Then use (6.11) and (6.12) to yield:

$$F(K) = C\{F(K), K + L[F(K), F_K - \delta + m]\} + \delta K. \tag{6.13}$$

Totally differentiating (6.13), and solving for dK/dm, the result is:

$$dK/dm = C_W L_i / [F_K(1 - C_Y - C_W L_Y)$$
$$- C_W(1 + L_i F_{KK}) - \delta], \quad \geq 0 \text{ or } \leq 0? \tag{6.14}$$

Therefore, as pointed out by Begg (1980), the *sufficient conditions* for super-neutrality must be:

$$C_W = 0, \tag{6.15}$$
$$L_i = 0. \tag{6.16}$$

If we can rule out these two conditions, there must be *non*-super-neutrality. Changes in the rate of growth of the money supply would affect both the equilibrium capital stock and the equilibrium level of output, one way or another.

Note, however, that we cannot tell immediately from Eq. (6.14) which way the results would go. If $dK/dm > 0$, this would represent the forced savings effect, or the Mundell–Tobin effect, in action. An increase in the rate of monetary growth, and therefore of inflation, would increase the capital stock and the steady-state level of output. On the other hand, if it could be shown that $dK/dm < 0$, there is still non-super-neutrality but that result would support the argument that inflation is bad for the economy. It might therefore, at least to some extent, justify an inflation targeting approach to monetary policy, or perhaps even the dire predictions of the Austrian view.

As for the two conditions for super-neutrality, to have $L_i = 0$ is quite implausible if the money is not interest-bearing, and that is the underlying assumption. This leaves the other condition $C_W = 0$. To make this specification would entail denying that there is any "wealth effect" on consumption. But, the existence of something like a wealth effect is the basic premise of the idea of forced saving in the first place. Therefore, to make this restriction would simply be *imposing* the conclusion that a forced saving effect cannot exist rather than proving it. Neither of the sufficient conditions is satisfied.

Stability Analysis

For the purposes of dynamic analysis, it is possible to identify two equilibrium *loci* in the model one of which relates to the market for "real capital", and the other to the money market.

To find out what these are, and again by successive substitution, we can identify the two dynamic equations describing the laws of motion of the system as:

$$F(K) = C(F(K), K + Z) + \dot{K} + \delta K, \qquad (6.17)$$

$$Z = L(F(K), F_K - \delta + m - \dot{Z}/Z). \qquad (6.18)$$

The two equilibrium *loci* in the steady-state in Z, K space (which exists when $\dot{K} = 0$ and $\dot{Z} = 0$) have slopes as follows:

$$dZ/dK|(\dot{K} = 0) = C_W/[F_K(1 - C_Y) - C_W - \delta], \qquad > 0 \text{ or } < 0? \quad (6.19)$$

$$dZ/dK|(\dot{Z} = 0) = L_Y F_K + L_i F_{KK}, \qquad > 0. \quad (6.20)$$

These expressions do seem somewhat analogous to textbook IS and LM equations, except that they apply to the long-run context with a variable capital stock. (They have real money balances and the capital stock on the axes, rather than interest rates and income.) The money market locus is upward sloping, however the capital market locus has an ambiguous slope. It could be either be upward sloping or downward sloping. Meanwhile, the direction of the "arrows of motion" in this problem can be discovered from the following partial derivatives of Eqs. (6.17) and (6.18), evaluated at their steady-state values:

$$\partial\dot{K}/\partial K = F_K(1 - C_Y) - C_W - \delta, \qquad > 0 \text{ or } < 0? \quad (6.21)$$

$$\partial\dot{Z}/\partial Z = Z/L_i(L_Y F_K + L_i F_{KK}), \qquad < 0. \quad (6.22)$$

There are therefore three possible cases for stability analysis illustrated in Fig. 6.1 through Fig. 6.3.

In Fig. 6.1, where the $\dot{K} = 0$ locus is upward sloping, and has a greater slope that the $\dot{Z} = 0$ locus, the model is completely unstable. This means that whatever the starting point in the diagram, the theoretical steady-state equilibrium levels of the capital stock (and of real money balances) can *never* be reached.

If both schedules are upward sloping, but the $\dot{K} = 0$ locus has a lesser slope than the $\dot{Z} = 0$ line, then the equilibrium will be a so-called saddle-point, as illustrated in Fig. 6.2. In this case there is a "stable arm", namely

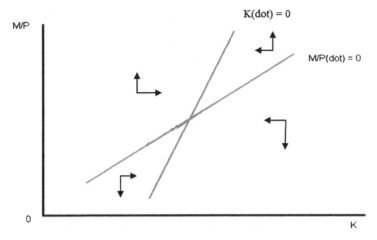

Fig. 6.1.   The model is unstable.

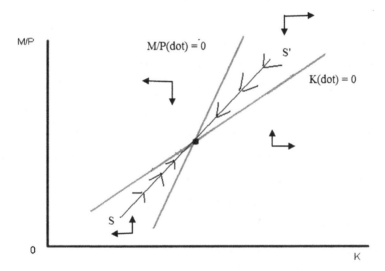

Fig. 6.2.   The model has a saddle-point (both schedules upward-sloping).

the line $S - S'$. If the amounts of real money balances and physical capital that are held initially happen to place the economy somewhere along that line, then the economy will proceed along it until the equilibrium is reached. Otherwise (if the economy starts *off* the $S - S'$ line), it is not immediately obvious how the equilibrium might be achieved.

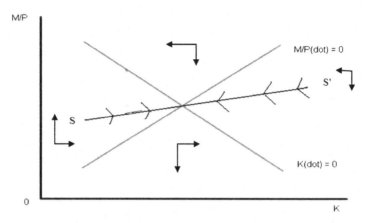

Fig. 6.3.   The model has a saddle-point (one schedule downward-sloping).

A final possibility is that the $\dot{K} = 0$ locus is downward sloping. In this case, the diagram does look a bit more like an IS/LM model in a textbook, and there is again a saddle-point solution, with one stable arm.

From the purely dynamic point of view therefore, the original three possibilities are reduced to two. Either the model is unstable *or* there is a saddle-point. The next question to ask is what are the implications of this? The pathological case of the *completely* unstable economy would presumably have to be ruled out both by mainstream economists (which is the most important issue here), but also by most heterodox economists, simply on the grounds of its implausibility in the context of this very simple theoretical model.

What however, are we to make of the saddle-point alternative? This issue is taken up in the next section.

Is the Existence of a Saddle-Point a Problem in Models Involving Both Monetary/Financial Assets and Real Assets?

In fact mathematical research by mainstream economists in the second half of the 20th century showed that many economic models incorporating both monetary/financial assets and real assets often do have the saddle-point property (Begg, 1982; Blanchard and Fischer, 1989; Burstein, 1995). The particular example above is actually just an illustration of the general principle.

When this problem was first discovered, some years before the publication of Begg's paper, the finding clearly had the potential to be something of an embarrassment to the neoclassical mainstream in economics. Certainly neoclassical economists would *like* to be able to argue that the capitalist economy *is* stable, in the tradition of Adam Smith's "invisible hand", and so forth. However, if in formal models we frequently find a saddle-point solution with only a single stable arm, it might seem that the logical conclusion is that the economy could only converge to the steady-state by accident. It has already been mentioned that the notion of forced saving was a historical example of a theoretical anomaly that was worrying to orthodox economists. This finding was potentially another one.

However during the 1970s and 1980s, when the concept of rational expectations (RE) was introduced, and widely discussed in academic economics, it turned out that a plausible "transversality condition" could be suggested, and was suggested by a number of authors (*e.g.*, Sargent and Wallace, 1973), which would solve the problem within the general set of assumptions of the RE model. Therefore, in the case of the present model (which assumes perfect foresight, a special case of RE) a similar type of argument may also be used.

The basic argument is illustrated in Fig. 6.4. In this figure, there is a downward-sloping $\dot{K} = 0$ locus and an upward-sloping $\dot{Z} = 0$ locus as was the case in Fig. 6.3, implying that the solution is again a saddle-point.

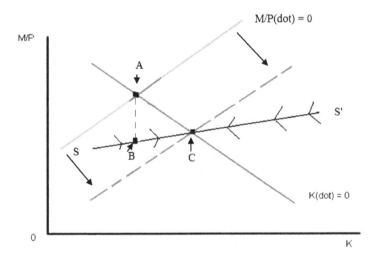

Fig. 6.4. The price level can be a "jump variable" in a saddle-point system.

Let the equilibrium be initially at point "A", without inquiring, in the first instance, *how* the economy got there. Then let there be an increase in the rate of growth of the money supply, which will shift the $\dot{Z} = 0$ locus down and to right. The thing to notice here is that the original point "A" is now left "high and dry". It now becomes a *disequilibrium* situation with respect to the new equilibrium position "C". Therefore it is *not* on the stable arm for the new configuration, $S - S'$.

The potential problem can be avoided, or so it has been argued, by realizing that at "A", real money balances ($Z = M/P$) are higher than would be required either at the point "B" on the stable arm, or indeed at the final equilibrium. The "rational" agent (and most certainly an agent with perfect foresight) should be aware of this, and can take action to remedy the situation. Specifically, the representative agent can always spend the excess money on goods, which drives up the price level on a "once-for-all" basis, and deflates real money balances to the required level. In effect, the price level is allowed to become a "jump variable" in the system, which can *always* adjust to put the economy on the stable arm. The reader should note the similarity of this argument to the monetarist analysis of the "overshooting" of the inflation rate that was previously discussed in Chapter 3.

Money in Non-Super-Neutral and the Mundell–Tobin Effect Holds

A more formal approach to stability analysis would start with the following linear approximation to the system around the steady-state values of K and Z. These are labeled K^* and Z^*.

$$d\dot{K} = \partial\dot{K}/\partial K(K - K^*) + \partial\dot{K}/\partial K(Z - Z^*), \qquad (6.23)$$

$$d\dot{Z} = \partial\dot{K}/\partial Z(K - K^*) + \partial\dot{Z}/\partial Z(Z - Z^*). \qquad (6.24)$$

The relevant partial derivatives are:

$$\partial\dot{K}/\partial K = F_K(1 - C_Y) - C_W - \delta, \qquad ? \qquad (6.25)$$

$$\partial\dot{K}/\partial Z = -C_W, \qquad < 0 \qquad (6.26)$$

$$\partial\dot{Z}/\partial K = Z/L_i(L_Y F_K + L_i F_{KK}), \qquad < 0 \qquad (6.27)$$

$$\partial\dot{Z}/\partial Z = -Z/L_i, \qquad > 0. \qquad (6.28)$$

Therefore, in matrix form, the approximate system will be:

$$\begin{vmatrix} d\dot{K} \\ d\dot{Z} \end{vmatrix} = \begin{vmatrix} [F_K(1 - C_Y) - C_W - \delta] & -C_W \\ [Z/L_i(L_Y F_K + L_i F_{KK})] & -Z/L_i \end{vmatrix} \begin{vmatrix} (K - K^*) \\ (Z - Z^*) \end{vmatrix}. \tag{6.29}$$

Denote the coefficient matrix, on the right-hand side (RHS) of (6.29), by the symbol Δ. The formal stability conditions for the system are therefore:

$$\text{Tr } \Delta < 0, \tag{6.30}$$

$$\text{Det } \Delta > 0. \tag{6.31}$$

The trace (Tr) is the sum of the terms along the NW-SE diagonal, and the determinant (Det) is the multiple of these same two terms, less the multiple of the terms along the NE-SW diagonal.

The stability conditions cannot both be satisfied simultaneously in the present model. As already seen in the graphical analysis, the only possibilities are that the model is completely unstable or that there is a saddle-point solution. The unstable case, which would occur if Tr $\Delta > 0$ and Det $\Delta > 0$ has to be ruled out for practical purposes. In the saddle-point case the determinant would have to be negative (Det $\Delta < 0$), or:

$$F_K(1 - C_Y - C_W L_Y) - C_W(1 + L_i F_{KK}) - \delta, \qquad < 0. \tag{6.32}$$

Now recall the solution given above in Eq. (6.14) showing the impact of a change in the rate of growth of the money supply. This is repeated as (6.33):

$$dK/dm = C_W L_i/[F_K(1 - C_Y - C_W L_Y) - C_W(1 + L_i F_{KK}) - \delta], \qquad > 0. \tag{6.33}$$

Therefore, given the result in (6.32) which is the only logical possibility for the neoclassical economist in this context if the model is not to be unstable, then that same economist would have no choice but to conclude that $dK/dm > 0$ and money is non-super-neutral.

An increase in the rate of growth of the money supply will permanently increase the capital stock and the equilibrium level of output. Moreover, the increase in the capital stock cannot be dismissed as "over-investment". It is the right level of investment from the technical point of view in the circumstances, and will persist. These are probably only slightly less palatable conclusions to many economists than the idea that a market economy might be unstable but, so far, are unavoidable.

It remains true that inflation in the steady-state is determined by the rate of growth of the money supply, or:

$$dp = dm. \qquad (6.34)$$

Therefore, the overall conclusion of this model putting (6.32), (6.33) and (6.34) together is that inflation caused by monetary growth can, and does cause a permanent increase in the capital stock (and therefore higher levels of output and consumption in the future). The forced saving argument goes through, and another way of putting this is that the Mundell–Tobin effect holds.

The results are also illustrated graphically in Fig. 6.5 where the equilibrium capital market locus is downward-sloping. The starting point in Fig. 6.5 is at point "A", where the stock of real money balances is $(M/P)_1$ and the physical capital stock is K_1. An increase in the rate of growth of the nominal money supply will increase the inflation rate and shift the "money market" locus down and to the right. The new equilibrium is at point "B", and the overall effect is to increase the capital stock to K_2, which will increase the permanent level of output and consumption and reduce holdings of real money balances (monetary wealth) to $(M/P)_2$. There is a possible analogy here to the case of the LM curve shifting to the right, in the Hicksian IS/LM model, but recall that the whole context of Fig. 6.5 refers to the "long run" or the "steady-state" rather than the Hicksian fix-price short run.

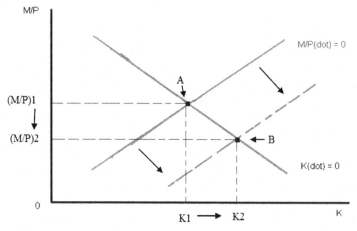

Fig. 6.5. An increase in the rate of money supply growth causes inflation and forced saving, and therefore increases the physical capital stock.

Interest Rate Determination

The concept of the so-called "natural rate" of interest was discussed in several previous chapters, and it is important, therefore, to note that there is *no such thing* as a natural rate of interest in the Begg model. This can be shown as follows. First, as stated, an increase in the rate of growth of the money supply will cause an increase in the capital stock:

$$dK/dm = C_W L_i / [F_K(1 - C_Y - C_W L_Y) - C_W(1 + L_i F_{KK}) - \delta], \qquad > 0. \tag{6.35}$$

Moreover, as this is indeed a "neoclassical" model, it remains true the real interest rate (whether this is a natural rate or not) will be equal to the marginal product of capital (MPK), plus the depreciation rate:

$$r = F_K + \delta. \tag{6.36}$$

The production function is subject to diminishing returns, so therefore an increase in the capital stock will cause the MPK to fall, and the real interest rate to fall, even on this purely materialist interpretation of what an interest rate is. This can be seen by totally differentiating (6.36) to obtain:

$$dr/dK = F_{KK}, \qquad < 0. \tag{6.37}$$

Then, to directly see the effect on a change in the rate of growth of the money supply on the real rate of interest, combine Eqs. (6.36) and (6.37) to yield:

$$dr/dm = F_{KK} C_W L_i / [F_K(1 - C_Y - C_W L_Y) - C_W(1 + L_i F_{KK}) - \delta], \qquad < 0. \tag{6.38}$$

An expansionary monetary policy *reduces* the equilibrium real rate of interest and *vice versa*. There is *no* natural rate and therefore, in effect, the theory involves what we have been calling a "monetary theory of the real rate of interest".

A Long-Run Phillips Curve?

Still another way of characterizing the results, obtained above, is that the long-run Phillips curve (LRPC) is *positively* sloped in p, Y space. There is, therefore, a permanent long-run trade-off between inflation and output.[4]

From the production function $Y = F(K)$, we have:

$$dY = F_K dK. \tag{6.39}$$

And so:

$$dY/dm = F_K(dK/dm). \tag{6.40}$$

As $dp = dm$:

$$dY/dp = F_K(dK/dm). \tag{6.41}$$

Finally, substituting in from Eq. (6.33):

$$dY/dp = F_K C_W L_i / [F_K(1 - C_Y - C_W L_Y) - C_W(1 + L_i F_{KK}) - \delta], \quad < 0. \tag{6.42}$$

Putting Eq. (6.42) the other way round therefore gives a positively-sloped relationship in p, Y space (which can be interpreted as the LPRC):

$$dp/dY = [F_K(1 - C_Y - C_W L_Y) - C_W(1 + L_i F_{KK}) - \delta]/F_K C_W L_i, \quad > 0. \tag{6.43}$$

This result is very clearly at odds with "textbook" monetary economics and macroeconomics. Recall that the main premise of textbooks, in both monetarist and neo-Wicksellian models, is that the long-run Phillips curve should be a vertical straight line.

Endogenous Money

One drawback of the model that has been presented so far is that it is somewhat "old-fashioned" (it is more than three decades old, after all) in the sense that the rate of growth of the money supply itself is treated as the direct monetary policy instrument. This was the usual procedure in the days of monetarism. However, as there is no natural rate of interest in the model this defect (from the modern point of view) is quite easily repaired. All that is required is to take the nominal interest rate, i, to be the monetary policy instrument instead of money supply growth, with the money supply endogenous. The monetary authorities will then have no difficulty in setting the real interest rate at whatever level they like, simply by continuously adjusting the nominal interest rate for changes in the perfectly foreseen inflation rate. The basic results of the model do not really change. Changes in monetary policy are still non-super-neutral. A deliberate reduction in real interest rates, for example, will immediately increase the capital stock, as shown in Eq. (6.44):

$$dK/dr = 1/F_{KK}, \qquad < 0. \tag{6.44}$$

Given the production function $Y = F(K)$, this means that steady-state level of output will increase when the real interest rate is reduced, as follows:

$$dY/dr = F_K/F_{KK}, \qquad < 0. \tag{6.45}$$

Simultaneously the "cheap money policy" (in real terms) will increase the inflation rate:

$$dp/dr = [F_K(1 - C_Y - C_W L_Y)$$
$$- C_W(1 + L_i F_{KK}) - \delta]/F_{KK} C_W L_i, \qquad < 0. \tag{6.46}$$

(Recall that the equilibrium is a saddle-point.)

Therefore we now have an endogenous money model with an interest rate instrument, and the results just reproduce the "forced saving" argument about inflation causing an increase in the capital stock and increases in output and employment. In fact, it was this precise sequence, starting with interest rates rather than the money supply, that originally provoked the strong dissent of the Austrians and others in the 1930s. The LRPC in p, Y space remains positively sloped.

"Micro-Foundations" and Monetary Super-Neutrality

As has already been made clear, the idea that inflation might increase the steady-state capital stock and the permanent level of consumption (and therefore be a "good thing"), is *not* a result that most economists, in the past or in the present, would be comfortable with. It goes against the grain. The more usual idea has been that inflation is unambiguously a "bad thing" and should be avoided. Therefore, theoretical demonstrations of the forced saving or Mundell–Tobin effect, such as that set out above, have always tend to be treated with suspicion. Walsh (1998, pp. 48–49) for example, puts forward a number of arguments against the various demonstrations of Mundell–Tobin effect such as that above, the most important of which is that:

> the ... behavioural relationships are *ad hoc* in the sense that they are not explicitly based on maximizing behaviour by the agents of the model. This limitation can lead to problems when we try to understand the

effects of changes in the economic environment, such as changes in the rate of inflation. The effects will depend in part, on the way in which individual agents adjust, so we need to be able to predict how the demand function for money changes if the underlying time series behaviour of the inflation process were to change ... (d)oing so will ... highlight channels leading to quite different predictions than Tobin found ...

It should be mentioned that the term *"ad hoc"* is typically used within mainstream/neoclassical economics as a dismissive criticism for a model with which the writer disagrees. By contrast to call something a "rigourous" treatment would be a term of approval. However, it must be said that this terminology is not actually correct as applied to mathematical models. A mathematical result is either right in its own terms if the correct algorithm has been applied, or wrong if it has not. Therefore, whenever a theory is described as *ad hoc* (even though mathematically correct) the real meaning can only be that it does not conform to some pre-approved/preferred methodology. Even though this sort of usage is very common, it should nonetheless be stressed that the mere use of these terms cannot reasonably be used simply to dismiss whatever results have been obtained by a theory that is not liked by the relevant peer group. Nor does either of the terms *rigourous* or *ad-hoc*, seem have any bearing on the relationship of the various theories with social reality. They give no information on whether, or not, the theory provides a good explanation.

Nonetheless the argument quoted above does seem to explicitly make the case that if that the model was "properly" constructed with microfoundations, optimizing behaviour, *etc.*, the forced saving, or Mundell–Tobin, effect would not apply. Therefore, there needs to be an answer to this, which will be presented in the next few sections of this chapter. It is possible to show that the attempt to appeal to micro-foundations to generate a particular result is not a valid argument. In the particular case of the Mundell–Tobin, effect, the key issue (whether the model is derived from neoclassical micro-foundations or not) remains the question of whether or not a "wealth effect" on consumption will be allowed (in terms of the model set out above, the issue is whether or not $C_W = 0$).

As it happens, long before Begg's paper was published the well-known contribution by Sidrauski (1967) had already shown that it is certainly *possible* to derive a model in which money is super-neutral (the desired result from Sidrauski's point of view), based on the optimizing behaviour of a "representative agent". In fact, this framework was often expounded in later graduate level textbooks (*e.g.*, Blanchard and Fischer, 1989; Walsh, 1998; Turnovsky, 2000) as a sort of baseline for the analysis of dynamic optimization models with money. Technically, the Sidrauski model was an example of the "money in utility function" (MIU) approach, one of a number of methods of introducing money into models that otherwise only deal with the "rational" allocation of real resources. A demand for money is justified by assuming that the decision-making agent directly gets "utility" from the holding of real money balances. It should be noted that, these days, the MIU method by itself is not all that popular among neoclassical economists, and the reasons for this are explained by Kam (2000, pp. 68–70). Basically, from the point of view of theorists of barter exchange it is difficult to understand why the holding of "barren money" (as they see it) should give any satisfaction or utility. Therefore there is a tendency to prefer other methods of bringing in the micro-foundations of money such as, for example, the CIA approach discussed in previous chapters. The issue clearly relates back to the disputes about the ontological status of money that were discussed in Chapter 1. On ontological grounds, however, it might be argued to the contrary that, *if* one has an understanding of money as a real social relation, and yet at the same time (for some reason) were also to insist on the micro-foundations approach to monetary theorizing,[5] then the MIU approach is probably the "least indefensible" method of introducing money into a barter exchange model. If "money is power" for example, why would one *not* get utility by possessing it?

Ultimately, however, the issues under discussion here do not depend on the *particular* method by which monetary factors are brought under the "microeconomics" umbrella. The MIU approach is at least one prominent method of deriving a monetary model from supposed micro-foundations, and it will suffice to illustrate the general point.

Therefore, using notation similar to that used in the Begg model earlier, it is useful to also write down a version of the Sidrauski model as follows:

$$\max: \int_0^\infty e^{-\theta t} U(C, Z) dt, \quad U_C, U_Z, > 0; \; U_{CC}, U_{ZZ} < 0; \; U_{CZ} = U_{ZC} = 0$$

$$(6.47)$$

subject to:

$$\dot{W} = Y + V - \delta K - pZ - C, \quad 0 < \delta < 1 \qquad (6.48)$$

$$W = K + Z, \qquad (6.49)$$

$$Y = F(K), \quad F_K > 0, \; F_{KK} < 0. \qquad (6.50)$$

In addition, there also has to be some appropriate "transversality condition" (Chiang and Wainwright, 2005, p. 634) as discussed earlier.

In this model, the "representative agent" is supposedly maximizing utility over an infinite time period. There are two arguments in the utility function, C, real consumption spending, and Z, real money balances. The time rate of discount applied to the continuous time problem is θ, the rate of time preference. Current output, Y, is a function of the capital stock, K. Real wealth is W, the sum of the two stocks of assets.

In the budget constraint equation (6.48) the rate of change of real wealth, $\dot{W}$, is shown as equal to current output, less capital depreciation at the rate δ, less the inflation tax on real money balances, less consumption spending, plus the value V of real money transfers to the representative agent (from the government or "central bank"). It is necessary to include the value of V for the model to be logically consistent (where does the money come from?), but V is not a choice variable from the representative agent's point of view. The model does not, in fact, discuss the question of how money gets introduced into the economy in at all a satisfactory way (Harkness, 1978; Smithin, 1983).

The "current value Hamiltonian" (Burmeister, 1970, pp. 238–249) for the problem is:

$$H = U(C, Z) + \lambda[F(W - Z) + V - \delta(W - Z)) - pZ - C] \qquad (6.51)$$

and the first-order conditions for a solution are:

$$H_C = 0, \qquad (6.52)$$

$$H_Z = 0, \qquad (6.53)$$

$$d\lambda/dt = -H_W + \lambda\theta, \qquad (6.54)$$

where λ is a co-state variable. These three equations can be re-written as:

$$U_C - \lambda = 0, \qquad (6.55)$$

$$U_Z - \lambda(F_K - \delta - p) = 0, \qquad (6.56)$$

$$d\lambda/dt = -\lambda(F_K - \delta - \theta). \qquad (6.57)$$

As shown by (Kam, 2000, pp. 30–33), in terms of the dynamic properties of the system the steady-state will be again be a saddle-point. The same two assets, K and Z, appear in this problem as in simpler Begg model, discussed earlier. On the same argument as above, therefore, we can move directly to the steady-state solution, in which:

$$\dot{W} = \dot{Z} = \dot{K} = \dot{\lambda} = 0. \qquad (6.58)$$

Using the familiar notation that m stands for the rate of monetary growth, p for the inflation rate, i for the nominal interest rate, and r for the real interest rate, the steady-state solution can therefore be characterized as:

$$U_Z/U_C = F_K - \delta + p, \qquad \text{(note: } F_K - \delta + p = i) \qquad (6.59)$$

$$C = F(K) - \delta K, \qquad (6.60)$$

$$F_K - \delta = \theta, \qquad \text{(note: } F_K - \delta = r) \qquad (6.61)$$

$$p = m. \qquad (6.62)$$

It can be seen immediately from Eq. (6.62) that the steady-state capital stock will *never* change, given the constant rate of time preference and a constant depreciation rate. We have:

$$F_{KK}dK = d\delta + d\theta = 0. \qquad (6.63)$$

Therefore, money must be super-neutral in the Sidrauski model, as, by definition:

$$dK/dm = 0. \qquad (6.64)$$

Increases in the rate of monetary growth have no effect on the capital stock, although they will, of course, continue to increase the inflation rate in accordance with the quantity theory of money:

$$dp = dm. \qquad (6.65)$$

As there is no change in the capital stock, there is, similarly, no effect of monetary growth and inflation on either output or consumption:

$$dY/dm = 0, \qquad (6.66)$$

$$dC/dm = 0. \qquad (6.67)$$

Moreover, the traditional idea of a natural rate of interest has been *re-imposed* on the structure of this model because:

$$r = \theta. \qquad (6.68)$$

The equilibrium real rate of interest cannot deviate from the exogenously given rate of time preference, and, therefore it fulfills the requirement or *desiderate* in neoclassical economics for the existence of an exogenous "natural rate" that can never be affected by monetary policy.

There is only actually one "real" effect of an increase in the rate of monetary growth. This occurs because, as money is non-interest bearing, holdings of "real" money balances Z will fall when the inflation rate increases. The result is that:

$$dZ/dm = -U_Z, \quad < 0. \quad (6.69)$$

Therefore although there is there is no forced saving *effect* as such, in the sense that (*e.g.*) Hayek would have understood this, as there is no actual over-investment, there are still losses of "utility" on the part of the original wealth-holders. So, although inflation does not affect output either way, from a distributional perspective the argument would still help to justify an anti-inflation policy, to some extent.

These results, therefore, do seem to be very neat from the point of the orthodox approach to monetary economics. Super-neutrality of changes in the rate of monetary growth, and hence of the inflation rate, is restored. Moreover, because a representative agent dynamic optimization problem has been used to obtain these results, it seems that the opinion from Walsh quoted earlier (that applying the "correct" method will obtain the "correct" results), is justified. There also remains some justification for a policy of keeping inflation low, (now on distributional grounds), even though it has no effect on the real economy.

However, a closer inspection of what is going on soon reveals that there is a major problem with these conclusions. The exercise does not really accomplish what it promised to do. It is true that the methodology has moved away from "*ad-hoc*" (non-utility maximizing) methods, but this is *not* actually the reason for the result that the forced saving effect "does not work". This has been accomplished, in fact, by exactly the same reasoning that would have ruled out forced saving in the earlier *ad-hoc* model, namely by disallowing even the *possibility* of any wealth effect. In the Sidrauski model, this was achieved quite simply by the assumption of an exogenous rate of time preference. It is this assumption, which ultimately ensures that there can never be any permanent changes in either the real rate of interest or the capital stock. It has nothing to do with the solution method.

Endogenous Time Preference

In fact, only a year or so after the first publication of Sidrauski's model, another quite well-known paper, by Uzawa (1968), had already shown that the non-neutrality results would not go through when the rate of time preference is made endogenous, instead of being assumed fixed. It may well be imagined, however, that this finding was not well received by many economists. Here is how Kam (2000, pp. 15–16) has described Uzawa's procedure:

> [Uzawa] assumes that time preference depends positively on the level of current utility, which itself is an increasing function of consumption. Monetary growth raises the opportunity cost of holding real balances and renders the initial equilibrium too costly. This *increases* the real interest rate and decreases the demand for real balances, which increases savings and the capital stock.

This procedure does restore the property of monetary *non*-super-neutrality. Moreover, because it does so in the context of an optimizing model, it is not subject to the type of criticism made by Walsh about (*e.g.*) Mundell–Tobin, and quoted above. In fairness to Uzawa's many critics, however, in truth the method that he suggested for making the rate of time preference endogenous, is not at all convincing. According to Uzawa, if consumption *increases* this is supposed to *increase* the rate of time preference, in other words, it will make the representative agent "impatient" for still more consumption. Reflecting on this, Persson and Svenson (1985, p. 45) say that the Uzawa specification is "... arbitrary and even counter-intuitive". Blanchard and Fischer (1989, p. 71) go further, and specifically warn budding economic theorists that:

> [although the] ... specification avoids the pathological results of the constant discount ↴rate case. Nonetheless, the Uzawa function, with its assumption (that the rate of time preference increases in instantaneous utility) is not particularly attractive as a description of preferences and is not recommended for general use.[6]

Kam (2000, 2005), however, building on a suggestion by Epstein and Hynes (1983), put forward an alternative, and far more intuitively plausible, method of making the rate of time preference an endogenous variable. In effect, this restores the wealth effect on consumption. The idea is simply to make the rate of time preference a positive function of total real wealth rather than consumption. Because the wealth effect on time preference is *positive*, this amounts to reinstating the idea that there is some sort of propensity to consume out of wealth, as well as out of income. The assumption is that as wealth accumulates time preference *increases*, so the representative agent is more willing to "spend" some of that wealth (simply put, the "representative agent" is not a miser). There is now a wealth effect entirely similar to that postulated in the Begg model, the only difference being this is now "rigourously" specified as part of the optimization problem. Following the treatment in Kam (2005) let:

$$\theta = \theta(W) = \theta(K + Z), \qquad \theta_W > 0. \tag{6.70}$$

Using this specification we will find that changes in the rate of monetary growth are not super-neutral. Equation (6.75) suffices to restore the Mundell–Tobin or "forced saving" effect, in a manner not subject to the sort of criticism levelled at Uzawa's specification. The dynamic properties of the modified system will be the same as in both the Begg and Sidrauski models (there will be a saddle-point), and the first-order conditions can be derived in the same manner as in the original Sidrauski problem. The new steady-state solution is therefore:

$$U_Z/U_C = F_K - \delta + p, \tag{6.71}$$

$$C = F(K) - \delta K, \tag{6.72}$$

$$F_K - \delta = \theta(K + Z), \tag{6.73}$$

$$p = m. \tag{6.74}$$

Totally differentiating:

$$(U_C U_{ZZ} dC - U_Z U_{CC} dZ)/U_C^2 = F_{KK} dK + dp, \tag{6.75}$$

$$dC = F_K dK - \delta dK, \tag{6.76}$$

$$F_{KK} dK = \theta_W dK + \theta_W dZ, \tag{6.77}$$

$$dp = dm. \tag{6.78}$$

Using this new equation system, the results are changed as follows.

First, the Mundell–Tobin/forced saving effect is restored, and money is non-super-neutral. An increase in the rate of monetary growth will increase the steady-state capital stock.

$$dK/dm = 1/\{[U_{ZZ}(F_{KK} - \theta_W)/U_C]$$
$$- [U_Z U_{CC}(F_K - \delta)/U_C^2] - F_{KK}\}, \qquad > 0. \tag{6.79}$$

Second, this implies that an "inflationary" policy will also increase steady-state output and consumption.

$$dY/dm = F_K/\{[U_{ZZ}(F_{KK} - \theta_W)/U_C]$$
$$- [U_Z U_{CC}(F_K - \delta)/U_C^2] - F_{KK}\}, \qquad > 0. \tag{6.80}$$

$$dC/dm = (F_K - \delta)/\{[U_{ZZ}(F_{KK} - \theta_W)/U_C]$$
$$- [U_Z U_{CC}(F_K - \delta)/U_C^2] - F_{KK}\}, \qquad > 0. \qquad (6.81)$$

Third, the so-called natural rate of interest disappears. An increase in the rate of monetary growth will reduce the equilibrium real interest rate.

$$dr/dm = F_{KK}/\{[U_{ZZ}(F_{KK} - \theta_W)/U_C]$$
$$- [U_Z U_{CC}(F_K - \delta)/U_C^2] - F_{KK}\}, \qquad < 0. \qquad (6.82)$$

As before, the final holdings of real money balances are decreased. The holders of real money balances pay the "inflation tax", and this is the method by which the real resources for increased investment are obtained.

$$dZ/dm = [(F_{KK}/\theta_W) - 1]/\{[U_{ZZ}(F_{KK} - \theta_W)/U_C]$$
$$- [U_Z U_{CC}(F_K - \delta)/U_C^2] - F_{KK}\}, \qquad < 0. \qquad (6.83)$$

Kam's (2000, 2005) results therefore, restore the age old argument that has been discussed through out this essay, to the effect that an inflationary policy can increase output through "forced saving". Moreover, they do so in a model that is *not* subject to the usual criticisms about micro-foundations and individual choice.

Endogenous Time Preference and Endogenous Money

There is one final point that needs to be discussed about the modified model with "Kam preferences", which is that Kam's model (like the original Begg and Sidrauski models), somewhat anachronistically takes the rate of growth of the money supply itself as being the primary monetary policy instrument, rather than a nominal interest rate.

However, as there again turns out to be no "natural" rate of interest in the model, there is no problem in turning this around to have the nominal interest rate, i, treated as the monetary policy instrument (with the money supply endogenous). In this case the monetary authorities can set the real rate by continuously adjusting the nominal interest rate for changes in observed inflation, as already discussed. This must, of course, be the rate of interest on *loans* of (base) money, as the money in the model itself continues to attract no interest. If we think of these monetary authorities as basically the "suppliers" of money, they can control the loan rate as they have the monopoly supply of base money.

To see the results of bringing Kam's model "up-to-date" in this way, simply set up the steady-state solution to the maximization problem in a slightly different way, as below.[7] In effect, this creates a model with *both* endogenous time preference and endogenous money. The steady-state solution can be characterized as:

$$U_Z/U_C = F_K - \delta + p, \tag{6.84}$$

$$C = F(K) - \delta K, \tag{6.85}$$

$$F_K - \delta = \theta(K + Z), \tag{6.86}$$

$$F_K - \delta = r. \tag{6.87}$$

Totally differentiating:

$$(U_C U_{ZZ} dZ - U_Z U_{CC} dC)/U_C^2 = F_{KK} dK + dp, \tag{6.88}$$

$$dC = F_K dK - \delta dK, \tag{6.89}$$

$$F_{KK} dK = \theta_W dK + \theta_W dZ, \tag{6.90}$$

$$F_{KK} dK = dr. \tag{6.91}$$

With a target real rate of interest as the focus of monetary policy, the results are therefore:

$$dK/dr = 1/F_{KK}, \qquad < 0. \tag{6.92}$$

A lower target real rate of interest will directly increase the capital stock. This will then also increase the steady-state level of output and consumption as, again, from the production function $Y = F(K)$, we can write:

$$dY/dr = F_K/F_{KK}, \qquad < 0 \tag{6.93}$$

$$dC/dr = (F_K - \delta)/F_{KK}, \qquad < 0. \tag{6.94}$$

The inflation rate and steady-state holdings of real money balances are affected by interest rate changes as follows:

$$dp/dr = 1/F_{KK}\{[U_{ZZ}(F_K - \theta_W)/\theta_W]$$
$$- U_Z U_{CC}(F_K - \delta) - F_{KK}\}, \qquad < 0 \tag{6.95}$$

$$dZ/dr = (F_{KK} - \theta_W)/F_{KK}\theta_W, \qquad > 0. \tag{6.96}$$

So, a cheap money policy, in the sense of lower real rates of interest, will increase the inflation rate, reduce holdings of real money balances and permanently increase the capital stock, output, and consumption.

This is exactly a description of the forced saving effect "in action" in the way that Hayek and others originally envisaged it (in their case as something to be avoided). A cheap money policy causes inflation, but the upside of this is that there will be more physical capital, and more output and consumption. Moreover, now no-one can object that this result has not been derived *via* a "rigourous" application of the micro-foundations methodology.

Conclusion

The upshot of the various mathematical exercises we have worked through in this essay is that the existence of economic forces operating along the lines of old "forced saving" effect (that in the 20th century was called the Mundell–Tobin effect) cannot be ruled out on the basis of choice-theoretic or "microeconomic" arguments alone. There is no assistance to be had, moreover, either from invoking questions of the dynamic stability of the model, or from the Austrian concept of "over-investment".

How then *would* it be possible to argue against "inflationism" of this type, as many economists would certainly be keen to do? Ultimately attention would have to revert to distributional questions in and of themselves. The argument would once again have to be made a question of the ethics of a situation in which the resources needed for making additional investments are not surrendered "voluntarily" by the wealth-holders, but are extracted from them by the method of inflation. As mentioned, this was always objectionable from the classical liberal point of view. Some individuals or groups do benefit by the economic expansion, but the interests of other groups are harmed by it. In essence, it is the idea that the "saving" is forced that is the sticking point.

It bears repetition that the combination of monetary and fiscal policy previously suggested by Smithin (1994, 2003, 2007a, 2009a) and taken up in Chapters 7 and 8 to follow, would *not* be vulnerable to criticism on this score. The important point that comes up in this discussion is that if, during the expansion, real interest rates on money remain *positive* (even while perhaps falling to "low" levels in absolute terms) the ethical strictures would simply no longer apply. (The society as a whole would be wealthier, and no individuals or groups could be identified as absolute losers from the process.) However, in the forced saving situations discussed in the present chapter it remains the case that there will always be some individuals whose real wealth has been reduced even when the economy as a whole is more prosperous.

In the appendix to this chapter, still another argument about the so-called "welfare costs of inflation" will briefly be discussed. However, the argument put forward there does not rebut the overall conclusion just stated. Later in Chapter 7, the issue of *outright* inflationary instability, if, when, and how that might become a problem, will be taken up in a slightly different context.

Notes

1. This term is in quotes because, in what really should be an obvious point, and was thought to be so at one time (Robinson, 1964; Harcourt, 1969; Hamouda and Harcourt, 1988; Cohen and Harcourt, 2003), it is actually impossible to give any concrete meaning to this in an aggregative model. What does K consist of? In theory, it is supposed to be a physical collection of machines, factories, vehicles, roads, computers, electronic cables, oil pipelines, and so on. However in empirical work in econometrics the definition shifts to the sum of money supposed to be the total market value of all these things divided through by some sort of price index. There is no logical connection whatsoever between these two definitions in terms of their supposed contribution to "output". It is easy enough to derive a theory based on the *assumption* that we *know* what K is, and what its physical properties are, as is done everywhere in this chapter for illustrative purposes. It is *impossible*, however, to put this theory into practice in the sense of submitting it to empirical tests. Essentially all empirical work involving estimates of "production functions" along the lines of $Y = F(K \ldots)$, and no matter how many other variables are included, should be regarded as highly dubious on logical grounds. The situation is different when comparing only quantities of "[real] money values [of flow variables] and quantities of employment" (Keynes, 1964/1936, p. 41).
2. See also Chapter 7.
3. The symbol Z used in this essay should not be confused with the term Z employed in Keynes's *General Theory* (and discussed earlier in Chapter 5). In the Keynesian context, Z was the symbol for the aggregate supply function.
4. The relationship between original Phillips curve relating unemployment and wage inflation, and other versions relating price inflation and growth, or price inflation and output, was discussed in Chapter 3.

5. This would seem, on the face of it, to be a somewhat inconsistent position to take, but see (for example), the views of Goodhart (2005), in a review of a book by Ingham (2004).

6. Interestingly enough, and as documented in detail by Kam (2005), these strictures about "Uzawa preferences" have not prevented this specification from being very widely used in the neoclassical/mainstream literature on the *open* economy. There is a reason for this. It is possible to "get away with" the Uzawa specification in the open economy context because then there exists *another* method of tying down the real rate of interest to something like a natural rate, namely assuming an exogenous "world" or global real interest rate.

7. The solution methods and dynamics are as before. Note that the V term from the original maximization problem is now redundant because of the assumption of endogenous money.

Appendix

Is it Possible to Make the Long-Run "Phillips Curve" (LRPC) Slope the Other Way (from the Mundell–Tobin Prediction)?

The short answer to this question is, yes. It will be recalled that one of the main assumptions in mainstream monetary and macroeconomic analysis, actually the centre-piece of most textbook models, is that the long-run Phillips curve (LRPC), in whatever graphical form it takes, is a vertical line. This is what accounted for the results of long-run super-neutrality in both monetarist and neo-Wicksellian models. The previous discussion, however, has shown that this position is not defensible, no matter how much this conclusion conflicts with received authority and the conventional wisdom.

Nonetheless, this situation must leave genuine opponents of "inflationism" in an awkward position. They would certainly still continue to feel that an outright inflationary policy is *not* desirable. Moreover, in a number of places (e.g., Smithin, 1994, 2003, 2007a, 2009a, 2010) the element of truth in that stance has been readily conceded. Consider the statement from Chapter 3, for example

> This is not to deny that money might be more useful in capitalism if its real value could be kept more stable. In this context, "real value" means the stability of purchasing power as measured by some sort of index of the average level of prices.

But, the quotation then does run on:

> [However,] to be able to preserve the real value of money in terms of its purchasing power, does *not* necessarily mean that the rate of inflation — the percentage *rate of change* of the price level — must itself always be zero. This stability could also be achieved if, for example, the interest rate paid on the nominal money balances ... were to keep pace with the inflation rate.

It can now clearly be seen, though, that in the context of Chapter 6, the real problem is that this not happening. That is why those worried by inflation are therefore more-or-less pushed back to a position that this is somehow unfair to the "rich". Faced with an argument that the forced saving effect works, but without access to the second part of the quote above, the only recourse must seem to be once again point out that this does not do strict justice to those who are already wealthy. This is not "wrong" against the argument of Chapter 6 (though it would be against that of Chapter 7) but from the point of politics and practical policy-making it is clearly *not* a convincing/persuasive rhetorical stance to take,

In fact, even the "vertical Phillips curve" itself was always something of a "weak reed" rhetorically and politically. If inflation does not "matter", in the sense of not changing the level or growth rate of real GDP or the unemployment rate, then why worry about it? The only answer is to go back to the fairness issue.

I think that is why another argument has sometimes been floated in the theoretical economics literature, which tries to turn the tables by pushing hard in the opposite direction. Milton Friedman (1977), for example, raised this issue in his famous Nobel prize lecture, and it also appeared frequently in the literature about the cash-in-advance (CIA) constraint during the 1980s and 1990s. The alternative strategy would be *not* to insist that there is that is "no trade-off", or that the forced saving effect "does not work", but to assert the opposite, that low inflation is actually a *pre-requisite* for an improved economy, lower unemployment, lower unemployment, higher growth, *etc.,* and not something which works against these outcomes. There is no real historical evidence for this position (in reality, all possible combinations of growth and inflation have occurred), but it can be demonstrated theoretically, at least, in the following simple CIA model:

$$Max: \sum_{0}^{\infty} \beta^t U(C_t, N_t), \qquad U'(C) > 0, \ U'(N) < 0 \qquad (A6.1)$$

subject to:

$$B = B_{-1} + WN + i(B_{-1} - M) - PC, \quad (A6.2)$$

$$M \geq PC. \quad (A6.3)$$

The notation here is similar to that used earlier and the terms C, N, W and B, mean consumption, employment, nominal wages and nominal financial assets, respectively. This is a discrete-time model with a representative agent, involving both a standard budget constraint and a CIA constraint.

Of particular importance in this problem are the timing assumptions, about when interest is paid, when portfolio choices must be made, when income can be spent and so forth. These are crucial to the results obtained in CIA models. The discount factor is the term β, given by:

$$\beta = 1/(1 + \theta), \quad (A6.4)$$

where $\theta =$ the rate of time preference.

Next, add two co-state variables, λ and α, one for each of the constraints, and the problem becomes:

$$\max : \sum_0^\infty \beta^t \{ U(C_t, N_t) + \lambda_t [W_t N_t + (1 + i_{t-1}) A_{t-1}$$

$$- i_t M_t - P_t C_t - A_t] + \alpha_t [P_t C_t - M_t] \}. \quad (A6.5)$$

The first-order conditions are therefore:

$$U'(C) - \lambda P + \alpha P = 0, \quad (A6.6)$$

$$U'(N) + \lambda W = 0, \quad (A6.7)$$

$$-\lambda i - \alpha = 0, \quad (A6.8)$$

$$\lambda_{+1}(1 + i) = \lambda, \quad (A6.9)$$

and the Euler equations are:

$$\beta U'(C)/P = [U'(C_{+1})/P_{+1}](1 + i), \quad (A6.10)$$

$$-U'(N) = [U'(C)(W/P)](1 + i). \quad (A6.11)$$

The model may be closed with the following additional assumptions about production:

$$Y = F(N), \qquad F'(N) > 0, \ F''(N) < 0 \qquad \text{(A6.12)}$$
$$W/P = F'(N), \qquad \text{(A6.13)}$$
$$Y = C. \qquad \text{(A6.14)}$$

And, the solution to the problem can be simplified by assuming (convenient) specific functional forms for the utility and production functions, as follows:

$$U = [(C)^{1-b}/(1-b)] - [(N)^{1-h}/(1-h)], \qquad (b > 0, \ h < 0) \quad \text{(A6.15)}$$
$$Y = Y_0(N)^a, \qquad (0 < a < 1). \quad \text{(A6.16)}$$

Now take logs, recalling that $i = r + (\ln P_{+1} - \ln P) = r + p^e_{+1}$. The log-linear version of the model is therefore:

$$\ln Y = \ln Y_{+1} + (1/b)(\theta - r), \qquad \text{(A6.17)}$$
$$\ln Y = \ln Y_0 + a \ln N, \qquad \text{(A6.18)}$$
$$\ln N = \ln N_0 + [1/(a-1)]w, \qquad \text{(A6.19)}$$
$$\ln N = \theta/h - (1/h)w + (1/h)p_{+1}, \qquad \text{(A6.20)}$$
$$p = m - (\ln Y - \ln Y_{-1}). \qquad \text{(A6.21)}$$

Here w is the log of the real wage rate, m is the rate of money growth, and N_0 is a composite term that involves the parameters of the specific functional forms suggested above. In the steady-state, therefore, the results may be summarized as:

$$r = \theta, \qquad \text{(A6.22)}$$
$$\ln Y = \ln Y^N + \{a/[h - a(1+b)]\}p, \qquad \text{(A6.23)}$$
$$p = m. \qquad \text{(A6.24)}$$

The term Y^N has to be interpreted again as the "natural rate" of output, but now only in the sense of the level of output which can be achieved when the inflation rate is *zero*. The interesting feature of Eq. (A6.23), however, is that when the inflation rate increases, the actual steady-state level of output will fall below this level. As inflation is caused by money supply growth, the model in Eq. (A6.22) through Eq. (A6.24) therefore exhibits non-super-neutrality of money. However, this is in the *reverse* direction to that of some of the models in the main text, because the term $\{a/[h - a(1 + b)]\}$ is negative.

This is therefore a result that, *if* it could be replicated in the real world, that would more than justify a strong anti-inflationary policy. In point of fact, however, it does no such thing because it has been achieved only by a fairly transparent analytical device or "trick". The reverse non-neutrality result occurs only because, in setting up the original budget and CIA constraints, the representative consumer was not allowed to spend current wage receipts in the current period but has to hold them over until next period. Therefore, an increase in the inflation rate acts as a "tax" on wages and hence on work effort. Most arguments against the distorting effects of inflation in the literature rely on something similar to this. However, such apparently strong results can easily be changed just by tweaking the model slightly, as discussed in the next section.

Different Timing Assumptions

In fact, by simply changing the timing assumptions from the problem in (A6.1)–(A6.3) the negatively sloped LRPC (in p, Y space) can be made to disappear, and the traditional vertical LPRC restored. Let the new problem be, for example:

$$\max \sum_0^\infty \beta^t U(C_t, N_t), \qquad U'(C) > 0, \ U'(N) < 0 \qquad (A6.25)$$

subject to:

$$WN + M \geq PC, \qquad (A6.26)$$
$$B = B_{-1} + WN + i(B_{-1} - M) - PC. \qquad (A6.27)$$

The key change here is now to allow the wage bill, WN, to also appear in the CIA constraint. The first-order conditions therefore become:

$$U'(C) - P(\lambda - \alpha) = 0, \qquad (A6.28)$$
$$U'(N) + W(\lambda - a) = 0, \qquad (A6.29)$$
$$-\lambda i - \alpha = 0, \qquad (A6.30)$$
$$\lambda_{+1}(1 + i) = \lambda. \qquad (A6.31)$$

Using the same functional forms and specification of production as before, a log-linear version of the overall revised model will therefore be:

$$\ln Y = \ln Y_{+1} + (1/b)(\theta - r), \qquad (A6.32)$$
$$\ln Y = \ln Y_0 + a \ln N, \qquad (A6.33)$$

$$\ln N = \ln N_0 + [1/(a-1)]w, \tag{A6.34}$$

$$\ln N = \theta/h - (1/h)w, \tag{A6.35}$$

$$p = m - (\ln Y - \ln Y_{-1}). \tag{A6.36}$$

In the steady-state, the model further reduces to a very familiar "classical" form consisting of the following three equations:

$$r = \theta, \tag{A6.37}$$

$$\ln Y = \ln Y^N, \tag{A6.38}$$

$$p = m. \tag{A6.39}$$

Therefore, the level output will now always return to its natural rate (regardless of the rate of inflation) and the super-neutrality of money is restored. The real rate of interest is also equal to its natural rate (the constant rate of time preference) and the inflation rate is dictated by the rate of monetary growth.

The "reverse" non-super-neutrality result has disappeared. In fact, it is shown up as simply an artefact of the way the original CIA model was set up in the first place. It is important to note that this *cannot* be said of the various "forced savings" results (that is results showing a positive relation between inflation and the level of output) that were derived in the main text.

CHAPTER 7

AN ALTERNATIVE MONETARY MODEL OF ECONOMIC GROWTH, THE BUSINESS CYCLE, INFLATION AND INCOME DISTRIBUTION

Introduction

This is Chapter 7 in the series *Essays in the Fundamental Theory of Monetary Economics and Macroeconomics*, and its goal is to develop an "alternative monetary model" (AMM) of economic growth, the business cycle, inflation and income distribution. This construct has had a number of antecedents over the years, for example, in Atesoglu and Smithin (2006, 2007) and Smithin (1994, 1997, 2003, 2005, 2009a, 2009c). The present version contains each of what were described in Chapter 2, as the "desirable" features of such a model. These are: (1) that money and credit creation are an essential feature of the way the economy works, not just a superfluous addition to a barter exchange economy, (2) the money supply is endogenous, (3) there is a *monetary* theory of the *real* rate of interest, (4) the monetary policy instrument used by the central bank is a nominal interest rate, the "policy rate", and, (5) monetary policy is non-neutral in both the short run, and over a longer time horizon. In context, this means that changes in the real inflation-adjusted policy rate affect both the ups and downs of the business cycle *and* the ongoing growth rate of the economy. The same thing can be said of changes in fiscal policy, meaning either changes in government spending as a percentage of GDP, or changes in the average tax rate. As shown in previous essays no other approach to monetary economics combines all of these features.

In what follows, the basic equations of the model are introduced and then it is explained how each is derived. Then the discussion moves on to the determinants of economic growth, the business cycle, and inflation in this framework. There is sufficient analytical material in these sections, I think, to fully identify and explain the factors that cause the economic fluctuations, episodes of boom and bust, periodic financial crises, and so on, that occur in reality, and how these might be mitigated or avoided.

In addition, however, I want to address the argument that is frequently made, particularly in difficult economic times, that the monetary production or "capitalist" economy is somehow inherently or *irremediably* unstable. The following section is therefore an investigation of the conditions that might make this "outright" instability a reality. The stability issue is shown to revolve *particularly* around questions of monetary policy, first and foremost, rather than (*e.g.*) either fiscal policy *or* financial regulation, as such. The argument is not meant to downplay the significance of either these matters as questions of practical statecraft. Fiscal policy *is* discussed in some detail *via* the impact of changes in g and t. Moreover, it goes without saying that the regulatory environment of banking and finance is important. (In North America, for example, compare the "safety and security" of the banking and financial system in Canada with that of the USA, historically and up to the present.) Nonetheless, the intent of this particular section of the essay is rather to pinpoint exactly the conditions that would *allow* for a really uncontrollable movement in either direction, rather than to repeat the eclectic and *ad hoc* discussions of "boom and bust" that take place around every historical episode.

The final two sections of the chapter will show how the model can be reduced to a simple three-equation construct for the purposes of a simplified graphical analysis, and discuss the impact of the same policy, and other changes, on the functional distribution of income, real wages, real interest rates and profits. The graphical framework provides a diagram directly comparable to the early 21st century textbook "new consensus" model (NCM) of economic orthodoxy (discussed in Chapter 4). It is then possible to examine several graphical applications of the AMM to assess the impact of monetary and fiscal policy, and other macroeconomic changes.

The model is worked out in the context of a theoretical closed economy but it has wider sphere of practical application. In principle, the results hold up in the following circumstances: (a) a closed economy under autarky, that is, an economy that does not trade with the rest of the world, (b) the world economy treated as whole, (c) an individual open economy with a floating exchange rate, (d) an economy with a "fixed but adjustable exchange rate regime" (Kam and Smithin, 2008, 2011), or (e) a regional economy with a common currency, but a floating common external exchange rate (such as the Euro-zone in the early 21st century).

However, it is left to a later essay (Chapter 8) to go into more detail about the issues arising from real exchange rate changes, the balance of payments, international capital flows, *etc.* What follows is intended as the basic theory of the enterprise economy in its own right, not dealing in detail (at this stage) with the specifically international complications (Smithin, 2009a).

The Alternative Monetary Model (AMM)

The latest version of the alternative monetary model, which Atesoglu and Smithin (2007) at one point (over-optimistically) called a "simple macroeconomic model" (SMM), consists of the following five equations:

$$y = d + g - t + \varepsilon k, \qquad 0 < \varepsilon < 1 \qquad \text{(economic growth)}, \qquad (7.1)$$

$$a = k + r + w \qquad \text{(income distribution)}, \qquad (7.2)$$

$$p = p_0 + w_{-1} - a \qquad \text{(inflation)}, \qquad (7.3)$$

$$w = w_0 + t + \eta y, \qquad 0 < \eta < 1 \qquad \text{(real wages)}, \qquad (7.4)$$

$$r = \mu + \sigma r'_B - (1 - \sigma)p, \qquad \mu > 0; \ 0 < \sigma < 1 \ \text{(real interest rates)}. \qquad (7.5)$$

The endogenous variables are y, the growth rate of real GDP, k the (expected) entrepreneurial profit share, r the real rate of interest on loans of money, w the logarithm of the real wage rate, and p, the inflation rate. The exogenous variables are, d the "net autonomous demand" of the private sector (as a percentage of GDP), g government spending (as a percentage of GDP), t the average tax rate, and r'_B, which is the inflation-adjusted real policy rate of the central bank (the notation is intended to retain a hint of the ancient term "bank rate") and lastly, a, the logarithm of aggregate labour productivity. The intercept term in the inflation equation, p_0, and also the intercept term in the wage curve, w_0, though derived from the underlying parameters of the behavioural variables, may also be considered exogenous variables from the point of view of policy analysis. It is possible to investigate the separate impact on the economy of each of these when they do change.

The term p_0 has to do with the idea of "liquidity preference" a well-known expression that is taken originally from Keynes. It means "sentiment in the money market", although in this case as applied specifically in an *endogenous money* context (In the *GT* itself, as we have seen,

Keynes wrongly assumed exogenous money.) A *decrease* in p_0 represents an *increase* in liquidity preference, or an increase in "bearishness" (Keynes, 1971a/1930, pp. 128–131), negative market sentiment. An increase in p_0 means a decrease in liquidity preference, an increase in "bullishness" in financial markets (Keynes, 1971a/1930, pp. 128–131).

The term w_0 involves essentially "real" cost factors, specifically having to do with the socio-political position of labour. An increase in w_0, for example, might represent such things as an increase in the political power of labour unions, legislation favourable to labour, an increase in "entitlements", *etc.* (and *vice versa*). The symbols ε, λ, η, μ and σ are the given parameters of the model. The restrictions on the signs and magnitudes of the parameters are based on considerations of empirical plausibility and also the logical requirements of the model.

A Keynesian Theory of Economic Growth

Equation (7.1) is essentially a Keynesian theory of economic growth. As explained elsewhere (e.g., Smithin, 2009a, 2007b, pp. 103–105) the "correct" growth theory is not the traditional Harrodian $y = s/O$ where s is the propensity to save, and O is the dubious concept of the "capital/output ratio".[1] Nor are any of the subsequent neoclassical theories correct. Instead, the basic growth equation should be simply:

$$y = d' - s, \tag{7.6}$$

where the term d' (not the same as d) is a portmanteau variable standing for "net total autonomous demand" as a percentage of GDP. Growth depends straightforwardly on whether, or not, and by how much, the demand parameter is greater that the impetus for saving (the growth if it occurs, is "financed" by credit creation, and the *incentive* for firms to provide the growth is profitability). Equation (7.1) above is simply an elaboration of (7.6) and can be formally derived from the following two equations:

$$Y = C + I + G, \tag{7.7}$$

$$C = cY_{-1} - T. \tag{7.8}$$

Equation (7.7) is the usual expenditure breakdown of real GDP, where Y stands for real GDP, C for real consumption spending, I for "investment" spending,[2] and G for government spending. Equation (7.8) is a Keynesian-type consumption function, with a lag for the sake of realism, as originally suggested by Hicks (1982a, p. 179). Lower case c is the Keynesian propensity to consume, and T is real value of total tax collections. Equation (7.8) states that planned consumption spending in real terms is some fraction of the level of income experienced in the previous period (taking into account the fact that there would have been taxation in that period also). It defines a sort of expected/desired standard of living based on what the mainstream literature calls "habit persistence". The equation also makes the assumption that this planned or desired level of consumption will have to be reduced by the full amount of the actual current tax burden. These are taken to be funds that are (literally) *not available* to be spent.

Hicks's idea of a simple lag in the consumption function is *all* that is required to generate a theory of economic growth which is entirely "Keynesian" in spirit, and quite different from all non-monetary classical or neoclassical theories of growth. To derive the complete growth equation, substitute Eq. (7.7) into Eq. (7.8) and divide through Y_{-1}, to yield:

$$Y/Y_{-1} = c + (1/Y_{-1})(I + G - T). \tag{7.9}$$

The, multiply the final term on the right hand side (RHS) by Y/Y, and rearrange the expression. Using the lower case notation from the previous section, this gives:

$$(1 + y)(1 - x - g + t) = 1 - s. \tag{7.10}$$

The symbol x stands for investment spending by the private sector (better "firm spending") as a percentage of GDP, so that $x = I/Y$. Similarly g is government spending as a percentage of GDP, and t is the average tax rate. The symbol s is the propensity to save, where $s = 1 - c$. Taking logs of Eq. (7.10) reduces the expression to:

$$y = x + g - s - t. \tag{7.11}$$

The next step is to specify an "investment function", such as:

$$x = (I/Y) = x_0 + \varepsilon k. \tag{7.12}$$

Investment as a percentage of GDP therefore depends upon profitability, and also on an autonomous component the intercept term, x_0. This corresponds to Keynes's (1964/1936, p. 161) "animal spirits". The "net autonomous expenditure" of the private sector can then be defined as $d = x_0 - s$ (animal spirits less the propensity to save), which leads directly to (7.1). The argument is that economic growth will increase if the expected profit share or mark-up increases (surely part of the fundamental logic of capitalism). Also, if there is an increase in either the net autonomous spending of the private sector, *or* in government spending as percentage of GDP. An increase in the average tax rate will reduce the rate of growth.

An Alternative Theory of Value and Income Distribution

Equations (7.1) was derived from the typical "expenditure breakdown" of GDP. Similarly, Eq. (7.2) can be thought of as log-linear version of the alternative "income-based" GDP breakdown. It is derived formally from the following two equations:

$$P_{+1} Y_{+1} = \Pi + (1 + i)PK + (1 + i)WN, \qquad (7.13)$$

$$Y_{+1} = AN. \qquad (7.14)$$

Equation (7.13) is the "income breakdown" of *expected future* nominal GDP $(P_{+1}Y_{+1})$ expressed purely in money terms. It allows for the fact that production takes time, and hence for an explicit interest charge on the costs of production. The expression $P_{+1}Y_{+1}$ represents *expected* money receipts from *current* production. The current money value of "variable capital" is WN (the nominal wage bill) while PK ($P \times K$) is the current money value of "constant capital", the initial money value of the raw materials and physical plant that is destined to be "used up" during the production process. These terms variable capital and constant capital are originally derived from Marx (Sweezy, 1970, p. 63), but have obvious analogies in neoclassical or mainstream economics (*e.g.*, the concepts of circulating and fixed capital). The interest charge on both variable and constant capital is i (a nominal rate of interest), and Π is the sum of expected money profit.

Equation (7.14), on the other hand, is a "Keynesian theory of aggregate supply" (Palley, 1996, 1997; Smithin, 1986). The main feature is a simple one-period production lag (strictly speaking, a "marketing" lag). This can therefore be thought of as quintessentially Keynesian idea because it means that *current* production is always being undertaken to satisfy expected *future* demand. The choice of specifically a one-period lag is merely the *simplest possible* way to capture the general idea. The term A is the "average productivity of labour" (the anti-log of a above), but such a definition requires some further thought as to what "productivity" actually means in the present context. Equation (7.14) simply maps some convenient measure of current employment into the total of "value added" that is *produced* in the current period, but only marketed (sold) in the next period. The expression in (7.14) explicitly mentions only the relation between labour input and output, but it should *not* therefore be inferred that this ignores the constant capital component. The contributions of the various machines, computers, buildings, raw materials, the state of technical knowledge, *etc.*, are "rolled up" in the term A. Any changes that occur in the physical conditions of production can be represented by changes in the term A itself. A technological innovation, for example, might be represented by an increase in A. On the other hand, a natural disaster which (say) destroys some of the physical equipment now in existence can be indicated by a decrease in A. Meanwhile, if we were to consider a situation in which "capital investment" is assumed to be going on, and, at the same time, the A term stays roughly constant, period by period, then this should be understood as implying that the investment in constant capital being undertaken is "just sufficient" to increase production and employ more labour at the existing average level of productivity.

On this same topic it should be noticed, however, that we can hardly think of the term A as being *only* a question of technology. What Eq. (7.14) actually shows is the relationship between the total of "value added" production expressed in (real) money terms, and some measure of labour input. Therefore, in *addition* to the purely technical aspects, the notion of productivity *must* also have a large subjective element. In a monetary economy any definition of "value added" (and therefore productivity) must involve at least some notion of what people "are prepared to pay for".

What emerges from the discussion is best described as something like a "labour theory of production" (rather than a labour theory of value). It is basically a rival to, or antidote for, the familiar "AK" model of neoclassical growth economics (Jones, 1998, pp. 148–150). Its most obvious feature is a full acceptance of Keynes's view that in macroeconomics it is best to restrict attention to "quantities of money value and quantities of employment" (Keynes, 1964/1936, p. 41). It specifically rejects any attempt at the quixotic task of trying to give concrete meaning to the vague notion of the "capital stock".

The underlying theory of value is ultimately *neither* the labour theory of value, *nor* neoclassical utility theory, but an "ontologically subjective" social theory of value (Ingham, 2004; Smithin, 2009a), which, in principle, is the same sort of idea that lies behind the calculation of index numbers in the national accounts.[3]

Returning now to Eq. (7.13) note that, unlike in the canonical neo-classical model, (or in Marx, or in Keynes), the representative firm is *not* assumed to be perfectly competitive. This is a fundamentally important issue as already discussed in Chapter 5. Given imperfect competition, conceptually a finite horizon or steady-state "growth equilibrium" must exist, in which entrepreneurial rates of profit are *not* necessarily "equalized" across firms and industries. Nonetheless, it is still reasonable to use the term equilibrium in describing the solution, because this steady-state, involving imperfect competition, and different profit rates in each industry, is presumed to stay in place at least until some new innovation or divestment occurs. Although there is no equalization of profits, nonetheless the same *interest rate* should still prevail everywhere in the steady-state equilibrium. This is simply because "money" itself can be moved around much more freely than any, and all, of the "firm-specific" attributes of the production process.

As discussed in other places (*e.g.*, Smithin, 2009a, 2009b, p. 5), it is not at all easy to arrive at the correct terminology to describe this finite horizon equilibrium. It would probably not be correct to call this simply a "long-run" equilibrium, in the sense that this term is used in intermediate textbooks (as opposed, for example, to some "very long-run" equilibrium, from neoclassical growth theory). The point is that in the AMM the growth rate has *already* been determined by the time the model gets into the finite horizon steady-state. Another alternative might be to use the expression "medium-run" from more recent mainstream economics (Blanchard, 2000; Solow, 2000), and to think of the time horizon in that literature as the empirical counterpart to our theoretical model.[4] In that case, however, and *unlike* anything in neoclassical economics, it is important to note that there would then be *no* other "long-run", or "very long-run", *except* the results realized empirically by the stringing together of the historical sequence of "medium-run" steady-state outcomes (Kalecki, 1971c; Marterbauer and Smithin, 2000, 2003). This is a fundamental issue in the application of any type of "equilibrium theory" to try to explain actual events.

Having discussed some of these conceptual issues, next introduce the new terms, $\pi' = \Pi/[WN(1+i)]$, and $k' = PK/WN$. The first of these is an analog to the Marxian notion of the "rate of surplus value" (as differentiated from the rate of profit). The second is similarly related to what Marx would have called the "organic composition of capital", the proportion between constant capital and variable capital (Sweezy, 1970, p. 66), or more simply the capital/labour ratio. Equation (7.13) can then be re-written in the form:

$$P_{+1}Y_{+1} = (1 + s' + k')(1 + i)WN. \tag{7.15}$$

This expresses total expected receipts, in money terms, as a mark-up over investment in the variable capital component, also measured in money terms. The overall mark-up therefore covers three main elements in the accounting scheme, the interest charge, depreciation on fixed or constant capital, and the net profit ("surplus value").

Finally, let the symbol k (different from k') stand for the "gross entrepreneurial profit share", such that $k = k' + s'$. The newly-defined mark-up factor, k, includes an allowance for both depreciation on physical capital and for the rate of surplus value. That is the sense in which it is a *gross* mark-up. Importantly though, from the perspective of theories of income distribution, it is now "net" of the nominal interest charge.

From a behavioural perspective, it is an advantage that k is the *expected* mark-up or profit share, as this is likely to be the most relevant consideration for economic decision-making. In equilibrium, actual and expected k will coincide, but whether in equilibrium or out, there always exists a subjective value of k, at *both* the firm level and the aggregate level. Aggregate k is derived simply by summation, as shown by (Kalecki, 1971a, pp. 47–48). This k is not an aggregate expected profit *rate* as profit rates, even in equilibrium, are different across different firms and industries. In specifying an aggregative behavioural model, the mark-up term k itself is the more useful concept. It is the most reasonable choice for the "incentive variable" in an aggregative equation, because an increase in k is a prerequisite for both an increase in the rate of surplus value itself and an overall increase *on average* in the various *ex ante* rates of return used by firms as individual decision metrics. (Each firm is also individually aware of the "depreciation allowances" that must be set aside under alternative business plans.) With the new notation, Eq. (7.15) becomes:

$$P_{+1}Y_{+1} = (1 + k)(1 + i)WN, \tag{7.16}$$

Substituting the lagged production function (7.14) into (7.16) and taking logs:

$$k = \ln A - [i - (\ln P_{+1} - \ln P)] - (\ln W - \ln P). \tag{7.17}$$

The term in square brackets, $[i - (\ln P_{+1} - \ln P)]$, is the nominal interest rate minus expected inflation, in other words, the real interest rate, r. Let lower case w stand for the log of the real wage rate ($w = \ln W - \ln P$), and recall that $a = \ln A$. Equation (7.2), the basic theory of profit, essentially an "adding up" theory in terms of logarithms or percentages, follows directly.

The Monetary Circuit, Profits, and an "Indirect" Money Demand/Supply Theory of Prices and Inflation

In the earlier discussion of the determinants of growth, there was brief reference to the fact that the $d' - s$ gap must necessarily be financed by credit creation. Apart from that, however, up to now, and as is unfortunately quite typical in macroeconomics, it has been possible to conduct the discussion almost entirely in so-called "real" terms. It is important, though, not to forget that this is only *half* the story. It is also necessary to trace out in detail the flows of money that must be occurring as the goods and services in the real economy are produced, marketed, and change hands. The reader is reminded that the money/credit mechanism is an integral part of the way in which profit is actually generated in capitalism, and that the real economy could not function without it. We are explicitly in an endogenous money environment, and credit creation and repayment are essential to any account of the way in which entrepreneurial profits are realized and disbursed (Seccareccia, 1996; Smithin, 2009a). This section therefore gives an account of the way in which the "monetary circuit" (Graziani, 2003; Parguez and Seccareccia, 2000; Smithin, 2011) can be made to work in the current framework.

Perhaps surprisingly, this same discussion also explains the derivation of Eq. (7.3) above. It will allow a theory of inflation to be added to the model in the tradition of the "cost-push" or "conflict inflation" approaches of the post-Keynesian literature. In another interesting twist, the discussion will *also* show how Keynes's important notion of "liquidity preference" fits into the AMM. It can be show that Keynes's idea retains its relevance even in a situation in which the money supply is not fixed, but is fully endogenous.

A starting point for thinking about the price level and inflation involves the two following simple "money demand and supply" equations, initially both assumed to have constant coefficients:

$$M^d = \psi PY, \qquad 0 < \psi < 1 \tag{7.18}$$

$$M^s = \phi W_{-1} N_{-1}, \qquad \phi > 1. \tag{7.19}$$

As in many theories of endogenous money, the supply of money in existence at any one time is seen as being closely related to the wage bill/production costs. This is shown in Eq. (7.19). In effect, the "circuit" begins as firms borrow sums of money that are *related* to the need to finance the wage bill (and also other cost items) to start the production process. It ends one period later (given the production/ marketing lag) as the output is sold, and the debts incurred can be paid off. This sequence is repeated every period.

It was pointed some time ago by Moore (1988, p. 232), that even if some individual firms do not directly borrow to finance their wage bill (or only partially finance their wage bill) nonetheless at the macroeconomic level it is likely that the *aggregate* coefficient ϕ, is greater than one ($\phi > 1$). Indeed, reverting to the theme of Chapter 1, this coefficient *must* be greater than one, in order for the system to be logically viable, and to validate the monetary circuit, $M - C - C' - M'$. Only then would firms *in aggregate* be able to realize positive monetary or accounting profits (Seccareccia, 1996; Smithin, 1994, 2003, 2009a). Fortunately for the feasibility of the monetary production economy this is at least a plausible condition in "normal" circumstances. This is because, in addition to the acquisition of working/variable capital by firms, all other forms of borrowing must also be taken into account. There are loans for fixed capital formation, consumption loans, and loans that are taken only to purchase financial securities. *The* main point to notice is that all of these are only likely to be granted *conditional* upon some income-based indicator of credit-worthiness and at the macro level the total wage bill is a good proxy for such an indicator. For firms, the wage bill is an indicator of size, for individuals, income. In an aggregative model, it is therefore, a reasonable strategy to express total lending as a *multiple* of the wage bill. The actual numerical value of ϕ can, of course, change spontaneously at any time, based on any and all factors that affect these estimations of credit-worthiness in the loan markets. If ϕ does change, then the effects that ensue in the financial and economic systems can be worked out in much the same way as the effects of (*e.g.*) changes the policy rate of interest, or labour productivity.

The money demand equation in Eq. (7.19) meanwhile gives the demand for money balances (that is, the demand for bank deposits) as a proportion ψ, of nominal GDP. This is obviously similar to the old fashioned quantity theory of money. In the terminology of Chapter 3, the theory is a straightforward Marshallian "cash balances" approach to the demand for money. This seems to become plausible once again, in the modern world of electronic money, because in this environment there is no reason why bank deposits themselves should not attract a market-determined interest rate. There can also be spontaneous changes in ψ, the money demand parameter, just as there are changes the supply coefficient, ϕ. In fact, it will be argued below that it is likely that the same sort of factors affect both the demand side and supply side of the "market for endogenous money".

Combining Eqs. (7.18) and (7.18) yields the aggregate price level:

$$P = [(\phi/\psi)W_{-1}]/A. \tag{7.20}$$

I call this an "indirect" theory of the price level, because strictly speaking a "cash balances" approach to the demand for money involves money that is *not* being spent and, presumably, the price level itself is actually determined by the amount of money that *is* offered in exchange for goods and services. Nonetheless, according to Eq. (7.21) the price level can always be *inferred* by the economic actors from what they know about the money demand and supply process, and from observation of the current levels of economic activity and previous costs. Taking logs of Eq. (7.20) and subtracting the term $\ln P_{-1}$ from both sides then gives Eq. (7.3) above, where $p = \ln P - \ln P_{-1}$, and p_0 is defined as $p_0 = \ln \phi - \ln \psi$. Inflation depends on the gap between lagged real wages and productivity and on a term involving the parameters on both the supply and demand side of the money market, ψ and ϕ, summed up in the term p_0. As already explained p_0 reflects called "liquidity-preference" Keynes (1964/1936, p. 194). Note that in the endogenous money case, liquidity preference involves *both* the overall willingness to borrow money on the one hand, illustrated by the term $\ln \psi$, and also the willingness to hold or absorb money balances, on the other, illustrated by the term $\ln \phi$. An increase in liquidity preference Keynes (1964/1936, p. 194) reflects an increased willingness to hold bank deposits and less readiness to borrow, and causes a fall in p_0. A reduction in liquidity preference on the contrary, means an increased willingness to both to borrow money and to spend money, and will increase p_0.

A "Classical" Theory of Real Wages

Equation (7.4) above might be called a "wage curve" and is intended to describe the macroeconomic behaviour of after-tax real wages. This is a different concept from a *labour supply curve*, as it has the (log of) the average real wage rate as the *dependent* variable, rather than as the *independent* variable. I have argued elsewhere that this is a more realistic way of approaching the issue, particularly at the macroeconomic level

(Smithin, 2009a, pp. 117–119). The basic suggestion is that there are two sorts of influences on the aggregate behaviour of real wages. First, whether or not the economy is growing. After-tax real wages will tend to rise with economic growth (y) because this increases the bargaining power of labour in the market-place, everything else equal. Second, there can be an autonomous rise or fall in the bargaining power of labour *not* connected with demand conditions in the labour market. That is, a change due to political, sociological or institutional considerations. Such an effect is captured by an index of the general socio-economic condition of labour (the w_0 term) the cumulative effect of labour legislation, social attitudes, and the strength or otherwise of labour unions, *etc.*

The idea that the level of real wages will tend to be higher in a growing, rather than stationary economy, goes all the way back to Adam Smith, as in the following passage from the *Wealth of Nations* (Smith, 1981/1776, p. 87):

> It is not the actual greatness of national wealth, but its continual increase which occasions a rise in the wages of labour. It is not accordingly in the richest countries, but in the most thriving, or in those which are growing rich the fastest, that the wages of labour are highest.

Smith's example was the observation of higher wages in the fast-growing North American colonies than in England at his time of writing (1776), the same year as the Declaration of Independence, even though England was obviously the absolutely richer country at the time. Moreover, it is clear that in modern terms) the passage definitely refers to real rather than nominal wages. Smith states that not only were money wages higher in the soon-to-be independent colonies, but also that "the price of provisions is everywhere much lower in North America than in England" (Smith, 1981/1776, p. 87). The argument illustrated by Eq. (7.4), then, is that this basic idea, that real wages will be higher the faster the growth rate, is still essentially the correct formulation. It is what might be called a "classical" theory of real wages.

The Transmission Mechanism of Monetary Policy and the Relationship between the Central Bank and Commercial Banks

To see how Eq. (7.5) is derived, let the symbol i_B stand for the nominal policy rate set by the central bank (essentially the rate at which the commercial can borrow reserves) and i for the nominal lending rate of the commercial banks themselves. As shown by Kam and Smithin (2012), and in Chapter 4, commercial banks having a "direct-clearing" relationship with the central bank will tend to respond by setting their own lending rates as:

$$i = \mu + \sigma i_B, \qquad (7.21)$$

where μ is the desired mark-up between commercial bank lending rates and deposit rates. This pass-through coefficient financial mark-up must be high enough to cover costs and earn a "normal" rate of return for the banks, given existing institutional arrangements and regulations. The term σ, meanwhile, is (something like) the subjective probability (in the view of commercial bank officials themselves) of their bank having negative settlement balances at the clearing house (and hence having to finance the shortfall at the policy rate). For example, if the bank was operating in an ergodic environment (Davidson, 2009, pp. 37–38) and the probability distribution was known to be "normal", the figure would be $\sigma = 0.5$ (Rymes and Rogers, 2000). However, neither of these conditions is likely to hold in reality, so the number simply "is what it is", so to speak. Consistent with some of the empirical evidence (Atesolgu, 2003/2004; Uddin *et al.*, 2011; Sran, 2012), the actual pass-through coefficient tends to be a higher number than 0.5, but still less than one (something like 0.7 or 0.8). Next subtract the *observed* inflation rate p from both sides of Eq. (7.21), and the result is:

$$i - p = \mu + \sigma r'_B - (1 - \sigma)p, \qquad (7.22)$$

where r'_B is the inflation-adjusted real policy rate, the current setting of the nominal policy rate less the currently reported inflation rate. An important point that must be made at this stage is that if the central bank were looking for a "monetary policy rule" to follow, it would be quite *possible* to set r'_B as a policy target (Smithin, 2007a). The procedure would be simply to always adjust the nominal policy rate for observed inflation. Therefore, it was not correct for Milton Friedman (1968, p. 5), for example, in his famous AER article, to have said of the central bank that "It cannot peg interest rates except for very limited periods". The statement is not true for this particular definition of the real rate. In effect, central bankers set r'_B every time they change the nominal policy rate, given that they do know what the current inflation rate (and are usually reporting it themselves on the same web-site.) There is, therefore, a real sense in which central bankers can, indeed, be held responsible for whatever r'_B is, whether or not they are consciously aiming at any particular value.

The term on the LHS of Eq. (7.22) meanwhile, is $i - p$. This is the inflation-adjusted real lending rate of the commercial banks. The interesting question here is whether or not there are circumstances in which the inflation-adjusted real rate will be taken as a proxy for the real interest rate itself by most economic actors, as has often been claimed, notably by Taylor (1993). This is more likely to be the case, the more the central bank is inclined to pursue a stable policy on r'_B. In such circumstances, we would arrive at the expression in Eq. (7.5) showing a negative underlying basic theoretical relationship between real interest rates and inflation, similar to the "Mundell–Tobin effect" discussed in Chapter 6. It is certainly the case, in any given period, that this relationship could be overturned, empirically, by the sort of monetary policy "reaction function" popular in central banking circles in the last years of the 20th century and early years of the 21st century, as discussed in Chapter 4. This neo-Wicskellian approach was supposed to insist on *raising* the real policy rate whenever observed inflation rose above some arbitrary target. All this would do (and did do), in practice, is to lead to frequent changes (instability) in observed real policy rates, and possibly a positive empirical relation between real lending rates and inflation for at least some time. However, this would be entirely spurious from the theoretical point of view (such a relation is solely policy-induced). It was therefore a valid criticism of the mainstream models of the early 21st century that their demand side is "vulnerable to collapse" (Coombes, 2009, p. 1, 2010).[5] Such an outcome can be avoided by sticking to the formulation in (7.5).

The Business Cycle, Inflation, and the Equilibrium Growth Rate in the AMM

Having now explained at length the derivations of Eqs. (7.1)–(7.5), it is possible to reduce the model to the single expression, in Eq. (7.23) below, by successive substitution. It is presumed that the average tax rate has remained unchanged between the previous period (-1) and the present, and reference to the μ term is omitted simply to reduce the amount of "clutter" in the algebra. The truncated version of the dynamic equation is therefore:

$$y = -[\varepsilon\eta(1 - \sigma)/(1 + \varepsilon\eta)]y_{-1} + [1/(1 + \varepsilon\eta)]\{(d + g)$$

$$- [(1 + \varepsilon\sigma)/(1 + \varepsilon\eta)]t - [\varepsilon/(1 + \varepsilon\eta)]r'_B$$

$$+ [\varepsilon\sigma/(1 + \varepsilon\eta)](a - w_0) + [\varepsilon(1 - \sigma)/(1 + \varepsilon\eta)]p_0. \quad (7.23)$$

Equation (7.23) is a first-order difference equation in the growth rate of real GDP, and it is thus a concise description of the "business cycle" in the world of the AMM. It is plausible as such because the difference equation is "convergent with oscillations". The coefficient on the lagged GDP growth term on the right-hand side (RHS) is a negative fraction $\{1 < [\varepsilon\eta(1 - \sigma)/(1 + \varepsilon\eta)] < 0\}$.

There are three key explicit *policy* variables that affect the ups and downs of the business cycle namely, g, government spending as a percentage of GDP, the average tax rate, t, and the inflation-adjusted real policy rate of interest, r'_B. These are all treated here as exogenous decision variables on the part of the fiscal and monetary authorities. It is true that, in any actual economy, it might always be argued that there can be "feedback" on each of these from other elements in the system. There may be a progressive tax system, government spending might "automatically" rise in a recession due to spending mandates, the central bank may be pursuing a reactive monetary policy rule and so on. However, the essential point of treating each of the three policy variables as *exogenous* is that they could all be made so if the relevant authorities wished it. A decision *not* to control these magnitudes is therefore as much a policy choice as setting them at any given level, and to put in place various feedback rules for the different instruments is also a *choice*. Therefore, even in an entirely empirical setting, the current levels of each policy instrument are what *have* been "chosen" by the society at large in a quite definite sense. In a theoretical treatment the likely impact of changes in these "effective" policy stances are what needs to be investigated.

According to Eq. (7.23), the initial effect of an increase in government spending as a percentage of GDP, is to set off a business cycle upswing, whereas an increase in the average tax rate will have the opposite effect. A reduction in the real policy rate of interest of the central bank represents an "expansionary" monetary policy, whose impact effect is to improve economic growth, whereas a higher real policy rate, or a "tight money policy", will provoke a downturn.

In addition to these strictly policy initiatives there are a number of other "Keynesian-type" influences on the cycle in Eq. (7.23) that also need to be discussed. An increase in, d, the "net autonomous demand" of the private sector (as a percentage of GDP), is another factor which might set off a boom. This could be the result of either an improvement in the "animal spirits" of the entrepreneurs, *or* a decline in the overall propensity to save (an increase in the propensity to consume). An *increase* in the propensity to save (Keynes's "paradox of thrift"), or a falling off entrepreneurial animal spirits, on the other hand, will reduce d, and cause a downturn. Clearly on the long-debated issues of the relationships between savings and investment, economic growth, the business cycle, *etc.*, the results of this model are firmly in the Keynesian rather than "classical" camp (Fletcher, 1987, 2000, 2007; Smithin, 2002b, 2009a).

In a similar vein, also note that an increase in "liquidity preference" on both sides of the money market (a fall in the p_0 term) is one of the changes that could set off a business cycle downturn. This is another issue on which Keynes's insights seem to have been well founded. Even though it was argued (in Chapter 2) that the *particular* form of liquidity preference theory that Keynes put forward in the *General Theory* did not work (in that case because of the assumption of a fixed money supply), it can be seen that the basic concept remains completely relevant in the more realistic endogenous money environment. Changes in liquidity preference, broadly defined, do seem to be entirely capable of contributing to economic difficulties in much the way that Keynes said that they would (Davidson, 2009, pp. 31–32).

Another type of macroeconomic change that could occur in our model is a spontaneous technological innovation (shown by an increase in the term a). According to Eq. (7.23) such an innovation will cause a business cycle upturn, whereas a fall in productivity, for any reason (a reduction in a) will lead to a downturn. Therefore, to use modern terminology, something of the logic of a "real business cycle" (RBC) model is present in this framework, along with the more demand-orientated factors. Perhaps a better way of putting this is that the model is able to *accommodate* a "Schumpeterian" or "Robertsonian" approach to cycles (Fletcher, 2007, pp. 67–70) in addition to those of the traditional opponents of such writers. There is an important difference between the discussion here, however, and that in much of the well-established literature on the possible real causes of cycles. In the present case, purely materialist concepts, in themselves, are not regarded as the *only* possible causal factors in the cycle. It is also crucially important that the monetary/financial background, which *enables* the working out and implementation of any technological changes, as and when they do occur, is fully articulated and described. This is the type of material often found missing in many of the so-called "real" theories of growth or business cycles.

Another possible cause of changes in real costs that will impinge on the business cycle can be represented by changes in w_0, the intercept term in the real wage equation. An increase in w_0 would have the opposite effect to that of an improvement in technical efficiency, and *vice versa*. An increase in w_0 represents an increase in production costs that occurs without any concomitant increase in productivity (perhaps due to labour legislation, an increase in the incidence of labour unionization, or an increase in "entitlements"). This will cause a business cycle downturn. A reduction in these costs, if this can be achieved by bargaining or otherwise will cause an upswing.

There is a similar expression to Eq. (7.23) that is, a similar difference equation, which involves the cyclical behaviour of the inflation rate. This is:

$$p = [[\varepsilon\eta(1-\sigma)/(1+\varepsilon\eta)]p_{-1}$$
$$+ [\eta/(1+\varepsilon\eta)](d+g) + [(1-\eta)]/[(1+\varepsilon\eta)]t$$
$$- [\varepsilon\sigma\eta/(1+\varepsilon\eta)]r'_B - [1/(1+\varepsilon\eta)](a-w_0) + [1/(1-\sigma)]p_0. \quad (7.24)$$

The inflation equation is also convergent. However, focusing initially on the impact effects, it can be seen how, depending of the source of the disturbance, sometimes the ups and downs of the business cycle are accompanied by changes in the inflation rate in the same direction, and sometimes *not*. Increases in d, g, t, and w_0, for example, will each tend to increase the inflation rate, but in the first two cases, we already know that this will be be accompanied by an increase in the economic growth rate. However, for tax increases and other real cost increases, an increase in inflation is associated with lower economic growth.

Increases in real interest rates can be caused either by central bank tight money policy (an increase in r'_B), or by an increase in liquidity preference (a fall in p_0), and, in both cases will reduce inflation but also reduce growth [from Eq. (7.23)]. Lower real interest rates, on the other hand, can help to set off an economic boom, but will also cause some inflation.

As already emphasized, these growth and inflation cycles are *not* taking place around some given "natural" rate of growth. The various policy changes and collective behavioural changes that drive the cycle, also lead to changes in very economic equilibrium, or steady-state, to which the economy is eventually tending. It is important to realize, moreover, that after undergoing the various oscillations described in Eqs. (7.23) and (7.24), these movements will all be in the same direction as the initial, or impact, changes. In the context of the AMM there is *never* any argument to be made that any policy initiatives or other changes, which "work" in the short run, will not work, or will be "automatically reversed", later on. This is a major difference from the sorts of arguments commonplace in economics textbook. In textbooks the usual idea is either to warn against too much "activism", or to reassure the reader that the economy will always "bounce back" to normal, however bad the situation may seem in the short term. In the AMM, however, it is quite clear that the forces which initially set off cycles in one direction or another, also impact the longer term growth path of the economy, eventually in the same direction.

The finite horizon steady-states are themselves, in principle, moving equilibria and will continue to change whenever any one of the exogenous variables changes. As already discussed, therefore, actual historical experience will just be the "stringing together" of all the short run and equilibrium changes (both completed and incomplete) that have in fact occurred. Nonetheless, the analytical solutions for finite horizon steady-state growth equilibria still provide further useful information for policy analysis. The solutions for the steady-state growth rate and the inflation rate are:

$$y = [1/(1 + \varepsilon\eta\sigma)](d + g) - [(1 - \sigma)/(1 + \varepsilon\eta\sigma)]t - [\varepsilon\sigma/(1 + \varepsilon\eta\sigma)]r'_B$$
$$+ [\varepsilon\sigma/(1 + \varepsilon\eta\sigma)](a - w_0) + \varepsilon(1 + \varepsilon\eta\sigma)p_0, \qquad (7.25)$$

$$p = [1/(1 - \varepsilon\eta\sigma)](d + g) + [(1 + \eta)/(1 - \varepsilon\eta\sigma)]t - [\varepsilon\eta\sigma/(1 - \varepsilon\eta\sigma)]r'_B$$
$$- [1/(1 - \varepsilon\eta\sigma)](a - w_0) + [1/1 - \varepsilon\eta\sigma]p_0. \qquad (7.26)$$

These results therefore allow for a number of different potential combinations of growth and inflation that last beyond the "short run", or the time horizon of the business cycle. An increase in autonomous demand ("animal spirits"), or in government spending as a percentage of GDP, therefore leads to a "permanently" higher growth rate, as well as to a "permanently" higher inflation rate. Higher taxes will lead to lower growth with higher inflation, and *lower* taxes lead to *higher* growth with *lower* inflation. An increase in real wage (or other) costs, without a matching increase in productivity, will lead to lower growth and higher inflation (stagflation). An increase in productivity, itself, however, will do the opposite (it will produce higher growth with lower inflation).

A "tight money" policy, in the sense of a higher real policy rate of interest, will reduce inflation but lead to lower growth, and *vice versa* for an expansionary monetary policy. An increase in Keynesian "liquidity preference" or "bearishness" in the financial markets, meanwhile, have the *same* effect on interest rates as a deliberate tight money policy (which, as mentioned, does seem to have been be one of the main points that Keynes himself was trying to get across in the *General Theory*).

The Potential for Outright Financial and Economic Instability

It is true that the results in the previous section pre-supposed that the monetary and fiscal authorities were pursuing a (somewhat) stable policy. What I mean by this is simply a policy of stabilizing the inflation-adjusted real policy rate of interest at (hopefully) some "low but still positive" level (Smithin, 1994, p. 201, 2003, p. 207). Frequently, when this sort of policy is suggested to academic economists (from all sides of the political spectrum), or to central bank and other government officials, financial markets participants, and others, the typical reaction is incredulity. Such a thing is "impossible", they say. How can central banks ever be expected to control a "real" interest rate? However, as we specifically mean the *inflation-adjusted* real policy rate, there is really no mystery, and such a response cannot be anything more than the result of some previous period of "conditioning" in the precepts of classical or neoclassical economics. In reality, it is not at all impossible to stabilize the real policy rate in the above sense, and actually a very simple thing. All that it means is that the central bank is continually adjusting the nominal policy rate to keep the inflation-adjusted real rate roughly constant. In these sort of circumstances (that is, if central bank is pursuing this type of policy) then even if the fiscal authorities have been running a budget deficit, for example, the mere existence of the deficit does *not* lead to instability *per se*, in spite of traditional popular prejudices on the topic, now greatly reinforced by nearly half-a-century of similar arguments from the mainstream economics profession. On the contrary, we have seen above that an increase in budgetary spending against the background of a stable *monetary* policy, meaning precisely a policy that ensures the stability of real interest rates, will certainly increase the economic growth rate. Moreover, while it also increases the inflation rate it will *not* lead to runaway instability in either variable. (An increase is presumably a "good thing" in the case of growth, and not so good in the case of inflation.)

Against the same monetary policy background, a tax cut holding spending constant, which *also* increases the deficit, will actually lead to *higher* economic growth with *lower* inflation (these are both presumably good things). What then might possibly be the cause of the irremediable financial and economic instability that has often thought to be a real danger in the context of a "capitalistic" economic system, whether in discussing the historical record or now, once again, in our own time? The simplest answer to this seems to be that such "irremediable" instability will occur if the central bank does *not* indeed pay very close attention to its interest rate policy.

Suppose, for example, that instead of taking care to stabilize real interest rates, the central bank simply sets the nominal policy rate at some given figure, then makes no further changes, and pays no attention to any subsequent economic developments. That is, they set the policy rate at:

$$i_B = z\%, \qquad (7.27)$$

where z is some given nominal target. It could be just 0%, as in some recent historical examples, or, 2%, 4%, 5%, or any other nominal figure thought reasonable at the time.

To find the dynamic equation system on this new premise is a little more difficult than it was in the previous section. Specifically, the formally correct definition of the real interest rate, $r = i - p_{+1}$, must now be used, wherever relevant, as the players in the financial markets have nothing else on which to base their expectations. Similarly, it must also be recognized that the money demand and supply equations (7.18) and (7.19) now give perhaps too mechanical a description of the monetary circuit in the new circumstances. There are now other reasons for speculation about future asset prices besides "bull" or "bear" sentiment, as such. Therefore, a convenient specification for the term, ϕ/ψ, the ratio of the demand and supply parameters in the money market, might now be as follows:

$$\phi/\psi = [(\phi_0/\psi_0)]e^{-\lambda(r-r_{-1})}, \qquad 0 < \lambda < 1. \qquad (7.28)$$

Equations (7.28) still reflects the point that in an endogenous money framework the concept of liquidity preference must be relevant to *both* sides of the money market. It adds expected changes in real interest rates to the mix because now the central bank is no longer attempting to moderate such change. An expected fall in real interest rates, for example, implying an expected capital appreciation of non-monetary financial assets, logically should increase the volume of borrowing in order to purchase such assets (it should increase ψ). The same expected fall in real rates should *also* reduce the willingness to hold the monetary residue of borrowing that is real money balances in the form of bank deposits (it should reduce ϕ). The formulation in Eq. (7.28), where e is the base of the natural logarithm and λ is a parameter, captures both of these influences.

Next, substitute (7.28) back into the equation for the price level (7.20), take logs, and subtract the term $\ln P_{-1}$ from both sides. The result is:

$$p = p_0 - \lambda(r - r_{-1}) + w_{-1} - a. \tag{7.29}$$

Then it is possible to substitute into (7.29) a lagged version of the wage equation (7.4). Setting the various exogenous variables temporarily equal to zero in order to work out the dynamics, we therefore obtain:

$$p = -\lambda(-p_{+1} + p) + \eta y_{-1}. \tag{7.30}$$

Also, from Eqs. (7.1), (7.2) and (7.21), another equation involving growth and inflation is:

$$y = [\varepsilon/(1 + \varepsilon\eta)]p_{+1}, \tag{7.31}$$

From (7.30) and (7.31), and using the symbol Δ to represent first differences, it is therefore possible to arrive at the following dynamic equation for the inflation rate:

$$p = \{[1 + \lambda(1 + \varepsilon\eta)]/[\lambda(1 + \varepsilon\eta)]\}p_{-1} - [\cdots]\Delta i_B + \cdots + \cdots. \tag{7.32}$$

This is an *unstable* difference equation in inflation as the term $\{[1 + \lambda(1 + \varepsilon\eta)]/[\lambda(1+\varepsilon\eta)]\}$ is greater than one. As explicitly shown, whenever a *change* is made in the nominal policy rate ($\Delta i_B \neq 0$), and then the new setting is maintained thereafter (*e.g.*, at $i_B = z$ as suggested above) the inflation (or deflation) will go on gathering speed forever. A cut in the nominal policy rate will set off an indefinite inflation, whereas an increase will cause an ongoing deflation.

The effects of changes in the other exogenous variables that affect inflation are not explicitly shown in (7.32), but we already know which way they will go from Eq. (7.24). It can be inferred that it now *is* the case that an increase in government spending will set off an uncontrollable inflation, for example. On the other hand, an improvement in productivity will cause prices to fall continuously.

One purpose in making these points, therefore, is to sharply distinguish between a "cheap money policy" that is specified in real terms (as in the previous section), and one that is simply specified in nominal terms. Consider, for example, the idea, which often does arise in times of economic distress, that the central bank should simply drop the nominal policy rate on loans of base money to 0% (or close to it) and keep it there. This is a very different proposition from any suggestion that the *real* interest rate should be kept "low" as in Smithin (1994, 2003, 2007a). The nominal interest cut in itself does causes inflationary instability and *vice versa*, as critics of easy money in this sense have always argued. Also notice that there is a still worse problem if the policy is to just leave the nominal interest rate at any particular value. It will then be the case that, in the future, *anything* can happen. If any *other* event touches off either inflation, or a deflation, and the central bank does not respond appropriately, then the subsequent inflationary or deflationary response will be uncontrollable. In the Great Depression of the 1930s, as one historical example, nominal interest rates were indeed close to zero, but real rates were very high, because of continuing deflation. This in turn, contributed to further deflation. On the other hand, if nominal interest rates are zero and then inflationary pressures arise from other causes, the real rate will fall continuously, adding still further inflationary pressure, and so on.

Another issue arising from the above examples is to notice that, in the circumstances described, whenever the inflation rate in unstable, the real economy *itself* will also be "unstable" (as also would be true of nominal asset prices, *etc.*). To illustrate the comparable unstable difference equation in *real economic growth* is:

$$y = \{[1 + \lambda(1 + \varepsilon\eta)]/[\lambda(1 + \varepsilon\eta)]\}y_{-1} - [\cdots]\Delta i_B + \cdots + \cdots . \qquad (7.33)$$

This means that a cut in nominal interest rates, for example, though it may be criticized as causing inflation to rise indefinitely, also appears to allow the *real* economy to grow indefinitely. An austerity programme for government expenditures on the other hand, would cause continuing deflation *and* depression. The reader will be able think of other examples, including ongoing stagflation or (more hopefully) non-inflationary growth.

Bringing in the behaviour of the real growth rate, in this way, shows up what has *always* been a fundamental difficulty in interpreting the whole question of what actually, is meant by such phrases as a "booming economy" an "inflationary boom", or a "prosperous economy", or on the other hand, a depression. Putting the point the other way round, it also calls into question precisely what terms like "economic *stability*" or "economic *instability*" are themselves supposed to mean.

In terms of Eqs. (7.32) and (7.33) we can certainly see that outright instability *in the downward direction* would indeed be a big problem. This would imply a deflation and a depression. However, why would anyone should anyone worry about "instability" when it occurs the other way round, when the real economy is growing? Remember that real GDP is measured in subjective value-added terms (Smithin, 2009a, pp. xvi–xvii) so that rapid growth or prosperity clearly does *not* automatically raise the question of "scarce resources" in any purely materialistic sense.

From the combination of Eqs. (7.32) and (7.33), we can see in the "boom" situation with the nominal policy rate of interest constant, even if inflation *does* go on accelerating for ever the growth rate will also go on rising for ever. In this unstable "inflationary boom" case, therefore, looking at the results at face value, the question can arise, surely *does* arise, why anyone should be worried about this? What, exactly, is the problem with inflation if also real economic well-being is continually increasing? Why not simply just "let the good times roll"? Historically, it seems to me, this has been an almost impossibly difficult question to answer, in the field of political economy. Hicks (2005/1967, p. 160), for example, writes that the classical economists:

> ... were *afraid* of that question, for they did not know the answer to it. Yet they felt in their bones that the suggestion in it was wrong. (emphasis added)

Moreover, and although, as we have seen, Hicks would definitely have been regarded by many economists as being firmly in the Keynesian camp, he does then goes on to say (Hicks, 2005/1967, p. 161) that actually the classical economists:

> ... were quite right in refusing to look that way, *though they did not quite know just why they were refusing.* (emphasis added)

I would similarly argue that this same question has *never* really been satisfactorily dealt with by any of the various theories of financial excess and breakdown continuously put forward from different quarters. Examples would be the Austrian theory of business cycles (Hayek, 1967/1935, 1994) discussed in earlier essays, or, at the other end of the political/economic spectrum, Minsky's later "financial fragility hypothesis" (Kindleburger, 1989; Toporowski, 2008).

The basic idea of the original Austrian-type theories (to focus on that version), seems to have been that if there is an inflationary boom, this must *inevitably* lead to a financial crisis and then to economic collapse. The argument is that the previous inflationary policy is actually the *cause* of the eventual depression (Hayek, 1995a, pp. 192–197) even though it might seem to have been a good thing in the short term. The problem with Hayek's and other similar arguments, however, is that the exact mechanism by which the one thing supposedly *inevitably* leads to other is *never* really spelled out. What is the turning point or tipping point? In the formal Eqs. (7.32) and (7.33), there does not actually seem to be any.

In Smithin (2009a, p. 19), I quoted a passage from Hayek (1994, p. 145) on this topic, which is worth repeating here. Hayek is asked by an interviewer about the supposed "inflationary boom", of the late 1940s, 1950s, and 1960s, of the 20th century. This, at the time, seemed to be a vindication of Keynesian, rather than Hayekian ideas. The questioner asks Hayek both to explain the sustained economic growth of that period (the so-called "golden age of capitalism"), and in particular why it did *not* lead to crisis and depression, as it *should* have done on supposedly Austrian principles. This, after all, was how "Austrian" and other like-minded economists had rationalized the events of the 1920s and 1930s and, naturally, very similar arguments have recently been revived to explain the economic events of the first decades of the 21st century. So, why did this narrative *not* work in the *mid*-20th century? Hayek explains as follows:

> The particular form I gave was connected with the mechanism of the gold standard which allowed a credit expansion up to a point and then made a certain reversal possible. I always knew that in principle there was no definite limit for the period for which you could stimulate expansion by rapidly accelerating inflation. But I just took it for granted that there was a built-in stop in the form of the gold standard, and in that I was a little (sic) mistaken in my diagnosis of the postwar development. I knew the boom would break down, but I didn't give it as long it actually lasted. That you could maintain an inflationary boom for something like 20 years, I did not anticipate. While on the one hand I never believed, as most of my friends did, in an impending depression, I anticipated an inflationary boom. My expectation was that the inflationary boom would last five or six years, as the historical ones had done, forgetting that then the termination was due to the gold standard. If you had no gold standard — if you could continue inflating for much longer — it was difficult to predict how long it would last. Of course, it has lasted very much longer than I had expected. The end result was the same.

This seems to be an admission, in so many words, that the Austrian analysis of how the workings of the market will eliminate "over-investment", and ultimately bring down any attempt to stimulate the economy, first by inflation, and then in a reaction and depression, *really* just boils down to assuming that a gold standard is in place. What is noticeable also is the way in which Hayek uses the words "rapidly accelerating inflation" to describe the events of this specific time period. This is an exaggeration by almost any later or earlier historical standards. It may have been reasonable to state that there was rapidly accelerating inflation in (say) the mid-to-late 1970s, but that was in the context of the later *stagflation*, not the long postwar boom. Finally, it is difficult to overlook that fact that no real explanation is given of *why* "the end result must be the same", when the "stop" of the gold standard is no longer relevant.

The significance of these points can be clarified by comparing the above discussion to the analytical results from both sets of Eqs. (7.23)–(7.24) and (7.32)–(7.33). The first pair of equations is oscillating, but ultimately generates, stable solutions, and is worked out on the assumption that monetary policy is stabilizing real interest rates. The second pair is unstable and monetary policy is not playing a helpful role.

Contrary to Hayek, there can clearly can be a permanently expansionary policy, one in which inflation does not get out of control, if the monetary authorities are willing to stabilize the real inflation-adjusted policy rate in the way suggested earlier. It must be conceded (obviously) that in "real life" nothing actually does go on forever. They are bound eventually to be *some* political, economic, natural, historical, ideological, or other reactions or obstructions, in the real world, that will set things off in another direction. In fact, there are more than enough candidates for the role of "efficient cause" of the business cycle in the two oscillating but stable Eqs. (7.23) and (7.24). These candidates include policy mistakes (no doubt high on the list in many actual historical situations) changes in business confidence, changes in sentiment in the financial markets, changes in the political environment (whether or not it is supportive of capitalism), and so on.

Nonetheless, three key analytical points can be made. First, that there is no real difficulty in explaining a 20-year "boom" with moderate inflation (just as there would be no difficulty in explaining other inflation/growth combinations whether positive or negative). Second, that in the assumed circumstances (given stabilizing monetary policy) there is no *inherent* mechanism in the economic or financial sphere, no inexorable market forces, that definitively brings the boom to an end. There is not an *inevitable* break-down in the sense that the passage from Hayek certainly implies. Third, the analysis already contained/summarized in (7.23) and (7.24) also immediately shows up various routes by which the situation might be rectified, that is various policy options, if things do get off track.

At the same time, however, going back to the *unstable* equations, we can also see how the narrative about "financial breakdown", and the specifically Hayekian case of an inflationary boom leading eventually to a crash and then a lingering depression, might gain the superficial plausibility that, in hindsight, was so puzzling to Sir John Hicks (2005/1967, p. 203). In fact, the narrative might work with or without the background of a gold standard, but *not* for the reasons that Hayek and others seemed to think.

In the case where monetary policy is *not* stabilizing real interest rates there is an (possible) explanation of a turning point or tipping point that might be thought of as immanent in the political system, but is *not* immediately a question of economic theory or "market forces". The main difference between the two pairs of equation systems in (7.23)–(7.24) and (7.32)–(7.33), is that in the first case the central bank (in some sense) "knows what it is doing". In the explosive case, however, it clearly does not.

For the simplest illustration of the drastically unstable case, suppose that there is an inflation going on in the economy, but the monetary authority (the central bank) pays no attention, and keeps the nominal policy rate at $i = z\%$. There will be a boom and inflation, but not now of a steady character. The boom will seem to be gathering pace all the time, and at the same time the inflation rate will also be accelerating according to (7.32). However wild a ride it may be, there is still nothing in the *mathematics* of (7.32) and (7.33) to stop this situation going on forever. What *is* reasonable to argue, in this case, is there might eventually be a largely *political* reaction to the now (apparently) unsustainable situation. Such a response would be consistent with the tenets of economic rationality, but would not be a question of "market forces" or "economic laws", as such.

The point simply is that in the inflationary case, with nominal interest rates held constant, real interest rates must be constantly falling. Therefore, even though production is "booming" there will certainly be rational economic objections to the situation from at least one quarter, those *wealth-holders* who find the real value of their money holdings falling. A likely probable reaction to the new unstable situation, therefore, would be a *political* campaign in the financial press and by orthodox economists, to return to a "tight money policy". In fact, even this, if it was just a question of going back to a policy of stabilizing real rates might do no harm. Suppose, however, that the relevant authorities are not very clear on this point, or that they definitely subscribe to the view that the nominal rate should be raised by *more* than enough to compensate for inflation, the so-called "Taylor principle" (Mankiw, 2001, 2003; Davig and Leeper, 2007, 2010; Farmer *et al.*, 2010), which was highly influential in the early 21st century. Furthermore, as is also very likely from the political point of view, suppose that budget "austerity" is thought to be a big part of the remedy.

With these sorts of reactions there *will* be a crash and a slump, and from the unstable inflationary boom situation, things can quickly turn around to an equally unstable situation with continuously falling growth rate and deflation, a potential depression. This is a description of a process that I elsewhere called the "revenge of the rentiers" (Smithin, 1996b).

Finally, if the turning or tipping point does occur in the unstable case, it also has to be stressed that, in principle, the resulting slump would *also* go on forever. It must continue until some deliberate policy counter-reaction sets in to reverse it. The slump would certainly not be anything resembling the healthy purgative for the economy which was the original conclusion of the over-investment theory. The downturn in economic activity will not eventually just work itself out. On the contrary, recover would have to wait until the sentiment that "something must be done" has once again gained the upper hand in policy circles.

What lessons are there for macroeconomic policy from the fact that these for situations of drastic financial and economic instability do have the potential to occur? The most obvious response would to seem to be to pursue those sorts of macroeconomic policies that do lead to stable and sustainable outcomes as in Eqs. (7.23) and (7.24). There would be no need for classical, or any other economists, to "refuse to look" in that particular direction. In actual crisis situations, unfortunately, many other types of solution are put forward, usually deriving from some pre-existing political agenda of one type or another. On the "left", for example, these might ranging from "abolishing capitalism" altogether, to be replaced some unspecified alternative, drastically increased regulation, in either the financial or industrial sphere, increased taxation for re-distributive purposes, "zero growth" on environmentalist grounds, *etc.* From the "right", one can imagine there would be calls for return to *"laissez-faire"*, for a strict "austerity" budget policy, for a tight monetary policy such as "inflation targeting", and many other variants. However, Keynes in the *General Theory* (1964/1936, p. 322) had the correct pre-emptive response to them all:

> The right remedy for the trade cycle is not to be found in abolishing booms and thus keeping us permanently is a state of semi-slump, but in abolishing slumps and keeping us permanently in a state of semi-boom.

I have quoted this passage previously (Smithin, 1996b, p. 132, 2009a), and to put aside, for a moment, the necessary discussion of technical details about the monetary system, it seems to me that in many ways this was the *essence* of the Keynesian approach to economic difficulties. Most of the other types of policies traditionally recommended, on all sides of the political spectrum, would do exactly the opposite. They would eliminate the business cycle, and "instability", by keeping the economy *permanently* in a slow growth, high unemployment mode. This is a situation itself, however, that could never be politically sustainable.

The AMM in Inflation/Growth Space

This section will show that the original AMM model in Eqs. (7.1)–(7.5), can be reduced to a simple three-equation graphical system in inflation/growth (p, y) space. In this form, it can then be directly compared, for example, to the new consensus model previously discussed in Chapter 4. A similar exercise was undertaken in Smithin (2009c), but in that case with an earlier and slightly different version of the model. Again, set $\mu = 0$ for notational convenience. The three-equation system is then as follows:

$$p = -[1/\varepsilon(1-\sigma)](d+g) + [(1+\varepsilon)/\varepsilon(1-\sigma)]t - [\varepsilon/(1-\sigma)](w_0 - a)]$$
$$+ [\varepsilon\sigma/(1-\sigma)]r'_B + [(1+\varepsilon\eta)/\varepsilon(1-\sigma)]y \quad \text{(DI)} \qquad (7.34)$$

$$p = p_0 + t + w_0 - a + \eta y_{-1} \qquad \text{(SRSI)} \qquad (7.35)$$

$$p = p_0 + t + w_0 - a + \eta y \qquad \text{(LRSI).} \qquad (7.36)$$

Equation (7.34) is derived by substituting (7.5), (7.4), and (7.2), into (7.3), and rearranging, to give an upward-sloping relationship between the inflation rate and the rate of growth. This is the same move as that made in deriving the new consensus model in early 21st century textbooks. However, in that context the relationship would have been downward-sloping, and would typically have be labeled an "aggregate demand curve" or similar, to stress the continuity with the earlier (static) textbook aggregate demand and supply (AD/AS) framework with a fixed money supply.

As far the AMM is concerned, it is important to realize that Eq. (7.34) cannot really be an aggregate demand curve for *output* in the conventional sense. In the first place, it relates the *rate of growth* of output to the inflation rate, rather than the *level* of output to the inflation rate. Even more significant, theoretically, is the fact that in the AMM the equilibrium growth rate can always be determined *independently* of the rate of inflation, as already shown in Eq. (7.25). Atesoglu and Smithin (2007) and Smithin (2009a) have, therefore, suggested that a more accurate interpretation of the p, y relationship in (7.34) is that it is "demand for inflation" (DI) curve. The question it asks is, given the growth rate, what rate of inflation will be tolerated (and, in that sense, "demanded") by the society, including investors in the financial markets? The upward slope suggests that, in general, the higher is the growth rate the higher will be the tolerance for inflation. This interpretation is strengthened if it is realized that to make the DI curve *downward* sloping, (as in the textbook new consensus model), the central bank would actually have to impose its own *contra* inflation preferences. It could do this *via* a monetary policy "reaction function" that mandates increases in the real policy rate whenever inflation gets above a certain target level (Mankiw, 2001, 2003; Romer, 2000; Taylor, 1993, 2000). In such a case, however, the negative slope of the curve arises *solely* as a result of policy choice (Barrows and Smithin, 2009; Smithin, 2009a, 2009c). In fact, it is correct to argue that in such models the demand side would be *indeterminate* unless the reaction function is in place (Coombes, 2009, p. 1, 2010). In the current version of the AMM, however, the central bank simply stabilizes real policy rates, and, to that extent acquiesces in the actual inflation preferences of the public (given that interest rate).

As there is a "demand for inflation" (DI) curve, in this economy, logically there must also be a "supply of inflation" (SI) curve. The question now being asked, is, what are the underlying forces *causing* the money supply to expand, and hence for inflation to increase, in an endogenous money environment? The short-run supply of inflation curve (SRSI) in Eq. (7.35) is derived simply by substituting (7.4) into (7.3). The rate of inflation "supplied" therefore depends on the growth rate itself, productivity, cost pressures, and the parameters of the money supply and demand equations. An important feature of the SRSI specification is that only exogenous variables and the lagged rate of output growth appear. The SRSI therefore shows up as simply a horizontal line in p, y space at any point in time. However, the SRSI also *shifts* over time as the growth rate changes. It behaves in a similar fashion to that of the typical horizontal short run "supply curve" of the

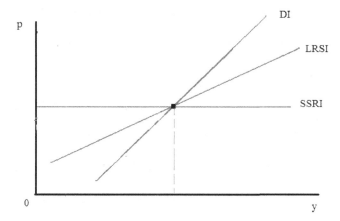

Fig. 7.1. The AMM in inflation/growth space.

new consensus model. Although the SSRI is *not* actually the supply curve for *output* in the traditional sense, it is similarly designed to illustrate the short run "stickiness" of the inflation rate. To derive the *long run* LRSI relation, simply neglect time subscripts in Eq. (7.35), to obtain (7.36), another positively-sloped relationship between inflation and economic growth.

The complete AMM is depicted graphically in Fig. 7.1. The intercept of the DI "curve" is $\{-[1/\varepsilon(1-\sigma)](d+g) + [(1+\varepsilon)/\varepsilon(1-\sigma)]t - [\varepsilon/(1-\sigma)](w_0 - a) + [\varepsilon\sigma/(1-\sigma)]r_B\}$, or, $F(d, g, t, w_0, a, r_B)$, with $F_t, F_a, F_r > 0$ and $F_d, F_g, F_w < 0$. It has a positive slope of $\{(1+\varepsilon\eta)/\varepsilon(1-\sigma)\}$. The SSRI curve is a horizontal line through the equilibrium point. The LRSI curve has an intercept of $[p_0 + w_0 + t - a]$ and a slope of η. All the SSRI curves are flat, and the DI curve has a steeper slope than LRSI. The intersection of the DI, SRSI and LRSI curves represents macroeconomic equilibrium, and determines the equilibrium (steady-state) growth rate, and the equilibrium inflation rate.

Some Graphical Applications

We now turn to examine a number of scenarios involving changes in the exogenous variables using primarily graphical techniques. Figure 7.2, for example, illustrates the result of a demand expansion, caused by an increase in government spending as a percentage of GDP that is *not* offset by any tax increases.

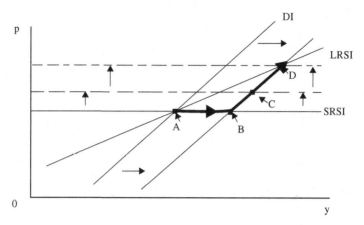

Fig. 7.2.   The effect of an increase in government spending.

The increase in g shifts the DI curve down and to the right. In the
short-run, the rate of inflation is "sticky" along the SRSI curve (it takes
time for the wage cost-push mechanism to operate) and there will be an
economic boom, but no immediate inflation, as the economy initially moves
out to point "B". After a while, however, the boom itself will lead to an
increase in cost pressures, the SRSI will begin shift up, and the inflation
rate will begin to rise. Nevertheless, the boom still continues (unless there
are deliberate attempts to choke it off) as shown by the move to the next
temporary equilibrium position at point "C". If left to itself, the economy
will finally settle to a long-run equilibrium at point "D" with (admittedly) a
higher inflation rate, but a permanently higher growth rate. The *short-run*
behaviour of the model is consistent with that of the new consensus model,
as far as both its initial impact on the real economy and the subsequent
impact on inflation, is concerned. The main difference in the final analysis,
however, is the fact that a boom caused by a demand expansion or "stimulus", although it does cause higher inflation, is never entirely dissipated or
eliminated. A key feature of the AMM model therefore is that it restores
basic "Keynesian" insights on policy for the longer term, as well as in the
short run.

Note that, for demand-side changes at least, we are back in the realm
of a permanent "trade-off" between inflation and growth. This is not really
the old Phillips curve logic however, as there is no actual causal relationship between inflation and growth. It would be more accurate to say that
inflation and growth are two *separate* processes that happen to be affected

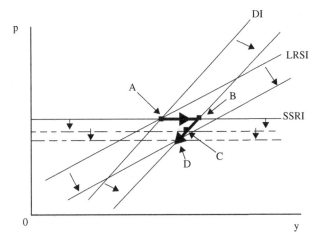

Fig. 7.3.   The effect of a tax cut.

by some of the same variables. To reinforce the point, recall that other possible combinations of inflation and growth are *also* accounted for by the model (in fact, *all* of the other possible combinations), and that there is a plausible explanation for each of them.

Figure 7.3 looks at the effects of another sort of fiscal policy, one that at different times has been favoured by both self-described Keynesians and "supply-side" economists — namely tax cuts *without* any corresponding reductions in government spending.

In Fig. 7.3, the reduction in the average tax rate shifts the SSRI and LRSI curves downwards, effectively reducing inflationary pressure at each growth rate. Simultaneously, it also shifts the DI curve to down and to the right. A tax cut will certainly increase growth, and the economy moves out to a point like "B" in the first instance. After this, the continuing reduction in inflationary pressures from lower taxation has to be taken into account. This means that the SSRI will shift down. At next stage, at point "C", therefore, the growth rate is still higher than at "A", but less than in the first phase of the boom. The final equilibrium position is at "D", with final steady-state growth falling again from where it was at "C", but *still* ending up higher than at the beginning of the process. The tax cut "works", in the sense that there is a permanent increase in growth, and it also brings about *lower* overall inflation. The economy moves along the path "A", "B", "C", "D".

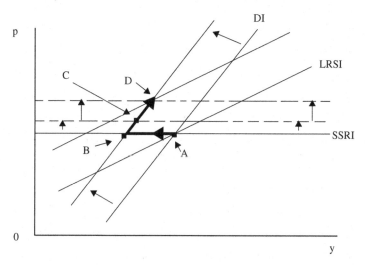

Fig. 7.4. A balanced budget increase in government spending.

Figure 7.4 next puts the spending and tax sides of fiscal policy together, looking at an example of an increase in government spending that is fully funded by tax increases. This might be called a "tax and spend" policy, to use the expression frequently heard in the contemporary political debate. Historically, it was known as the "balanced budget multiplier". The graphical figure immediately show that the balanced budget multiplier here operates in a very different way to the theory that Samuelson (1964, p. 245) once called a subject for "advanced treatises".[6] According to Samuelson, the balanced budget multiplier was *positive* and increase in government spending, covered by an equal increase in taxes, would still increase overall demand. Therefore, tax and spend policies were thought to be very much to the point. Samuelson actually went so far as to argue (for example) that to avoid inflation when government spending is increased, "taxes would probably have to be increased by *more than enough to balance the budget*" (original emphasis). In retrospect, from the vantage point of subsequent political developments, this seems not to have been a very promising beginning for the advocacy of Keynesian policies, as Keynes had specifically argued in the *General Theory* for a fiscal policy of "loan expenditure", defined as "a convenient expression for the net borrowing of the public authorities on all accounts whether on capital account or to meet a budgetary deficit" (Keynes, 1964/1936, pp. 128–129, Footnote 1). Samuelson, however, was proposing an out and out "tax and spend" policy even to the point that taxes should be larger than spending.

However, it can be seen that in terms of the analysis of Fig. 7.4 neither of Samuelson's propositions are true. In Fig. 7.4, the balance budget multiplier is actually negative, and the higher taxes lead to higher inflation, not lower inflation. Samuelson's supposedly "Keynesian" policy would therefore actually have led to lower growth with higher inflation, in fact, to stagflation. The depressing effect of higher taxes on demand growth outweighs any positive impact of the spending, and the inflationary effect of both changes is in the same direction. The economy moves along the path "A", "B", "C", "D". There is initially a recession, then something of a recovery, with inflation also rising, but the final growth path still ends up lower than it was to start with. In short, "tax and spend" does *not* work. The underlying economic issue illustrated here is that discussed in a number of earlier essays, to the effect that the fiscal authorities *must* be prepared to run a deficit of some kind if their activities (tax cuts or spending increases) are to have any sort of positive impact on the economy. In and of themselves *either* a balanced budget, or a budget, surplus would *both* have a depressing effect. Therefore, if a government does accept the notion that balancing its budget, or running a surplus, is a desirable goal, a very commonly expressed opinion these days, they really should be asked how this can be attempted *without* damaging the economy. The answer would have to be the government budget or surplus must be offset by some other sector of the economy going into debt, such as domestic firms, or domestic or foreign consumers.

It cannot be claimed, and should not be claimed, that it is actually *impossible* to have a healthy economy if the government is balancing the budget. However, if we are indeed to have *both* a good economy and a balanced budget, then the necessary impetus for borrowing and spending must be coming from elsewhere. This is a case that was argued in Chapter 1, and has now been demonstrated in an analytical context. Conservatives might perhaps argue the mere existence of budget balance would itself fill the entrepreneurs and consumers with the necessary confidence to take on the implied risk. However, this does not alter the basic arithmetical logic in the slightest.

Figure 7.5, meanwhile, turns to the impact of monetary policy on the economy. It looks specifically at the case where there is an *increase* in the inflation-adjusted real policy rate r'_B. This means a deliberate "tight money" policy. In Fig. 7.5, the increase in the real policy rate shows up as a higher intercept value for the DI curve, which shifts up and to the left.

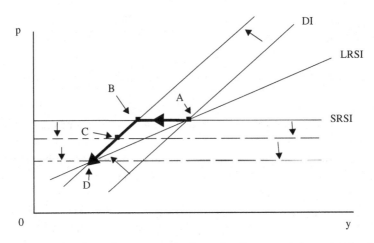

Fig. 7.5.   The effect of an increase in the real policy rate of the central bank.

In the short run, the economic growth rate falls, along the flat SRSI schedule, initially to point like "B".

In orthodox theory, the argument would usually have been that, from this point onwards, the very fact of the short-term recession will reduce wage and other cost pressures, and the inflation rate will begin to fall. Thereafter, there would (supposedly) be no problem for the economy to recover back to the original rate of growth, but with a lower inflation rate. The usual idea is that a tight money policy can stop inflation without causing any permanent damage to the real economy.

However this optimistic view does not work out at all in the present model. In Fig. 7.5, there is lower inflation after point reaches points "B". However, both the average growth rate and the inflation continue to fall as the economy moves along the path "A", "B", "C", "D". The end result of a sustained high interest rate policy, therefore, is certainly to reduce the inflation rate, but also to permanently reduce the growth rate.

Figure 7.6, on the other hand, does not consider any specific policy change, but the effects of a spontaneous increase in productivity, such as might be caused by a technological innovation. This might be thought of as the "Schumpeterian" side of the AMM. One of Schumpeter's arguments was that an important feature of capitalism is that there are always incentives for innovation, of this sort, on the individual firm level. He also thought that major *economy-wide* innovations, appear "periodically" in "swarms" (Schumpeter, 1983/1934, p. 214). In the AMM, an economy-wide innovation

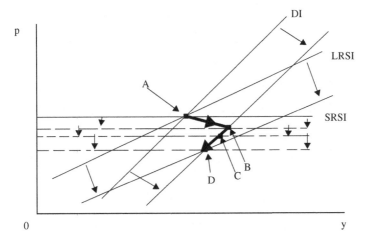

Fig. 7.6.   The effect of an increase in productivity.

that increases the (log of) average labour productivity (the term a) can therefore be interpreted as similar to the ideas of Schumpeter.

An increase in "a" shifts both the SRSI and LRSI curves downward. This increases the growth rate in the short run, and even more so in the long run, as the economy moves along the path "A", "B", "C", "D". Higher growth is actually combined with a *lower* inflation rate. The DI curve also shifts downward (reflecting the fact that productivity improvements will increase profits and therefore increase effective demand). However, this is not enough to offset the overall fall in inflation. The diagram thus illustrates what was once called the "new economy" scenario (anachronistic as it now seems at this point in history). For example, it was claimed that this was what happening in the 1990s in the USA. In summary, the argument is that an exogenous technological improvement leads to both higher growth and lower inflation.

In contrast, Fig. 7.7 provides an explanation of so-called "stagflation" (a term originally applied to the combination of high inflation and high unemployment/low growth that first seemed to appear in the 1970s). It explains how such a thing might occur in the world of the AMM. An increase in w_0, for example, the intercept term in the wage curve, will increase real costs and shift both the SRSI and LRSI upwards. This does tend to reduce growth *and* to increase inflation. In the diagram, there is also a shift back of the DI curve as profit (and therefore firm spending) falls. However, this does not offset the overall inflationary (and hence "stagflationary") tendency.

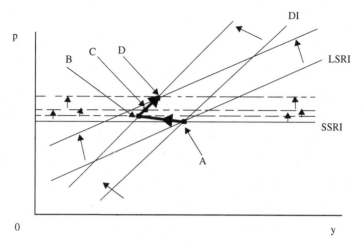

Fig. 7.7.   The effect of an exogenous cost increase.

The economy moves over time along the path "A", "B", "C", "D", with rising inflation and falling growth. The same logic will also apply to any other exogenous increase in "costs", and, in fact, a *fall* in productivity (the opposite case to that in Fig. 7.6) would also have similar effects to those shown in Fig. 7.7.

As a final exercise, it is interesting to look at how Keynes's notion of an increase in liquidity preference, or "bearishness", in the financial markets will affect the inflation rate and the growth rate. An *increase* in liquidity preference means a more negative attitude on the part of participants in the financial markets, and is shown, in the AMM, by a *fall* in the p_0 term. There is a decline in both the willingness to borrow to acquire financial assets, and also to part with (that is, spend) bank deposits. The fall in confidence affects both sides of the "money market".

In terms of Fig. 7.8, the fall in p_0 shifts LRSI downwards and to right, and also shifts down the original SRSI curve. Simultaneously, the DI curve shifts back to the left, because of the effect on interest rates. Both inflation and growth begin to fall, initially to the position at "B". Thereafter, they keep falling along the path "A", "B", "C", "D". So, Keynes's concerns about the potential for shifting sentiment in the financial markets to cause problems are definitely borne out in the AMM (and therefore in the endogenous money environment generally). Although earlier (in Chapter 2) it was argued that the *particular* model of liquidity preference put forward by Keynes in the *General Theory* did not work out, because of the

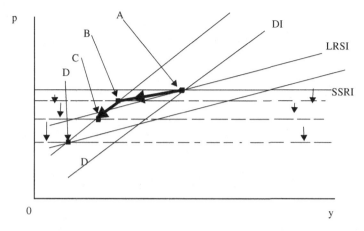

Fig. 7.8. An increase in liquidity preference or "bearishness".

assumption of a fixed money supply, it is clear, nonetheless, that the basic
idea remains an important part of the overall explanation of how economic
problems can arise, or, alternatively, of how they may be intensified once
they have occurred (Davidson, 2009).

The mechanism by which "bear sentiment" negatively affects the economy is by causing the real interest rate as perceived by economic decision-
makers to rise. This is, again, in line with Keynes's basic intuitions. A more
"bullish" or confident attitude in financial markets, would have the reverse
effects, interest rates would fall, and growth and inflation would rise.

Income Distribution

One of the advantages of the AMM framework is that questions of income
distribution are made explicit. Solutions for the after-tax entrepreneurial
profit share, the after-tax real wage rate, and the after-tax real rate of
interest can be obtained. In the model set out above actually only the wage
bill was explicitly "taxed". However, this makes no difference to effective
tax incidence. Therefore, the results for k and r (the entrepreneurial profit
share and the real interest rate) can be interpreted as being "net of tax".
The after-tax real wage is $[w - t]$. The results are:

$$k = -[\eta\sigma/(1 + \varepsilon\eta\sigma)](d + g) - [\sigma(1 - \varepsilon\eta)/\varepsilon(1 + \varepsilon\eta\sigma)]t$$
$$- [\sigma/(1 + \varepsilon\eta\sigma)]r'_B + [\sigma/(1 + \varepsilon\eta\sigma)](a - w_0) + [1/(1 + \varepsilon\eta\sigma)]p_0.$$
$$(7.37)$$

$$[w - t] = [\eta/(1 + \varepsilon\eta\sigma)](d + g) - [\eta(1 - \sigma)/(1 + \varepsilon\eta\sigma)]t - [\varepsilon\eta\sigma/(1 + \varepsilon\eta\sigma)]r'_B$$
$$+ [\varepsilon\sigma/(1 + \varepsilon\eta\sigma)]a + [1/(1 + \varepsilon\eta\sigma)]w_0 + [\eta/(1 + \varepsilon\eta\sigma)]p_0 \qquad (7.38)$$
$$r = -[1 - \sigma/(1 - \varepsilon\eta\sigma)](d + g) - \{[1 - \sigma(1 + \eta)]/(1 - \varepsilon\eta\sigma)\}t$$
$$+ [\sigma(1 - \varepsilon\eta)/(1 - \varepsilon\eta\sigma)]r_B + [(1 - \sigma)/(1 - \varepsilon\eta\sigma)](a - w_0)$$
$$- [(1 - \sigma)/(1 - \varepsilon\eta\sigma)]p_0. \qquad (7.39)$$

An increase in the inflation-adjusted real policy rate of interest tends to *reduce* both real wages and entrepreneurial profits, but will ultimately increase the reward to rentiers (the equilibrium real interest rate). A tax cut has the opposite effect. It will increase profits and real wages, but reduce the real interest rate. A demand expansion, caused either by an increase in government spending or in the autonomous spending (animal spirits) of the private sector, will increase real wages and real interest rates, but cuts into profit.

It is possible therefore that this last result may provide insight into the sometimes paradoxical attitude of "business interests" to Keynesian economics (specifically to government spending increases) that was noticed long ago by Kalecki (1971b). One would have thought that a booming economy is "good for business", but if it *is* true that profits tend to fall during a demand-led boom, even if wages and employment are increasing and the economy is generally healthy, this might explain at least some part of the scepticism on the part of business. Kalecki called this a "difficult and fascinating question" (Kalecki, 1971b, p. 138). A counter-argument might, however, stress that fact that the possibility of an eventual fall in the overall profit *share* may not be a "front burner" issue for individual businesses and individual commentators (as compared, for example, to real or imagined concerns about inflation, or the sustainability of deficits, *etc.*). Although the profit *share* may fall, businesses as a whole will still *be* profitable, more *individual* businesses will be making profits, and the private enterprise system will continue to function. As Keynes (1964/1936, p. 374) remarked in a somewhat different context:

> It is not necessary ... that the game should be played for such high stakes as at present ... lower stakes will serve the purpose equally well, as soon as the players are accustomed to them.

As for the distributional effects of other macroeconomic changes, an increase the w_0 term (caused, *e.g.*, by an increase in labour militancy or pro-labour legislation) will certainly tend to increase the after-tax real wage rate for workers. However, such a change will also *reduce* real interest rates and profits, reduce the level of employment, and slow the growth rate. In thinking about this result, notice that, generally speaking, in the present model, there is actually a *positive* relationship between real wages and economic growth/employment (not negative). This is why from the point of view of the wage-earner, an expansionary policy, and continued economic growth and full employment, are not only "good things", but essential. However, in the *specific* case of an increase in the w_0 intercept, there is an opposite relation between growth and real wages. This is explained by the fact that an increase in real wages not due to an increased demand for labour, and which occurs without any corresponding change in productivity, has really just been "awarded" due to the political power of the recipients. This directly cuts into profits and thereby reduces incentives for investment and induces stagflation. In the end, some people do end up with higher than average wages, but others will have lost their jobs.

The opposite case to this, a "Schumpeterian" economy-wide technological innovation will tend to increase both profits and real wages, and increase real interest rates. (This is part of traditional case *for* "private enterprise" and capitalism.) Finally, an increase in liquidity preference increases real interest rates simply as a defensive strategy on the part of financial wealth-holders, but reduces profits and real wages.

Conclusion

The AMM is an "alternative monetary model", with endogenous money and an interest rate instrument for monetary policy. It generates "non-neutrality" results in both the short run *and* in the model's steady-state. It can be reduced to a simple three-equation framework in inflation/growth space that can be directly compared to recent textbook models. The AMM also generates explicit solutions for the distribution of income.

Signs for the complete set of steady-state "multipliers" are reported in Table 7.1. There is no suggestion in Table 7.1 that there exists any "natural" growth rate for a capitalist economy, or any single value relationship between growth and inflation. Instead, there are a wide variety of alternative steady-state growth/inflation combinations, each of which could potentially occur. The co-movements of inflation and growth depend on the source of the initial disturbance to the economy and on the other parameters of the system. For each of monetary policy (interest rate) changes, changes in

Table 7.1.   Summary of comparative static results for the AMM.

	dd	dg	dt	dr'_B	da	dw_0	dp_0
dy	+	+	−	−	+	−	+
dp	+	+	+	−	−	+	+
dk	−	−	−	−	+	−	+
$d[w-t]$	+	+	−	−	+	+	+
dr	−	−	−	+	+	+	−

government spending, changes in private-sector autonomous demand and changes in liquidity preference, there is a positive relation between growth and inflation. However, any form of "cost increase" (including tax increases, wage increases without concomitant changes in productivity, or failing off of productivity), could be one of the possible causes of "stagflation". If there are innovations in productivity, tax cuts or real wages "concessions", on the other hand, it is possible for growth to be accompanied by falling inflation.

As for distributional issues, a low (real) interest policy pursued by the central bank would clearly benefit both entrepreneurial business and labour, but will reduce the real return to the financial/rentier interests. A demand expansion *either* in the private or the public sector, will improve economic growth and real wages, but tends to reduce the entrepreneurial profit share and reduce real interest rates. An improvement in productivity, or a deliberate tax cut, will increase after-tax profits, after-tax real wages, and after-tax real interest rates. Wage concessions will improve profitability and increase real interest rates, but obviously do not increase the after-tax real wage itself. A fall in confidence in financial markets will increase interest rates, but reduce profitability and real wages.

Notes

1. It is dubious because of the problems involved in giving any coherent meaning to the value magnitude, K. If $O(=k/y)$ however, is a constant, and "investment" contrary to Footnote 1 is defined as the change in the capital stock, we have $I = O(Y - Y_{-1})$ and $sY = V(Y - Y_{-1})$. Dividing through by Y_{-1}, and with lower case y standing for the real growth rate of GDP, this illustrates the formula first suggested by Harrod (1970, p. 47), $y = s/O$. The reason that this formula was (and is) antithetical to Keynesian ideas about growth, is just a question of the algebra. A higher savings rate is "associated" with higher growth, which points straight

back to the pre-Keynesian logic that savings are the key to growth. To be fair, this was not Harrod's original intention. His idea was that of a *hypothetical* equilibrium requirement that, given the capital/output ratio and the saving propensity, would allow balance between them (Sen, 1970, p. 14). Whether or not this is the correct interpretation of Harrod, once the idea of a positive association between the savings rate and the growth rate was in play, it was inevitable that neoclassical economists would find an appropriate adjustment mechanism to show how "market forces" can ensure that the equilibrium growth rate is not just a benchmark, but can actually be achieved.

2. In Smithin (2009a, pp. 124–125), I expressed some reservations about using the term I to stand for "investment" as this might be taken to apply *only* to purchases of physical capital equipment, This is necessary because, as Davidson (1994, p. 33, 2011) has pointed out, the terminology is misleading from the point of view of the theory of *effective demand*. Keynes (1964/1936, p. 29), at one stage simply called the two categories, $D1$ and $D2$, and argued that $D1$ was important mainly because this was the portion of total demand dependent on current employment, whereas $D2$ was the portion of demand not so dependent. Even if $D2$ is identified primarily with *business spending*, these purchases need not always represent physical increments to the productive capital stock as assumed in neoclassical models (Smithin, 2003, 2005, p. 6). What if, for example, firms make large investments but these fail to generate the future returns expected? What if executives decide to redecorate the boardroom, organize a sales conference at a golf resort, or buy a proverbial "corporate jet"? All these things are relevant to aggregate demand, but not necessarily to productivity, as such. In this chapter, I use the traditional notation of I to mean "spending by business firms", but these important caveats should be noted.

3. A similar notion lay behind Keynes's (1964/1936, p. 41) concept of the "wage unit".

4. According to Solow (2000, p. 137), "... (t)here must be a medium run, five-to-ten year time scale at which some ... transitional model is appropriate".

5. Coombes (2009, p. 1, 2010) also claims that the model of Atesoglu and Smithin (2007) suffer from a similar drawback, but this is not accurate.

6. This is also different from the "balanced budget multiplier" in Marterbauer and Smithin (2000, 2003). I now think that the formulation used here is the correct one (e.g., Solow, 1970).

CHAPTER 8

CAPITALISM IN ONE COUNTRY?: A RE-EXAMINATION OF MONETARY MERCANTILISM FROM THE FINANCIAL PERSPECTIVE

Introduction

Kam and Smithin (2008, 2011) used the term "monetary mercantilism" not to refer to *protectionism* as such, but rather (specifically in the context of the open or international economy) to a general policy of stimulating aggregate demand, and trying to bring about full employment, economic growth, general prosperity, *etc.*, by various financial and monetary techniques. These techniques might include, for example, a monetary policy delivering low and stable real interest rates (Smithin, 2003, 2007a, 2009a), or Keynesian-type expansionary fiscal policy involving "loan expenditure" (Keynes, 1964/1936, pp. 128–130). In previous chapters, the detailed impact of such policies has been investigated from various points of view, including those of the various schools of thought arguing that such polices would be ineffective or even damaging. In the course of the discussion, the views of the members of the different schools, on such things as exchange rates and the balance of payments, have also been discussed.

However, in Chapter 7, which appears immediately before this one, there was a detailed explanation of the type of theory advocated as the most plausible alternative to orthodoxy that was carried out in context of a theoretical closed (self-sufficient) economy. This was an important step in setting out basic principles.[1] Nonetheless, it is clear that the discussion must move on from there. The purpose of the present chapter, the eighth and last in the series with the overall title *Essays in the Fundamental Theory of Monetary Economics and Macroeconomics* is therefore to extend the argument to the more fully realistic open economy case.

Having brought up the whole question of the open or international economy, and even mentioned the term "mercantilism", it is important to stress the point that the argument has really nothing to do with the advocacy of tariff or non-tariff "barriers to trade", that is with "protectionism" as such. It is entirely reasonable to argue that *conventional* protectionist measures are unlikely to achieve the results claimed for them. Most likely they would have *negative* macroeconomic impacts similar to those of (*e.g.*) high taxes, as already discussed in Chapter 7.

On this question of terminology it is interesting to note that Humphrey (1998) has also used the expression mercantilism (although without the qualifier "monetary") in similar way to the usage here. Humphrey cast the entire history of economic thought as a contest between "mercantilism" in the monetary sense, and "classical economics". Figures like Law, Stueart, Tooke, Keynes and Kaldor, were on the mercantilist side, and Hume, Smith, Thornton, Ricardo and Friedman, on the other. According to Humphrey (1998, p. 2):

> This policy prescription [protectionism] was, of course, the mercantilists main claim to fame. But the hallmark that secures them a permanent niche in the history of monetary doctrines was their contra- or anti-quantity theory of money.

As far as the specifically international repercussions of their policy preferences are concerned, presumably the expectations of those pursuing "mercantilist" strategies (as now defined) would have been that, along with higher domestic growth, such policies would also lead to a strong current account and the building up of a foreign *credit* position, rather than becoming indebted either, to other nations, or to international financial institutions. This would occur most easily and obviously under a system of flexible exchange rates. However, Kam and Smithin (2008, 2011) have also suggested that, historically, whether under flexible exchange rates or not, and whether or not the issues were fully understood/articulated by the relevant decision-makers at the time, strategies that might be characterized as monetary mercantilism were indeed employed by many of the nations that *did* succeed in achieving stronger economic growth, and ultimately a prominent global geo-political position, in the capitalisms of their day.

In the present chapter, and as I have argued on a number of previous occasions, a main objective is to show that similar policy options *continue* to exist even in "modern" conditions created by globalization, increasing economic integration, increased capital mobility, and so forth (Palley, 2004, 2012; Parguez, 1999; Smithin, 1999; Kam and Smithin, 2004,

2008, 2011; Smithin, 2003, 2009a). Or rather, they will continue to exist *if* certain preconditions are met.

The preconditions are firstly, the domestic political situation. Specifically there needs to be a certain type of domestic political "settlement" or bargain (Ingham, 2004; Kam and Smithin, 2004; Smithin, 2009a; Kim, 2011) that is conducive to the development of the necessary domestic financial and business infrastructure and therefore the "correct" set of (social) relationships between the governmental authorities, the central bank, commercial banks, and financial markets. There must also be some sort of settlement, including the legal aspects, of the relationship between business and labour. Second, there must be an *independent* currency. Third, there must *either* be flexible exchange rates, or, if it is (misguidedly) insisted that there should be fixed or "pegged" nominal exchange rates (*e.g.*, for political reasons) then, at least, there should remain in existence sufficient residual friction, or perceived remaining currency risk, such that the conditions of a "virtual" flexible exchange rate system are replicated (Kam and Smithin, 2008, 2011). Any attempt at a "hard peg" or "irrevocably fixed" exchange rate will be disastrous, and similarly attempts to establish a common currency between *different* political jurisdictions. It seems clear from the lessons of history that the idea of any objective "international standard" (Keynes, 1971b/1930, p. 348), such as the supposed "international gold standard" of the late 19th century, is a fallacy. The meaning of the expression "capitalism in one country" (a sort of pun on Stalin's notion of "socialism in one country") is to summarize the various arguments that can be made along these lines.

I do not think it would be correct to describe the monetary mercantilist approach as a "beggar-thy-neighbour" policy, as many writers, both in the past and currently, have certainly been inclined to do. As shown below, it is true that if one country, alone, pursues the type of policy suggested here, and others do not, this is certainly to the first mover's sole advantage. They may eventually gain a hegemonic position and build up a commercial and/or political empire, *etc.*, as has frequently been the case historically. However, I would also argue that the principles of monetary economics, as correctly understood, suggest that the world economy is not, in principle, a "zero sum" game. Therefore, if each nation, given the necessary socio-political pre-conditions in all of them, were to pursue the same *types* of policies simultaneously, the result would simply be higher overall world growth, with balance across both the current and capital accounts of the balance of payments (Kam and Smithin, 2008, 2011). There seems to be nothing, therefore, to preclude offering similar policy advice to each jurisdiction separately. It is up to the decision-makers in each individual polity to decide whether, or not, to accept the advice, and thereby whether they end up as either creditors, debtors, or "in balance". As the saying goes, "on their own head be it" (Smithin, 2011). It should be emphasized, nonetheless, that the formal mathematical analysis undertaken below does relate to one jurisdiction only, acting alone.

The underlying premise of this chapter is a heterodox, rather than mainstream, approach to monetary and financial issues. Specifically it is the approach of Chapter 7. The concepts of endogenous money, and the importance of credit creation for the generation of profit, are strongly emphasized. Also prominent is the key idea that both the real interest rate and the real exchange rate are *monetary* variables. They are not predetermined beforehand by such things as the rate of time preference, in the one case, or the barter terms of trade, in the other (Kam, 2005; Kam and Smithin, 2004, 2008, 2011; Smithin, 2003a). Overall, the chapter illustrates that policy views on international economic relations, quite as much as those on the domestic economy, differ essentially depending on the underlying social ontology of money, and on the theory of money and finance that is adopted (Bougrine and Seccareccia, 2008; Smithin, 2009a).

In what follows a formal macroeconomic model of the open economy is presented. The topics discussed include the role of flexible versus fixed exchange rate regimes, and how changes in the general level of aggregate demand, changes in domestic monetary and fiscal policy, and innovations in productivity, spill over into the global economy.

Aggregate Demand and Economic Growth in the Open Economy

In this section, we repeat the derivation of an equation for economic growth similar to that previously deployed in Chapters 4 and 7. The difference here is that the analysis is now extended to the open economy. Therefore, start with the standard expenditure breakdown of real GDP including a term for net exports.

$$Y = C + I + G + (EX - IM). \tag{8.1}$$

The notation, as before, is that Y = real GDP, C = real consumption expenditure, I = real investment, and G = real government spending. The term

$(EX - IM)$ = real net exports. Next, reintroduce the "Keynesian-type" consumption function from Chapter 7:

$$C = cY_{-1} - T, \quad 0 < c < 1, \tag{8.2}$$

where T stands for total tax collection, and c is the modified version of the Keynesian "propensity to consume". Therefore:

$$Y = cY_{-1} - T + I + G + (EX - IM). \tag{8.3}$$

Divide through by Y_{-1}:

$$Y/Y_{-1} = c - T/Y_{-1} + I/Y_{-1} + G/Y_{-1} + (EX - IM)/Y_{-1}. \tag{8.4}$$

Next, multiply some of the terms on the LHS by the expression $Y/Y(= 1)$. This gives:

$$Y/Y_{-1} = c + (Y/Y_{-1})[-T/Y + I/Y + G/Y + (EX - IM)/Y]. \tag{8.5}$$

Recall the notation that $y = (Y - Y_{-1})/Y_{-1}$ = the growth rate of real GDP, $t = T/Y$ = the average tax rate, $g = G/Y$ = government expenditure as a percentage of GDP, and $x = I/Y$ = investment (firm spending) as a percentage of GDP. Similarly, let $(ex - im) = (EX - IM)/Y$ = net exports as a percentage of GDP. By definition, $c = 1 - s$, where s = the "propensity to save". Equation (8.5) can therefore be re-written as:

$$(1 + y)[1 + t - x - g - (ex - im)] = 1 - s. \tag{8.6}$$

Taking logs Eq. (8.6) reduces to:

$$y = g + x + [ex - im] - t - s. \tag{8.7}$$

This expression therefore shows how the growth rate of real GDP is influenced by such things as the tax rate, the savings rate, investment, the trade balance, *etc.*

These magnitudes, in turn, must be influenced by other economic variables such as interest rates, exchange rates, and so on. To derive a complete growth equation for open economy, it is necessary therefore to specify both an investment function, as done in earlier essays, and now also a net exports function. For example:

$$x = x_0 + \varepsilon k, \qquad 0 < \varepsilon < 1 \tag{8.8}$$

$$(ex - im) = -\alpha q, \qquad \alpha > 1. \tag{8.9}$$

In Eq. (8.8), the familiar argument is that investment (firm) spending (as a percentage of GDP) depends on the "animal spirits" of the private sector (the x_0 term) and, on profitability, (k). Equation (8.9) uses the most obvious specification for the trade balance. The trade balance as a percentage of GDP depends on the (log of) the real exchange rate q. A real depreciation (making domestic goods more competitive) should weaken the trade balance, whereas a real appreciation should improve it. Using (8.9) and (8.10) in (8.7) the growth equation in an open economy is therefore:

$$y = g + x_0 - s - t + \varepsilon k - \alpha q. \tag{8.10}$$

As a final simplification, define d as "total net domestic autonomous expenditure", so that:

$$d = g + x_0 - s. \tag{8.11}$$

The basic equation for growth therefore reduces to:

$$y = d - t - \alpha q + \varepsilon k. \tag{8.12}$$

The next step is to recall how the k term, the aggregate profits share, is determined. Therefore repeat the simple "adding up" theory of income distribution discussed in the previous chapter. This started with a simple "aggregate production function" with a one-period production lag:

$$Y = AN_{-1}, \tag{8.13}$$

where A is average labour productivity, and N_{-1} is the labour input to the production process made in the previous period. A *forward-looking* (expected) pricing equation, relevant both at the firm level and (in summation) for the domestic economy as a whole, is therefore:

$$P_{+1}Y = (1 + k)(1 + i)WN. \tag{8.14}$$

This assumes that the "representative firm" is imperfectly competitive and faces a downward-sloping demand curve for its own product. The term i is the nominal rate of interest, and the multiple WN is the nominal wage bill (of the *current* period). Takings logs of Eqs. (8.13) and (8.14) then gives two more equations:

$$\ln Y = \ln A + \ln N, \tag{8.15}$$

$$\ln P_{+1} - \ln Y = k + i + \ln W + \ln N. \tag{8.16}$$

Recalling the notation that $\ln P_{+1} - \ln P = p_{+1}, \ln W - \ln P = w$, and $\ln A = a$, substitute (8.15) into (8.16), and then subtract $\ln P$ from both sides. This yields:

$$p_{+1} = k + i + w - a. \tag{8.17}$$

Equation (8.17) describes the expected inflation rate for next period as the sum of the expected profit share plus the log of the current nominal interest rate, plus the log of the current real wage rate less the log of average labour productivity. The real rate of interest is define as $r = i - p_{+1}$, as perceived from the current period. Therefore, Eq. (8.17) can be re-written as:

$$k = a - r - w. \tag{8.18}$$

The profit share is equal to the log of labour productivity, less the real rate of interest, less the log of the real wage rate.

It now has to be asked how real wages will are determined in an open economy. This can be thought of, essentially, as asking the question what is likely to be the "target" real wage for domestic workers, in a world in they buy *both* domestic and foreign consumer goods. The log of the "real product wage" for domestic goods is:

$$w = \ln(W/P) = \ln W - \ln P. \tag{8.19}$$

However, in the open economy it is also necessary to define a more comprehensive "consumer price index" (say Π) which also includes the price of foreign goods. For example:

$$\Pi = P^{1-\theta}(P^*/E)^{\theta}, \qquad 0 < \theta < 1. \tag{8.20}$$

Where E is the nominal exchange rate (the foreign currency price of one unit of domestic currency), P^* is the foreign price level and θ is the proportion of foreign goods in the "consumption bundle" of domestic consumers. A specification for the "target wage", consistent with the discussion of real wage determination in previous chapters, is therefore to suggest that the *after-tax* target real wage is given by:

$$W(1-t)/\Pi = [(W/\Pi)_0](1 + \eta y), \qquad \eta > 0. \tag{8.21}$$

This expression has an intercept term $(W/\Pi)_0$, which is the consumer real wage that would be "insisted on" in a static economy (a sort of "base" real wage), and thereafter the target real wage rate will increase if the economy is growing, as argued previously. If we define $\ln(W/\Pi)_0$ as w_0 and take logs, the result is:

$$\ln W - \ln \Pi - t = w_0 + \eta y. \tag{8.22}$$

Then, from (8.20):

$$\ln \Pi = (1 - \theta) \ln P + \theta \ln P^* - \theta \ln E. \tag{8.23}$$

Using (8.23) in (8.22):

$$\ln W = (1 - \theta) \ln P + \theta \ln P^* - \theta \ln E + t + w_0 - \eta y. \tag{8.24}$$

Now, recall that definition of the real exchange rate, Q, is given by:

$$Q = EP/P^*. \tag{8.25}$$

In a log-linear version:

$$q = \ln E + \ln P - \ln P^*. \tag{8.26}$$

"Normalize" the foreign price level at $P^* = 1$, so that $\ln P^* = 0$. Equation (8.26) simplifies to:

$$q = \ln E + \ln P. \tag{8.27}$$

Next, (8.27) can be substituted into (8.24) to obtain:

$$\ln W = (1 - \theta) \ln P + \theta \ln P^* - \theta \ln E + t + w_0 - \eta y. \tag{8.28}$$

As $\ln W - \ln P = w$, the equation shows how the *domestic real product wage* is determined (the real wage as viewed from the point of view of domestic employers), as is:

$$w = w_0 + t - \theta q + \eta y. \tag{8.29}$$

This takes into account the effect of the international "cost of living" on domestic wage demands. The expression determining the profit share of domestic firms in an open economy is therefore:

$$k = a - r - w_0 - t - \theta q - \eta y. \tag{8.30}$$

Finally, substitute (8.30) into (8.12):

$$y = d - t - \alpha q + \varepsilon(a - r - w_0 - t - \theta q - \eta y). \tag{8.31}$$

Re-arranging (8.31) then results in the expression for real economic growth in the open economy, which is:

$$y = [1/(1 + \varepsilon\eta)]d - [(1 + \varepsilon)/(1 + \varepsilon\eta)]t - [(\alpha - \varepsilon\theta)/(1 + \varepsilon\eta)]q$$
$$+ [\varepsilon/(1 + \varepsilon\eta)](a - w_0 - r). \tag{8.32}$$

So in the open economy it is still the case that an increase in domestic demand as a percentage of GDP, will increase the growth rate, and that an increase in the average tax rate will *decrease* it. Similarly improvements in productivity will increase the growth rate, but an increase in the base level of real wages, not matched by increases in productivity, will reduce growth. Higher real interest rates will also reduce growth.

The new element in the growth equation in the open economy setting is the effect of changes in the relative price of foreign and domestic goods, that is, changes in the (log of) the real exchange rate q. What is the impact of a change in q? There are two competing influences. If the real exchange rate depreciates, there is an obvious tendency for an improvement in the trade balance, as exports rise and imports fall. However, this may (at least partially) be offset by the tendency for costs to increase for domestic employers, as a result of the depreciation. This occurs if workers can get higher real wages in terms domestic product prices, to compensate for the loss of purchasing power that occurs as the imported goods they consume become more expensive. In the notation used here α represents the proportional influence of the exchange rate on the trade balance (as a percentage of GDP), and ε continues to represents the sensitivity of investment spending by domestic firms to an increase in costs. The proportion of foreign goods in the consumption bundle of domestic workers is θ. In the algebraic terms, therefore, the question is whether, or not, the term $[- (\alpha - \varepsilon\theta)]$ is negative, (that is, $\alpha - \varepsilon\theta$ is positive). Will a depreciation of the real exchange rate tend increase the domestic growth rate, or to decrease it?

There seems to be an analogy here to the so-called "Marshall–Lerner conditions" from non-monetary international trade theory. This involves thinking about the likely empirical magnitudes of the relevant elasticities. In the present case, if the trade balance is at least somewhat elastic (responsive) to changes in the real exchange rate, and the terms ε and θ have magnitudes within the bounds of empirical plausibility, it seems likely that the first term, (which is a percentage) will be greater than the multiple of the second two (which are also percentages). Then we would have $\alpha - \varepsilon\theta > 0$. In that case, according to Eq. (8.32) a *depreciation* of the real exchange rate will *increase* economic growth, and *vice versa*. This will be the assumption from now on.

We have seen that higher real interest rates continue to reduce growth in the open economy, but that brings back the question of how domestic interest rates themselves are determined. The argument in previous chapters has been that (essentially) they are determined by the monetary policy of the domestic central bank and "liquidity preference". Recall that the transmissions mechanism of monetary policy is represented by an expression such as:

$$r = \mu + \sigma r'_B - (1 - \sigma)p, \qquad \mu > 0, \ 0 < \sigma < 1, \qquad (8.33)$$

where r'_B is the inflation-adjusted real policy rate (the nominal policy rate set by the central bank less the observed inflation rate). The term r, similarly, is the inflation-adjusted "real" lending rate of the commercial banks. As discussed in Chapter 7, the transmission mechanism illustrated in (8.33) gives a fairly detailed story about how domestic interest rates and domestic financial markets behave. The complexity was an advantage in that context, because (in particular) it did allow us to separately to identify the impact of Keynesian-style changes in liquidity preference on the macro-economy in addition to the direct influence of monetary policy.

However, the present open economy context is surely *already* sufficiently complicated because of the international dimension. It will therefore simplify matters to assume that the domestic monetary authorities have at least (some) of the intuitive understanding necessary to take account of the various complicating factors in domestic financial markets. We might imagine, for example, that the central bank actually tries to stabilize the inflation-adjusted lending rate of the commercial banks, itself, rather than simply targeting the inflation-adjusted policy rate. If they do try to stabilize the inflation-adjusted commercial *bank* real lending rate at a certain level, $r = r'$, this can be achieved by keeping to the monetary policy rule:

$$r'_B = (1/\sigma)(r' - \mu) + [1 - \sigma)/\sigma]p. \qquad (8.34)$$

In these circumstances, the growth equation for the open economy emerges simply as:

$$y = [1/(1 + \varepsilon\eta)]d - [(1 + \varepsilon)/(1 + \varepsilon\eta)]t - [\varepsilon/(1 + \varepsilon\eta)]r'$$
$$- [(\alpha - \varepsilon\theta)/(1 + \varepsilon\eta)]q + [\varepsilon/(1 + \varepsilon\eta)](a - w_0). \qquad (8.35)$$

If this schedule were to be graphed in p, y (price/inflation space), it would be a vertical line. This is different to either the upward-sloping line in p, y

space of Chapter 7, or the downward-sloping schedule of the new consensus model discussed in Chapter 4. The vertical "slope" arises simply because the authorities are pursuing the specific monetary policy goal in Eq. (8.35). There is always action by the central bank, as really there should be, to try to offset the effects of changes in inflation.

Although the behaviour of the monetary authorities is somewhat more "sophisticated" than was assumed earlier, the formulation still retains the essence of what we have learned previously about the *general* effects of changes in interest rates. It is still the case, for example, that changes in the real interest rate target itself (a change in r') will have the same effects that both policy-induced and "financial market-induced" changes had in Chapter 7. In short, a reduction in r' will increase the growth rate of real GDP, whereas an increase in r' will reduce it.

Money Supply and Demand, the Price Level, and the Inflation Rate in the Open Economy

The growth equation (8.35) was determined independently of the inflation rate, so the argument now turns to a discussion of how inflation is determined in an open economy. The argument made in earlier chapters was that in any (realistic) version of a capitalist economy it must be accepted that the money supply is endogenous, and credit creation drives the system. This must remain true in the open economy under *both* flexible and fixed exchange rates. At the same there must still be a coherent "demand for money function", which makes the demand for deposits created by the banking system consistent with the current price level and inflation rate. The simplest theory of money demand and (endogenous) money supply, as discussed in previous essays, consists of the following:

$$M^s = \phi WN, \qquad \phi > 1 \tag{8.36}$$

$$M^d = \psi P_{+1} Y, \qquad 0 < \psi < 1 \tag{8.37}$$

(where both of these expressions continue to make use of the one-period lag in the production process). Equating money supply and demand then gives:

$$\psi P_{+1} Y = \phi WN. \tag{8.38}$$

Taking logs, and re-arranging:

$$\ln P_{+1} = \ln \phi - \ln \psi + \ln W - \ln Y + \ln N. \tag{8.39}$$

Then, subtract the term $\ln P$ from both sides:

$$\ln P_{+1} - \ln P = \ln \phi - \ln y + (\ln W - \ln P) - (\ln Y - \ln N). \quad (8.40)$$

Next, define p_0 as $p_0 = \ln \phi - \ln \psi$, and use the previous definitions of p, w, and a:

$$p_{+1} = p_0 + w - a. \quad (8.41)$$

Substituting in from (8.29):

$$p_{+1} = p_0 + t + w_0 - a - \theta q + \eta y. \quad (8.42)$$

Equation (8.42) therefore states that the expected inflation rate for next period depends upon the parameters of the money demand and supply equations (rolled up together in the p_0 term), the average tax rate, the state of labour relations, the average productivity of labour, the real exchange rate and the growth rate of real GDP.

A Complete System with Flexible Exchange Rates

There are now two separate equations that describe domestic economic conditions in the open economy, as partly determined by what is going on in the rest of world. Equation (8.35) looked at the determinants of economic growth, including the impact of changes in the real exchange rate. Equation (8.42) shows how economic growth affects inflation, and also takes into account the effect of real exchange rate changes. In order to complete the open economy model two further equations need to be added (Paschakis, 1993; Paschakis and Smithin, 1998; Kam and Smithin, 2004, 2008). Firstly, there must be an expression explaining the evolution of the balance of payments (BOP) itself. Second, there must be an expression that describes the determinants of international capital flows. This means it is necessary to specify an "arbitrage condition" for the international capital market.

This section deals specifically with the case of flexible exchange rates, and in context, it should be noted that if exchange rates truly are freely floating, the overall balance of payments (BOP) as such will *always* balance. There will be no need for any changes in foreign exchange reserves as the capital account (KA), of the balance of payments, will be equal and opposite in sign to the current account (CA).

Change in foreign exchange reserves (sometimes called "official financing" or OF) usually occur when the overall balance of payments is in deficit or surplus. They increase when the overall BOP is in surplus and fall when it is in deficit. The general equation for the BOP is:

$$OF = BOP = CA + KA. \tag{8.43}$$

But, with flexible/floating exchange rates, there is no *need* for the central bank ever to intervene in the foreign exchange markets to preserve the nominal exchange rate. Therefore, under floating exchanges rates:

$$OF = BOP = 0, \tag{8.44}$$

$$KA = -CA. \tag{8.45}$$

To repeat the point with a more detailed description of the flows of funds involved, let B equal the real foreign debt position denominated in domestic currency (the total of bonds outstanding held by foreigners, denominated in domestic currency). In a world of endogenous money, flexible exchanges rates, and a "deliberate" central bank monetary policy (as described above), the average real interest rate paid on outstanding foreign debt (denominated in *domestic* currency), will be just the domestic real interest rate itself. Net exports are given by the expression $X - IM$, and Eq. (8.44) can therefore be re-written as:

$$B_{+1} - B = -[EX - IM] + r'B. \tag{8.46}$$

Now divide through by Y, and let $b = B/Y$ *and* $b_{+1} = B_{+1}/Y$, *etc.* The term, b, "foreign debt as a percentage of GDP" is thus defined relative to a given base year, rather than in relation to current year GDP.[2] Net exports relative to GDP can be written $(ex - im)$ as before, so that:

$$b_{+1} - b = -(ex - im) + r'b. \tag{8.47}$$

Then, substitute in from (8.9), to give:

$$b_{+1} - b = \theta q + r'b. \tag{8.48}$$

This expression describes the balance of payments situation and consequent changes in the foreign debt position as a percentage of GDP, under the situation of flexible exchange rates.

The final step in building up an open economy model is to *separately* describe the determinants of international capital flows. To this end, recall that the standard covered interest parity (CIP) condition in international capital markets, is given by:

$$i - i^* = (E - F)/E. \tag{8.49}$$

That is, differential between domestic and foreign interest rates is equal to the forward discount, or approximately:

$$i - i^* = \ln E - \ln F. \tag{8.50}$$

It has already been explained, however, in Chapter 3, and in Smithin (1993, 2002/03, 2003), that if exchange rates are "floating" then, even if CIP holds, it is most *unlikely* that the stronger condition of uncovered interest parity (UIP) will also hold. The existence of UIP would imply, not only that $i - i^*$ is equal to $\ln E - \ln F$, but also that is equal to $\ln E - \ln E_{+1}$. In that case, the forward exchange rate, F, would exactly equal to the expected future nominal spot exchange rate E_{+1}. This is not, however, a reasonable description of how the forward exchange market might work in the case of floating exchange rates. As E_{+1} is *not* known, there must be a "currency risk premium" included in the forward price of foreign exchange. This can be denoted by the symbol z, and therefore in logarithmic terms:

$$\ln F = \ln E_{+1} + z \tag{8.51}$$

implying that:

$$i - i^* = \ln E - \ln E_{+1} + z. \tag{8.52}$$

This relationship can also be expressed in "real" terms. Note from Eq. (8.26) that $q = \ln E + \ln P$. Using this expression, plus the definitions of domestic and foreign real interest rates, in Eq. (8.52), it must also be true that:

$$r' - r^* = q - q_{+1} + z. \tag{8.53}$$

On what does the risk premium, z, depend? In Smithin (1994, 2002/03, 2003), I have argued that main determinant is likely to be the foreign debt position itself. The reasoning behind this is that the *larger* is the debt denominated in domestic currency in real terms, the *greater* is the incentive for the domestic monetary authorities to pursue policies that may cause the currency to depreciate, and *vice versa*. Paschakis (1993) provided early empirical evidence that something along the lines of this mechanism is, in fact, operative in the real world. The most convenient specification to capture this effect in the present model is to argue that the currency risk premium increases with the level of debt as percentage of base year GDP, b, so that:

$$z = \zeta b, \qquad \zeta > 1. \tag{8.54}$$

Substituting (8.54) into (8.52) and, rearranging, we therefore have:

$$q_{+1} - q = r^* - r' + \zeta b. \tag{8.55}$$

Equation (8.55) therefore describes how international capital flows affect real exchange rates. The earlier equation, (8.46), described the determination of the overall balance of payments. Combining these two equations with Eqs. (8.34) and (8.42) that explain the growth rate and the inflation rate, it is then possible to write down a complete "discrete-time" system of a small open economy, under flexible exchange rates. The complete system is:

$$y = [1/(1 + \varepsilon\eta)]d - [(1 + \varepsilon)/(1 + \varepsilon\eta)]t - [\varepsilon\sigma/(1 + \varepsilon\eta)]r'$$
$$- [(\alpha - \varepsilon\theta)/(1 + \varepsilon\eta)]q + [\varepsilon/(1 + \varepsilon\eta)](a - w_0), \tag{8.56}$$

$$p_{+1} = p_0 + t + w_0 - a - \theta q + \eta y, \tag{8.57}$$

$$b_{+1} - b = \alpha q + r' b, \tag{8.58}$$

$$q_{+1} - q = r^* - r' + \zeta b. \tag{8.59}$$

In the following section we turn next to the dynamic and static analysis of an approximation to the above system, but in "continuous time" rather than discrete time.

A Continuous-Time Model of the Small Open Economy with Flexible Exchange Rates

As it is easier to work out the stability properties of a system expressed in continuous time than in discrete time (using differential rather than difference equations), the next step is to approximate the system in (8.55) to (8.58) with its continuous time analogue. The continuous time approximation consists of the following four equations:

$$y = [1/(1 + \varepsilon\eta)]d - [(1 + \varepsilon)/(1 + \varepsilon\eta)]t - [\varepsilon/(1 + \varepsilon\eta)]r'$$
$$- [(\alpha - \varepsilon\theta)/(1 + \varepsilon\eta)]q + [\varepsilon/(1 + \varepsilon\eta)](a - w_0), \tag{8.60}$$

$$p = p_0 + t + w_0 - a - \theta q + \eta y, \tag{8.61}$$

$$\dot{b} = \alpha q + r' b, \tag{8.62}$$

$$\dot{q} = r^* - r' + \zeta b. \tag{8.63}$$

This system includes theories of economic growth and inflation in an open economy, and also equations explaining the dynamics of the foreign debt position and the real exchange rate, under a floating exchange rate system. The terms $\dot{b}$ and $\dot{q}$ are the time derivatives of the foreign debt position, and of the (log of) the expected future real exchange rate, respectively. Recall that $(\alpha - \varepsilon\theta) > 0$. Also, for mathematical convenience, the foreign price level will be "normalized" at the level $P^* = 1$. Therefore the foreign inflation rate is $p^* = 0$.

Set the values of all exogenous variables temporarily equal to zero. The pure dynamic system is reduced to:

$$\dot{b} = \alpha q, \qquad\qquad\qquad (8.64)$$

$$\dot{q} = \zeta b. \qquad\qquad\qquad (8.65)$$

This can be re-written in matrix form:

$$\begin{vmatrix} \dot{b} \\ \dot{q} \end{vmatrix} = \begin{vmatrix} 0 & \propto \\ \zeta & 0 \end{vmatrix} \begin{vmatrix} b \\ q \end{vmatrix}. \qquad\qquad (8.66)$$

Let the symbol Δ stand for the coefficient matrix on the right-hand side (RHS) of (8.67). Stability of the system would require that $\operatorname{tr}\Delta < 0$ and $\det\Delta > 0$. However, in reality, we have:

$$\operatorname{tr}\Delta = 0, \qquad\qquad\qquad (8.67)$$

$$\det\Delta = -\zeta\alpha, \qquad < 0. \qquad\qquad (8.68)$$

The system therefore has a saddle-point solution. As previously explained in Chapter 6, and also (*e.g.*) in Kam and Smithin (2004), this means that is just one stable path to equilibrium (the "stable arm") and all other possible trajectories of the system are unstable. As discussed earlier, in the modern mainstream economics literature, this sort of finding in itself has *not* usually been regarded as a problem. On the contrary, it is actually thought of as sufficient justification for proceeding to a comparative static analysis of the system around the steady-state. This is on the grounds that even if a saddle-point is discovered it is usually possible to invoke the existence of a plausible "jump variable" within the system, based on the likely behaviour of the various players in it. This variable is supposed capable of literally "jumping" (changing very quickly) when circumstances demand it, and thereby in mathematical terms, of being able to quickly shift the economy on to the single "stable arm".

Although such reasoning is, by now a "standard practice" in the mainstream economic theory, it should be noted that as a general proposition, and *a fortiori* in the context of the present chapter, it is not really such an overwhelming convincing argument as graduate level textbooks make it seem. In mathematical jargon it requires specifying a plausible "transversality condition" (grounded in the actual behaviour of the supposed actors in the system) to achieve the desired goal. In reality (as opposed to working through a purely mathematical exercise), there may well exist several scenarios in which it is not possible to do this.

In the present case of flexible exchange rates, however, as the problem specifically involves the behaviour of this *particular* asset market, it does seem possible to appeal to the likely behaviour of market participants to provide the solution. Players in the market for foreign exchange will surely be constantly involved in valuing, revaluing and rearranging their portfolios. Hence, it does become plausible to suggest that the asset values can always be either quickly inflated, or deflated, sufficiently, as the case may be, such that the system lands on the "stable arm".[3] If this is a legitimate argument, it is then possible to proceed directly to comparative static analysis of the steady-state multipliers, as below.

The complete equilibrium solution for the flexible exchange rate case in continuous time is as follows:

$$y = [1/(1 + \varepsilon\eta)]d - [(1 + \varepsilon)/(1 + \varepsilon\eta)]t - [\varepsilon/(1 + \varepsilon\eta)]r'$$
$$- [(\alpha - \varepsilon\theta)/(1 + \varepsilon\eta)]q + [\varepsilon/(1 + \varepsilon\eta)](a - w_0), \qquad (8.69)$$

$$p = p_0 + t + w_0 - a - \theta q + \eta y, \qquad (8.70)$$

$$0 = \alpha q + r'b, \qquad (8.71)$$

$$0 = r^* - r' + \zeta b. \qquad (8.72)$$

Totally differentiating, we obtain:

$$dy = [1/(1 + \varepsilon\eta)]dd - [(1 + \varepsilon)/(1 + \varepsilon\eta)]dt - [\varepsilon/(1 + \varepsilon\eta)]dr'$$
$$- [(\alpha - \varepsilon\theta)/(1 + \varepsilon\eta)]dq + [\varepsilon/(1 + \varepsilon\eta)](da - dw_0), \qquad (8.73)$$

$$dp = dp_0 + dt + dw_0 - da - \theta dq + \eta dy, \qquad (8.74)$$

$$0 = \alpha dq + r'db + bdr', \qquad (8.75)$$

$$0 = -dr' - \zeta db. \qquad (8.76)$$

In the above dr^* has been set at $dr^* = 0$, indicating that, by assumption, the foreign or "world" interest rate is not changing. The system can then be written in matrix form as:

$$
\begin{vmatrix} dy \\ dp \\ db \\ dq \end{vmatrix}
\begin{vmatrix}
1 & 0 & 0 & (\alpha - \varepsilon\theta)/(1+\varepsilon\eta) \\
-\eta & 1 & 0 & \theta \\
0 & 0 & r' & \alpha \\
0 & 0 & \zeta & 0
\end{vmatrix}
$$

$$
=
\begin{vmatrix}
1/(1+\varepsilon\eta) & -(1+\varepsilon)/(1+\varepsilon\eta) & -\varepsilon/(1+\varepsilon\eta) & \varepsilon/(1+\varepsilon\eta) & -\varepsilon(1+\varepsilon\eta) & 0 \\
0 & 1 & 0 & -1 & 1 & 1 \\
0 & 0 & -b & 0 & 0 & 0 \\
0 & 0 & 1 & 0 & 0 & 0
\end{vmatrix}
\begin{vmatrix} dd \\ dt \\ dr' \\ da \\ dw_0 \\ dp_0 \end{vmatrix}.
$$

$$(8.77)$$

Next, work out the comparative static derivatives using Cramer's Rule. These are:

$$dy/dd = 1/(1+\varepsilon\eta), \qquad dy/dr' = -\varepsilon/(1+\eta), \qquad dy/dw_0 = -\varepsilon/(1+\varepsilon\eta),$$
$$dy/dt = -(1+\varepsilon)/ \qquad dy/da = \varepsilon/(1+\eta), \qquad dy/dp_0 = 0,$$
$$(1+\varepsilon\eta),$$
$$dp/dd = \eta/(1+\varepsilon\eta), \qquad dp/dr' = -\eta/(1+\varepsilon\eta), \qquad dp/dw_0 = \eta/(1+\varepsilon\eta),$$
$$dp/dt = \eta(1+\varepsilon)/ \qquad dp/da = -\eta/(1+\varepsilon\eta), \qquad dp/dp_0 = 1$$
$$(1+\varepsilon\eta),$$
$$db/dd = 0, \qquad db/dr' = 1/\zeta, \qquad db/dw_0 = 0,$$
$$db/dt = 0, \qquad db/da = 0, \qquad db/dp_0 = 0,$$
$$dq/dd = 0, \qquad dq/dr' = -(\zeta b + r'), \qquad dq/dw_0 = 0,$$
$$dq/dt = 0, \qquad dq/da = 0, \qquad dq/dp_0 = 0.$$

$$(8.78)$$

The signs of the comparative static derivatives are summarized in Table 8.1.

Looking first at the results in the third column (involving changes in the real rate of interest) we note that, for example, that a reduction in the real policy rate of interest, which might be thought of as the classic

Table 8.1.   Signs of the comparative static derivatives in the floating exchange rate case.

	dd	dt	dr'	da	dw_0	dp_0
dy	+	−	−	+	−	0
dp	+	+	−	−	+	+
db	0	0	+	0	0	0
dq	0	0	?	0	0	0

"monetary mercantilist" policy in our sense does tend to increase growth. Thus, the results do show that lower real interest rates on money do work out much as the old-time mercantilists might have suggested. Inflation does increase, but notice that inflation will not "accelerate" further (that is, get out of control) after the initial increase. This is therefore a situation in which there once again a "trade-off" between inflation and growth, at least as far as changes in monetary policy are concerned. Meanwhile, if a lower rate of interest can be achieved, then, in addition to the direct effects on growth this will cause capital outflow which, in turn, means that the current account of the balance of payments will improve. The foreign debt position will be reduced (or the credit position increased). The real exchange rate simply adjusts as necessary.

Returning to the first two columns of the table, Column 1 shows the effect of a change in the demand parameter, d, which would include such things as a change in the ratio of government spending to GDP, or an upturn in the animal spirits of the business community. Column 2 documents the effect of a change in the average tax rate. Therefore, for example, an expansionary fiscal policy, by means of an increase in government spending as a percentage of GDP, will increase the growth rate, much as a "Keynesian" advocate of "stimulus" would argue. As a result of the expansion, there will indeed be a somewhat higher inflation rate, but, as already mentioned, not an "ever-accelerating" rate of increase.

A reduction in the average tax rate, rather than an increase in spending, would probably also be called a "stimulus" in current parlance. (Either way there is an increase in the budget deficit or a reduction in a budget surplus.) In the open economy with flexible exchange rates, therefore, tax cuts continue to have the effect of *increasing* the rate of real GDP growth. In the case of lower taxes, however, this is not just a question of increasing aggregate demand. The tax cut actually works *via* a combination of demand side and incentive (supply-side) effects. In fact, when taxes are reduced the inflation rate falls (rather than rises), because of the impact of lower taxes on production costs. This is the main difference between the effects of spending increases and tax cuts, and this holds up for an open economy with flexible exchange rates.

According to Table 8.1, however, and now looking at the effects on international economic relations it seems that changes in the fiscal policy variables, *unlike* changes in interest rates caused by monetary policy, ultimately have *no* effect on either the real exchange rate or the foreign debt position. (There are "zeros" everywhere in the last two rows of the first two columns of Table 8.1.) These seem to be very strong results from the theoretical point of view. Therefore, although nonetheless it appears that an expansionary fiscal policy is also a viable "monetary mercantilist" policy, we must also ask the question of how best to interpret the null results.

In fact, the *particular* results present in the first two columns of Table 8.1 come about because in the background the monetary authorities are assumed to be pursuing the interest rate rule in Eq. (8.34). This means that the central bankers always respond when inflation "threatens" and (in particular) never *allow* inflationary tendencies to reduce the real lending rates of the commercial banks. The only situation in which commercial bank real interest rates are allowed to fall is when there is a deliberate monetary policy choice to do so. For this reason, unless the central bank wants it to happen, there will be no change in the real exchange rate or foreign debt position.

These strong results at least have the advantage of reinforcing the point that the real exchange rate itself, just like the real interest rate, is above all a *monetary* variable. Once this point is understood, however, it is then also fairly easy to work out what is likely to happen to both real interest rates and the real exchange rate if the monetary authorities do not pursue such a well-defined policy (as will usually be the case in reality).

Suppose, for example, that instead of following the rule in (8.34), we think of the authorities simply setting the inflation-adjusted real policy rate r'_B at some arbitrary level as was the assumption in Chapter 7. What will then happen when there is, for example, an increase in government spending as a percentage of GDP? As before, the growth rate will increase at the cost of a somewhat higher inflation rate, so the "stimulus" continues to work. The difference now, however, is that the real lending of the commercial banks, r, is allowed to fall because of the increase in inflation, *via* Eq. (8.33). The fall in interest rates will presumably give a still further boost to the economy. More to the present point, the foreign credit position and the current account improve as before. In this case, expansionary fiscal policy itself appears directly in the guise of a "monetary mercantilist" policy, which *lowers* interest rates, and improves the current account. This is actually the *opposite* result to much of the conventional wisdom on the international effects of fiscal policy. The more usual argument has been that an increase in government spending will increase real interest rates, and cause the real exchange rate to appreciate. This was the prediction, for example, of the old Mundell–Fleming model, as discussed in Chapter 5. In the present "mercantilist" interpretation of the likely international effects of an expansionary fiscal policy the credit position will improve and the real exchange rate could go either way.

In the case of tax cut, rather than a spending increase, if this is also allowed to have an impact on the real rate of interest (and thereby on the foreign debt position and the real exchange rate) the actual effects will be slightly different. Tax cuts are still an expansionary policy and the rate of economic growth will increase, but now there is *lower* rather than higher inflation. The tendency must be, therefore, to increase, rather than decrease, the real lending rate charged by the commercial banks. So, in the case of expansionary fiscal policy *via* a tax cut, although this does stimulates growth, there would be a worsening of the current account of the balance of payments, and an increase in foreign indebtedness (unless the central bank takes action to prevent this).

Returning now to Table 8.1 itself, the effects of an increase in productivity (an increase in the exogenous variable, a) are shown in the fourth column. The improvement in productivity leads to an increase in the economic growth rate, together with a fall in the inflation rate. Once again, against the backdrop of the stabilizing monetary policy of Eq. (8.34), and therefore with no interruption in the provision of financing, there would be no effect on either the real exchange rate, or on the foreign debt position. If, on the other hand, the change were allowed to have some impact on real interest rates (if the central bank does not react comprehensively with the stabilizing interest rate rule) the lower inflation rate would allow the real interest rate to rise. The current account balance will therefore worsen. It is a very traditional argument that an improvement in productivity increases growth and profits, but not that it also has a negative effect on the foreign debt position.

The opposite case to an improvement in productivity would be a cost increase *via* a change in the wage intercept, w_0. This would lead, not to improved growth and lower inflation, but rather to "stagflation", with falling growth and rising inflation. If the change is not allowed to impact real interest rates, there are again "zeros", in Table 8.1, against the real exchange rate and the foreign debt position. If, however, the rising inflation rate is allowed to cause the real interest charged by commercial banks to increase, the current account and foreign debt position would deteriorate.

The final column in Table 8.1 shows the impact of a change in the term p_0. This is the intercept term in the inflation equation. In Chapter 7 it was also interpreted as indicating changes in the state of liquidity preference, in the sense in which Keynes used that term. Changes in liquidity preference, by definition, affect both the supply of money (the willingness to borrow) and the demand for holding bank deposits. In Table 8.1, it seems that the only effect of an increase in liquidity preference, a fall in p_0, is to cause a fall in the inflation rate. It does *not* seem to affect any of the real economic variables either domestically or internationally. Once again, though, the very strong result comes about because of the detailed interest rate rule that the central bank is assumed to be following. If the central bank were not so strict, or conscientious, the likelihood is that a fall in inflation would also tend to increase real interest rates. Then we would get the quintessentially Keynesian result that an increase in liquidity preference causes interest rates to rise. There would not only be lower inflation, but also lower growth. In the open economy there would be still further contractionary effects and a worsening of the current account of the balance of payments.

Overall, the results in Table 8.1, "strong" as they are, and when suitably modified to allow for a less stringent monetary regime, seems to give a good indication of how macroeconomic policy changes will affect inflation, growth, and the international position of the domestic economy. Generally, a policy of monetary mercantilism, as now defined, involves the pursuit of expansionary policies which delivers higher growth and causes the current account to improve, and for there to be capital outflow. In reality, this is actually the way both commercial and political empires arise. They happen if only *one* nation is pursuing the right type of policy, and others are not. Ironically, if all the players could be persuaded that what "seems commonsense is commonsense" (in one of Keynes's well-known phrases), that is, they all pursue full employment/growth policies simultaneously then, this is what would lead to the "wealth of nations" (plural). Note that these are the opposite of the recommendations that Adam Smith made in his attack on the "mercantilist system" of two and a half centuries ago.

The System under an "Irrevocable" Fixed Exchange Rate Regime

The preceding discussion dealt with a situation in which the nominal exchange rate of the relevant national currency is flexible or floating. Throughout economic history, there has always been a large of opinion body among economists, politicians and the public, that this should *not* be the case. Frequently one of the pillars of ideas about "sound finance" has been the idea that the exchange rate should be fixed. This was certainly the idea behind the 19th century international gold standard, for example. If each national currency is defined to be equivalent to so many grains of gold, this means a *de facto* fixed exchange rate regime between the national currencies themselves. One of the supposed advantages of the gold standard, moreover, was that it was a "hard peg". As long as central banks honoured their obligation to redeem national currencies in gold the exchange rate regime would turn out to be "irrevocable", as the common expression has it.

In reality the gold standard eventually collapsed, but notwithstanding this factual discrepancy, it has also been argued that many of more *recent* attempts at fixing exchange rates should also try to be "hard pegs" or "irrevocable". This was the objective of advocates of the various "currency board" arrangements of recent decades, for example. It is also true in the case of the contemporary Euro-zone of the European Union (EU). In the latter the nations involved share a "common currency" under the control of a central bank, supposedly independent of any of the national governments. There are no formal provisions for any of the members to withdraw from the currency union and therefore, effectively, they have a *permanent* one-for-one exchange rate against each other. Also, there is no system at all of "the fiscal federalism" which makes life bearable for the provinces in genuine federal systems such as Canada. The Euro-zone is therefore an "irrevocable" fixed exchange rate regime in quite a precise sense.

The purpose of this section is to consider this polar opposite to the case of the pure floating/flexible exchange rate regime. It investigates a scenario in which the nominal exchange rate of the domestic currency is believed to be *irrevocably* fixed against that of some other currency. In these circumstances (and if formally "separate" currencies continue to be in existence) the domestic central bank must undertake to always buy, or sell, their own currency in exchange for foreign exchange reserves, to whatever extent is required to keep the nominal exchange rate at the pre-determined level. In this situation, in contrast to the example of the pure floating rate, the main theoretical point is that it cannot now be guaranteed that there will ever be "overall balance" in the balance of payments.

If there is an overall BOP deficit, for example, there will be an outflow of foreign exchange reserves. If there is a surplus, foreign exchange reserves will accumulate. In general, we can revert to the expression:

$$OF = BOP = KA + CA. \tag{8.79}$$

The outflow of foreign exchange reserves (FE), also known as the official financing (OF) of the balance of payments deficit, is equal to the deficit itself, across both the current account and capital account. The opposite would be true in the case of a surplus. As exchange rates are now fixed changes in foreign exchange reserves will usually be occurring in one direction or another.

Some new notation must now be introduced to define three new expressions to be used in the analysis. These are:

FDN = the real foreign debt net of foreign exchange reserves (denominated in domestic currency), such that $FDN = B - FE$.

v = the ratio of net real foreign debt to real foreign exchange reserves, $FDN/FE = v$.

f = real foreign debt *net of* real foreign exchange reserves (both denominated in domestic currency) as a percentage of *base-year* GDP.

The evolution of the balance of payments in the irrevocable fixed exchange rate case can be therefore be written as:

$$FDN - FDN_{-1} = -(EX - IM) + r(1 + v)FDN, \qquad v > 0. \qquad (8.80)$$

As before, divide through by Y to yield:

$$FDN/Y - (FDN_{-1})/Y = -(EX - IM)/Y + r(1 + v)(FDN/Y). \qquad (8.81)$$

Using the lower case notation just introduced, (in addition to that described earlier), this becomes:

$$f - f_{-1} = -(ex - im) + r(1 + v)f. \qquad (8.82)$$

Therefore, recalling Eq. (8.9), the following expression can be thought of as a reasonably concise description of the evolution of the "net foreign debt position" in the case of a "hard peg" for the nominal exchange rate:

$$f - f_{-1} = \theta q + r(1 + v)f. \qquad (8.83)$$

Equation (8.83) is clearly comparable to the similar Eq. (8.46) for the flexible exchange rate case. However, it is important to keep in mind the difference between the definitions of b in the earlier expression and that of f above.

As, by assumption, the fixed rate regime is irrevocable, the exchange rate is not, and cannot ever, be expected to change. If it is "really" believed to be unchangeable, market participants must think that there is no chance at all that this expectation might be wrong. It must therefore be true that both:

$$E_{+1} - E = 0, \qquad (8.84)$$

$$z = 0. \qquad (8.85)$$

The "arbitrage condition" for international capital markets under irrevocably fixed exchange rates thus reduces to a single simple requirement. This is that domestic nominal interest rates will be equal to the comparable foreign or "world" rates. It is not possible for the domestic monetary authorities to set nominal interest rates at different levels to those prevailing elsewhere. They lose control over the monetary policy instrument (having replaced all of monetary policy with the single-minded exchange rate objective). In short:

$$i = i^*. \qquad (8.86)$$

How will this work in terms of *real* interest differentials? Once again, normalizing the foreign price level *at* $P^* = 1$ (and, therefore, assuming that the foreign inflation rate is zero) from the definitions of domestic, and foreign, real interest rates, we can immediately write:

$$r - r^* = -p_{+1}. \qquad (8.87)$$

The most general expression for evolution of the real exchange rate, as discussed, is:

$$q_{+1} - q = r^* - r - z. \qquad (8.88)$$

Using Eqs. (8.85) and (8.87) in (8.88) we can see that (logically enough) under irrevocable fixed nominal rates the real exchange rate can only change because of differences in inflation:

$$q_{+1} - q = p_{+1}. \qquad (8.89)$$

The complete system, in discrete time, for the irrevocable fixed exchange rate regime, therefore consists of the following four equations drawing on (8.35), (8.42), (8.83) and (8.89):

$$y = [1/(1 + \varepsilon\eta)]d - [(1 + \varepsilon)/(1 + \varepsilon\eta)]t - [\varepsilon/(1 + \varepsilon\eta)]i^*$$
$$- [(\alpha - \varepsilon\theta)/(1 + \varepsilon\eta)]q + [\varepsilon/(1 + \varepsilon\eta)](a - w_0)$$
$$+ [\varepsilon/(1 + \varepsilon\eta)]p_{+1}, \qquad (8.90)$$

$$p_{+1} = p_0 + t + w_0 - a - \theta q + \eta y, \qquad (8.91)$$

$$f - f_{-1} = \theta q + r(1 + v)f, \tag{8.92}$$

$$q_{+1} - q = p_{+1}. \tag{8.93}$$

This is comparable to, but not identical with, the similar four equation system with flexible rates set out in Eqs. (8.53) to (8.59). As in that case, it is more convenient to work with a continuous time approximation to the system, and this is taken up in the next section.

Stability in the Irrevocable Fixed Exchange Rate Case

The continuous time approximation to the system with irrevocable fixed exchange rates is:

$$y = [1/(1 + \varepsilon\eta)]d - [(1 + \varepsilon)/(1 + \varepsilon\eta)]t - [\varepsilon/(1 + \varepsilon\eta)]i^*$$
$$- [(\alpha - \varepsilon\theta)/(1 + \varepsilon\eta)]q + [\varepsilon/(1 + \varepsilon\eta)](a - w_0)$$
$$+ [\varepsilon/(1 + \varepsilon\eta)]p, \tag{8.94}$$

$$p = p_0 + t + w_0 - a - \alpha q + \eta y, \tag{8.95}$$

$$\dot{f} = \theta q + r(1 + v)f, \tag{8.96}$$

$$\dot{q} = p. \tag{8.97}$$

Now recall that, previously, in the section on flexible exchange rates, the notion of saddle-point "stability" in monetary models was discussed. Frequently, the only possible equilibrium solution to a dynamic system turns out to be a saddle-point, meaning there is only one unique dynamic "path" that the economy can take if equilibrium is ever to be achieved. There needs to be a plausible transversality condition somewhere in the system to make this happen.

In the particular case of the system with irrevocable fixed exchange rates, it can immediately be seen that the existence of any kind of equilibrium solution must rest on Eq. (8.97), stating that the time derivative of the real exchange rate is equal to the inflation rate. Therefore, the only possibility of equilibrium in a credible fixed exchange rate system, (in which, by assumption, the rest of the world is *not* inflating) would be if there is "zero inflation" in the domestic economy also. It must be true that:

$$p = 0. \tag{8.98}$$

Just to make this statement, however, evidently does not in any way explain how the desired result is actually to come about. Zero inflation is a necessary condition for equilibrium, but there is no obvious "transversality condition", that could be inferred from an examination of Eq. (8.97) alone, to ensure this result.

By a similar logic, given that we have already assumed that the foreign price level is normalized at $P^* = 1$, it must also be the case that the only possible equilibrium value for the real exchange rate involves "purchasing power parity" (PPP). Therefore, by definition, for equilibrium it would also have to be true that:

$$q = 0. \qquad (8.99)$$

Continuing in the same vein, it is, moreover, also obvious that there cannot be an equilibrium solution if the level of net foreign debt as a percentage of base-year GDP (the term f), continues to change. Equilibrium must entail that:

$$\dot{f} = 0. \qquad (8.100)$$

Given Eqs. (8.100), (8.99), (8.96) the foreign debt ratio itself must also be zero:

$$f = 0. \qquad (8.101)$$

The *only* equilibrium level of net foreign debt consistent with it "not changing" as *per* (8.100) is zero. Eventually there must be no foreign debt.

By now the essential features of the equilibrium solution for a credible "irrevocable" fixed exchange rate regime are becoming clear. As a practical matter, they seem impossibly strict. Next, apply Eqs. (8.98) and (8.99) to Eq. (8.95). The result is an expression for GDP growth in the domestic economy, as follows:

$$y = (1/\eta)(a - w_0 - t - p_0). \qquad (8.102)$$

At first sight, this seems like something similar to the neoclassical "natural rate" of growth, extensively discussed in previous chapters. However, in reality, the term natural is a misnomer in this case. There is nothing at all natural about the putative equilibrium growth rate, because it has been *imposed*, artificially, by the nature of the exchange rate regime.

According to Eq. (8.102), the only *policy* variable that can now affect the GDP growth rate is a change in the average tax rate t, which fits in with the general idea of "supply side" economics. A cut in taxes will increase the GDP growth rate because of incentives, and *vice versa*, as in the usual argument. However, there is a major flaw in this artificially imposed version of supply-side economics. This can be seen by noting that there is another expression which also seems to explain the growth rate, namely the original Eq. (8.94). The equilibrium model is, in fact, "over-determined", and for it to work there would have to be some way to reconcile the *faux* "natural rate" of growth in (8.102) with that implied by (8.94). Substituting (8.102) into (8.94), we arrive at the expression:

$$(1/\eta)(a - w_0 - t - p_0) = [1/(1 + \varepsilon\eta)]d - [(1 + \varepsilon)/(1 + \varepsilon\eta)]t$$
$$- [\varepsilon/(1 + \varepsilon\eta)]i^* + [\varepsilon/(1 + \varepsilon\eta)](a - w_0). \quad (8.103)$$

This can be simplified down to:

$$(1/\eta)(a - w_0) + \varepsilon i^* - (1/\eta)(1 + \varepsilon\eta)p_0 = d - t. \quad (8.104)$$

At this stage, the inconsistency of the supposed equilibrium solution is glaringly obvious. On both sides of the expression there are only exogenous variables. This is no endogenous variable that can "automatically" adjust make the equation hold. The only possibility to make it work is that one, or both, of the two policy variables in the equation must be *consciously* changed to offset any spontaneous changes that occur in any of the other variables. The policy variables are, g, government spending as a percentage of GDP (which is part of the overall demand parameter, d) and the average rate t. We have arrived at the conclusion that if the necessary fiscal policy adjustments are not made the unique saddle-point equilibrium will never to be reached. There is no "jump variable" to place the system on the saddle-path automatically. In effect, the system, in practice, will be unstable.

It is clear that this conclusion, about the need to subjugate fiscal policy to the stability of the exchange rate regime, sounds uncannily like the sort of advice that *is* often given to nations involved in schemes such as the contemporary Euro-zone at the time of writing, or historically, the restored gold standard of the 1930s. There are also echoes of the "austerity policies" that have often been urged on "developing" or "emerging" nations, by the International Monetary Fund (IMF), at several times in the last few decades. This is hardly a coincidence.

To see the basic problem, start initially from an assumed situation in Eq. (8.104) in which the LHS of the equation is momentarily equal to the RHS. Then, suppose that there is a tax cut with the objective of increasing the growth rate as suggested by Eq. (8.102). The problem is that according to Eq. (8.104), this would have to immediately be offset by equal spending cuts. It would not be possible to run a government budget deficit *at all* without the economy becoming unstable.

Alternatively, suppose there is a spontaneous increase in domestic real wages through the term w_0. This might seem like good news for the "workers", but again under fixed exchange rates the real wage increase would have to be immediately offset by either cuts in government spending, or an increase in taxes. As a final puzzle, ask what happens if interest rates increase in the rest of the world (a situation than with a fixed exchange rate, the domestic authorities have no control over)? In that case, the authorities may actually have to run a budget *deficit* (however psychologically unprepared they may for this eventuality). Now, either government spending must be *increased* or taxes *cut*, or both.

Interestingly, therefore, although on the surface some of the statements made above may seem to be merely familiar propositions about the need to "carefully manage the public finances" the actions required are far more detailed, and specific, than the usual slogans about fiscal responsibility tend to imply. Sometimes, strictly speaking, the measures taken must even be in the opposite direction to what these slogans are usually taken to mean, (although it is no doubt true that most frequently it will be budget cuts and austerity measures that will be recommended). It is important to note that these complicated rules for fiscal policy are not imposed by "market forces" or anything of the kind, just the opposite. They are necessary *only* because of the commitment by the governmental authorities to the exchange rate regime. In effect, a supine willingness to continually adjust/manage the government budget in whatever direction is necessary, in response to whatever economic changes occur, takes the place of a formal transversality condition in the mathematical system.

There is a virtually impossible "balancing act" to perform, both and financially and politically, if the elusive (and self-imposed) straight-Jacket of an equilibrium is ever to be attained. Both current events, and the historical record, seem to bear out the theory that politics is unlikely to be able to solve the underlying mathematical problem. The main practical conclusion to be drawn is that a supposedly "credible" or "irrevocable" system is, nonetheless, eventually likely to break down in some sort of crisis, such as a classic foreign exchange crisis.

One possible objection to the underlying argument that (any of) a hard peg, a gold standard, common currency, *etc.*, will eventually come crashing down, might be to invoke the ubiquitous "rational agents" of neoclassical economics. Why would such a person initially believe in the system, and welcome it, if they thought (or even dimly suspected) that it could all ultimately end in crisis. However "rational expectations", in themselves, are clearly not enough to make this type of decision. To foresee the eventual demise the policy-makers and market participants would also have to be working with the *correct* model of the economy. It seems obvious, however, that many persons in the real world, no matter how they form expectations, are certainly *not* working with the correct model. Otherwise, how is it possible to explain why over the years there could ever have been so many "expert" advocates of such things as currency unions, currency boards, "dollarization", the gold standard, other commodity standards, or a single world currency.

The International System in the Case of a "Fixed but Adjustable" Exchange Rate Regime

Perhaps ironically, a fixed exchange rate regime that is initially perceived as *less* secure than a "hard peg" may in reality have a greater chance of longevity. The reason for this is that a currency risk premium will re-emerge in such circumstances, which then allows the domestic monetary authorities a greater degree of control over both interest rate and fiscal policy (if they can manipulate the value of this premium by their activities). A related argument would be that the introduction of various frictional elements into the system (some form of capital controls being the most obvious example) would also allow more room to manoeuvre on the part of the domestic policy-makers. For example, the old "Bretton Woods" system of 1944–1971, was explicitly called a "fixed but adjustable" exchange rate regime, so there must have been some remaining, currency risk premium in the system. It also retained various capital control provisions.

In the formal mathematics of this section we will suppose that there is a regime in which the nominal exchange is fixed "for the time being", but that there remains some doubt about whether or not this will be a permanent state of affairs. In short, the exchange rate regime *is* fixed but adjustable. Kam and Smithin (2008, 2011) have shown that policy-makers in this type of situation may be able to replicate some of the results achievable under floating exchange rates, and have labeled this case a "virtual floating rate" scenario.

From the historical point view this would explain why some nations with pegged or fixed exchange rates (which the previous section indicated might lead to big problems) have nonetheless been able to pursue, at least for some time, what we have here been calling "monetary mercantilist" policies.[4] This does not, however save the argument for fixed exchange rates. Even if there are "loopholes" in an actual system of fixed exchange rates, enabling the domestic authorities to operate for some time without difficulty, there is no real point to this. If "money" cannot maintain its value without being pegged, or fixed, to some other country's money, or to some purely external standard, it is not *really* money itself. The only way to make a "real money", as opposed to Alain Parguez's (1999, p. 63) concept of a "false money", is to preserve the real value of the money by making sure that domestic real interest rates are stabilized at "low but still positive" levels (Smithin, 1994, 2003, 2007a). At the same time, there must be sufficient confidence enough to allow the exchange rate to float (Smithin, 2011). There is no point in trying to gain an *ersatz* credibility by hitching to someone else's star.

We now turn to the mathematics of the fixed but adjustable exchange rate regime. Once again let the expression *FDN* equal the real foreign debt net of foreign exchange reserves (all denominated in domestic currency), so that, as before $FDN = B - FE$, $FDN/FE = v$, and $FDN/Y = f$. The balance of payments equation *per se* will therefore not much be different than it was in the case of a "hard peg", and we can simply repeat Eq. (8.63) above, as:

$$f - f_{-1} = \theta q + r(1 + v)f. \qquad (8.105)$$

As for the arbitrage condition in international capital markets the argument now, is that the exchange rate is still not actually *expected* to change, but that there is some definite "risk" that the expectation might be wrong. Because it is formally a fixed exchange rate regime, we can still write:

$$E_{+1} - E = 0. \qquad (8.106)$$

However, the "expectation" of E_{+1} is not 100% certain. As in the pure flexible exchange case, there must therefore be a currency risk premium in the pricing of forward exchange contracts:

$$z \neq 0. \qquad (8.107)$$

The risk premium z itself will presumably depend on the same sorts of factors discussed earlier, so we can also write:

$$z = \zeta f, \qquad \zeta > 0. \qquad (8.108)$$

The parameter ζ has been re-introduced, and now stands for the sensitivity of the currency risk premium to real foreign debt net of real foreign exchange reserves, as a percentage of base-year GDP. The definition of f is somewhat different to that of b in the flexible exchange rate case, where b stood simply for the outstanding foreign debt in the case of *no* foreign exchange reserves. However, in the course of operating a "fixed but adjustable" exchange rate regime, the authorities will be accumulating or de-cumulating reserves. Therefore, it will be changes in the value of f (rather than b) that, in the minds of participants in the foreign exchange markets, is most likely to induce the domestic monetary authorities to devalue or revalue their own currency. Next, recall the uncovered interest parity (UIP) condition:

$$i - i^* = \ln E - \ln E_{+1} + z. \tag{8.109}$$

We can see from (8.108) and (8.109) that although exchange rates are formally "fixed" the upshot is that there is no "hard peg". Therefore, nominal interest rates domestically and abroad can differ by:

$$i - i^* = \zeta f. \tag{8.110}$$

From the definitions of real interest rates and real exchange rates, therefore it must be true that:

$$q_{+1} - q = r^* - r + \zeta f. \tag{8.111}$$

Meanwhile, as nominal interest rates can be made to differ from those abroad, there is actually nothing to stop the domestic authorities from pursuing a real interest rate rule similar to that suggested above:

$$r'_B = (1/\sigma)(r' - \mu) + [1 - \sigma)/\sigma]p. \tag{8.112}$$

In which case, Eq. (8.111) can be rewritten as:

$$q_{+1} - q = r^* - r' + \zeta f. \tag{8.113}$$

The discrete time system for a fixed exchange rate regime, with continuing currency risk therefore consists of the following four equations:

$$y = [1/(1 + \varepsilon\eta)]d - [(1 + \varepsilon)/(1 + \varepsilon\eta)]t - [(\alpha - \varepsilon\theta)/(1 + \varepsilon\eta)]$$
$$+ [\varepsilon/(1 + \varepsilon\eta)](a - w_0 - r'), \tag{8.114}$$
$$p_{+1} = p_0 + t + w_0 - a - \theta q + \eta y, \tag{8.115}$$

$$f - f_{-1} = \alpha q + r(1 + v)f, \tag{8.116}$$

$$q_{+1} - q = r^* - r' + \zeta f. \tag{8.117}$$

As usual, we turn next to a continuous time approximation to this system.

Stability in the Case of "Fixed but Adjustable" Exchange Rates

The following set of equations represents the continuous time version of the system with fixed but adjustable exchange rates

$$y = [1/(1 + \varepsilon\eta)]d - [(1 + \varepsilon)/(1 + \varepsilon\eta)]t - [(\alpha - \varepsilon\theta)/(1 + \varepsilon\eta]q$$
$$+ [\varepsilon/(1 + \varepsilon\eta)](a - w_0 - r'), \tag{8.118}$$

$$p = p_0 + t + w_0 - a - \theta q + \eta y, \tag{8.119}$$

$$\dot{f} = \alpha q + r(1 + v)f, \tag{8.120}$$

$$\dot{q} = r^* - r' + \zeta f. \tag{8.121}$$

This is almost the same as the model outlined in (8.60) through (8.70). There is one main difference, which is that the nominal exchange remains fixed and is not *expected* to change, albeit with some perceived risk that these expectations will *not* be fulfilled.

Setting all exogenous variables equal to zero, the dynamic system becomes:

$$\dot{f} = \alpha q, \tag{8.122}$$

$$\dot{q} = \zeta f. \tag{8.123}$$

In matrix form:

$$\begin{vmatrix} \dot{f} \\ \dot{q} \end{vmatrix} = \begin{vmatrix} 0 & \alpha \\ \zeta & 0 \end{vmatrix} \begin{vmatrix} f \\ q \end{vmatrix}. \tag{8.124}$$

As before, let Δ = the RHS coefficient matrix. Full stability requires $\operatorname{tr} \Delta < 0$ and $\det \Delta < 0$. However, in fact:

$$\operatorname{tr} \Delta = 0, \tag{8.125}$$

$$\det \Delta = -\zeta\alpha, \qquad (< 0). \tag{8.126}$$

Therefore, the equilibrium of the dynamic system is again a saddle-point, but, as there is a similar transversality condition to that of the floating exchange rate case (the possibility of devaluation or revaluation) there is a plausible mechanism by which the equilibrium may be reached.

Comparative Statics for the Fixed but Adjustable Exchange Rate Regime

In the case of fixed but adjustable exchange rates, the equilibrium solution will therefore be:

$$y = [1/(1 + \varepsilon\eta)]d - [(1 + \varepsilon)/(1 + \varepsilon\eta)]t - [(\alpha - \varepsilon\theta)/(1 + \varepsilon\eta)]q$$
$$+ [\varepsilon/(1 + \varepsilon\eta + \gamma)][a - w_0 - r'], \tag{8.127}$$

$$p = p_0 + t + w_0 - a - \theta q, \tag{8.128}$$

$$0 = \alpha q + r'(1 + \upsilon)f, \tag{8.129}$$

$$0 = r^* - r' + \zeta f. \tag{8.130}$$

Totally differentiating:

$$dy = [1/(1 + \varepsilon\eta)]dd - [(1 + \varepsilon)/(1 + \varepsilon\eta)]dt - [\varepsilon/(1 + \varepsilon\eta]\delta r'$$
$$- [(\alpha - \varepsilon\theta)/(1 + \varepsilon\eta)]dq + [\varepsilon/(1 + \varepsilon\eta](da - dw_0), \tag{8.131}$$

$$dp = dp_0 + dt + dw_0 - da - \theta dq + \eta dy, \tag{8.132}$$

$$0 = \alpha dq + r' db + b dr', \tag{8.133}$$

$$0 = -dr' + \zeta db. \tag{8.134}$$

Next, again work out the comparative static derivatives, which are:

$$
\begin{array}{lll}
dy/dd = 1/(1 + \varepsilon\eta), & dy/dr' = -\varepsilon/(1 + \eta), & dy/dw_0 = -\varepsilon/(1 + \varepsilon\eta), \\
dy/dt = -(1 + \varepsilon)/ & dy/da = \varepsilon/(1 + \eta), & dy/dp_0 = 0, \\
\quad (1 + \varepsilon\eta), & & \\
dp/dd = \eta/(1 + \varepsilon\eta), & dp/dr' = -\eta/(1 + \varepsilon\eta), & dp/dw_0 = \eta/(1 + \varepsilon\eta), \\
dp/dt = \eta(1 + \varepsilon)/ & dp/da = -\eta/(1 + \varepsilon\eta), & dp/dp_0 = 1 \\
\quad (1 + \varepsilon\eta), & & \\
df/dd = 0, & df/dr' = 1/\zeta, & df/dw_0 = 0, \\
df/dt = 0, & df/da = 0, & df/dp_0 = 0, \\
dq/dd = 0, & dq/dr' = -(\zeta b + r')/\alpha\zeta, & dq/dw_0 = 0, \\
dq/dt = 0, & dq/da = 0, & dq/dp_0 = 0.
\end{array}
\tag{8.135}
$$

The signs of the comparative static derivatives are then summarized in Table 8.2.

The most obvious point about Table 8.2 is that, qualitatively, the results simply replicate those of the flexible exchange rate case, discussed earlier. This shows that the reintroduction of the currency risk premium, in

Table 8.2. Signs of the comparative static derivatives in the fixed but adjustable exchange rate case.

	dd	dt	dr'	da	dw_0	dp_0
dy	$+$	$-$	$-$	$+$	$-$	0
dp	$+$	$+$	$-$	$-$	$+$	$+$
df	0	0	$+$	0	0	0
dq	0	0	$?$	0	0	0

this case because of the possibility of exchange rate adjustments, can recreate the conditions of a "virtual" floating exchange rate regime.[5] Therefore, in practice, at least for some time and to some extent, the regime still provides the necessary degrees of freedom for domestic policy-makers to pursue their own domestic interests, *via* "monetary mercantilist" policies.

Conclusion

The framework set out in this last chapter has been able to illustrate several of the growth scenarios for an open economy suggested by a number of different schools of economic thought, including those of the original "mercantilists". Also, to predict the impact of "monetary mercantilist" policies on such things as the real exchange rate and the foreign debt position. The key to "capitalism in one country", to return to our original expression, is the existence of a separate monetary and financial system, with either a floating exchange rate regime (preferably), or at least one in which adjustments can be made as frequently as required without excessive political or other difficulties. It also explains the problems often been experienced by jurisdictions that are not in a comparable situation, and are trapped in the situation of an irrevocably fixed exchange rate.

Notes

1. See Barrows and Smithin (2009), Kam and Smithin (2008), and Smithin (2009a, 2003).
2. The purpose of this is to avoid carrying around an awkward term $(r' - y)$ — the real interest rate minus the growth rate — which might appear in some of the comparative statics. The term can be either positive or negative (most likely negative in a "healthy" economy). In previous work, authors such as Paschakis and Smithin (1998) and Kam and Smithin (2004) have shown that this is just a minor irritation in

the mathematical analysis, and does not change any of the important results.

3. This is not the same argument as that which states that "stabilizing speculation" will tend to reduce nominal exchange rate volatility, as in Friedman (1953). In the present model, nominal exchange rates will need to change to whatever extent is necessary to achieve the eventual *real* exchange rate equilibrium. The real exchange rate itself is considered to be a monetary variable. See also Iwai (2011).

4. The most obvious course of action for the domestic monetary authorities, in this case, would be simply to peg the nominal exchange rate such that the starting real exchange rate is undervalued at current foreign and domestic prices.

5. The same would hold true for the introduction of other frictional elements.

BIBLIOGRAPHY

Aristotle (2006). Politics: Ethics. In *Early Economic Thought: Selected Writings from Aristotle to Hume*, AE Monroe (ed.), pp. 3–29. Mineola, NY: Dover Publications.

Asimakopolous, A (1988). The aggregate supply function and the share economy: Some early drafts of the general theory. In *Keynes and Public Policy after Fifty Years: Theories and Method*, Vol. 2, O Hamouda and J Smithin (eds.), pp. 70–80. Aldershot: Edward Elgar.

Atesoglu, HS (2003/2004). Monetary transmission — Federal funds rate and prime rate. *Journal of Post Keynesian Economics*, 26, 357–362.

Atesoglu, HS and J Smithin (2006). Real wages, productivity, and economic growth in the G7, 1960–2002. *Review of Political Economy*, 18, 1–11.

Atesoglu, HS and J Smithin (2007). Un modelo macroeconomico simple. *Economia Informa*, 346, 105–119.

Atesoglu, HS and J Smithin (2008). Canadian monetary policy and the US federal funds rate. *Applied Economics Letters*, 15, 899–904.

Barro, R (1984). *Macroeconomics*. New York: Wiley & Sons.

Barrows, D and J Smithin (2006). *Fundamentals of Economics for Business*. Toronto: Captus Press.

Barrows, D and J Smithin (2009). *Fundamentals of Economics for Business*, 2nd edn. Toronto and Singapore: Captus Press and World Scientific Publishing.

Begg, DKH (1980). Rational expectations and the non-neutrality of monetary policy. *Review of Economic Studies*, 47, 293–303.

Begg, DKH (1982). *The Rational Expectations Revolution in Macroeconomics: Theories and Evidence*. Baltimore: John Hopkins University Press.

Bell, S (2005). The role of the state and the hierarchy of money. In *Concepts of Money: Interdisciplinary Perspectives from Economics, Sociology and Political Science*, G Ingham (ed.), pp. 496–510. Cheltenham: Edward Elgar. (First published in *Cambridge Journal of Economics*, 2001)

Blanchard, OJ (2000). What do we know about macroeconomics that Fisher and Wicksell did not? *Quarterly Journal of Economics*, 115, 1375–1409.

Blanchard, OJ and S Fischer (1989). *Lectures on Macroeconomics*. Cambridge, MA: MIT Press.

Bougrine, H and M Seccarecccia (2001). The monetary role of taxes in the national economy. Paper Presented at the Annual Meetings of the Canadian Economics Association, Montreal, June.

Bougrine, H and M Seccarecccia (2008). Financing development: Removing the external constraint. Paper Presented at An International Conference Financing Development: Where Do We Find the Money? Laurentian University, Sudbury, Ontario, October.

Bougrine, H and M Seccarecccia (2010). What is money? How is it created and destroyed? Editors' introduction. In *Introducing Macroeconomic Analysis: Ideas, Questions, and Competing Views*, H Bougrine and M Seccareccia (eds.), pp. 33–34. Toronto: Esmond Montgomery Publications.

Burmeister, E (1970). *Capital Theory and Dynamics*. Cambridge: Cambridge University Press.

Burstein, ML (1963). *Money*. Cambridge, MA: Schenkman Publishing Co.

Burstein, ML (1995). *Classical Monetary Economics for the Next Century*. Toronto: York University.

Caldwell, B (ed.) (1995). *Contra Keynes and Cambridge, Essays, Correspondence. The Collected Works of F.A. Hayek*. Indianapolis: Liberty Fund.

Cagan, P (1956). The monetary dynamics of hyperinflation. In *Studies in the Quantity Theory of Money*, M Friedman (ed.), pp. 25–117. Chicago: University of Chicago Press.

Cecchetti, SJ (2006). *Money, Banking and Financial Markets*. New York: McGraw Hill.

Chiang, AC (1974). *Fundamental Methods of Mathematical Economics*. New York: McGraw-Hill.

Chiang, AC and K Wainwright (2005). *Fundamental Methods of Mathematical Economics*, 4th edn. New York: McGraw-Hill.

Chick, V (1983). *Macroeconomics after Keynes: A Reconsideration of the General Theory*. Cambridge, MA: MIT Press.

Chick, V (2000). Money and effective demand. In *What is Money?* J Smithin (ed.), pp. 124–138. London: Routledge.

Cohen, A and GC Harcourt (2003). Whatever happened to the Cambridge capital controversies? *Journal of Economic Perspectives*, 17, 199–214.

Collins, R (1986). *Weberian Sociological Theory*. London: Routledge.

Coombes, T (2009). Comment on the Taylor-Romer and Atesoglu-Smithin models. School of Economics and Finance, Victoria University, Australia.

Coombes, T (2010). Taylor-Romer-Phillips model. School of Economics and Finance, Victoria University, Australia.

Davidson, P (1994). *Post Keynesian Macroeconomic Theory*. Aldershot: Edward Elgar.

Davidson, P (2003/2004). Setting the record straight on a histroy of post Keynesian economics. *Journal of Post Keynesian Economics*, 26, 245–272.

Davidson, P (2009). *The Keynes Solution: The Path to Global Economic Prosperity*. New York: Palgrave Macmillan.

Davidson, P (2011). *Post Keynesian Macroeconomic Theory Second Edition: A Foundation for Successful Economic Policies for the Twenty-First Century.* Cheltenham: Edward Elgar.

Davidson, P and E Smolensky (1964). *Aggregate Demand and Supply Analysis.* New York: Harper and Row.

Davig, T and EM Leeper (2007). Generalizing the Taylor principle. *American Economic Review,* 97, 603–635.

Davig, T and EM Leeper (2010). Generalizing the Taylor principle: Reply. *American Economic Review,* 100, 618–624.

Dillard, D (1988). The barter illusion in classical and neoclassical economics. *Eastern Economic Journal,* 14, 299–318.

Dofinger, P and S Debes (2010). A primer on unconventional monetary policy. Working Paper No. 7785, Center for Economic Policy Research, March, 24 pp.

Dow, SC and J Smithin (1999). The structure of financial markets and the first principles of monetary economics. *Scottish Journal of Political Economy,* 46, 72–90.

Epstein, LG and JA Hynes (1983). The rate of time preference and dynamic economic analysis. *Journal of Political Economy,* 91, 611–635.

Farmer, REA, DF Waggoner and T Zha (2010). Generalizing the Taylor principle: Comment. *American Economic Review,* 100, 608–617.

Fleming, JM (1963). Domestic financial policies under fixed and under floating exchange rates. *IMF Staff Papers,* 9, 369–379.

Fletcher, G (1987). *The Keynesian Revolution and Its Critics: Issues of Theory and Policy for the Monetary Production Economy.* London: Macmillan.

Fletcher, G (2000). *Understanding Dennis Robertson: The Man and His Work.* Cheltenham: Edward Elgar.

Fletcher, G (2007). *Dennis Robertson: Essays on his Life and Work.* London: Palgrave.

Fisher, I (1896). *Appreciation and Interest.* New York: American Economic Association.

Fisher, I (1911). *The Purchasing Power of Money.* New York: Macmillan.

Fontana, G and M Setterfield (eds.) (2009). *Macroeconomic Theory and Macroeconomic Pedagogy.* London: Palgrave.

Friedman, BM (2000). The role of interest rates in Federal Reserve policymaking. NBER Working Paper 8047, December.

Friedman, M (1953). The case for flexible exchanges rates. In *Essays in Positive Economics.* Chicago: University of Chicago Press.

Friedman, M (ed.) (1956). The quantity theory of money — A restatement. In *Studies in the Quantity Theory of Money,* pp. 3–21. Chicago: University of Chicago Press.

Friedman, M (1960). *A Program for Monetary Stability.* New York: Fordham University Press.

Friedman, M (1968). The role of monetary policy. *American Economic Review,* 58, 1–17.

Friedman, M (1974a). A theoretical framework for monetary analysis. In *Milton Friedman's Monetary Framework: A Debate with his Critics,* RJ Gordon (ed.), pp. 1–62. Chicago: University of Chicago Press.

Friedman, M (1974b). Comments on the critics. In *Milton Friedman's Monetary Framework: A Debate with his Critics*, RJ Gordon (ed.), pp. 132–77. Chicago: University of Chicago Press.

Friedman, M (1977). Nobel lecture: Inflation and unemployment. *Journal of Political Economy*, 85, 451–472.

Friedman, M (1983). Monetarism in rhetoric and in practice. *Bank of Japan Monetary and Economic Studies*, 1, 1–14.

Friedman, M (1989). Quantity theory of money. In *The New Palgrave: Money*, J Eatwell, M Milgate and P Newman (eds.), pp. 1–40. London: Macmillan.

Friedman, M and R Friedman (1980). *Free to Choose*. New York: Harcourt Brace Jovanovich.

Friedman, M and AJ Schwartz (1963). *A Monetary History of the United States, 1867–1960*. Princeton: Princeton University Press.

Friedman, M and AJ Schwartz (1982). *Monetary Trends in the United States and the United Kingdom: Their Relation to Income Prices, and Interest Rates, 1867–1975*. Chicago: University of Chicago Press.

Goodhart, CAE (2002). The endogeneity of money. In *Money, Macroeconomics and Keynes: Essays in Honour of Victoria Chick*, P Arestis, M Desai and S Dow (eds.), pp. 14–24. London: Routledge.

Goodhart, CAE (2005). What is the essence of money? *Cambridge Journal of Economics*, 29, 817–825.

Graziani, A (1990). The theory of the monetary circuit. *Economies et Societies*, 24, 7–36.

Graziani, A (2003). *The Monetary Theory of Production*. Cambridge: Cambridge University Press.

Gronewegen, P (1995). *A Soaring Eagle: Alfred Marshall 1842–1924*. Cheltenham: Edward Elgar.

Hahn, F (1983). *Money and Inflation*. Cambridge, MA: MIT Press.

Hamouda, O and GC Harcourt (1988). Post Keynesianism: From criticism to coherence? *Bulletin of Economic Research*, 40, 1–33.

Harkness, J (1978). The neutrality of money in neoclassical growth models. *Canadian Journal of Economics*, 11, 701–713.

Harcourt, GC (1969). Some Cambridge controversies in the theory of capital. *Journal of Economic Literature*, 7, 369–405.

Harrod, R (1970). An essay in dynamic economic theory. In *Growth Economics*, A Sen (ed.), pp. 43–64. Harmondsworth: Penguin.

Hayek, FA (1941). *The Pure Theory of Capital*. Chicago: University of Chicago Press.

Hayek, FA (1967). *Prices and Production*, 2nd edn. New York: Augustus M. Kelley. (First published 1935)

Hayek, FA (1991). Introduction. In *An Inquiry into the Nature and Effects of the Paper Credit of Great Britain*, H Thornton and FA von Hayek (eds.), pp. 11–63. New York: Augustus M. Kelley.

Hayek, FA (1994). *Hayek on Hayek: An Autobiographical Dialogue*, S Kresge and L Wenar (eds.). Chicago: University of Chicago Press.

Hayek, FA (1995a). The paradox of saving. In *The Collected Works of F.A. Hayek: Contra Keynes and Cambridge, Essays, Correspondence*, B Caldwell (ed.), pp. 74–120. Indianapolis: Liberty Press.

Hayek, FA (1995b). Reflections on the pure theory of money of Mr. J.M. Keynes. In *The Collected Works of F.A. Hayek: Contra Keynes and Cambridge, Essays, Correspondence*, B Caldwell (ed.), pp. 121–146. Indianapolis: Liberty Press.

Hayek, FA (1995c). Reflections on the pure theory of money of Mr. J.M. Keynes (continued). In *The Collected Works of F.A. Hayek: Contra Keynes and Cambridge, Essays, Correspondence*, B Caldwell (ed.), pp. 174–197. Indianapolis: Liberty Press.

Hicks, J (1946). *Value and Capital: An Inquiry into Some Fundamental Principles of Economic Theory*, 2nd edn. Oxford: Clarendon Press. (First published 1939)

Hicks, J (1982a). *Money, Interest and Wages: Collected Essays on Economic Theory: Volume II*. Oxford: Basil Blackwell.

Hicks, J (1982b). A suggestion for simplifying the theory of money. In *Money, Interest and Wages: Collected Essays on Economic Theory: Volume II*, pp. 46–63. Oxford: Basil Blackwell.

Hicks, J (1982c). IS/LM an explanation. In *Money, Interest and Wages: Collected Essays on Economic Theory: Volume II*, pp. 318–331. Oxford: Basil Blackwell.

Hicks, J (1989). *A Market Theory of Money*. Oxford: Oxford University Press.

Hicks, J (2005). *Critical Essays in Monetary Theory*. Oxford: Clarendon Press. (First published 1967)

Heilbroner, R (1992).*Twenty-First Century Capitalism: The Massey Lectures 1992*. Toronto: House of Anansi Press.

Heilbroner, R (1999). *The Worldly Philosophers*, 7th edn. New York: Touchstone.

Heilbroner, R and W Milberg (1995). *The Crisis of Vision in Modern Economic Thought*. New York: Cambridge University Press.

Heinsohn, G and O Steiger (2000). The property theory of interest and money. In *What is Money?* J Smithin (ed.), pp. 67–100. London: Routledge.

Hume, D (1987). Of money. In *Essays, Moral Political and Literary*, EF Miller (ed.), pp. 281–294. Indianapolis: Liberty Classics. (First published 1752)

Howitt, P (1992). Interest rate control and non-convergence to rational expectations. *Journal of Political Economy*, 100, 776–800.

Howson, S (1989). Cheap money. In *The New Palgrave: Money*, J Eatwell, M Milgate and P Newman (eds.), pp. 93–96. London: Macmillan.

Humphrey, TM (1993a). The real bills doctrine. In *Money Banking and Inflation: Essays in the History of Monetary Thought*, pp. 21–31. Cheltenham: Edward Elgar.

Humphrey, TM (1993b). Can the central bank peg real interest rates? A survey of classical and neoclassical opinion. In *Money Banking and Inflation: Essays in the History of Monetary Thought*, pp. 35–44. Cheltenham: Edward Elgar.

Humphrey, TM (1993c). The early history of the real/nominal interest rate relationship. In *Money Banking and Inflation: Essays in the History of Monetary Thought*, pp. 66–74. Cheltenham: Edward Elgar.

Humphrey, TM (1993d). Fisherian and Wicksellian price stabilization models in the history of economic thought. In *Money Banking and Inflation: Essays in the History of Monetary Thought*, pp. 303–312. Cheltenham: Edward Elgar.

Humphrey, TM (1993e). Non-neutrality of money in neoclassical economic thought. In *Money Banking and Inflation: Essays in the History of Monetary Thought*, pp. 251–263. Cheltenham: Edward Elgar.

Humphrey, TM (1998). Mercantalists and classicals: Insights from doctrinal history. Annual Report, Federal Reserve Bank of Richmond Economic Review, 1–27.

Ingham, G (2000). Babylonian madness: On the historical and sociological foundations of money. In *What is Money?* J Smithin (ed.), pp. 16–41. Londres et New York: Routledge.

Ingham, G (2004). *The Nature of Money*. Cambridge: Polity Press.

Ingham, G (2005). Money is a social relation. In *Concepts of Money: Interdisciplinary Perspectives from Economics, Sociology and Political Science*, G Ingham (ed.), pp. 221–244. Cheltenham: Edward Elgar. (First published in *Review of Social Economics*, 1996).

Innes, AM (2004). What is money? In *Credit and State Theories of Money*, LR Wray (ed.), pp. 14–49. Cheltenham: Edward Elgar. (First published in *Banking Law Journal*, 1913).

International Monetary Fund (IMF) (2001). *World Economic Outlook*. Washington DC: International Monetary Fund.

Iwai, K (2011). The second end of laissez-faire: The bootstrapping nature of money and the inherent instability of capitalism. In *New Approaches to Monetary Theory*, H Ganssman (ed.), pp. 237–266. London: Routledge.

Jones, CI (1998). *Introduction to Economic Growth*. New York: W.W. Norton & Co.

Kahn, RF (1931). The relation of home investment to employment. *Economic Journal*, 41, 173–198.

Kaldor, N (1982). *The Scourge of Monetarism*, 2nd edn. Oxford: Oxford: University Press.

Kaldor, N (1983). Keynesian economics after fifty years. In *Keynes and the Modern World*, DN Worswick and JR Trevithick (eds.), pp. 1–27. Cambridge: Cambridge University Press.

Kaldor, N (1985). *Economics without Equilibrium*. Armonk, NY: M.E. Sharpe.

Kalecki, M (1971a). Costs and prices. In *Selected Essays on the Dynamics of a Capitalist Economy 1933–1970*, pp. 43–61. Cambridge: Cambridge University Press.

Kalecki, M (1971b). Political aspects of full employment. In *Selected Essays on the Dynamics of a Capitalist Economy 1933–1970*, pp. 138–145. Cambridge: Cambridge University Press.

Kalecki, M (1971c). Trend and the business cycle. In *Selected Essays on the Dynamics of a Capitalist Economy 1933–1970*, pp. 165–183. Cambridge: Cambridge University Press.

Kam, E (2000). Three essay on endogenous time preference, monetary non-superneutrality and the Mundell–Tobin effect. PhD Thesis in Economics, York University, Toronto.

Kam, E (2005). A note on time preference and the Tobin effect. *Economics Letters*, 89, 137–142.

Kam, E and J Smithin (2004). Monetary policy and demand management for the small open economy in contemporary conditions with (perfectly) mobile capital. *Journal of Post Keynesian Economics*, 26, 679–694.

Kam, E and J Smithin (2008). Unequal partners: The role of international financial flows and the exchange rate regime. *Journal of Economic Asymmetries*, 5, 125–137.

Kam, E and J Smithin (2011). Capitalismo en un sólo país? Una re-valoración de los sistemas mercantilistas desde el punto de vista financier. In *Las Instituciones Financieras y el Crecimiento Económico en el Contexto de la Dominación del Capital Financiero*, NL Orlik and TL González (eds.), pp. 37–58. Mexico City: Juan Pablo.

Kam, E and J Smithin (2012). A simple theory of banking and the relationship between commercial banks and the central bank. *Journal of Post Keynesian Economics*, 34, 545–549.

Kane, T (2009). The macro war. Available at http//:www.growthology.org/growthology/2009/09/the-macro-war [accessed on 15 September 2009].

Keynes, JM (1923). *A Tract on Monetary Reform*. London: Macmillan.

Keynes, JM (1933). *Essays in Biography*. London Macmillan.

Keynes, JM (1937). The general theory of employment. *Quarterely Journal of Economics*, February.

Keynes, JM (1939). Professor Tinbergen's method. *Economic Journal*, 49, 558–568.

Keynes, JM (1964). *The General theory of Employment, Interest and Money*. London: Harcourt Brace. (First published 1936)

Keynes, JM (1971a). *The Collected Writings of John Maynard Keynes, V, A Treatise on Money, I, The Pure Theory of Money*, D Moggridge (ed.). Cambridge: Cambridge University Press. (First published 1930)

Keynes, JM (1971b). *The Collected Writings of John Maynard Keynes, V1, A Treatise on Money, II, The Applied Theory of Money*, D Moggridge (ed.). Cambridge: Cambridge University Press. (First published 1930)

Keynes, JM (1973). *The Collected Writings of John Maynard Keynes, XIII, The General Theory and After, Part 1, Preparation*, D Moggridge (ed.). Cambridge: Cambridge University Press.

Kim, J-C (2011). Identity, money, and trust: Three essays on the origin, ontology, and politics of early-modern paper money in England, 17th–Early 19th Century. PhD Thesis in Political Science, York University, Toronto.

Kindleburger, C (1989). *Manias, Panics and Crashes: A History of Financial Crisis* (Revised edn.). New York: Basic Books.

King, J (2012). *The Microfoundations Delusion*. Cheltenham: Edward Elgar.

Knapp, GF (1973). *The State Theory of Money*. Clifton, NJ: Augustus M. Kelley.

Krugman, P (2009). How did economists get it so wrong? *New York Times*, 6th September.

Krugman, P (2012). Gadgets versus fundamentals (wonkish). *New York Times*, 13th July. Available at http://krugman.blogd.nytimes.com/2012/03/13. [accessed on 13 March 2012].

Laidler, D (1996). Wage and price stickiness in historical perspective. In *Monetary Economics in the 1990s*, F Capie and GE Wood (eds.). London: Macmillan.

Laidler, D (1999). *Fabricating the Keynesian Revolution: Studies in the Inter-War Literature on Money, the Cycle and Unemployment*. Cambridge: Cambridge University Press.

Lau, JYF and J Smithin (2002). The role of money in capitalism. *International Journal of Political Economy*, 32, 5–22.

Lavoie, M (1992). *Foundations of Post-Keynesian Economic Analysis*. Aldershot: Edward Elgar.

Lavoie, M (2007). *Introduction to Post Keynesian Economics*. London: Palgrave Macmillan.

Lavoie, M (2010). Changes in central bank procedures during the sub-prime crisis and their repercussions on monetary policy. *International Journal of Political Economy*, 39, 2–23.

Lavoie, M and M Seccareccia (eds.) (2004). *Central Banking in the Modern World: Alternative Perspectives*. Cheltenham: Edward Elgar.

Leeson, R (2002). Expectations augmented Phillips curve. In *An Encylopedia of Macroeconomics*, B Snowden and HR Vane (eds.). Cheltenham: Edward Elgar.

Leeson, R (ed.) (2003a). *Keynes, Chicago and Friedman*, Vol. 1. London: Pickering & Chatto.

Leeson, R (ed.) (2003b). *Keynes, Chicago, and Friedman*, Vol. 2. London: Pickering & Chatto.

Leijonhufvud, A (1968). *On Keynesian Economics and the Economics of Keynes*. New York: Oxford University Press.

Leijonhufvud, A (1981a). Keynes and the Keynesians: A suggested interpretation. In *Information and Coordination: Essays in Macroeconomic Theory*, pp. 3–15. New York: Oxford University Press.

Leijonhufvud, A (1981b). The Wicksell connection: Variations on a theme. In *Information and Coordination: Essays in Macroeconomic Theory*, pp. 131–202. New York: Oxford University Press.

Leijonhufvud, A (1989). Natural rate and market rate. In *The New Palgrave: Money*, J Eatwell, M Milgate and P Newman (eds.), pp. 268–272. London: Macmillan.

Leijonhufvud, A (2004). The long swings in economic understanding. In *Macroeconomic Theory and Economic Policy: Essays in Honour of John-Paul Fitoussi*, KV Lupillai (ed.), pp. 115–127. London: Routledge.

Lerner, AP (1943). Functional finance and the federal debt. *Social Research*, 10, 38–51.

Lerner, AP (2005). Money as a creature of the state. In *Concepts of Money: Interdisciplinary Perspectives from Economics, Sociology and Political Science*, G Ingham (ed.), pp. 467–472. Cheltenham: Edward Elgar. (First published in *American Economic Review*, 1947)

Lewis, MK and PD Mizen (2000). *Monetary Economics.* Oxford: Oxford University Press.

Lucas, RE (1981). *Studies in Business-Cycle Theory.* Cambridge, MA: MIT Press.

Lucas, RE (1987). *Models of Business Cycles.* Oxford: Basil Blackwell.

MacKinnon, KT and J Smithin (1993). An interest rate peg, inflation and output. *Journal of Macroeconomics*, 15, 769–785.

McCallum, BT (1985). Bank deregulation, accounting systems of exchange and the unit of account: A critical review. Carnegie-Rochester Conference Series on Public Policy, 23, 13–46.

McCallum, BT (1986a). On real and sticky-price theories of the business cycle. *Journal of Money, Credit, and Banking*, 18, 379–414.

McCallum, BT (1986b). Some issues concerning interest rate pegging, price level determinacy, and the real bills doctrine. *Journal of Monetary Economics*, 17, 135–160.

McCallum, BT (1989). *Monetary Economics: Theory and Policy.* New York: Macmillan.

McCallum, BT (1991). Inflation: Theory and evidence. NBER Reprint No. 1581. August.

Mankiw, NG (2001). US monetary policy during the 1990s. NBER Working Paper 8471, September.

Mankiw, NG (2003). Program report: Monetary economics. NBER Reporter, pp. 1–5. Spring.

Marshall, A (2003). *Money, Credit, and Commerce.* Amherst, NY: Prometheus Books. (First published 1923)

Marterbauer, M and J Smithin (2000). Fiscal policy in the small open economy within the framework of monetary union. WIFO Working Paper 137, Vienna, November.

Marterbauer, M and J Smithin (2003). The balanced budget multiplier for the small open economy in a currency union, or for a province in a federal state. In *Dollarization: Lessons from Europe and the Americas*, L-P Rochon and M Seccareccia (eds.), pp. 101–112. London and New York: Routledge.

Marx, K (1970). *A Contribution to the Critique of Political Economy.* Moscow: Progress Publishers. (First published 1859)

Marx, K (1976). *Capital: A Critique of Political Economy*, Vol. I. London: Pelican Books. (First published 1867)

Meltzer, AH (1988). *Keynes's Monetary Theory: A Different Interpretation.* Cambridge: Cambridge University Press.

Meltzer, AH (2003). *A History of the Federal Reserve, Volume I: 1913–1951.* Chicago: University of Chicago Press.

Meltzer, AH (2009a). *A History of the Federal Reserve, Volume II: Book 1: 1951–1969.* Chicago: University of Chicago Press.

Meltzer, AH (2009b). *A History of the Federal Reserve, Volume II: Book 2: 1970–1986.* Chicago: University of Chicago Press.

Mendoza España , AD (2012). Three essays on money, credit, and philosophy: A realist approach per totam viam to monetary science. PhD Thesis in Economics, York University, Toronto.

Menger, C (1892). On the origin of money. *Economic Journal*, 2, 239–255.

Mill, JS (1987). *Principles of Political Economy*. Fairfield, NJ: Augustus M. Kelley. (First published 1848)

von Mises, L (1980). *The Theory of Money and Credit*. Indianapolis: Liberty Press. (First published 1934)

Moore, BM (1988). *Horizontalists and Verticalists: The Macroeconomics of Credit Money*. Cambridge: Cambridge University Press.

Mundell, RA (1963a). Inflation and real interest. *Journal of Political Economy*, 71, 280–283.

Mundell, RA (1963b). Capital mobility and stabilization policy under fixed and flexible exchange rates. *Canadian Journal of Economics and Political Science*, 2, 475–485.

Nell, EJ and M Forstater (eds.) (2003). *Reinventing Functional Finance: Transformational Growth and Full Employment*. Cheltenham: Edward Elgar.

Okun, A (1962). Potential GNP: Its measurement and significance. *Proceedings of the American Statistical Assocation*, 7, 98–111.

Palley, T (1996). *Post Keynesian Economics: Debt, Distribution and the Macro Economy*. London: Macmillan.

Palley, T (1997). Expected aggregate demand, the production period, and the Keynesian theory of aggregate supply. *The Manchester School*, 295–309.

Palley, T (2004). The effectiveness of monetary policy in open-economy macroeconomics: Dornbusch versus Tobin. In *Central Banking in the Modern World: Alternative Perspectives*, M Lavoie and M Seccareccia (eds.), pp. 211–225. Cheltenham: Edward Elgar.

Palley, T (2012). *From Financial Crisis to Stagnation: The Loss of Shared Prosperity and the Role of Economics*. Cambridge: Cambridge University Press.

Parguez, A (1999). The expected failure of the European economic and monetary union: A false money against the real economy. *Eastern Economic Journal*, 25, 63–67.

Parguez, A and M Seccareccia (2000). The credit theory of money: The monetary circuit approach. In *What is Money?* J Smithin (ed.), pp. 101–123. London: Routledge.

Paschakis, J (1993). Real exchange rate control and the choice of an exchange rate system. PhD Thesis in Economics, York University, Toronto.

Paschakis, J and J Smithin (1998). Exchange risk and the supply-side effects of real interest rate changes. *Journal of Macroeconomics*, 20, 703–720.

Patinkin, D (1948). Price flexibility and full employment. *American Economic Review*, 38, 543–564.

Patinkin, D (1974). Friedman on the quantity theory and Keynesian economics. In *Milton Friedman's Monetary Framework: A Debate with His Critics*, RJ Gordon (ed.), pp. 111–131. Chicago: University of Chicago Press.

Patinkin, D (1976). *Keynes's Monetary Thought: A Study of its Development.* Durham, NC: Duke University Press.

Patinkin, D (1982). *Anticipations of the General Theory? And Other Essays on Keynes.* Chicago: University of Chicago Press.

Phillips, AW (1958). The relation between unemployment and the rate of change of money wages in the United Kingdom. *Economica*, 27, 1–32.

Pigou, AC (1943). The classical stationary state. *Economic Journal*, 53, 343–351.

Persson, T and LEO Svenson (1985). Current account dynamics and the terms of trade: Harberger-Laursen-Metzler two generations later. *Journal of Political Economy*, 93, 43–65.

Radford, RA (2005). The economic organization of a POW camp. In *Concepts of Money: Interdisciplinary Perspectives from Economics, Sociology and Political Science*, G Ingham (ed.), pp. 20–32. Cheltenham: Edward Elgar. (First published in *Economic Journal*, 1945)

Ricardo, D (2004). *The Principles of Political Economy and Taxation.* Indianapolis: Liberty Fund. (First published 1817)

Rima, IH (1996). *Development of Economic Analysis*, 6th edn. London: Routledge.

Robbins, L (1998). *A History of Economic Thought*, WJ Samuels and SG Medema (eds.). Princeton, NJ: Princeton University Press.

Robertson, DH (1940). *Essays in Monetary Theory.* London: P.S. King & Son.

Robertson, DH (1948). *Money.* London: Nisbet & Co. (First published 1922)

Robinson, J (1970). Quantity theories old and new: Comment. *Journal of Money, Credit, and Banking*, 2, 504–512.

Robinson, J (1964). *Economic Philosophy.* London: Pelican Books.

Robinson, J (1979). Introduction. In *A Guide to Post-Keynesian Economics*, AS Eichner (ed.), pp. xi–xix. White Plains, New York: M.E. Sharpe.

Rochon, L-P (1999). *Credit, Money and Production.* Cheltenham: Edward Elgar.

Rogers, C (2006). Doing without money: A critical assessment of Woodford's analysis. *Cambridge Journal of Economics*, 30, 293–306.

Romer, D (2000). Keynesian macroeconomics without the LM curve. *Journal of Economic Perspectives*, 14, 149–170.

Rothbard, MN (1998). *The Ethics of Liberty.* New York: New York University Press.

Rowthorn, R (1977). Conflict inflation and money. *Cambridge Journal of Economics*, 1, 215–239.

Rymes, TK (1998). Keynes on anchorless banking. *Journal of the History of Economic Thought*, 20, 71–82.

Rymes, TK and C Rogers (2000). The disappearance of Keynes's nascent theory of banking between the Treatise and the General Theory. In *What is Money?* J Smithin (ed.), pp. 255–269. London: Routledge. (First published, 1954)

Salant, W (1985). Keynes and the modern world: A review article. *Journal of Economic Literature*, 23, 1176–1185.

Samuelson, PM (1964). *Economics: An Introductory Analysis*, 6th edn. New York: McGraw-Hill.

Sargent, TJ (1979). *Macroeconomic Theory.* New York: Academic Press.

Sargent, TJ and N Wallace (1973). The stability of models of money and growth with perfect foresight. *Econometrica*, 41, 1043–1148.

Scarth, WM (1996). *Macroeconomics: An Introduction to Advanced Methods*, 2nd edn. Toronto: Dryden.

Schumpeter, JA (1983). *The Theory of Economic Development: An Inquiry into Profits, Capital, Credit, Interest, and the Business Cycle*. New Brunswick, NJ: Transactions Publishers. (First published 1934)

Schumpeter, JA (1994). *History of Economic Analysis*. London: Routledge. (First published 1954)

Shackle, GLS (1967). *The Years of High Theory: Invention and Tradition in Economic Thought 1926–1939*. Cambridge: Cambridge University Press.

Searle, J (1995). *The Construction of Social Reality*. New York: Free Press.

Searle, J (1998). *Mind Language and Society: Philosophy for the Real World*. New York: Basic Books.

Searle, J (2005). What is an institution? *Journal of Institutional Economics*, 1, 1–22.

Searle, J (2010). *Making the Social World: The Structure of Human Civilization*. New York: Oxford University Press.

Seccareccia, M (1996). Post Keynesian fundism and monetary circulation. In *Money in Motion: The Circulation and Post Keynesian Approaches*, G Deleplace and EJ Nell (eds.), pp. 400–416. London: Macmillan.

Sen, A (ed.) (1970). Introduction. In *Growth Economics*, pp. 9–40. Harmondsworth: Penguin.

Sidrauski, M (1967). Rational choice and patterns of growth in a monetary economy. *American Economic Review*, 57, 534–544.

Simmel, G (2005). *The Philosophy of Money*. New York: Routledge.

Simons, H (1936). Keynes's comments on money. *The Christian Century*, 22nd July, pp. 1016–1017.

Smith, A (1981). *An Inquiry into the Nature and Causes of the Wealth of Nations*. Indianapolis: Liberty Fund. (First published 1776)

Smithin, J (1980). On the sources of the superneutrality of money in the steady-state. Working Paper No. 80-14, Department of Economics, McMaster University, October.

Smithin, J (1982). The incidence and economic effects of the financing of unemployment insurance. PhD Thesis in Economics, McMaster University.

Smithin, J (1983). A note on the welfare cost of perfectly anticipated inflation. *Bulletin of Economic Research*, 35, 65–69.

Smithin, J (1984). Medio and Musu's Keynesian analysis of money wage changes: a comment. *Economic Notes*, 12, 167–170.

Smithin, J (1985). On the definition of involuntary unemployment in Keynes's general theory: A note. *History of Political Economy*, 17, 219–222.

Smithin, J (1986). The length of the production period and effective stabilization policy. *Journal of Macroeconomics*, 8, 55–62.

Smithin, J (1988). On flexible wage policy. *Economies et Societies–Oeconomia*, 22, 135–153.

Smithin, J (1990). *Macroeconomics after Thatcher and Reagan: The Conservative Policy Revolution in Retrospect.* Aldershot: Edward Elgar.

Smithin, J (1991). Review of Hicks, *A Market Theory of Money* (1989), *Eastern Economic Journal*, 17, 377–379.

Smithin, J (1993). La pensee monetaire de Milton Friedman face aux theories contemporaines. In *Milton Friedman et son ouvre*, M Lavoie and M Seccareccia (eds.), pp. 83–99. Montreal: Presses de l' Universite de Montreal.

Smithin, J (1994). *Controversies in Monetary Economics: Ideas, Issues and Policy.* Cheltenham: Edward Elgar.

Smithin, J (1995). Geldpolitik und demokratie. In *Europaische Geldpolitik zwischen Marktzwangen und Neuen Institutionellen Regelungen: Zur Politischen Okonomie der Europaische Wahrungintegration*, C Thomasberger (ed.), pp. 73–96. Marburg: Metropolis-Verlag.

Smithin, J (1996a). Hicks on Keynes and Thornton. *Canadian Journal of Economics*, 29, 235–241.

Smithin, J (1996b). *Macroeconomic Policy and the Future of Capitalism: The Revenge of the Rentiers and the Threat to Prosperity.* Aldershot: Edward Elgar.

Smithin, J (1997). An alternative monetary model of inflation and growth. *Review of Political Economy*, 9, 395–409.

Smithin, J (1999). Money and national sovereignty in the global economy. *Eastern Economic Journal*, 25, 49–61.

Smithin, J (2000). What is money? Introduction. In *What is Money?* J Smithin (ed.), pp. 1–15. London: Routledge.

Smithin, J (2002a). Phillips curve. In *An Encylopedia of Macroeconomics*, B Snowdon and HR Vane (eds.), pp. 581–585. Cheltenham: Edward Elgar.

Smithin, J (2002b). Review of Fletcher, *Understanding Dennis Robertson: The Man and His Work* (2000): *Eastern Economic Journal*, 28, 440–442.

Smithin, J (2002/2003). Interest parity, purchasing power parity, risk premia and post Keynesian economic analysis. *Journal of Post Keynesian Economics*, 25, 219–235.

Smithin, J (2003). *Controversies in Monetary Economics: Revised Edition.* Cheltenham: Edward Elgar.

Smithin, J (2004a). Keynes, Friedman and Chicago: a review essay. *Journal of Economic Studies*, 31, 76–88.

Smithin, J (2004b). Interest rate operating procedures and income distribution. In *Central Banking in the Modern World: Alternative Perspectives*, M Lavoie and M Seccareccia (eds.), pp. 57–69. Cheltenham: Edward Elgar.

Smithin, J (2004c). Macroeconomic theory, (critical) realism and capitalism. In *Transforming Economics: Perspectives on the Critical Realist Project*, PA Lewis (ed.), pp. 53–75. London and New York: Routledge.

Smithin, J (2005). The real rate of interest, the business cycle, economic growth and inflation: An alternative theoretical perspective. *Journal of Economic Asymmetries*, 2, 1–19.

Smithin, J (2007a). A real interest rate rule for monetary policy? *Journal of Post Keynesian Economics*, 30, 101–118.

Smithin, J (2007b). Aggregate demand and supply. In *Post Keynesian Macro-economics: Essays in Honour of Ingrid Rima*, M Forstater, G Mongiovi and S Pressman (eds.), pp. 108–128. London and New York: Routledge.

Smithin, J (2009a). *Money, Enterprise and Income Distribution: Towards a Macroeconomic Theory of Capitalism*. London: Routledge.

Smithin, J (2009b). Interest and profit. *Chinese Business Review*, 8, 1–13.

Smithin, J (2009c). Teaching the new consensus model of modern monetary economics from a critical perspective: Pedagogical issues. In *Macroeconomic Theory and Macroeconomic Pedagogy*, G Fontana and M Setterfield (eds.), pp. 255–272. London: Palgrave.

Smithin, J (2009d). Review of Fletcher, *Dennis Robertson: Essays on His Life and Work* (2007): *Eastern Economic Journal*, 35, 269–271.

Smithin, J (2010). The importance of money and debt-credit relationships in the enterprise economy. In *Introducing Macroeconomic Analysis: Issues, Questions, and Competing Views*, H Bougrine and M Seccareccia (eds.), pp. 49–60. Toronto: Esmond Montgomery Publications.

Smithin, J (2011). Max Weber's last theory of capitalism and heterodox approaches to money and finance. In *New Approaches to Monetary Theory: Interdisciplinary Perspectives*, H Ganssmann (ed.), pp. 67–82. London: Routledge.

Smithin, J (2012). Inflation. In *The Elgar Companion to Post Keynesian Economics*, 2nd edn., JE King (ed.), pp. 288–293. Cheltenham: Edward Elgar.

Smithin, J and BM Wolf (1993). What would be a Keynesian approach to currency and exchange rate issues? *Review of Political Economy*, 5, 365–383.

Solow, RM (1970). A contribution to the theory of economic growth. In *Growth Economics*, A Sen (ed.), pp. 161–192. Harmondsworth: Penguin.

Solow, RM (2000). Towards a macroeconomics of the medium run. *Journal of Economic Perspectives*, 14, 151–158.

Sran, G (2012). An empirical estimation of the relationship between commercial bank's prime interest rate and the Bank of Canada's overnight policy rate. Economics Research Workshop Presentation, Graduate Programme in Economics, 11 pp, York University, Toronto, March.

Sweezy, PM (1970). *The Theory of Capitalist Development: Principles of Marxian Political Economy*. New York: Modern Reader Paperbacks.

Tabassum, A (2007). Three Essays on the Impact of Financial Evolution on Monetary Policy. A dissertation proposal submitted to the Faculty of Graduate Studies in partial fulfillment of the requirements for the degree of Doctor of Philosophy, Graduate Programme in Economics, York University, Toronto.

Taylor, JB (1993). Discretion versus policy rules in practice. *Carnegie-Rochester Conference Series on Public Policy*, 39, 195–214.

Taylor, JB (2000). Teaching modern macroeconomics at the principles level. *American Economic Review*, 90, 90–94.

Taylor, JB (2007). *Principles of Macroeconomics*, 5th edn. Boston: Houghton Mifflin.

Tcherneva, PR (2009). Bernanke and his fights against deflation and intergenerational government debt: Can he win both? Paper Presented at the 4th Bi-Annual Cross-Border Post Keynesian Conference, Buffalo State College, Buffalo NY, October.

Tilley, G (2005). Keynes's theory of liquidity preference and his debt management and monetary policies. University College, London.

Tilley, G (2010). *Keynes Betrayed*. London: Palgrave Macmillan.

Tobin, J (1958). Liquidity preference as behavior towards risk. *Review of Economic Studies*, 25, 65–86.

Tobin, J (1965). Money and economic growth. *Econometrica*, 33, 671–674.

Tobin, J (1981). The monetarist counter-revolution today: An appraisal. *Economic Journal*, 91, 29–42.

Thornton, H (1991). *An Inquiry into the Nature and Effects of the Paper Credit of Great Britain*. Fairfield, NJ: Augustus M. Kelley. (First published 1802)

Toporowski, J (2008). Minksy's induced investment and business cycles. *Cambridge Journal of Economics*, 32, 725–737.

Turnovsky, SJ (2000). *Methods of Macroeconomic Dynamics*, 2nd edn. Cambridge, MA: MIT Press.

Uddin, M, MG Ahsan and K Kabir (2011). Real interest rate rule: An empirical assessment. Paper submitted in partial fulfillment of course requirements for ECON 5500, Advanced Monetary Economics, 25 pp, York University, Toronto, April.

Uzawa, H (1968). Time preference, the consumption function, and optimal asset holdings. In *Value, Capital, and Growth: Essays in Honour of Sir John Hicks*, JN Wolfe (ed.), pp. 485–504. Edinburgh: Edinburgh University Press.

Walsh, CE (1998). *Monetary Theory and Policy*. Cambridge, MA: Cambridge University Press.

Walsh, CE (2009). Foreword. In *Macroeconomic Theory and Macroeconomic Pedagogy*, G Fontana and M Setterfield (eds.), pp. xix–xx. London: Palgrave.

Weber, M (2003). *General Economic History*. Mineola, NY: Dover Publications. (First published 1927).

Weintraub, S (1958). *A General Theory of the Price Level, Output, Income Distribution and Economic Growth*. Philadelphia: Chilton.

Weintraub, S (1961). *Classical Keynesianism, Monetary Theory, and the Price Level*. Chilton: Philadelphia.

Wicksell, K (1907). The influence of the rate of interest on prices. *Economic Journal*, 17, 213–220.

Wicksell, K (1965). *Interest and Prices: A Study of the Causes Regulating the Value of Money*. New York: Augustus M. Kelley. (First published 1898)

Wicksell, K (1969). The influence of the rate of interest on commodity prices. In *Selected Papers on Economic Theory*, E Lindahl (ed.), pp. 67–89. New York: Augustus M. Kelley. (First published 1958)

White, LH (1984). *Free Banking in Britain: Theory Experience and Debate 1800–1845*. Cambridge: Cambridge University Press.

Woodford, M (1998). Doing without money: Controlling inflation in a post-monetary world. *Review of Economic Dynamics*, 1, 173–219.

Woodford, M (2003). *Interest and Prices: Foundations of a Theory of Monetary Policy.* Princeton, NJ: Princeton University Press.

Woodford, M (2010). Robustly optimal monetary policy with near-rational expectations. *American Economic Review,* 100, 274–303.

Wray, LR (1990). *Money and Credit in Capitalist Economies: The Endogenous Money Approach.* Aldershot: Edward Elgar.

Wray, LR (1998). *Understanding Modern Money: The Key to Price Stability and Full Employment.* Cheltenham: Edward Elgar.

Wray, LR (2000). Modern money. In *What is Money?* J Smithin (ed.), pp. 42–66. London: Routledge.

Wray, LR (2012). *Modern Money Theory: A Primer on Macroeconomics for Sovereign Monetary Systems.* London: Palgrave Macmillan.

INDEX

a monetary variable, 39
abstract pure exchange system, 11
accelerating inflation, 244
accelerationist aggregate supply
    equation, 118
acceptability feature, 6
Adam Smith's invisible hand, 195
adaptive expectations, 80
after-tax entrepreneurial profit share,
    257
after-tax real rate of interest, 257
after-tax real wage rate, 257
after-tax real wages, 230, 231
aggregate demand, 51, 144
aggregate demand and supply, 115,
    142, 168
aggregate demand function, 154
aggregate supply "curve", 68
aggregate supply function, 153
alternative monetary model, 219, 221
alternative theories of inflation such
    as cost-push and/or conflict
    theories, 53
animal spirits, 223, 258, 268
appreciation, 268
arbitrage, 99
assumed exogeneity of the supply of
    money, 49
austerity, 246, 290
Austrian capital theory, 186
Austrian theory of the business cycle,
    104

average labour productivity, 255
average productivity of labour, 224
average tax rate, 219, 224, 251, 289

balance of payments, 98, 171, 172,
    263, 265, 274
balance of payments surplus (deficit),
    44
balance sheet of the central bank, 75
balance sheet operations, 22, 75
balanced budget, 159, 253
balanced budget multiplier, 158, 252
balancing the budget, 178
Bank Act of 1844, 44
bank balance sheets, 104
bank deposits, 15, 16, 26, 75, 229
bank loans, 105
bank money, 45
Bank of Canada, 25
bank rate, 22, 53, 104
bank reserves, 20, 75
banking, 48, 56, 134, 220
banking and financial system, 75
banking firms, 52, 132
banking ratios, 76
banking system, 53, 136, 148, 149
banknotes in bottles, 145
bargaining power of labour, 231
barter exchange, 2, 94, 100, 126, 142
barter exchange economy, 11, 48
base money, 117
bearishness, 222

bearishness in the financial markets,
    256
bonds, 127
boom and bust, 220
booms and depressions, 104
Bretton Woods system, 30, 292
brute facts, 94
brute facts, physical facts, or the laws
    of nature, 8
budget constraint, 127, 204
budget deficit, 15, 58, 290, 291
budget surplus, 253
bullishness, 222
business cycle, 47, 65, 219, 234
business cycle downturn, 236
business cycle upswing, 234
business cycle upturn, 235
business firms, 132

Canada, 220
capital, 136
capital controls, 292
capital inflow, 171
capital mobility, 264
capital outflow, 171
capital stock, 186, 188, 197, 210
capitalism, 142
capitalism in one country, 263, 265,
    297
capitalist system, 149
cash to deposits ratio, 76
cash-in-advance, 93–95, 214
Central and South America, 44
central bank, 46, 248, 265
central bank is the "monopolist" in
    base money, 22
central bank liabilities, 75
central bank reaction function, 113,
    118, 130
central banking, 48
central banks' monopoly supply of
    money, 117
changes in interest rates, 127
changes in money wages, 151
chartalist, 48

chartalist and "neo-chartalist"
    schools, 20
cheap money policy, 26, 241
classical monetary economics, 43
classical theory of real wages, 231
collateral, 17
collective intentionality, 8
combinations of inflation and growth,
    56
command economy, 10
commercial bank balance sheet, 133
commercial bank lending rates, 135
commercial banks, 19, 75, 132, 232
commercial society, 12
commodity, 44
commodity standard, 3, 292
commodity theory of money, 4
common currency, 285
comparative static concepts, 157
competing monetary networks, 29
compulsory saving, 186
computer entries, 45
conflict inflation, 56, 162, 228
constant capital, 224
constant velocity, 63
constitutional state, 56
consumer-led boom, 15
consumption, 128, 144, 207, 210
consumption expenditure, 266
consumption function, 118, 222
consumption spending, 118, 156, 222
contractionary monetary policy, 46
Controversies in Monetary
    Economics, 34
convertible, 19
cost-push, 228
cost-push and conflict inflation, 160
cost-push inflation, 56
cost-push theories of inflation, 49
covered interest parity, 99, 275
credible fixed exchange rate system,
    288
credit, 56
credit and money creation, 48

credit creation, 26, 117, 142, 219, 222, 228, 266, 273
credit creation and money creation, 5, 53
credit economy, 75, 76
credit or "claim" theory of money, 4, 35
crowding out, 168
Crusoe Economy, 9
cumulative process, 55
currency in the hands of the non-bank public, 19
currency in the hands of the public, 75
currency principle, 44, 45
currency risk, 265
currency risk premium, 276, 292, 296
currency unions, 292
cyclical behaviour of the inflation rate, 236

debt, 128
debt management, 28
debt pyramid, 18
definition of money, 5
deflation, 45, 49, 54, 107, 241, 242
deliberate monetary policy response, 123
demand for inflation, 248
demand for money, 46, 49, 77
demand side changes, 116
demand-pull inflation, 56
depreciation, 268
depreciation allowances, 227
depression, 187, 242, 246
discount factor, 95
discount rate, 22, 104
discrepancy between the policy rate and the natural rate, 113
disequilibrium, 110, 123, 154, 196
dynamic optimization, 94, 127
dynamic optimization problem, 125, 128

economic growth, 57, 235, 263
economic growth rate, 254
economic instability, 242
economic sociology, 52, 132
economic stability, 242
effective demand, 142, 143
efficient markets, 100
electronic money, 229
electronic payments system, 126
empirical problems, 56
endogenous money, 48, 56, 161, 200, 201, 221, 229, 235, 266, 275
endogenous money approach, 36
endogenous money theory, 175
endogenous supply of money, 105
endogenous time preference, 206, 210
endogenous variable, 36
enterprise economy, 100
entrepreneur, 143, 153, 235
entrepreneur economy, 48
equilibrium condition, 129
equilibrium level of output, 96
equilibrium real interest rate, 114
Euler equations, 128
Euro, 30
Euro-zone, 21, 220, 285, 290
excessive credit creation, 16
exchange rates, 263
exogenous money, 63
exogenous variable, 36
expansionary monetary policy, 46, 234
expectations, 48, 66
expectations-augmented Phillips curve, 87
expectations error, 86
expectations operator, 91
expectations theory of the term structure of interest rates, 27
expected real rate of interest, 24
exports, 271
external equilibrium, 172

fall in real interest rates, 239
false money, 293

federal funds, 20
federal funds rate, 22, 104
Federal Reserve System, 53
fiat money, 21
financial, 229
financial and economic instability, 239
financial asset, 194, 128, 129
financial breakdown, 245
financial crises, 220
financial fragility hypothesis, 242
financial institutions, 115
financial mark-up, 232
financial markets, 116, 222, 248, 256, 265
financial regulation, 220
financial speculation, 17
finite horizon steady-state, 226
fiscal policy, 50, 119, 174, 211, 219, 220, 252
fiscal responsibility, 291
Fisher, 139
fixed but adjustable exchange rate regime, 292
fixed but adjustable exchange rates, 296
fixed exchange rate, 98, 174, 177
fixed supply of money, 44, 116
flexible exchange rates, 137, 172, 173, 264, 265, 274, 277
floating exchange rate system, 30
floating exchange rates, 98
forced investment, 186
forced saving, 185
foreign credit position, 282
foreign debt, 275, 283, 289, 294
foreign exchange reserves, 274, 285, 294
formal and substantive validity of money, 4, 7
formal validity, 3
formal validity of money, 21
forward discount, 276
forward exchange market, 276
forward exchange rate, 99, 276

fully-fledged barter exchange economy without money, 13
functional finance, 58
future "spot" exchange rate, 99

General Theory, 164
General Theory of Employment Interest and Money, 48
global capital market, 99
global economy, 44
global monetarism, 97
globalization, 264
gold, 44
gold coins, 45
gold reserves, 44, 45
gold standard, 3, 244, 245, 285, 292
government expenditure multiplier, 157
government spending, 69, 118, 156, 222, 234, 266
Great Depression, 66, 187, 241
growth gap, 88
growth rate, 115, 277
growth rate of real GDP, 118

habit persistence, 223
hard peg, 265, 285
Hayek, 104, 186, 243
helicopter drop, 47
Hicks, 149, 164, 242
Hierarchical notions of money, 18
high powered money, 20
high real policy rate, 26
horizontalist theory, 27

imperfect competition, 52, 152
imports, 271
income distribution, 57, 219, 224, 257
increases in real interest rates, 236
index numbers, 225
infinitely lived representative agent, 94
inflation, 45, 47, 107, 198, 219, 228, 241

inflation-adjusted real interest rate, 24
inflation-adjusted real policy rate, 25, 55, 58, 108, 238
inflation-adjusted real policy rate of interest, 234
inflationary boom, 242, 243, 246
inflation expectations, 80
inflation rate, 78, 178, 254, 273, 277
inflation targeting, 246
inflation targeting policy, 122
inflation tax, 209
inflationism, 211
inflation — the percentage rate of change of the price level, 7
instability, 212, 220, 233, 238, 241, 242
Interest and Prices, 103
interest elasticity of money demand, 80
interest elasticity of the demand for money, 49
interest elasticity of the demand for real money balances, 80
interest rate channel, 23, 40
interest rate operating procedures, 76
interest rate policy, 22
interest rate rule, 103, 112, 129
interest rates and inflation, 104
internal equilibrium, 172
international capital flows, 275, 277
international capital markets, 287
international debt pyramid, 29
international financial markets, 29
international gold standard, 284
international markets, 29
International Monetary Fund, 290
international monetary relations, 28
international reserve currency, 29
international standard, 265
inverted yield curve, 28
investment, 144, 266
investment multiplier, 157
investment spending, 118, 156, 222

irrevocable fixed exchange rate regime, 284
irrevocably fixed exchange rate, 297
IS, 165
IS (investment/savings) curve, 117
IS curve, 136, 167
IS/LM model, 163, 166

John Maynard Keynes, 48
jump variable, 278, 290

Kam preferences, 209
Keynes, 6, 104, 139, 150, 154, 221, 252
Keynesian economics, 139, 140
Keynesian theory of aggregate supply, 224
Keynesian theory of economic growth, 222
Keynesian/mercantalist-type theory, 61
Knut Wicksell, 52, 103

labour productivity, 229
labour supply curve, 230
labour theory of production, 225
labour theory of value, 225
laissez-faire, 246
law of one price, 97
legal tender, 21
Leijonhufvud, 50, 149
level of employment, 151
level of output, 115, 129
liabilities of the central bank, 19
liquidity effect on interest rates, 85
liquidity preference, 49, 50, 164, 221, 228, 230, 235, 239, 256, 283
liquidity preference theory of interest rates, 49
liquidity trap, 77
LM curve, 166, 167
loan expenditure, 59, 252, 263
loanable funds, 117
loans, 134, 209
loans of base money, 241
loans of money, 127

long position in goods and services, 14

low and stable real interest rates, 263

low real policy rate, 26

LRSI relation, 249

Lucas supply curve, 85

macroeconomic policy management, 17

main refinancing rate, 22

marginal product of labour, 96, 128

marginalism, 51, 52

mark-up, 153, 161, 224

market for endogenous money, 230

market forces, 123, 244, 291

Marshall–Lerner conditions, 271

Marshallian microeconomics, 50

Marx, 14, 224

Max Weber, 11

means of payment, 7, 95

means of payment recognized, 6

medium of exchange, 2, 7, 95, 126

mercantilism, 264

methodological *obiter dicta*, 93

Mexico, 44

micro-foundations, 53, 94, 131, 141, 201

micro-foundations of macroeconomics, 94, 125

Milton Friedman, 45, 214

model, 201

models without money, 127

monetarism, 45, 61

monetarist versus Keynesian debates, 49

monetary, 229

monetary base, 20, 22, 39, 75

monetary circuit, 14, 228, 229

monetary demand, 15

monetary economy, 6

monetary growth, 101

monetary macroeconomics, 141

monetary mercantilism, 263, 284

monetary mercantilist, 297

monetary misperceptions theory of the business cycle, 86

monetary neutrality, 42

monetary neutrality *versus* non-neutrality, 50

monetary policy, 46, 174, 219

monetary policy instrument, 39, 200, 209, 219

monetary policy reaction function, 114

monetary policy rule, 132, 232

monetary policy transmission mechanism, 135

monetary production, 35, 140, 141, 229

monetary profits, 45, 142

monetary super-neutrality, 201

monetary targeting experiments, 113

monetary theory, 136

monetary theory of a real rate of interest, 108

monetary theory of the real exchange rate, 57

monetary theory of the real rate of interest, 37, 38, 49, 57, 111, 149, 164, 219

money, 44

money and credit creation, 39

money as a social relation, 8

money as creature of the state, 23

money circuit, 56

money demand and supply, 228

money in utility function, 203

money multiplier, 23, 39, 75, 134

money of account, 6

money supply, 22, 39, 63, 75, 273

money supply growth, 64

money supply rule, 89

monopoly supply of base money, 209

Mr. Keynes's special theory, 149

Mundell–Fleming model, 170

Mundell–Tobin effect, 185, 201, 233

national income identity, 69

natural level of employment, 96

natural rate, 54, 105, 131

natural rate of growth, 112, 289
natural rate of interest, 37, 40, 44, 55, 105, 124, 165, 199
nature and functions of money, 48
negative real interest rates, 26
negative real return, 26
negative settlement balance, 133, 232
neo-Wicksellian theory, 110
neo-Wicskellian approach, 233
neoclassical economics, 123, 129
neoclassical economics of wage and price flexibility, 151
neoclassical equilibrium, 110
neoclassical growth model, 186
neoclassical growth theory, 226
neoclassical theories of growth, 223
neoclassical theory, 149
net autonomous demand, 118, 235
net exports, 275
neutral, 48
neutral money, 63
neutrality versus non-neutrality, 88
new consensus model, 52, 103, 115, 220
new-classical theory, 61
nominal exchange rate, 29, 97
nominal interest rate, 24, 84, 99
nominal rate of interest, 107
nominal wage and price "stickiness" or "rigidity", 140
nominal wage bill, 162
nominal wage or price rigidities, 51, 178
non-neutral, 47
non-neutrality, 42
non-superneutral, 47, 208
non-superneutrality, 218
North America, 44
not actually led to the disappearance of money, 3

observed inflation rate, 232
Okun's law, 88

ontology of money, 1, 35, 46, 48, 56, 266
open economy, 137, 170, 263
organic composition of capital, 226
over-investment, 186, 211, 244
overnight call rate, 22
overnight rate, 22
overshooting, 82

paper money, 45
pass-through, 232
Paul Krugman, 33
payments structure, 129
perfect capital mobility, 171
perfect competition, 51, 151
perfect foresight, 195
perfectly elastic supply of money, 149
Phillips curve, 86, 118, 199, 250
physical capital, 193
Pigou effect, 49
policy irrelevance, 93
policy rate, 22–24, 40, 53, 104, 133, 219, 231, 232
political economy, 121
political nation states, 29
possible methods of obtaining provisions, 9
Post-Keynesian literature, 228
power of the state to levy taxes, 21
price level, 115, 143, 160, 228, 230, 273
price level determination, 63
process analysis, 157
production function, 128
production lag, 224, 268
production process, 229
profit, 224, 226, 228, 229, 258
profit maximization, 132
profit rate, 227
profit share, 227
propensity to consume, 146
propensity to save, 222, 235
protectionism, 264
proxy for expected inflation, 114
public finances, 158, 291

purchasing power, 3
purchasing power of money, 42
purchasing power parity, 99
pure theory of capital, 105

quantitative easing, 28
quantity theory of money, 44, 45, 61, 68, 161, 229

rate of growth, 248
rate of growth of the money supply, 190, 200
rate of interest, 148
rate of profit, 226
rate of surplus value, 226, 227
rate of time preference, 44, 95, 207
rational expectations, 85, 90, 91, 100, 195, 291
rational expectations revolution, 89
rational expectations theory, 61
real and nominal interest rates, 108
real balance effect, 49
real bills doctrine, 16
real business cycle (RBC) model, 126, 235
real costs, 236, 255
real depreciation, 29
real economic growth, 241, 271
real effective exchange rate, 29
real exchange rate, 29, 39, 97, 171, 268, 271
real exchange rate appreciation, 29
real GDP, 41, 62, 266
real interest rate, 24, 99, 105, 123, 135, 258
real interest rate on money, 187
real interest rate parity, 100
real interest rate rule, 26, 135, 294
real money balances, 190, 210
real natural rate, 110
real policy rate, 55, 258, 272
real rate, 107
real rate of interest, 36, 130, 136

real rate of interest on, 44
real theory of the real exchange rate, 38
real theory of the real rate of interest, 37, 54
real wage rate, 151
real wages, 162, 258
realization of money profit, 101
recession, 187, 254
rejection of idealist metaphysics, 9
relative prices, 101, 126, 187
rentiers, 258
repayment of debt, 126
representative agent, 125, 127, 204
representative economic agents, 125
representative money, 48
reserves, 133, 232
reserves to deposits ratio, 76
revenge of the rentiers, 246
rigidity or "stickiness" of nominal prices, 45
risk, 19, 135
risk premium, 19, 177, 276
Rogers, 125

saddle-point, 192, 194, 204, 278, 288, 295
Samuelson, 155, 157, 252
saving, 145, 235
savings propensity, 119
Say's Law, 144
short-run supply of inflation, 248
short-term interest rate, 22
social facts, 94
social institutions, social relations, or social facts, 8
social ontology, 21, 125
sound finance, 284
sound money, 116
sources of inflation, 56
South Africa, 44
spot exchange rate, 29, 276
stability, 79, 197, 220, 295
stable arm, 192, 278

stagflation, 57, 237, 244, 255, 283
state theory of money, 21
steady-state, 79, 96, 121, 190, 210, 226, 237
steady-state equilibrium, 78
stimulus, 69, 281, 282
store of value, 7
subject of finance, 47
subjectivist theory of value, 52
substantive validity of money, 3, 21
super-neutral, 47, 48
supply creates its own demand, 63
supply of inflation, 248
supply of money, 229
supply of money is not fixed, 56
supply side, 116, 143
supply side economics, 289
system, 220, 299

target real wage, 163, 269
tax, 156, 169, 223
tax and spend, 58, 159, 252, 253
tax burden, 223
tax cut, 158, 239, 253, 283, 290
tax incidence, 257
tax multiplier, 157
Taylor principle, 120, 131
Taylor rule, 114
technical knowledge, 225
technical monetary detail, 48
technological innovation, 225, 235, 254
temporary equilibria, 122
temporary wage rigidities, 50
the generation and realization of monetary profits, 14
the idea of credit money, or debt money, 4
the market economy, 11
the multiplier, 157
the neoclassical theory of capital, 185

theory of banking, 132
theory of inflation, 106, 107
theory of value, 224
Thornton, 52, 103
tight money policy, 234, 253
time preference, 136
trade balance, 268
trade-off between inflation and growth, 281
trade-off between inflation and unemployment, 87
traditional economy, 10
transactions demand for money, 78
transmissions mechanism, 132
transmissions mechanism for monetary policy, 117
transmissions mechanism of monetary policy, 23, 231, 272
transversality condition, 195, 203, 279, 288

uncontrollable inflation, 240
uncovered interest parity, 99, 276, 294
undershooting, 84
unemployment, 74, 150
unemployment gap, 88
unit of account, 6, 7, 126
US Federal Reserve System, 16
utility, 132, 204
utility theory, 225

value added, 225
variable capital, 224
variable velocity version of the quantity theory, 78
velocity of circulation, 14, 62, 77
virtual floating exchange rate regime, 297
voluntary exchange in a free market, 10

wage bill, 229
wage curve, 154, 230, 255

wage unit, 146
wealth, 128, 186, 191, 207, 211
wealth effect, 191, 202
Wicksell-type theory, 55, 61, 139, 164
Woodford, 125
world price level, 44

zero inflation, 55, 57, 124, 288
zero inflation in a growing economy, 111